THE BEST SHOW IN
FOOTBALL

THE BEST SHOW IN
FOOTBALL

THE 1946–1955 CLEVELAND BROWNS
PRO FOOTBALL'S GREATEST DYNASTY

ANDY PIASCIK

TAYLOR TRADE PUBLISHING
Lanham • New York • Boulder • Toronto • Plymouth, UK

Published by Taylor Trade Publishing
An imprint of The Rowman & Littlefield Publishing Group, Inc.
4501 Forbes Boulevard, Suite 200, Lanham, Maryland 20706

Estover Road
Plymouth PL6 7PY
United Kingdom

Distributed by NATIONAL BOOK NETWORK

Library of Congress Cataloging-in-Publication Data

Piascik, Andy, 1957–
  The best show in football : the 1946–1955 Cleveland Browns, pro football's greatest dynasty / Andy Piascik.—1st Taylor Trade Pub. ed.
       p.   cm.
  Includes bibliographical references and index.
  ISBN-13: 978-1-58979-360-6 (cloth : alk. paper)
  ISBN-10: 1-58979-360-9 (cloth : alk. paper)
  1. Cleveland Browns (Football team : 1946-1995)—History.   I. Title.
  GV956.C6.P54 2007
  796.332'640977132—dc22
                                                        2006021546

∞™The paper used in this publication meets the minimum requirements of American National Standard for Information Sciences—Permanence of Paper for Printed Library Materials, ANSI/NISO Z39.48-1992.

Manufactured in the United States of America.

*To the first Browns fan I ever knew, my father Frank,
who was there from the very beginning.*

Contents

Foreword

Ara Parseghian

GROWING UP IN AKRON in the 1930s and 1940s, I was very aware of the football accomplishments of Paul Brown. My high school teammates and I used to go to watch Brown's Massillon High teams, and it was clear to us then that we were seeing high school football at its very best. Almost seventy years after the fact, I still vividly remember a scrimmage in which Massillon took apart the Kent State University varsity team.

Brown continued his success at Ohio State, guiding the Buckeyes to a national championship in just his second year in Columbus. College football was king in those days, and although Brown was only thirty-four at the time, it seemed that there were no more football worlds for him to conquer. Little did we know.

Needless to say, I was thrilled when Brown signed me to a contract with the Cleveland Browns in 1948. He had assembled a great group of players that had won the first two championships of the All-America Football Conference. Among them were Otto Graham, Marion Motley, Lou Groza, Dante Lavelli, Bill Willis, Mac Speedie, Lou Rymkus, Horace Gillom—the list is so long I could go on and on and still leave out some pretty good ones.

Pro football is a difficult, exacting business, and when you're in the middle of it you can't allow yourself to think about whether any particular team, even the team you're playing for, is the best ever. Written from the distance of many years, I think Andy Piascik makes a very strong case for those Browns teams. It's hard to argue with seven championships in ten years, a record no other team has matched.

In the same way, we were too focused on winning to reflect at any length on the role of Marion Motley, Bill Willis, and Horace Gillom as groundbreakers. To us, they were first and foremost great football players.

Without them, it's doubtful the Browns would have been as successful as they were.

Here, too, Piascik does an excellent job of illuminating just how important the presence of Motley, Willis, Gillom, and the other African American players on the Browns was to the team's success and, in no small part, to helping change American society. Their accomplishments as players and the important role the Browns played in ending the color line in pro football are an integral and riveting part of *The Best Show in Football*. Looking back, I am just as proud to have been a part of pro sport's first integrated team of the modern era as I am to have been a part of the great Browns dynasty.

One of the most memorable moments in football history, when Cleveland defeated the Philadelphia Eagles 35–10 in their first NFL game, came not long after I retired from the Browns. I was working in Ohio as an assistant coach at the time, but a part of me was in Philadelphia that night. When I heard the news I was filled with a great sense of pride as well as a little bit of regret: pride that the Browns had proved unquestionably that they—we—were a great football team, and had been all along, and regret that I could not have been a part of what may have been the team's finest hour.

I don't know if the Browns were the greatest dynasty in pro football history, but Andy Piascik certainly makes a good case that they were. I was very impressed with his research, his arguments, and his sense of history. Reading *The Best Show in Football* brought back a lot of great memories of an important period in pro football. I hope you enjoy it as much as I did.

Acknowledgments

THE RESOURCES of the Professional Football Researchers Association were invaluable. The PFRA not only publishes a newsletter, *The Coffin Corner*, it also has a website, it has published a game summary/line score project for the game's early decades, and it has published such gems as "The Progression of NFL Records," compiled by Ken Pullis. The articles from *The Coffin Corner* listed in the sources section only hint at the great work that organization does.

Thanks to employees at the New York Public Library and the Brooklyn Public Library. Special thanks to John Soltis, Gerald Sabo, and Ronald Fontaine of the Bridgeport Public Library; Anne Marie Carey, Mary Coe, Jennifer Dayton, Paula Herzlinger, and Cliff Smith of the Fairfield Public Library; Melinda Schafer and Elmer Turner of the Cleveland Public Library; and Lynn Bycko, Joanne Cornelius, and Vern Morrison of Special Collections at the library at Cleveland State University for the help they provided.

Thanks to Joanne Chirco of Corbis, and special thanks to Dulcie Wilcox at Taylor Trade Publishing. Thanks to Kevin Carroll, author of *The Houston Oilers: The Early Years*, for sharing insights with me from the many interviews he did with Lou Rymkus, former Browns player and Oilers coach.

A hearty thanks to all the players I interviewed for this book. To a man they were gracious, generous with their time, and full of good stories and insights. Thanks to Lou Sossamon for putting me in touch with some of his New York Yankees teammates. Special thanks to Ara Parseghian, both for sharing his time and observations in conversations and correspondence and for writing the foreword.

Lastly, I had the opportunity to briefly interview Edgar "Special Delivery" Jones. Edgar was more than happy to talk when I called, and it was only after we had spoken for a while that he informed me he had gone for a dialysis treatment that morning and was feeling tired. I apologized and told him I would call back another time. Edgar died a short while later. May you always walk in sunshine, Special Delivery.

Notes on Terms

HROUGHOUT THIS BOOK, references are made to championships. That seems a safe enough term, but because of the many changes in pro football over the decades, it requires some clarification. References to conference or division championships are just that, a team that finished first in its conference or division.

More important are the championships that signify pro football supremacy in a given year. As used here, *championships* refers to the following: the team that finished atop the standings of the National Football League (originally known as the American Professional Football Association) from 1920 through 1932, the winner of the NFL Championship Game from 1933 through 1965, the winner of the All-America Football Conference Championship Game from 1946 through 1949, the winner of the American Football League Championship Game from 1960 through 1965, and the winner of the Super Bowl from 1966 through the present.

Championships won in the same season in two major leagues that did not play each other are both recognized as championships. Thus from the years 1946 through 1949 and 1960 through 1965, two teams are recognized as having won championships. League championships won in the NFL and AFL from 1966 through 1969 are not considered championships in the sense of pro football supremacy unless that team also won the Super Bowl. So, for example, the 1969 AFL champion Kansas City Chiefs won a championship, but the 1966 AFL champion Chiefs did not.

Also, when records and individual achievements in league Championship Games are discussed, those games are accorded the same status as the Super Bowl. In its endless efforts to promote the Super Bowl, the NFL, in its publications and releases, instead treats those pre-1966 league

Championship Games as the equivalent of today's conference championship games. That is an insult to the players who played in those games, to the historical record, and to the game itself.

The terms *division* and *conference* have both historically been used as names for one half, or approximately one half, of a league's teams. *Conference* has been used for a far longer period of time and is still in use today in the same way (National Football Conference and American Football Conference). For the sake of simplicity and continuity, *conference* and *conference champion* are used even for the pre-1950 period when what we know as conferences were called divisions.

For three seasons beginning in 1950, the NFL's conferences were the American and National. For the rest of the time in question, they were known as the Eastern and Western. Where it is necessary for the sake of clarity, Eastern and Western are used for those three seasons.

There were four different American Football Leagues in the twentieth century. All are referred to within. In discussions of the first three, the one in question is specifically referred to by the years it operated or as AFL I, AFL II, or AFL III. All references to the American Football League that do not include such designations are to the AFL of 1960–1969.

For most of pro football history, calculations of team winning percentages disregarded tie games. More recently, a system was adopted that counts a tie game as half a win and half a loss. Although the current system is more accurate, the old system is used throughout because that was the one in use during the period under discussion. To maximize the accuracy of comparisons, the winning percentages of teams of more recent vintage have been recalculated using the old style.

Finally, readers will note that the team and individual records from the All-America Football Conference are treated throughout on the same level as those of the NFL and the AFL of the 1960s (i.e., as those of a major league). The Browns, for example, are referred to at various times as the first and only team to ever win four and then five consecutive championships and as holders of the record for the longest unbeaten streak.

Similarly, Lou Groza's thirteen field goals in 1946 are referred to as, at the time, an all-time pro record, and Mac Speedie is referred to as the first player to ever accumulate 1,000 receiving yards in two different seasons. Those references are not "mistakes," they are intentional. The NFL's refusal to recognize these AAFC team and individual records is the mistake. Putting those AAFC records on the same level as those accomplished in the NFL and AFL is true to the historical record, and it is done for that reason.

"The Best Show in Football," the source of the title, was a slogan the Browns used in the 1950s in highlight films and other publicity.

Introduction

THEY WERE DANTE, Emerson, and Horace; the Rivet, the Rabbit, and Rock. They were Shula, Noll, and Parseghian; and Lou the Toe, Lou the Heel, and Captain Lou.

They were Lil' Abner, Chet the Jet, and the Kid; and Tony Adamle, MD, Bob Kolesar, MD, Les Horvath, DDS, and Hal Herring, PhD. They were Special Delivery and Dub; Otto, Bob, and Bill.

They were Mo, Mo, and Big Mo; and Mike, Len, and Marion. They were Dippy, Dopey, and Iggie; and Tom Jones and Tommy James.

They were Chubby, Curly, and Chick; and Pete, Lin, and Ken. They were Pinky, Flip, and Spud; and Warren, Abe, and Mac.

They came from all over the United States, from places like North Tonawanda, New York, and East Bridgewater, Massachusetts. They came from Council Bluffs, Iowa, and Carrier Mills, Illinois, from Augusta, Kansas, and Nashua, New Hampshire.

They came from Swoyersville and Mount Zion in Pennsylvania, from Humboldt and Kyles Ford in Tennessee. They came from New Village and Hackensack and Wenonah in New Jersey and from Elk City, Ponca City, and Chickasha in Oklahoma.

They came from Weimar, Nixon, and Pilot Point, Texas, and they came from all over the state of Ohio, from Sugar Creek, Mt. Vernon, Martin's Ferry, and any number of other places. They came from dozens of small towns and from farms, and they came from big cities such as New Orleans, Boston, Chicago, Kansas City, St. Louis, Pittsburgh, Milwaukee, Dallas, and, yes, Cleveland.

They were Hungarian, Czech, and Irish; Polish, Italian, and Armenian. They were Slovenian, Greek, and Lebanese; Slav, Lithuanian, and, significantly, African American. Many grew up poor during the Great

1

Depression, and they were overwhelmingly sons of the working class; one was the son of sharecroppers.

They were 118 in all, men who played for the Cleveland Browns during a ten-year period from 1946 through 1955. Many were World War II combat veterans for whom the aggression and rigors of pro football were a step down from war and death. They had gone to large state colleges, like the University of Texas and Ohio State, and small schools, like Waynesburg, Findlay, and Superior State Teachers College.

Together they created the greatest dynasty in the history of pro football. Some played only briefly, while four were there for the entire ten years. Almost one in ten is in the Pro Football Hall of Fame; others toiled far from the spotlight, their value known primarily to their teammates and to the players from the teams they so consistently defeated.

They played in glorious old stadiums, uniquely shaped ballparks set in the middle of urban neighborhoods. Of the seventeen they played in, few remain standing, and only Soldier Field is still used for pro football. They played in an era when pro football trailed far behind baseball and college football in popularity, when the select group who called themselves fans followed their team primarily via newsreels, radio, and newspapers.

They played at a time when white footballs were used for night games and when players would help remove the tarpaulin from the field before a game. They played at a time when a corporate box was something one dropped a donation into during the holidays, and the highest paid among them earned $25,000. They played in and dominated two leagues, hastening the demise of one and ushering in the golden age of the other.

They won more championships in a decade than all but a handful of franchises have won in their entire histories. They conquered an established league as no first-year team in any sport ever has, yet the accomplishments of their earlier teams that were just as good remain officially unrecognized and thus foolishly doubted. They were coached by a man who changed football in a number of significant ways, and many followed their playing years with careers as coaches in both colleges and the pros, including some who are among the greatest of all time.

They were the Cleveland Browns in the decade after World War II. Many are no doubt surprised to see them dubbed pro football's greatest dynasty. Other great teams of more recent vintage are far better known, and the fact that Cleveland won games and championships with greater frequency than any of them will be an eye-opener to many.

The claim of greatest is not made lightly. A great deal of information is presented, both pro and con, and I believe it is presented in a fair and objective manner. The evidence is what ultimately led me to the conclusions I draw. Actually, the most startling thing about the research is how much new (to me) evidence I uncovered that led back to the Browns as the best.

I knew, for example, that the Browns were one of the first teams to break the color line in pro sports for good. What was especially revealing, however, was the degree to which practically every team's performance in the postwar era correlated to how quickly and to what degree they signed black players. Without the trailblazing role the team played in signing black players, it is extremely difficult to imagine the Browns winning enough to have been the game's greatest dynasty.

Similarly, I knew that the All-America Football Conference was a major league. Relative to the NFL, for example, it was far stronger than the American Football League of the 1960s was in its early years—and stronger than that league was for most, if not all, of its existence. Still, I was surprised to learn how well former AAFC players did in the NFL in 1950 and beyond after the merger of the two leagues. There, too, was a correlation that was stunning in its exactness: The NFL teams with the most AAFC players all improved in 1950, while those with the fewest all got worse.

Accomplished football historians have reached different conclusions and may continue to do so. I hope, however, the evidence presented here will expand the discussions and debates about which dynasty was the greatest.

Ultimately, though, this book is only partly a historical documentation of football's greatest dynasty. To a greater degree, it is the story of a group of football players who collectively played at a phenomenal level of excellence for a long time. Some are among the best ever, while most were "merely" good enough to have productive pro careers. Their hopes, frustrations, happy memories, slights, camaraderie, disappointments, triumphs, and injuries are also part of the story.

Perhaps most lasting of all is the solidarity and support they gave each other as the first integrated major league team in the modern era of pro sports. This part of their story in many ways surpasses the far better known drama of Jackie Robinson's joining the Brooklyn Dodgers, and not only because it happened a year earlier. Unlike the Dodgers, for example, not one white Cleveland player is known to have acted in opposition to having black teammates or demanded to be traded.

Overwhelmingly, in fact, the white Cleveland players speak of the team's first two black players, Bill Willis and Marion Motley, with the utmost respect and fondness. For their part, Willis and Motley appear not to have ever mentioned any incidents of racial hostility on the part of their teammates in all of the interviews they did over a course of decades. And in a sport where the threat of serious physical injury is far greater than anything Robinson faced, the Browns rallied to ensure that the racially motivated blows directed at their black teammates—and there were many—did not go unanswered.

For all of that, the vast majority of the Browns from those ten years, Willis, Motley, and the other blacks included, point to the winning and the camaraderie most of all. Friendships were formed that last to this day, and the players who have participated in the many team reunions held over the years speak of those occasions as very special ones. Even those who have stayed relatively out of touch speak fondly of those years, both of the collective accomplishments on the playing field and of the togetherness.

CHAPTER 1

The Beginning

PAUL BROWN is the single most important figure in the history of the Cleveland Browns. His innovations and accomplishments are matched by few in the long history of professional football. As head coach, general manager, and part owner, Brown guided the Browns to seven championships and compiled a winning percentage of .767. Brown will forever be linked to the team that bears his name and that he led during their ten years of glory.

Without the daring of Arch Ward and Leo "Mickey" McBride, however, it is unlikely that Brown would have accomplished all that he did. Certainly he would not have done all that he did without the extraordinary circumstances he operated under at the beginning of his pro career. Except for the foresight of Ward and McBride, there might not have been a Cleveland Browns franchise. In fact, Ward, the visionary behind the All-America Football Conference, and McBride, the majority owner of the Browns at the team's inception, are among the most overlooked of the men who helped shape pro football in the pivotal years after World War II.

It is easy to imagine Paul Brown achieving success without Ward, McBride, and the AAFC. Few people have been as driven to succeed in football as Brown. By the age of 35 he had already helped resurrect football at Ohio State University, long one of the elite programs in college football, coaching the Buckeyes to a national championship in just his second year as head coach.

There is no doubt, however, that Brown benefited greatly from what was an almost ideal situation in Cleveland. McBride was a money man who, at least where football was concerned, didn't mind remaining in the background. Among other traits, he was smart enough to know what he didn't know.

McBride was a fan drawn to the game late in life when his son enrolled at Notre Dame. He was attracted by the spectacle and excitement of the game and saw that it might also be a way to make money. McBride didn't pretend to know the game. When he hired Brown, he did so precisely because he wanted someone to run the football side of the team. And in Brown he got someone who was both extremely knowledgeable and fanatically dedicated to success, someone who came with an already developed corporate organizational approach that would forever change pro football.

Arch Ward was the sports editor of the extremely influential *Chicago Tribune*, one of the largest-circulation daily newspapers in the United States. The *Tribune* was especially influential throughout the upper Midwestern part of the country. At the time, when virtually no one had a television and many people did not own radios, that influence was still quite exceptional.

By the 1930s, Ward had achieved a great deal of power at the *Tribune*. In addition to writing a regular column on the sports page, he had linked the *Tribune*'s name to two hugely successful and popular innovations: baseball's All-Star Game and football's College All-Star Game.

Begun in 1933, the major league All-Star Game was, by 1944, one of baseball's hallowed traditions. In the first game played at Chicago's Comiskey Park, Babe Ruth hit the very first home run of all-star competition. And in the decade since, the midsummer classic had already featured other fabled moments of the game's history such as Carl Hubbell striking out five of the game's best hitters in succession in 1934 and Ted Williams's game-winning, bottom of the ninth home run in the midst of his great 1941 season. After just a few years, the game initiated by Ward was one that baseball fans looked forward to every season.

College football was second to baseball in popularity in 1934, and when the first College All-Star Game was played that year, it also was a rousing success. The game pitted the best of the previous year's college seniors against the champions of the National Football League in an exhibition game played each summer in Chicago.

The game attracted interest in no small part because it brought together on the same field the two parts of the football world that had coexisted, sometimes uncomfortably, for decades. The first was the collegiate amateur game that had predominated since the first two football teams squared off against each other. The other was the professional game, consolidated in a league begun in 1920 and still struggling but slowly becoming more popular.

College seniors considered it an honor to be selected to play in the game. Elroy Hirsch said that being introduced in a spotlight in a darkened stadium before the game, with his college song playing over the loudspeakers, was the biggest thrill of a career that included an NFL championship and induction to the College and Pro Football Halls of Fame. For many of the collegians, it was a last hurrah for football, a chance for one last taste of gridiron glory.

Although they had only a few weeks of practice together before the game, the college all-stars had done fairly well in the game's first decade. In the first ten games, the NFL champs had won five, the college all-stars three, and there had been two ties. Three of the all-stars' defeats had been by fewer than 10 points.

And the game was more popular than even Ward had probably imagined when he first broached the idea. Ten of the first twelve games were played at massive, historic Soldier Field. The average attendance at those ten games was 85,000, and one year the game drew over 100,000.

But once-a-year all-star games were one thing. Starting a whole new sports league, as Ward proposed in 1944 with the All-America Football Conference, was something else altogether. There had been three such challenges to the National Football League in the quarter century after that league's formation. By any account, the three previous ventures had all been failures. All had been dubbed the American Football League. None had lasted more than two seasons.

AFL I of 1926 begat a New York Yankees team (the briefly famous team of Red Grange and C. C. Pyle) that was absorbed into the NFL and then went under a short time later. AFL II had produced the Cleveland Rams, a franchise that went into the NFL in 1937 after one year of play even while AFL II continued for a second season before folding. AFL III of 1940–1941 had come and gone without making any visible impact on the NFL.

So the track record was not promising. Further clouding the prospects of success for a new professional football league was the frequently unstable nature of the NFL itself during its first twenty-five years. From a high of twenty-two franchises in 1926, the same year AFL I operated with an additional nine teams, the NFL was pared to ten teams by 1931. Many of the NFL's franchises in smaller cities had gone under because of fan bases that were just not large enough, while others from larger cities fell by the wayside as the Great Depression deepened.

What stability the NFL had gained was again tossed upon rocky waters by the entry of the United States into World War II in 1941. Hundreds of NFL players and would-be players from the college ranks went into the military and thus watered down the talent available. Teams had to contend with travel restrictions and wartime shortages. Attendance declined and franchises struggled. Several teams merged and played for a while as one entity. Several others suspended operations.

Thus, late 1943 and early 1944 seemed an especially unlikely and risky time for Ward to propose a new league. Not only was the talent of the available player pool down appreciably, but some of the league's teams were to be located in cities that already had struggling NFL teams. That meant competition for a declining fan base.

And since Ward from the outset emphasized that the new league would be national in scope (by which he meant it would include teams on the West Coast and in the Deep South, parts of the country the NFL had either ignored or failed in), an additional potential obstacle to success was created. For even if the war was over and travel restrictions lifted when play began, there remained the heretofore prohibitive costs of travel to points beyond the nation's northeastern quadrant.

But Ward was a man with a vision, a healthy dose of tenacity, and, at least in some respects important to the new venture, a finger on the pulse of the country. He also seems to have familiarized himself with and learned from the mistakes of the three previous failed leagues, not to mention some of the NFL's mistakes. For one thing, he was in touch with a group of men of means who wanted to own football teams and were willing to tolerate some initial financial setbacks.

Tony Morabito is a prime example. Rebuffed by the NFL in his efforts to bring a team to his native San Francisco, Morabito eagerly joined Ward's venture early on. He became the backbone of the 49ers franchise for the first thirteen years of its existence and helped prove that San Francisco, derided by some in the NFL as a college football town, could support major league sports. And along with Los Angeles, the San Francisco experience would prove that with the rise of air travel, cities west of the Mississippi could be successfully integrated into a national sports league.

In addition, although the war would last until the summer of 1945, by 1944 Allied victory seemed inevitable. The announcement of the AAFC's formation came at almost the same time as the Normandy invasion on D-Day. Ward was astute enough to realize that the time for laying the foundation for a new league was as the war was entering its final stages, not after it was over.

An organization with its planning completed that was ready to go at war's end, Ward knew, would be better positioned to get off to the critical fast start than one that waited until peace was declared. Originally scheduled to begin play in 1945, Ward and the AAFC team owners wisely chose to wait another year. That allowed teams to develop more thoroughly, and it allowed the league to benefit from the sports attendance boom that followed demobilization as well as from the large numbers of players available in 1946 who would not have been the year before.

Ward also accurately anticipated, either through luck or foresight or some combination of both, some of the key sociological trends of the immediate postwar period. Unlike after World War I when, for a period of about five years, the United States experienced the economic depression that swept the globe, the downturn that hit the country after World War II was relatively short and far less severe. That was partly because the working class was better organized, or at least unionized to a greater degree. And while thousands of the country's best organizers from the Industrial Workers of the World and the Socialist Party were in prison at the end of World War I for antiwar work, no similar repression of the working class took place during World War II.

The winter and spring of 1946 were, to be sure, very difficult for many people. There was a widespread sense among workers that they had done the work of winning the war, in the factories and on the battlefields, while many corporations had unfairly earned unprecedented profits. At one point in 1946 there were more workers on strike in the United States than there had ever been anywhere, before or since, in all of history.

But labor peace was soon the order of the day. Unions born amid the militancy of the 1930s were, by 1945–1946, consolidated under captains of labor who sought peace with their cohorts in industry. Much that had been won was surrendered. Much more that might have been won was bargained away. What was gained, although it was not really a larger percentage of the pie given that the pie had grown so much larger during the war, was, anyway, more pie in the form of wages and a material living standard higher than workers anywhere had ever had.

Lots of people suddenly had both more money and more time. *Leisure time* entered the sociological lexicon. Advertising became one of the country's most conspicuous growth industries. Especially intrusive was advertising that stressed the desirability, the civic responsibility even, of spending one's money and leisure time on entertaining oneself. As men were far more likely to be both sports fans and higher wage earners, entertainment often took the form of attending sports events. The All-America Football Conference was just one of the beneficiaries of a huge sports attendance boom that began in 1946.

Dozens of men who would play in the AAFC and thousands of others who would be among the league's paying customers were in the military well past the war's official end on September 2, 1945. By the opening of the 1946 football season a year later, however, the vast majority of them were home. During that time the AAFC's ownership groups signed coaches and players, rented stadiums, sold tickets, and publicized the league's coming.

Ward had originally envisioned the new league as a partnership with the NFL modeled after the relationship between the National and American Leagues in baseball. In Ward's conception of the venture, the two leagues would have a common draft, interleague play, salary limits for players, and no raiding. Begun by separate interests twenty-five years apart, major league baseball's two leagues reached agreement after several years of intense warfare at the beginning of the twentieth century.

Almost half a century later, the two leagues still played separate schedules, were overseen by separate management structures, and met on the field only in exhibitions, the All-Star Game, and the World Series. Yet they existed under one umbrella, and Ward's rather naive hope was that sooner rather than later the NFL would welcome the AAFC in as an equal partner.

The NFL quickly shot down the possibility of any such relationship with the AAFC. Almost from the outset, then, the new league was in competition with the NFL for players, newspaper and radio exposure, and, in the four cities where the leagues would compete head to head, fans. And despite an official policy to the contrary, the AAFC was very aggressive in pursuing NFL players.

The NFL's rejection of the AAFC, stated in particularly unflattering terms by Commissioner Elmer Layden when he suggested that the new league "get a football first," was perhaps the opening salvo in the war between the leagues. But it was the AAFC's aggressive pursuit of players coming out of college as well as those already belonging to NFL teams that escalated matters to the acrimonious level that would mark the relationship between the two leagues until the end of 1949.

Like Tony Morabito, Mickey McBride had actively sought ownership of an NFL franchise. His efforts to buy the Cleveland Rams from millionaire supermarket heir Dan Reeves came to naught. Having caught the football bug while his son was a student at Notre Dame, McBride was not easily deterred, however. He had been through newspaper circulation wars in Chicago at a time when those wars were quite literally shooting ones, and he did not flinch at the prospect of going up against the National Football League. McBride had known Ward in Chicago, and when he learned that Ward was putting together a new football league, he enthusiastically put up the money for a franchise for Cleveland.

In his mid-fifties at the time, McBride was a wealthy man. His first big money came as he climbed his way up the Hearst newspaper organization. After establishing himself in Chicago, McBride went to work for Hearst in Cleveland. He settled there, continued to do well financially, and along the way became the principal owner of the Yellow-Zone Cab

Company. After the Browns got started and Paul Brown had extra players beyond the roster limit that he wanted to hold onto and not risk losing to other teams, McBride put them on the Yellow-Zone payroll and the "taxi squad" was born.

Utilizing his newspaper connections, McBride also began operating a wire service that provided horse racing information. Perhaps then, or perhaps earlier in Chicago, he also became acquainted with and had business relations with organized crime figures. In the 1950s, while still the majority owner of the Browns, McBride was called to testify before the Kefauver Commission, a Senate committee headed by Estes Kefauver that was investigating organized crime. McBride was never arrested or indicted as a result of the investigations, but he did sell his interest in the Browns not long after being called to testify.

Notre Dame was in the midst of its greatest period of success in the 1940s, and McBride's first candidate for the head coaching job of his new Cleveland franchise was Fighting Irish coach Frank Leahy. Already a legendary figure as both player and coach at Notre Dame, Leahy was then on leave from his job and in the Navy. McBride aggressively pursued Leahy, and the two shook hands over an agreement that would make Leahy coach and general manager.

High-level administrators at Notre Dame objected as soon as they got wind of the deal, however. They appealed to McBride's sense of loyalty to his first football love and the old alma mater (his son's, anyway). McBride backed off, and Leahy eventually coached Notre Dame to still further glory in the late 1940s.

With Leahy out of the picture, McBride then asked Cleveland sportswriter John Dietrich whom he should consider for the coaching job. Without hesitating, Dietrich recommended Paul Brown. Not knowing much about Brown, McBride got in touch with Ward and asked his opinion. Ward replied that he thought Brown an excellent choice. Working at the largest newspaper in Big Ten country, Ward knew very well who Brown was from his accomplishments at Ohio State.

Ward knew, if McBride did not, that Brown was Ohio through and through. Brown was born and raised in Norwalk, about halfway between Cleveland and Toledo. He had attended first Ohio State and then Miami University in Oxford, where he played quarterback on the football team. For nine years he coached one of the most successful high school football teams in the country, Washington High School in Massillon (commonly known as Massillon High).

During Brown's tenure, Massillon compiled an 81–7–2 record and won six state championships. Brown's teams were so dominating that a number of Ohio's other high school coaches petitioned Ohio State to hire Brown when the Buckeyes head job became vacant in 1941. Massillon was a tremendously popular team at the gate. In fact, after the school's stadium was enlarged in the late 1930s, the team averaged more than 20,000 per home game—a figure that was higher than every college in Ohio except Ohio State and a number of NFL teams.

Because of his great success at Massillon and in three years at Ohio State (one of which was a national championship season), Brown was, by the time McBride was looking for a coach, the most visible and respected football figure in Ohio. And Ohio was the birthplace of professional football. The American Professional Football Association, forerunner of the NFL, had been founded just a few miles from Massillon in Canton in 1919.

In fact, Ohio had established itself as the country's hotbed of football. People in the state's large cities, in its small towns, and on its farms were passionate about the game. Ohioans followed baseball and other sports too but seemed to care first and foremost about football. They were ahead of their time in that sense, anticipating by decades the love affair with the game that would blossom in the country as a whole after the midpoint of the century.

In several different seasons in the first ten years of the NFL, as many as seven of the league's franchises had been based in Ohio. In all, ten different cities in the state had been represented by an NFL team for at least one season. Ohio, Ward knew, was a place where lots of people loved football, and with a team based in what was then the state's largest city, one that held great potential for the success of his new league.

So the hiring of Brown to coach the AAFC's Cleveland franchise made sense to Ward, not just because of Brown's outstanding football credentials but also because of the iconic status he had achieved in his home state. That would mean spectators, perhaps lots of them. Those spectators might help tilt the balance in the AAFC's favor, for Cleveland was one of the places where the new league would be going head to head with the NFL.

A new team would need every advantage in a battle with the Rams. Brown's reputation and following would be important to the AAFC's efforts to overcome the advantages the Rams enjoyed from having played in the city for almost a decade. It would be additionally important because Cleveland was the smallest of the four venues where the AAFC would take on the NFL.

Although near its population apex with approximately 900,000 residents as World War II was ending, Cleveland was nowhere near as populous as New York, Chicago, and Los Angeles, the three other cities where the AAFC would compete directly with the older league. Those other cities were large enough that more than one team might be able to survive, perhaps even thrive. Compounding matters in Cleveland was the fact that fans there had thus far been quite frugal in their support of the pro game.

One additional factor that would soon become apparent and aid the AAFC cause was Brown's fanatical commitment to football success. He was no aging legend, coasting and looking back at the best of his coaching accomplishments. He was only in his mid-thirties, young for a pro coach, and he was hungry and determined. Football and the desire to be the absolute best consumed Brown as it did few others, and when he did eventually arrive in Cleveland, he was on a mission for new, greater football worlds to conquer.

Those looking ahead to the possibility that there might be only one survivor in an AAFC-NFL war in Cleveland were proven correct, and far more quickly than anyone anticipated. Months before the Browns played their first game and just weeks after the Rams won the 1945 NFL championship, the matter was resolved when the Rams left for Los Angeles. It was an early and decisive victory for the new league, one gained with nary a shot being fired.

Although the Rams' primary reason for leaving was that they never really achieved box office success in Cleveland, the groundswell of support that grew under McBride and Brown's new team was a major contributing factor. Much of that support was due to the reputation of Paul Brown in Ohio and the way he went about putting together the pieces of the new franchise.

Actually, Brown's popularity and football acumen were the source of some controversy when it was announced he was forsaking a return to

Ohio State from the Navy to accept a pro job. The Buckeyes, after all, were the first love of many football fans in Ohio. The pro and semi-pro teams that came and went in the industrial cities and the small towns were a definite part of the state's football landscape, but, on five or so Saturdays every autumn, Ohio Stadium in Columbus was the place for football.

Ohio State was the big time, bigger than all those NFL teams in Toledo and Canton and Akron and Cincinnati put together. Yet suddenly there was Brown, the very man who had brought Ohio State to glory just a few years before and who, it was certain, once the war was over and he was back on the sidelines, would lead the school and the state to even greater heights, leaving to take a job in some pro league that few people even knew much about.

Brown had left Ohio State after three seasons to go into the Navy. His assumption was that he would return to Columbus after his military service, and university officials verbally assured him that that was the case. Matters became more complicated, however, after Ohio State had an outstanding season in 1944, the first season after Brown's departure.

Behind Heisman Trophy winner Les Horvath, Brown's successor Carroll Widdoes coached Ohio State to an unbeaten season, a conference championship, and a number two ranking behind Army in the national polls. It was then, according to Brown, that Ohio State athletic director Lynn St. John began to equivocate about Brown's return in 1945.

Around the same time, Ward, at the behest of McBride, showed up at the Great Lakes Naval Center in Illinois where Brown was stationed and, to nobody's surprise, was the head football coach. Ward pitched the new league, McBride, the credibility and enthusiasm of the other ownership groups, and the possibilities in Cleveland. Brown liked what he heard and was not happy with the response from Ohio State when he pressed further about his return there.

In no time McBride and Dan Sherby, one of the franchise's minority owners, met with Brown to talk terms. Their offer was unprecedented for a professional football coach: $25,000 per year for five years guaranteed, no matter what happened to the franchise or the league; a 5% owner's share of the franchise; and a monthly stipend of $1,500 that would begin immediately and continue for as long as Brown was in the Navy.

Of equal or even greater importance to Brown, McBride agreed to

Brown's demand that he have absolute control of the football part of the organization. He had had much, but not all, of that kind of control at Massillon and Ohio State. With a pro franchise, if he didn't have to answer to the owner, he could build a team and not have to worry about trustees, administrators, alumni, or anybody else.

There would still be tests to pass, rules to follow, and standards to meet, but Brown and nobody else would devise and implement them. He would be his own administration and board of trustees and, since the team was just starting, the alumni, too. McBride could promote the team, sell tickets, advertise, attend league meetings, hire front office staff, and do anything and everything else on the business side. But Paul Brown and only Paul Brown would make all decisions regarding the team. Once the contracts were signed, for all intents and purposes right down to its name, the team was Paul Brown's.

The reaction among some in Ohio was to accuse Brown of betraying the state's number one football institution. While Brown blamed St. John and traded potshots with Widdoes, the brunt of the criticism was directed at him. The vituperation would eventually die down, only to rise again when Brown signed a number of Ohio State players who had college eligibility remaining to Cleveland contracts. The hard feelings of some alumni persisted for years.

In spite of that, at several times during the early years of Brown's tenure with Cleveland, stories would surface of his possible return to the head coaching job at Ohio State. Brown later said that he seriously considered returning when the AAFC hit particularly rocky waters in 1949. He never did, however, and the legacy of Paul Brown in Columbus among the university community of the 1940s was a mixed one. He had guided the team to a national championship, but, in the eyes of the Buckeyes' biggest supporters, he also left prematurely and took some of the school's best players with him.

Brown did not wait for his Navy discharge to begin the business of building an organization. Virtually all of the coaches and a vast majority of the players he signed were men he had seen in action first-hand somewhere in his time as a coach. Players and coaches from Massillon, Ohio State, and Great Lakes (the military was abundantly rich in football talent during the war) and players those teams played against would make up the backbone of the early Cleveland teams.

Of Cleveland's original coaching staff, Blanton Collier was probably Brown's most significant hire. Collier was as fanatically obsessed with the technical aspects of football as Brown was with the organizational. A Kentucky native, Collier had starred in football at Georgetown College in his home state, after which he began a long stretch as football and basketball coach at a nearby high school.

Collier entered the Navy during the war and ended up at Great Lakes. He attended the football practices there and met Brown when Brown grew curious about who this spectator was who was so intently watching his team practice. Collier would work a long stint as a Cleveland assistant, would have a very successful stint as the head coach of the Browns after succeeding Brown, and would work in an informal capacity for the team after his retirement from coaching almost until his death in 1983.

Collier's original post with the Browns was as backfield coach, and his specialty was pass defense. His work was largely responsible for the fact that from 1946 until the late 1950s, Cleveland's defense against the pass was football's best. Collier's knowledge of virtually anything and everything having to do with football so impressed Brown, however, that the head coach quickly granted Collier free reign with all of the team's players.

Collier's demeanor was very different from Brown's. He was patient and kind, and he went out of his way to be considerate of the feelings of the players. In contrast to the biting sarcasm Brown often employed, Collier favored constructive suggestions. He seems to have believed that just about anybody good enough to make it as far as a pro football training camp could learn the skills required to become at least a serviceable pro player. Oddly enough, that attitude was both in contradiction to and a reinforcement of a prime tenet of Brown's that held that just about every player was a replaceable part of the overall machine.

"Everything had to be perfect; he was a stickler on perfection—but at the same time, he had great patience," Otto Graham said of Collier. "If I made a mistake, we would keep working—he would try to draw it out of me—give me every possible chance."

When former players talk about Collier, they invariably use words like *fatherly* to describe his relationship with them. Others likened him to a favorite old college professor. Several different generations of Cleveland players, men like defensive tackle Don Colo and defensive end Bill Glass, thought Collier a football genius, while others including Graham considered him "brilliant."

"He taught us how important defensive football was, at a time when people weren't talking about defense," defensive back Tom Colella, an original Brown, said of Collier. "He and Paul Brown made defensive football what it is today. The other teams all copied them, and today everybody emphasizes defense."

"He was absolutely amazing in his ability to teach the details of all 22 positions," said Dick Schafrath, a standout offensive tackle in the 1960s. "I don't think anyone has ever concentrated so much on the teaching aspect of athletics."

The patience and thoughtfulness Collier showed the players seems, on the surface, to be a luxury only an assistant can afford. Part of Brown's job, and the job of any head coach, was to be the tough guy that enforces the rules and makes the hard decisions that some players invariably resent.

According to many players who played for Collier during his eight years as Cleveland's head coach, however, that appears not to have been true in his case, or at least nowhere near as true as with other coaches. He was a player's coach and a highly successful one, both as an assistant and as head man, and the contributions he made to Cleveland's ten-year dynasty in his first stint with the Browns were enormous.

Another of the assistant coaches Brown hired was Fritz Heisler. Heisler played for Brown at Massillon and was an undersized but outstanding guard at Miami University. He then worked under Brown at both Massillon and Ohio State before going into the service, where he coached football at DePauw University under the Navy's V-5 program.

At DePauw, Heisler coached Bob Steuber, a back who had played previously at the University of Missouri. Under Heisler, Steuber led the nation in scoring in 1943, and Brown signed Steuber to play for Cleveland in 1946 at Heisler's urging.

Heisler began as a guard coach with the Browns and remained with the team until 1970. In his early years with the team, which were also the last years of single platoon football, he worked with the team's guards on both offense and defense. In the 1950s, when the evolution to the two platoon system was complete, he became the offensive line coach. Few teams have had as many outstanding linemen over an extended period as the Browns did during Heisler's tenure.

Many of the players he coached credited Heisler with playing a key role in their success. On defense, he tutored Bill Willis, Weldon Humble, and others who played in the middle of Cleveland's great defense. Even after he became strictly an offensive coach, Heisler would offer tips to defensive players. Paul Wiggin, a defensive end in the 1960s, said of Heisler that "he was one of the most brilliant technicians that ever walked the face of the earth."

It was on offense that Heisler really made his mark, though. Cleveland's guard play on offense was as important a factor in the team's success in their dynasty years as any. Lin Houston, Ed Ulinski, Bob Gaudio, Abe Gibron, and Humble were among those who opened holes for Marion Motley and Cleveland's other backs. Motley won rushing titles in 1948 and 1950 and compiled the highest career yards per carry average in the game's history.

Heisler's guards were also an instrumental part of revolutionizing pass protection with the pass pocket, or cup, as it was originally called. Previously, pass blocking was done haphazardly. Brown, Heisler, and the players on the Cleveland line coordinated it, and pass protection as it is done to this day was born.

"Nobody touches Graham" was the line's chant as the line broke huddle, and for ten years they were as good as their word. That protection was a significant part of the great advances by the Browns as they ushered in the modern passing game. Heisler's tutelage, although like the play of the line itself often overlooked, was crucial.

The first player Brown contacted about playing for his team was quarterback Otto Graham, a native of Waukegan, Illinois. Graham was the son of music teachers and as a boy was proficient at several instruments, most notably the French horn. He was also an outstanding all-around athlete who, in addition to his football prowess, excelled in basketball. He played basketball as well as football at Northwestern University, and he played for the 1945–1946 Rochester Royals, champions of the

National Basketball League, one of the major league predecessors of the National Basketball Association.

Graham was an even better football player. He led Northwestern as a three-year starter and was runner-up for the 1943 Heisman Trophy. He was drafted by the Detroit Lions of the NFL, but he entered the service upon graduation before signing a contract or playing a pro game.

Brown remembered Graham from Ohio State's games with Northwestern, as the Graham-led Wildcats were one of the few Big Ten teams to defeat the Buckeyes during that time. Brown particularly remembered a play where Graham stopped and turned after running to his left and threw accurately and with authority to complete a long pass back to his right.

In talking of the other skills that led him to build his new team around Graham, Brown mentioned "poise, ball-handling, and distinct qualities of leadership." He was also impressed by his quarterback's great peripheral vision. Ara Parseghian played halfback alongside Graham for two years and said that as a passer, in addition to arm strength and accuracy, Graham also "had the kind of touch for a quarterback that was way ahead of his time."

"He threw a beautiful ball," Parseghian said. "He had the ability to lead you perfectly, or to drop the ball just over the defenders into your hands."

"Oh they were soft," Dante Lavelli said of Graham's passes. "I used to catch a lot of them one-handed. He had great touch in his hands."

Graham "could feather the short one, throw a bullet over the middle, and launch the long ball, all with equal finesse," Browns broadcaster Ken Coleman said. "Graham was the best all-around athlete I ever saw."

Longtime teammate Lou Groza noted that "Otto was physically and mentally tough." That statement was born out by the penchant Graham would develop for leading his team back from deficits to victory, as well as by the remarkable fact that in an era when quarterbacks, like other players, were fair game for being hit just about anytime anywhere, Graham never missed a game in his ten-year pro career.

"I remember a couple of games, I mean he really took some shots," halfback Chet Hanulak recalled. "He was the type of guy, no matter how bad he was getting beat up, you would never know it. He never got upset." That toughness and refusal to criticize or blame teammates,

Hanulak thought, was one of the traits that made Graham such a great leader.

"I don't think anybody ever let up or let him down because you knew he always gave 100%," Hanulak said. "And if he did, you were certainly going to do the same thing. And I think that was the attitude we had on offense, that he was the leader and the ultimate leader, and he kind of set the pace and you better follow the pace."

"Otto instilled the desire to win right there on the field," is how Lin Houston put it.

As he would do with several players he really wanted, Brown offered Graham a contract that, like his own, included a monthly payment for the duration of Graham's military stint as well as a salary and a signing bonus that were both higher than the NFL standard. Overwhelmed, Graham immediately signed, forsaking the established NFL. He would look back on his decision to go with the Browns and the AAFC as one of the best and most important of his life.

Martins Ferry, Ohio, native Lou Groza was busy as a surgical technician in Leyte and Okinawa and other points east in 1945. Like Graham, Groza was an outstanding athlete. He led his high school to state championships in both basketball and football. His brother Alex was one of the best basketball players of that era and enjoyed a distinguished career at the University of Kentucky, where he gained All-American honors and played on two national championship teams. Groza had played only freshman football as a tackle and placekicker at Ohio State before going into the service, but nonetheless he made a lasting impression on Brown.

One day, in between taking care of wounded soldiers, Groza received a package from Brown. It contained some footballs, a contract, and a letter encouraging him to keep his strong right leg in shape. Groza did so by kicking the balls up and down the various Pacific beaches he and his platoon were in the process of securing. Groza, too, signed with little hesitation. When he returned to the States, he began what remains the second longest playing career in the history of pro football.

Dante Lavelli was another player signed by Cleveland who had played at Ohio State during the Paul Brown era. Lavelli was a sophomore end on the Buckeyes' 1942 national championship team and went into the Army the following spring. Upon returning from Europe, Lavelli attended an NFL game between the New York Giants and Washington

Redskins at the Polo Grounds in 1945. He was pleasantly surprised to find his former Ohio State teammate Sam Fox, a player who had played behind him on the Buckeyes, playing end for the Giants.

"I thought if he could make the grade, so could I," Lavelli said. "So when Paul offered me the chance, I was ready."

Something else that Lavelli saw in that game became an important part of Cleveland's passing game beginning the following year. Steve Bagarus was one of Sammy Baugh's favorite receivers with Washington at the time. Lavelli watched as time and again, Bagarus got open on sideline patterns. A relatively simple pattern, it was something new in pro football, where the running game was still the preferred mode of moving the ball. When he returned to his home in Ohio after being discharged, Lavelli spent many hours on his own practicing and improvising on the sideline pattern.

That kind of tenacity would not have surprised anyone who played with Lavelli. As an infantryman, Lavelli had survived the horror of the Battle of the Bulge. Expecting to come of age at a leafy college campus, he had instead done so with his life on the line. Years later he would joke that in all his years as a player he had never run as fast on a football field as he had in the forests of France. But, in those horrific wintry months of December 1944 and January 1945, it had not been funny at all.

Six-foot-three-inch, 200-pound end Mac Speedie from Utah was another player Cleveland signed early on. Speedie was afflicted with Perthes disease as a boy, a serious leg condition that required him to wear a brace for four years. He eventually made a complete recovery, although he was left with one leg that was shorter than the other. A few years after overcoming the disease, one that could have left him unable to walk for life, Speedie became proficient at sports.

Speedie was one of the best athletes in Salt Lake City schoolboy history and in the history of the University of Utah. He excelled at basketball and football and was one of the fastest NCAA low and high hurdlers in the early 1940s. Once, he finished second in a race in which the winner set an NCAA record.

Speedie entered the Army in 1942 and played against Great Lakes, where Brown was impressed with his skills. He was big and strong, had great speed and jumping ability, and possessed the strong but soft hands that are the hallmark of the great receivers. According to Lavelli, the bout with Perthes may have benefited Speedie as a football player in that "it gave him an odd gait in which he could fake plays without even trying."

Speedie also had a healthy combination of determination and boyish enthusiasm. The determination helped him through his childhood ailment, while the enthusiasm was best expressed when he said, "I didn't know whether I was good enough to play with the big boys or not. I've never got over the feeling of happiness that hit me when I found I was."

Very quickly, Speedie became one of the biggest boys in all of pro football. Writers seeing him for the first time regularly likened him to Don Hutson, the absolute highest praise for a receiver of the postwar era. Browns linebacker Tony Adamle said Speedie was "the guy I think was the greatest end who ever lived," an opinion seconded by longtime Browns defensive back Tommy James.

"I covered the guy every day in practice [and] I never saw a better receiver than Mac Speedie," James said. Linebacker Alex Agase called Speedie a "gamebreaker" and recalled the difficulty the outstanding Cleveland linebacking corps had containing him in practice.

"We tried to jam those people in practice all the time," Agase said of Speedie, Lavelli, and Dub Jones. "You couldn't touch Mac Speedie. He was like a ghost. He was quick and he could just fake you out and everything. He was one of the premier receivers of that time."

Perhaps more than any of his teammates, Speedie also had an independent spirit that led him to occasionally clash with Brown. The two would eventually part acrimoniously, apparently never seeing or speaking to each other in the almost four decades from Speedie's departure until Brown's death. But in his time with the Browns, Speedie was the best receiver in football.

One of the assistant coaches Brown hired was John Brickels. While Brown was still in the Navy in 1945, Brickels signed a number of players to Cleveland contracts. Among them were center Frank Gatski and guard Ed Ulinski.

From Farmington, West Virginia, and Marshall University, Gatski came from a family whose male members virtually all worked in the area's coal mines. Gatski had been a miner himself before going into the Army. As coach of an opposing high school, Brickels saw Gatski play several times, spoke highly of him to Brown, and signed him at Brown's urging once Gatski returned from Europe.

Gatski was quick and, like Graham, incredibly durable. He never missed a practice or a game in high school, college, or a pro career that lasted twelve years. Gatski was also very strong, perhaps the strongest player on the Browns during his time with the team.

Once he stepped into the center job on a full-time basis after Mo Scarry was forced to retire because of an injury, Gatski anchored Cleveland's offensive line for a decade. Groza called him a "Rock of Gibraltar," while tackle Derrell Palmer, who played against Gatski for three years with the New York Yankees and then with him for five years, said he was the "best center I ever played with or against."

Pittsburgh native Ulinski had played for Brickels in high school and with Gatski at Marshall. His signing with the Browns was the beginning of a long association with the team, first as a player and then as an assistant coach. Brown remembered Ulinski as "one of the most dedicated players I ever had" and "one of my all-time offensive guards."

"He had real quickness and he had an elbow block that was a good block," Palmer said of Ulinski. He was an excellent player for the Browns for four years. Later, as a coach, Ulinski worked with Heisler mentoring Cleveland's many outstanding offensive linemen of the 1950s and 1960s, men such as Groza, Schafrath, Gatski, Gibron, Mike McCormack, Jim Ray Smith, Gene Hickerson, John Wooten, John Morrow, and Monte Clark. Ulinski's brother Harry was a standout at Kentucky and played several seasons for the Redskins.

Tackle Lou Rymkus was one of the best of the players the Browns signed away from the NFL. After starring in high school in Chicago and at Notre Dame, Rymkus played for an outstanding Eastern Conference champion Redskins team in 1943. He was a first-team selection to the *Chicago Herald-American*'s all-pro team as a rookie.

It was while he was in the Navy that Rymkus was tendered a contract offer by Brown in 1945. Washington owner George Preston Marshall refused to match the offer, derided the AAFC project to Rymkus, and questioned whether the new league would ever even begin play. Rymkus signed with Cleveland and immediately became a valuable member of their great offensive line.

"Lou Rymkus was one of the best offensive tackles I ever played against," Palmer said. Brown called Rymkus "the best pass protector I've ever seen" and considered him Cleveland's best tackle in every season he played with the Browns, quite a statement given that the tackle on the other end of the line for most of that time was Groza, a future Hall of Famer.

Rymkus was also tough. He played the entire 1946 season, offense and defense, fifty-plus minutes a game, with a knee injury so serious that it required surgery immediately after year's end.

Back Edgar "Special Delivery" Jones of Scranton, Pennsylvania, was another of the early Browns who excelled in more than one sport. In addition to his prowess in football at the University of Pittsburgh, Jones was an outstanding pitcher who attracted the attention of several major league teams while in high school. At seventeen he pitched against Joe Medwick, Johnny Mize, and the rest of the Gashouse Gang St. Louis Cardinals in an exhibition game in Scranton.

Jones earned his nickname on the football field for consistently making big plays, including against Brown's Ohio State teams. Even though he played alongside Marion Motley, the best fullback of that era, Jones earned a reputation as a runner who was especially good in short yardage and goal line situations.

"He could really cut and he was a rough one to bring down," said Graham. Lavelli remembered Jones not just as an excellent player but also as a leader and a positive force on the team.

"He brought everybody close together," Lavelli said. "And he wasn't afraid to talk back to Paul Brown." That alone was probably sufficient to earn Jones the respect of most if not all of his teammates.

Illinois native Lou Saban played against Brown's Ohio State teams as a blocking back and linebacker for Indiana University. Signed by Cleveland after a hitch in Asia in the Army where, among other things, he was a Chinese interpreter, Saban was one of the team's best defensive players in its early years.

Linebacking mate Agase said Saban was "a great player," while Groza remembered him as "intense." George Terlep played both with and against Saban. "He was one of the two hardest hitting men I've ever seen in pro football," Terlep said of Saban. "Him and Buckets Hirsch. They just put it to you."

Saban's skill, intensity, and leadership qualities led Brown to name him team captain in 1947, a title he held until he retired. Those same qualities also enabled Saban, like so many of Cleveland's players who played under Brown, to enjoy a long and successful college and pro coaching career.

In addition to Rymkus, some of the other original Cleveland Browns who had played in the NFL were end Alton Coppage of the Chicago Cardinals and tackle Jim Daniell and back Bob Steuber of the Chicago Bears (Edgar Jones actually played one game for the Bears in 1945 as well). Daniell was another of Cleveland's original team who played for Brown at Ohio State. In addition, there were five players who refused to go to Los Angeles when the Rams left who ended up with the Browns.

Those five players—backs Gaylon Smith, Tom Colella, and Don Greenwood; center Mike "Mo" Scarry; and tackle Chet Adams—claimed their contracts were with the *Cleveland* Rams and that they were under no legal obligation to play for the team in Los Angeles. Brown was interested in the five, and they were interested in remaining in Cleveland to play for the Browns, so he signed them to contracts.

The players went to court to be freed of their Rams contracts, Rams owner Dan Reeves went to court seeking to have those same contracts upheld, and eventually matters were resolved in favor of the players. Rams coach Red Conkwright also ended up signing with the Browns.

Of the five ex-Rams, Scarry and Cleveland native Adams had NFL credentials that were particularly noteworthy. Scarry had been all-pro in 1945 and was captain of the 9–1 Rams that year even though it was just his second pro season. He also had played in the first football game ever televised in 1939 while at Waynesburg College. Adams, meanwhile, was a veteran of five seasons and had been named all-pro while playing for the Green Bay Packers in 1943, a season that the Rams suspended operations because of war-related financial difficulties. And with the Rams having won the NFL title in 1945, the five brought a degree of a winning attitude to their new team. None would play more than three seasons with the Browns, but each would contribute to the team's earliest championships.

Several NFL veterans who seemingly had come over to the Browns and the new league had a change of heart and went back to their respective teams. One was Vince Banonis, a center and linebacker who played for the Cardinals for several seasons beginning in 1942. While in the Navy,

Banonis came to terms with the Browns and began receiving a monthly stipend that was to last until he was discharged.

When Cardinals owner Sonny Bidwill got wind of the deal, however, he gave Banonis a raise commensurate with his Cleveland contract. Banonis informed the Browns of his change of heart and returned the money he had received up to that point. He went on to have a fine career, playing with the Cardinals during their best years in the late 1940s and with Detroit Lions teams that would beat the Browns in two consecutive Championship Games in the 1950s.

Green Bay Packers fullback Ted Fritsch actually made it to training camp before he had a change of heart. He returned to the Packers without the Browns putting up any resistance. In part that was because it was not clear whether they had any legal leg to stand on. The jumping of some players resulted in legal action, and when players jumped and then jumped back, that, too, sometimes resulted in legal action—but very rarely. A new league competing with the NFL had suddenly introduced a whole new dynamic that many players took advantage of in a variety of ways.

Having successfully signed away Rymkus, the five players from the Rams, and others, Brown may have simply decided to pull in his horns and not fight over Banonis and Fritsch. His chances of winning legally were very slim anyway. Besides, as more and more military personnel came to the end of their obligations, the pool of available football talent grew on a weekly if not daily basis. And as good as Banonis and Fritsch were, Brown knew it would not be good in the building of his new team to have players on the team who didn't want to be there.

Players would continue to jump leagues through 1949 without much in the way of legal recriminations. Looking back, defensive back Tommy James, who jumped to the Browns from the Lions in 1948, would marvel that he was able to do so without the hindrance of a lawsuit, especially given that he continued to be treated by Detroit's team doctors for an arm injury after he had reached terms with Cleveland.

Still, there were legal battles, and they weren't just between the two leagues. Guard Bill Radovich was a five-year veteran of the Lions who signed with the AAFC Los Angeles Dons in 1946. After playing two years with the Dons, he sought a return to the NFL. He was barred from playing, however, and not just in the NFL. None of the teams in the Pacific Coast League would have him, either. Radovich sued and, after several lower court defeats, was upheld in the Supreme Court. He was awarded $105,000 but never played in the NFL again.

When the very first Cleveland Browns training camp opened in 1946 at Bowling Green University, it was full of hungry football players. They had grown up during the Great Depression, and many had just returned from distant battlefields. If they were not to make it in pro football, and most of them would not, it would not be for lack of trying.

There was also a certain symmetry in these men finding themselves on a football field not many months after having been at war. Not in the sense of the cliché that equates football with war, but rather in the opposite effect that being a soldier can have.

There was a certain existential derring-do at work, a pronounced tendency to live in the moment because the future was so uncertain. In the war their lives were quite often on the line, whereas in camp the stakes were nowhere near as high. Still, the opportunity to play football at the highest level was there, and it was a much brighter prospect than any of them faced elsewhere.

"I didn't know what was going to happen," Gatski said of his leaving a coal-mining camp in West Virginia to hitchhike to Bowling Green. "I just went up there to see what would happen."

Gatski had been in the infantry for three and a half years. Eighteen months of that time had been spent in various parts of Europe battling the soldiers of the collapsing Third Reich. Two of the possibilities for the future, Gatski knew, were football and a life of work in the mines, the very same mines in which his father had been killed in an accident. Fighting Nazis and working in coal mines can toughen people, crystallize their desire to do something else, and drive them that much more to go after what they want.

While dozens of others fell by the wayside in the weeks of training camp, Gatski persevered. Still, he was on the margins at first, a backup center who also filled in on defense. Gatski's attributes were his physical skills and his willingness to not be outworked by anybody. He deployed his work ethic, persevered, and walked away from pro football a dozen years later, destined for the Hall of Fame after having played on more championship teams than any player in the game's history.

That first training camp made a lasting impression on a number of players. "It was a tough, dog-eat-dog situation, and you really had to hustle," Groza said. Back Gene Fekete was competing with his own brother.

"The toughest game I ever played in was the first intrasquad scrimmage game" is how Lavelli remembered Bowling Green. "Nobody talked to each other for two days." Lavelli also recalled that a number of players arrived in camp in their military uniforms and that most came by bus, by train, or, like Gatski, by hitchhiking. Few young men in those days owned cars.

The competition was stiff, and Lavelli, like so many who would not only make it but also have great careers, faced an uphill climb at the outset. Lavelli had played only through part of his sophomore year in college. At Bowling Green, in addition to the immensely talented Speedie, he found himself competing with a number of ends that included a lanky speedster who had played both college and service football (John Harrington), an All-American from powerhouse Notre Dame (John Yonakor), a veteran starter for three seasons with the NFL Cardinals (Coppage), and a Duquesne University All-American and veteran of three collegiate all-star games (John Rokisky). The competition made Lavelli and the others who survived better players, and the Browns were a stronger team for it.

There were two other players at that first training camp in Bowling Green. The football exploits of each, while not a part of the national sports consciousness, were certainly well-known to many in Ohio in the summer of 1946. One had been an All-American at Ohio State and had played on the Buckeyes' national championship team. The other had been a dominant player in high school in Canton and then in college in the relative obscurity of Reno, Nevada.

Despite their credentials and their physical skills, which, as the football world would soon discover, were myriad, neither had received so much as a look from the NFL. The reason was simple: They were African American, and African Americans were not welcome in the NFL.

Brown knew them both well and invited them to camp. As soon as they stepped on the field with the others assembled, it was clear that they were very special football players. The NFL's loss because of its collective ignorance was the gain of the Cleveland Browns, their fans, professional football, and, it is not an exaggeration to say, the United States.

When September rolled around and both were in the Cleveland starting lineup, another small but important step in the direction of progress was taken. The two men were Bill Willis and Marion Motley.

Willis, Motley, and the Fall of the Color Line

HEN PAUL BROWN invited Bill Willis to come to camp that summer of 1946, he apparently did not speak to either Arch Ward or Mickey McBride beforehand about his intention to do so. He certainly did not ask either of them permission. It would never have occurred to him to do that.

The Browns were his team in a way they could never be McBride's regardless of how much money McBride had. And Ward had encouraged him to become a part of the All-America Football Conference with the idea that the league would take on the NFL with all guns firing. Paul Brown was determined to put together the best team that anybody had ever seen, he was going to do so with black players, and nobody was going to have anything to say about it.

It would be wrong to think that Brown came to such a point simply through the sheer force of his own will. The World War II years had been a time of great upheaval in the United States. In the midst of global cataclysm, many of the rules that governed human societies no longer made sense. Many of those rules fell by the wayside. Nothing seemed set in stone anymore.

People began to think and act differently and have different, more ambitious aspirations. In some instances, entrenched and powerful reactionary forces proved stronger than those aspirations, at least in the short run. The forced exodus of women from many of the workplaces they had moved into during the war is one striking example.

For African Americans, the war years were a period of struggle and of some progress. Although not as dramatic as the struggle and progress that would come less than a generation later, it was an important period nonetheless. And even though the world of sports has historically been presented as being above politics, it was there that some of the era's most dramatic breakthroughs occurred.

In December of 1945, Jackie Robinson (a great football player at UCLA who would have immediately improved any pro team, NFL or AAFC, had any chosen to sign him) was signed to a contract with the baseball Brooklyn Dodgers by Branch Rickey, the team's general manager and part owner. Robinson played with Brooklyn's top minor league affiliate in Montreal in 1946 and then, in 1947, became the first black player in the major leagues since the nineteenth century.

In the spring of 1946, the newly relocated Los Angeles Rams signed Kenny Washington and Woody Strode, teammates of Robinson on UCLA's football team, to contracts. And several months later, Brown offered Willis a contract to play for his new football team, then several months later signed Marion Motley.

Although Brown was probably as certain of his rightness in all things as Branch Rickey or anyone else who ever lived, he was also different from Rickey in important ways. He never considered himself a crusader on the race issue, nor did he do anything to call attention to his role in breaking the color barrier in sports. As Jim Brown put it, Brown "integrated football the right way—and no one was going to stop him."

"Paul Brown integrated pro football without uttering a single word about integration," Jim Brown said. "He just went out, signed a bunch of great black athletes, and started kicking butt. That's how you do it. You don't talk about it. Paul never said one word about race."

Rickey, on the other hand, constantly played up his role as a racial pioneer to whoever would listen. Rickey was nicknamed the Mahatma after Mohandas Gandhi by New York sportswriters for his penchant for addressing them condescendingly in long-winded parables. His accomplishments were great, and he is remembered for his pioneering role in a way Brown is not, in part because of the greater popularity of baseball, but also to a great degree because Rickey was expert at blowing his own horn, something completely alien to Paul Brown. Yet it was Willis and Motley (and Washington and Strode) who broke the major league sports color line for good more than a half a year before Robinson.

There were important differences, too, in the way integration took place in Cleveland and the AAFC under Brown's leadership and the way it happened in Los Angeles and the NFL with the Rams. In contrast to the Browns, the Rams were essentially forced to sign Washington and Strode. To not have done so, as events unfolded, would have meant financial disaster for owner Reeves and perhaps even the death of his franchise.

Reeves moved the Rams to Los Angeles in January of 1946 despite having won the NFL championship just a month before when it became clear that the franchise was losing the popularity battle in Cleveland to the Browns of the upstart AAFC. Reeves was so desperate to move that he did so despite the opposition of the other NFL owners. One of the arguments he used in making his case was the danger the NFL might face if it completely ceded California to the AAFC. Still the other owners would not budge, and it was only when Reeves made it clear that he would not comply with any attempt to make him stay that the other owners reluctantly went along with Reeves's plan.

With the Rams organization taking root in Los Angeles and its ties to Cleveland cut, Reeves began negotiating with various Los Angeles officials about the Rams' use of the Los Angeles Memorial Coliseum as their home stadium. With much of Los Angeles ecstatic about the city's first breakthrough into major league sports, Reeves assumed that his team's use of the Coliseum was a foregone conclusion.

It was an important moment for the Rams. Los Angeles was a sprawling, rapidly growing megalopolis. Like many cities in the United States, its population had swelled during the war, with people arriving from all over to work in the area's many weapons-related businesses. The large influx of people also created a need for more service workers, workers like Jackie Robinson's mother, who moved to the city when Robinson was a young boy. By 1946, Los Angeles had passed Philadelphia and Detroit and was the third most populous city in the country.

For this and other reasons, as risky as Reeves's move west was, it was also one fraught with great possibilities. The size of the city, the increased leisure time, the warm climate, the passion the citizenry had shown for college football, the excitement of having a local pro team—all undoubtedly had Reeves salivating at the potential for his franchise. The Coliseum had a larger seating capacity than any arena, stadium, or ballpark of any kind in the country. The prospect of it being filled with the kinds of crowds that UCLA and USC football games drew, the kinds of crowds that had proved so elusive in Cleveland, was daunting.

Still, the risks were very real. Those very same UCLA and USC teams would be competition for fans. In addition, the other NFL owners, highly displeased with Reeves for his defiance of them, extracted concessions from him whereby the Rams would pay for the added cost of travel to the West Coast. And although the Rams' move meant they would not be engaged in a potentially deadly fight with the Browns, they had not escaped the AAFC. Millionaire Ben Lindheimer and a group of Hollywood celebrities including Don Ameche, Bob Hope, and Louis B. Mayer had been awarded an AAFC franchise and were also seeking to rent the Coliseum.

Use of the Coliseum was imperative to the success of the Rams. Other facilities like Wrigley Field and Gilmour Stadium just would not do. Reeves and the Rams were thus in a somewhat vulnerable position, and that vulnerability did not go unnoticed by some in Los Angeles. Under pressure from Los Angeles's black populace, some city and Coliseum officials seized the opportunity to press the Rams to integrate their roster.

In fact, that stipulation became a part of the negotiations: Use of the Coliseum was contingent on the Rams' abandonment of the whites-only policy that had been in force in the NFL for thirteen years. So it was that Washington, a UCLA legend and one of the best college football players of the late 1930s, and Bruins teammate Strode became NFL players. Just like that, from pressure from the outside that threatened the league financially and not from any sense of enlightenment, the color line in the NFL fell for good like the proverbial house of cards.

Willis played middle guard for Brown at Ohio State and had been one of the best players on the best team in the country. He was also a sprinter in high school in Columbus and in college, a marvelous athlete.

Somewhere along the way he probably dreamt of playing football beyond college. But when he did graduate from Ohio State in 1945, he came up against the harsh reality of racial exclusion.

Although blacks were not welcome in the NFL, there was nothing in writing where it was spelled out, no contract or other written agreement between the league's owners. But there was an understanding firmly in place since 1933 that each of the owners unwaveringly adhered to.

Prior to 1933, that had not been the case. Even then most NFL teams did not employ blacks, but a few did. Outstanding black players like Duke Slater and Fritz Pollard made an important contribution to the game that went well beyond their small numbers.

It's not exactly clear what changed in 1933, but the arrival of George Preston Marshall as owner of the then-Boston Redskins the year before is often cited as an important turning point. Marshall was a segregationist from Washington, DC. He would own the Redskins for more than thirty years, and his franchise would bear the shame of not hiring a black player until 1962, the last pro football team to do so.

The Marshall explanation has merit but hardly provides the entire answer. Men like George Halas, whose life was football and who had struggled through so many difficult times to keep the NFL alive, willingly and decisively ceded to the newcomer Marshall. The NFL's other established owners were likewise all too quick to go along with Marshall. The number of blacks in the NFL had declined steadily in the seven years prior to 1933, indication that many owners were not exactly enthusiastic about integration to begin with.

Perhaps Halas and the other owners were infected with the view, increasingly popular during the Great Depression, that blacks should not be allowed to work while whites were unemployed. Or perhaps more likely, the outlook Marshall overtly expressed was one that resonated with the other owners because it was theirs as well, and Slater, Pollard, and other blacks had been allowed in despite the owners' better judgment and not because of it. Even the circumstances surrounding Dan Reeves, Kenny Washington, and the final desegregating of the NFL, events that were unfolding while Brown was building his team, bear this sad fact out.

So as Willis entered the years when his physical skills would reach their peak, his playing career appeared to be at an end. He worked as the head football coach at Kentucky State College, an all-black school in

Frankfort, in the fall of 1945. Still itching to play, Willis was on the verge of accepting an offer to play for the Montreal Alouettes when Brown contacted him about playing for Cleveland in that momentous summer of 1946.

There was a risk involved, Willis knew. Brown's invitation to come to camp was just that. There was no guarantee that he would make the team. And Willis knew that if he didn't make the team, or if the racial environment was intolerable, or if things didn't work out for any reason, by camp's end it would be too late to go to Canada or return to Kentucky State.

But Willis also knew that he could play football. And he knew Paul Brown. Willis knew that Brown was not one to do anything having to do with football unless he was dead serious about it. An offer to make the Cleveland team was just that, not an orchestrated stunt that someone less determined than Brown might have pulled to placate public pressure or to lure black fans.

Through a complicated intersection of circumstances, Willis had been presented a unique opportunity. Convinced he would be given a fair chance, Willis kicked down the door of opportunity. He scuttled his plans to go to Montreal and put aside his thoughts about coaching. He set out for Bowling Green with a suitcase and a determination to be as good a football player as anybody else in camp.

Willis made an impression in his very first days. With his great speed, strength, quickness, and intelligence, he was ideally suited to play middle guard, a position that tapped into all of those skills. A middle guard lined up in a down position over center and usually charged forward like other linemen. But the middle guard—at least as Willis played it—also dropped off the line and played like a linebacker, with the responsibilities of pass coverage and pursuit of running plays to the outside.

Not all middle guards played the position with the versatility of Willis. Contemporaries Ed Neal and Les Bingaman were stationary 300-pounders who neither dropped into coverage or pursued laterally. Even other mobile middle guards did not cover the field the way Willis did. His mobility and other skills gave the Browns yet another advantage over other teams, and as with other players Brown devised his team's style of play around his personnel. When defending against an inside running game, Willis played as a down lineman in the middle of a five- or six-man front; against outside running plays and passes, he went sideline to sideline and back into coverage like a linebacker.

Center Mo Scarry had played two NFL seasons, had been captain of the Rams' 1945 championship team, and was named second-team all-pro that same season. He would be the Browns' center for their first two years until his career was cut short by an injury. At Bowling Green, Scarry became the first of many offensive players in the pros to experience the frustration of going up against Bill Willis.

On a number of consecutive plays during drills in practice, Scarry, after centering the ball, had Willis go by without being able to impede him in any serious way. Incredulous that Willis or anybody else could beat him that thoroughly that often, Scarry asserted that Willis was offside. Much of the other activity of practice stopped. Players and coaches gathered around to watch the confrontation between the two men. Scarry was a good and respected player who came with an NFL pedigree. But who was this Willis?

The man watching most intently was Paul Brown. He knew Willis had been an excellent player at Ohio State, but this was something else altogether. In Scarry, Willis was dominating someone who was better than anybody he had ever played against in college. After a few more plays, the verdict of Brown and the other coaches was that Willis was not offside, he was simply that quick.

"Incredibly quick," Agase said of Willis. "*He was quick.* I don't think there was anybody as quick at that position, or any position for that matter. He came off that ball *with* that ball as quick as anything you would want to see. And he had a lot of power. He wasn't the heaviest guy in the world but he had great strength. He was one of the great players of all time, no question about it."

"He never gave you a rest the whole game," said Banonis, who would play center against Willis for four years after the Browns joined the NFL. "He came at you a mile a minute. He was a goer. He would come at you and come and he had such great stamina."

"Quick as the devil and very difficult to handle" is how Charlie Ane, offensive lineman for the Lions, put it.

Mike McCormack joined the Browns the year after Willis retired with the unenviable task of stepping into his shoes at middle guard. He would play there one season and then switch to offensive tackle, where, like Willis, he forged a career that earned him a spot in the Pro Football Hall of Fame. Watching Willis on film in 1954, he saw that on play after play, "by the time the ball was snapped, he would be around the running back, ahead of the quarterback."

McCormack also recalled a sequence of photographs he had seen in a newspaper of Willis going against center John Rapacz of the Giants. "He hit John so hard, it drove him back and caused Charlie Conerly to bobble the ball. He picked up the ball, dropped back, Bill hit him and came out and intercepted the pass. Just imagine that: great, great quickness, and cat-like agility."

"No one could block him," Lavelli said. "He was across the line before the other guy was making the blocks."

"It was my first year with Green Bay," Hall of Fame center Jim Ringo recalled of a 1953 game, "and we opened up against the Cleveland Browns. I was a twenty-one-year-old kid and I had to play against Bill Willis. He was all over me."

"He was just so quick, they couldn't block him," Parseghian said of Willis. "He was gone. I mean, gone."

Browns broadcaster Ken Coleman recalled that even in the latter years of Willis's career, Brown would have to remind officials before games of Willis's quickness and caution them to be absolutely sure before calling him offside. And that was more than a coach working an officiating crew for an edge, several Browns players said, for the league office had confirmed by looking at game films that Willis was occasionally flagged in error.

Unlike Jackie Robinson's first weeks with the Dodgers, there was no moment of truth in the integration of pro football that has been passed down and told and retold about Willis and that first camp. In the case of the Dodgers, the moment of truth came when a group of Brooklyn players circulated a petition stating their objections to playing with a black teammate. In essence, their demands were that Robinson and other blacks not be allowed to play and, failing that, that they, the white players, be traded to other teams. When manager Leo Durocher got wind of the petition, he quelled the mutiny with an impassioned late-night speech to a hotel room full of Dodgers.

Paul Brown laid down the law much as Durocher did, only he did it before there was any hint of an insurrection. Graham remembered

Brown's edict to the team as, "If you don't like playing with a black man, get out of here."

Also, unlike the baseball Dodgers, the Browns were a brand new franchise in a fledgling league. Most of the players had no pro experience; the jobs they were fighting for had just been created only months before. To make an issue of having a black player in camp, to demand a trade or seek a tryout somewhere else, would have been a laughingly suicidal career move. As far as is known, no player did.

There were several other factors that worked to the advantage of Willis and Brown. Unlike minor league baseball, college football in most of the country was not segregated. Although there weren't many blacks playing college football in the 1940s, there was a history of whites and blacks playing together. This was especially true in Willis's case. He had played not only with the Ohio State players in camp but also against many of the others who came from colleges throughout the Great Lakes area.

"I had played against most of those guys in the Big Ten," Willis said, "so it was old home week when I joined the Browns."

Whatever the whites in camp felt about playing with a black player, after only a short while it was obvious to all that Willis was a special player who would help them win football games. As Durocher had said of Robinson in his inimitable way in his late-night speech, "He's gonna put a lot of money in your fuckin' pockets." It proved true of Robinson, and it proved just as true of Willis and Marion Motley.

It was after camp was under way that Brown got in touch with Motley and invited him to come to Bowling Green. Motley had played against Brown's Massillon teams at Canton's McKinley High School, and then for him at Great Lakes. Motley said that Brown rebuffed an earlier request for a tryout and contacted him only when it became clear that Willis was going to make the team and was in need of a roommate.

Brown's claim is that he had Motley in mind all along. Perhaps he appraised the fullback talent in the first days of camp and decided Motley was better than anybody there, especially after Fritsch returned to the Packers. The fact is that camp was under way when Brown contacted Motley, a fact that supports Motley's version of the chain of events.

Born in Georgia and raised in Canton, Motley attended all-black South Carolina State College and then the University of Nevada in Reno, where he starred in football. He went into the Navy and ended up at

Great Lakes, where Brown secured his services for the football team. Motley excelled for Great Lakes, as he had everywhere else he played.

Collier remembered Motley's defensive play in a game between Great Lakes and a group of college all-stars in 1944. "We finally went into a seven man line, with Motley as the linebacker, in an effort to hold them," Collier said. "Pretty soon it developed into a struggle between Marion and the All-Star offense—and you can believe me when I say it was a standoff."

Like Willis, however, Motley returned to civilian life after being discharged from the Navy without hope of a career in pro ball. He was working at a steel mill in the Canton area in the summer of 1946, having decided to return to Nevada-Reno in September, when word came from Bowling Green about a tryout. Motley could not have known what to expect upon arriving at a training camp that was several weeks in progress. Did Brown, in fact, want him primarily because Willis needed a roommate?

Motley was taking the same kind of risk as Willis. If he was injured or cut near the end of camp, he would have missed his chance to return to college and play football that fall. The chance to achieve a dream that had only recently seemed impossible, however, drove Motley. How others treated him or whether he got a fair shake was, to some degree, out of his hands. All he could do was play his best. Motley was determined to do so.

"I knew this was the one big chance in my life to rise above the steel mill existence, and I really wanted to take it," Motley said. "I had no doubt I could make the team because I had played against some of the best competition during the war, and I had measured up pretty well in my own mind."

At six foot two and 235 pounds and as fast as just about anybody in football, Motley, like Willis, made an immediate impression. The six-foot-three-inch, 240-pound Groza remembered his first encounter with Motley.

"I tackled Motley head-on, and I thought a truck had run over me," Groza said. "It was just like a load of something fell on me."

Motley was twenty-six, had played college and service ball, and had built up his strength working the most difficult jobs in a segregated steel mill. He was at the peak of his physical skills. To Groza, who was twenty-two and had played only a few freshman games, Motley "was a man; most of us were still boys."

Hall of Fame coach Bud Grant played with Motley for Brown at Great Lakes. Grant would later be an outstanding end for the University of Minnesota, the Philadelphia Eagles, and in Canada. Upon arriving for practice at Great Lakes, however, Grant was eighteen, not long out of high school, and fancied himself a fullback. That notion lasted until he saw Motley, who was seven years older and about forty pounds heavier.

"[A]t that moment I became an end because there was no way I was going to beat Marion Motley," Grant said. "I didn't know him and hadn't heard of him, but I knew he was awfully tough."

Tom Landry, another Hall of Fame coach, played against Motley as a defensive back with the AAFC New York Yankees and the NFL Giants before embarking on his long and successful tenure with the Dallas Cowboys. He thought Motley "perhaps the best all-around fullback ever to play the game." Motley "not only helped break the color barrier in professional football, he broke a few opponents' helmets with his punishing runs and devastating blocks."

"Motley was the greatest I've ever seen," said Otto Schnellbacher, who also played defensive back with the Yankees and Giants. "I thought he was in a class by himself. He ran over me my rookie year. We were playing a 5-3-3 and I was the safety. The hole opened and the linebackers were gone and here comes Motley. He cuts toward the sidelines and I'm gonna push him out of bounds, but he doesn't go out of bounds, he turns suddenly. He puts an elbow in my nose, breaks my nose, knocks me out, steps on me, and goes on and scores. I woke up and the coach says, 'You'll get killed tackling like that.' I said, 'Tell me about it.' I was very much impressed with Marion Motley."

"I remember him because he was coming down the sidelines and I was gonna bump him out," said George Hekkers, a tackle who played for the Miami Seahawks, Baltimore Colts, and Lions. "Forget it. He knocked me five feet."

"Motley had quick feet and good running sense," teammate Parseghian said of some of the skills that made Motley great. "A great back is one who comes into the hole and still makes yardage even if the hole is one hole away. . . . Motley could bowl you over, but he could also find the hole."

As great a defensive player as Dick "Night Train" Lane spoke of bringing Motley down as a Herculean accomplishment. "He looked like a big truck rolling down on me," Lane said of an encounter that took place near the end of Motley's career. "I saw a few stars but I felt good because I tackled Marion Motley." Second-generation black players like Lane undoubtedly also felt a bit of a thrill playing against the ground-breaking Motley and Willis in the same way that Willie Mays, Hank Aaron, and Ernie Banks were thrilled when they found themselves playing against Jackie Robinson.

Many of the players who played with and against Motley echoed Landry, Schnellbacher, Groza, and Lane. Others agreed with Brown's assessment that he was the best fullback ever to play the game. Collier and longtime football writer Paul Zimmerman went one better and called Motley the best all-around player ever.

For Zimmerman, Motley's blocking skills helped set him apart. He "pass-blocked like no other back who ever played the game," Zimmerman said, utilizing "a numbing, paralyzing head-and-shoulders shot that would lift defensive ends and tackles and dump them on their behind."

Schnellbacher echoed those sentiments. "He could sit back there and pass block for Otto Graham and it didn't matter how big those guys were coming in . . . he could sit there and take it. He was a great blocking fullback."

Then there was Motley's skill on the other side of the ball. As he had in the Great Lakes game that so impressed Collier, Motley often played linebacker in short yardage and goal line situations throughout his career with the Browns. Brown said Motley was a good enough linebacker to have made the Hall of Fame had he played strictly that position. And in much the same way that Brown came to appreciate Motley's greatness, Motley appreciated the tone the coach set in 1946.

"[T]here were a few who weren't too happy," Motley said of his white teammates at Bowling Green. "Paul addressed that at the first meeting. He said, 'If you can't get along with your teammates, you won't be here.' He didn't have to spell it out, everyone knew what he meant."

Cleveland's signing of Willis and Motley was part of a historic change in pro sports. For years, the color line in sports had been under attack, and finally in 1946 the whole thing collapsed without so much as a lawsuit or a countermovement. By 1950, pro football, basketball, and baseball were all integrated, and players like Robinson, Willis, Motley, Joe Perry, Roy Campanella, and Larry Doby had established themselves as all-time greats.

The struggle continued for many years after 1946, however. Black players faced tremendous hostility on the field for years, and many were held to a special code of behavior off the field that often hindered and even ended careers. And for many years after 1946, there was a quota and stacking system in place that limited the number of black players and confined them to certain positions.

Still, 1946 was an important year in which huge strides were made. Although Willis and Motley never achieved the iconic status of Jackie Robinson, they are remembered respectfully by the 1940s and 1950s generation of black players whose careers they helped make possible. And almost to a man, their white teammates remember Willis and Motley both as tremendous football players and as men whose presence on the team helped make the whites better human beings.

Significantly, it also quickly became obvious that the early jump the Browns (not to mention the Rams and the baseball Dodgers) got in the signing of blacks made them better than almost all of their rivals. In fact, it is difficult to imagine the Browns achieving the success they did had they not so thoroughly outpaced other teams in the signing of blacks. So although Paul Brown's racial attitudes were seriously flawed in a number of ways, his steadfast determination to build the best team he possibly could contributed both to the breaking of the color line and to his team's becoming the greatest dynasty in football history.

Unlike Willis and Motley, the great Kenny Washington did not have many moments in the sun as a pro. He occasionally showed flashes of brilliance, but in 1946 he was no longer the player he had been when he played so brilliantly for UCLA in the late 1930s. So as with Josh Gibson, Cool Papa Bell, and so many other African American baseball greats, we are left to wonder at all Washington might have accomplished and rue the ignorance that prevented him from doing so.

As criminal as the color line was, Washington also endured the equally egregious racism that kept him on the bench after the color line was broken. Despite averaging a phenomenal 7.4 yards per carry in 1947, for example, he was underutilized by a team that had not really wanted him in the first place, carrying the ball only sixty times that season. So at the same time that it's true that Washington's talents had eroded because of knee injuries, it is also true that he faced an additional set of obstacles that remained prevalent in 1946 and well after.

Although the end of Washington's life was not as haunting or as tragic as that of Josh Gibson's, in some ways it eerily paralleled that of the great catcher. Friends and observers reported that the denial of opportunity ate at Washington over the years and affected his health. He was just fifty-two when he died in 1971, just a little more than a year before his college teammate and friend Jackie Robinson died at age fifty-three.

C H A **3** T E R

The First Season

1946 Roster: Chet Adams (T), Al Akins (HB), Ernie Blandin (T), George Cheroke (G), Tom Colella (HB), Alton Coppage (E), Jim Daniell (T), Fred "Dippy" Evans (HB), Gene Fekete (FB), Frank Gatski (C), Otto Graham (QB), Don Greenwood (HB), George Groves (E), Lou Groza (T), John Harrington (E), Lin Houston (G), Edgar Jones (HB), Alex Kapter (G), Bob Kolesar (G), Dante Lavelli (E), Cliff Lewis (QB), Bill Lund (HB), Mel Maceau (C), Marion Motley (FB), John Rokisky (E), Lou Rymkus (T), Lou Saban (LB), Mike "Mo" Scarry (C), Bud Schwenk (QB), Gaylon Smith (FB), Mac Speedie (E), Bob Steuber (HB), Ray Terrell (HB), Ed Ulinski (G), Bill Willis (G), John Yonakor (E), George Young (E)

PENING DAY for the Browns, the Miami Seahawks, and the All-America Football Conference was Friday night, September 6, 1946, at Cleveland's Municipal Stadium. It was a year and four days after the end of World War II and two weeks before opening day in the National Football League. It was also Labor Day weekend, and as tens of thousands of fans streamed into the cavernous stadium on the banks of Lake Erie, it was clear that Mickey McBride and the Browns front office had done as good a job promoting the new team as Paul Brown had done constructing it.

In the seasons they had called Cleveland home, before departing for Los Angeles, the Rams had played all but two of their home games at League Park. The Rams had not drawn well throughout their Cleveland tenure, and it was just as well that they did not use Municipal Stadium more often. A stadium with 60,000 empty seats would not have been a beneficial atmosphere to play in.

There was no such concern about empty seats on that warm late summer evening in 1946, however. A new era was about to begin, and 60,135 were on hand to witness that beginning. In retrospect, the enormity of the crowd was only fitting, as the home team was about to begin a ten-year stretch of greatness unmatched in the annals of pro football.

Vast crowds have become so commonplace in professional football in the years since 1946 that one of 60,135 would be a disappointment in most places. At that time, however, there had been only one larger crowd in the game's history: the 68,000 that had gathered at the Polo Grounds to see the Giants and Bears in one of the feature games of Red Grange's rookie season. By contrast, although League Park was significantly smaller than Municipal Stadium, the Rams had been able to draw as many as 30,000 fans on only two occasions in Cleveland.

In fact, the capacity crowd of 35,964 that the Browns had attracted to Akron's Rubber Bowl in their only preseason game, a 35–20 victory over the Brooklyn Dodgers, was larger than every single home crowd the Rams had drawn in eight seasons. Perhaps the success of the date in Akron should have prepared the Browns for what was to come. Whether it did or didn't, it was clear right from the first game that Cleveland and much of the surrounding area had taken to the new team in a big way.

Because of the size of the crowd, the Cleveland and Miami players who took the field that night must have felt absolutely certain that they had made the right decision in signing with the AAFC. Based on the size of the crowd, *this* was the big leagues. McBride, other AAFC owners, and the league office undoubtedly felt equally satisfied when word of the attendance got out.

Lou Groza would play twenty-one years in front of numerous crowds in the same stadium that were far larger, yet the turnout for the game against the Seahawks made a lasting impression. "The first game we played there, I came out on the field and just felt like a midget," Groza said. "There was a lot of hoopla, a lot of excitement. It was overwhelming, the noise and everything."

"It was really a sensation playing in front of a crowd that large," Groza went on. After the initial sense of awe passed, Groza realized the great size of the crowd could be an advantage to the home team. "Just that alone gave you inspiration."

One aspect of the attendance success that the Browns enjoyed that night and in the years that followed was the presence of large numbers of black fans attracted in large part by the presence of Willis and Motley. Estimates place the number of blacks at the Seahawks game at 10,000. Significantly, the game also drew a large number of reporters from black-owned newspapers that were then immensely popular and influential in black communities around the country.

Editors and writers from many of those newspapers had been calling for an end to the color line in sports for years. Together with radicals like Lester Rodney, sports editor of the New York–based *Daily Worker*, the national daily newspaper of the Communist Party with a circulation of over 100,000, those editors and writers had focused most of their attention on baseball. But when the first breakthrough came not in baseball but in football, they were there in force to cover the Browns and their two black players.

That coverage further fueled excitement in a number of cities with AAFC teams, most notably Cleveland, New York, and Los Angeles. The AAFC's hiring of black players far outstripped the NFL's and remains one of the important legacies of the upstart league. And although to a lesser degree because of the greater popularity of baseball, the Browns joined the baseball Dodgers as the most popular teams among blacks throughout the United States in the years after World War II.

If the Browns team that took the field for that first AAFC game represented the progressive face of pro sports, the Miami Seahawks represented the opposite. In their desire to create a league that was truly national, the AAFC's founders awarded a Miami franchise to Harvey Hester. Miami in 1946 was a bastion of white supremacist attitudes; had anyone so much as dared to think that a black might play for the Seahawks, it would have required the passage of new legislation, for that kind of integration was quite literally against the law in the state of Florida. In fact, even blacks on opposing teams were barred from play-ing in Seahawks games in the Orange Bowl, as the Browns would dis-cover in December.

In building his team, Hester's original plan was for the Seahawks ros-ter to be made up entirely of players from the South. A lack of talent in training camp required the team to hire players from other parts of the country, but Hester was not deterred. In spirit and attitude, he was deter-mined that the Seahawks be a team of the South.

Hester's attitude is reflected in some remarks he directed Paul Brown's way on the field prior to the opening game. "Boy, I feel sorry for you in this league," Hester said. "You don't have enough Southern boys on your team."

The Seahawks were polar opposites of the Browns in other ways, too. In contrast to the corporate precision Brown applied to all things foot-ball, the Seahawks were disorganized. And at the same time much of the football world discovered that the Browns were an enormously talented team, they discovered that the Seahawks were severely lacking in talent. They were one of the worst teams in football that year, and they drew the fewest number of fans.

Even Providence seemed to be against the Seahawks. Several games had to be rescheduled because of hurricane-like conditions, and torren-tial rains fell during several others. The team was also under pressure from various religious congregations concerned about Sunday football games, and Hester scheduled all of Miami's games on weeknights. Such a schedule might have worked, but by the time the Seahawks played their first home game, they were 0–3; by the time they played their second, they were 1–7.

The Browns received the opening kickoff and so began on offense, and the starting lineup that took the field was as follows: Mac Speedie (left end), Jim Daniell (left tackle), Ed Ulinski (left guard), Mo Scarry (center), Bill Willis (right guard), Chet Adams (right tackle), Alton Cop-page (right end), Edgar Jones (left halfback), Don Greenwood (right half-back), Gene Fekete (fullback), and Cliff Lewis (quarterback).

The unlimited substitution rules used today were still several years away. Until then, teams were limited in when they could make substitu-tions and in how many players could be substituted at a time. Not only did players have to play both ways, therefore, but coaching decisions about whom and when to substitute were an important part of game strategy as well.

The talent discrepancy between the two teams was evident immediately as the Browns built a 27–0 halftime lead en route to a 44–0 victory. The Browns defense overwhelmed Miami, while the offense was led by a multitude of players. Mac Speedie scored the first touchdown in Cleveland and AAFC history on a 19-yard touchdown pass from Lewis, Groza scored 14 points including three field goals, Tom Colella scored on a 50-yard run, and Graham and Lavelli hooked up for the first of their many touchdown connections. The defense got in on the scoring as Ray Terrell set a team record that stood for fourteen years when he returned an interception 76 yards for a score.

Perhaps more disturbing than Miami's dismal performance on the field was the fact that Hester and the team left town without paying any of their bills. Thus began four years of financial troubles that would dog the AAFC. The Browns paid the bill, and another pattern began in which the AAFC's better-heeled, more successful franchises would make money available to the unsuccessful ones in order to keep the league going.

There were two other games on the AAFC slate that first weekend. At Kezar Stadium, 35,000 fans saw the New York Yankees defeat the 49ers in the first ever major league football game in San Francisco. And at Civic Stadium (later to be renamed War Memorial Stadium), 25,000 people welcomed major league football back to Buffalo after a seventeen-year absence and saw the Brooklyn Dodgers defeat the homestanding Bisons, 27–14.

The Browns again played a Friday-night game the following week, and for the second time in two games they played before a crowd of historic proportions. Going up against the Chicago Rockets at Soldier Field, the Browns won 20–6 in front of 51,962, the largest crowd ever to see a pro football game in Chicago. That was quite a beginning in the city that figured to be the toughest for the new league to gain a toehold.

And given that the seating capacities of Wrigley Field and Comiskey Park where the Bears and Cardinals played their home games were significantly smaller than Soldier Field, the Rockets' home park, the two NFL teams that had called Chicago home for more than twenty-five years undoubtedly took note. In fact, Soldier Field held as many people as the city's two other stadiums combined. If the Rockets got off on the right foot and Chicago football fans responded as they did for the game against Cleveland, the Bears and Cardinals knew, the Rockets could gain a substantial financial edge over their two rivals.

The big crowd and the sense that the AAFC might make a real go of it in Chicago could not obscure a more disturbing aspect of the game that night. Perhaps more than any game the Browns played that year, the match with the Rockets was marred by a preponderance of late hits and cheap shots directed at Willis and Motley. The Browns retaliated frequently, and by some accounts the tactics of the Chicago players rallied the white Cleveland players behind their black teammates to a greater degree than before.

Despite the backing of their teammates, the game was just one of many over the next eight years where Willis and Motley would face physical and verbal abuse directed at them because of the color of their skin. They would endure having their hands stepped on, late blows from forearms and elbows, and racist slurs of all kinds. Even the most hardened players and game officials were shocked by some of what they saw and heard in the Rockets game.

Still, in some ways the experience may have made the Browns a better team. Once exposed to the kind of behavior the Rockets exhibited, many of Cleveland's white players came to understand that unless they stood together, serious injury to their two teammates was a distinct possibility. And as both Willis and Motley had already proven themselves to be among the best players on the team, it would also hurt the team's prospects. Some of the Browns were repulsed that anyone would have to endure the kind of abuse the Rockets were meting out. Willis remembered that then and later, Lou Rymkus and several others were more than willing to retaliate when necessary.

But if the Rockets game was the first exposure of some of Cleveland's white players to racially motivated dirty play, that was not the case for Willis and Motley. They had experienced such things before and had even come to expect it. The retaliatory blows struck by their teammates were both welcome and necessary, but Cleveland's two black players were not about to be pushed around by anyone.

They got back at the opposition in several ways. Motley was fast and, at 235 pounds, bigger than not only all backs in football at the time but most linemen as well. When he ran with the ball, he dished out far more punishment than he received. In the game against the Rockets, he also made his presence felt when he scored the first touchdown of his illustrious career.

Willis was already establishing himself as one of the best, hardest-hitting defensive players in the game. He covered ground like no one else who played his position, and he often required double-team blocking that further disrupted offenses. Before the 1946 season was very old, it was clear that Willis and Motley could inflict pain both with their bruising style of play and with the high quality of their skills, which would prove instrumental to so many Cleveland victories. Or as Motley so eloquently put it, "They found out that while they were calling us niggers and alligator bait, I was running for touchdowns and Willis was knocking the shit out of them. So they stopped calling us names and started trying to catch up with us."

More history was made that second AAFC weekend. About the time the Browns-Rockets game was ending, the Dodgers and Dons kicked off in the Los Angeles Memorial Coliseum. It was the first major league football game ever played in that stadium, and the first by a Los Angeles team in twenty years, beating the Rams' debut by sixteen days. The Dons marked the occasion with a 20–14 win, but the crowd of 19,500 was quite a bit less than was hoped for. The following night, 40,606 welcomed pro football back to Yankee Stadium as the Yankees defeated the Bisons 21–10.

The Browns made the short trip to Buffalo on September 22 for their third game and defeated the Bisons 28–0. As they would so often in the next ten years, the Browns showed their all-sided superiority in dominating the Bisons. Motley led the ground game, and the Browns' passing game was on display as Graham threw two early touchdown passes. Then the defense took over, stifling Buffalo throughout and adding a clinching touchdown on a 25-yard run by Chet Adams after a fumble recovery.

Cleveland rolled through the first half of the season, winning four more games to bring their streak to seven. Included in the winning streak were two victories over New York's Yankees. Both were the kind of hard-fought games that were to be the hallmark of the brief rivalry between the two teams. The two losses were the first suffered by the Yankees, who at midseason already sat comfortably atop the AAFC East.

Many preseason prognosticators had dubbed the Yankees the AAFC's best team. That was in part because the Yankees came into the new league as an already existent organization, owner Dan Topping having brought his Brooklyn Dodgers/Tigers franchise over from the NFL. Among the Yankees players were perennial NFL all-pros and future Hall of Famers Bruiser Kinard and Ace Parker (the NFL's MVP in 1940) and others who had been Brooklyn standouts like Pug Manders and Perry Schwartz.

Topping's decision to throw in with the new league was the end result of a complex set of circumstances that unfolded at the same time Arch Ward and the earliest AAFC owners were launching the new league. Topping, owner of the Dodgers since 1931, was dissatisfied with the situation of his team. With the exception of 1940–1941, the team had floundered throughout its fifteen years, and the Dodgers had never been able to make a breakthrough attendance-wise.

By 1945, Topping and partners Del Webb and Larry MacPhail also owned the baseball Yankees. A move of his football team to Yankee Stadium in the Bronx appealed to Topping, both because it would allow him to easier consolidate his two teams under one umbrella and because he believed it would afford the Dodgers a greater chance to succeed. Yankee Stadium, after all, was newer and far larger than Ebbets Field, the park the Dodgers had called home since the franchise's inception.

The baseball Yankees were the crown jewel of sports franchises, and part of Topping's thinking undoubtedly was that that success might rub off on his football team if they were to call Yankee Stadium home. Many of the Yankees' regular fans were Topping's kind of people—sophisticated, well heeled, used to success—and they hailed from his kind of places (Manhattan, Westchester County, and the Bronx's more upscale neighborhoods).

Brooklyn, on the other hand, was, to people like Topping, an outpost, a place one went to only if absolutely necessary. There are many things that could be and have been said about Brooklynites of that era, specifically the denizens of Ebbets Field; "sophisticated," "well heeled," and "used to success" are not among those things.

So a move to Yankee Stadium made sense to Topping, a man who was used to getting what he wanted. While still a part of the NFL, he went about making plans for the move for the 1946 season (the Dodgers, renamed the Tigers in 1944, combined with the Boston Yanks for the 1945 season). There was only one problem: New York Giants owner Tim Mara.

Mara had been through this fight several times since founding the Giants in 1925. He had successfully opposed the efforts of Red Grange and C. C. Pyle to place an NFL team in Yankee Stadium in 1926, leading to the formation of the first American Football League. When AFL I folded after just one season, Mara agreed to allow Grange and Pyle's Yankees into the NFL and Yankee Stadium under the condition that the vast majority of their games be played on the road.

With Grange unavailable most of the time because of serious injuries, those Yankees never caught on and folded after the 1928 season. Mara next beat off an attempt to place a team in the Bronx less than two years before Topping's proposed move. In 1944, Mara successfully prevented Ted Collins from placing his new Yanks franchise in the Bronx (the same Yanks that Topping's Dodgers merged with in 1945), and they settled in Boston instead. After twenty years in the NFL, Mara was one of the most senior owners, and his invocation of his "territorial rights" was respected by the league's other owners and Commissioner Elmer Layden.

The other owners recognized the fact that a stable, successful team in the country's largest city was a boon to the NFL. Mara was willing to go along with franchises in Brooklyn and Staten Island (the NFL Staple-tons had played in that part of New York City from 1929 through 1932), but he was unwilling to go along with having a team play in Yankee Sta-dium. He had seen how the balance of power had shifted between the baseball Giants, his co-tenants at the Polo Grounds, and the baseball Yan-kees in the years since the opening of Yankee Stadium in 1923.

Whereas before 1923 the baseball Giants had been the preeminent franchise in all of sports, the Yankees had quickly surpassed them and then left them far behind after moving into their new ballpark. After never having won a World Series before 1923, the Yankees had won ten in the twenty-three seasons since, and in those years they featured Babe Ruth, Lou Gehrig, and Joe DiMaggio, three of the greatest and best-known players of all time. The Giants, on the other hand, while still suc-cessful, had won only one World Series in that time, and only twice in those twenty-three years had they been able to outdraw the Yankees.

Once the Yankees acquired Ruth and the city committed to con-structing Yankee Stadium, there was not much baseball Giants owner Charles Stoneham could have done to prevent the dramatic power shift. Mara, on the other hand, was recognized to have exclusive NFL rights to New York (which meant essentially that no other team could take up residence in the Polo Grounds or Yankee Stadium without his agreement). That gave him an advantage that Stoneham did not enjoy, and he utilized that advantage with Topping as he had with first Grange and Pyle and then Collins by successfully nixing the move of the Dodgers/Tigers to the Bronx.

The existence of the AAFC, however, gave Topping leverage he would not otherwise have had. Shortly after the AAFC's formation, reports began to appear in New York of the new league's wooing of the Brooklyn owner. When those reports intensified in 1945, NFL commissioner Layden and the other team owners began to pressure Mara. Much as they respected Mara's territorial rights, the other owners and Layden recognized that a Topping defection would be a serious blow.

Reluctantly, Mara agreed to Topping's request for a move to Yankee Stadium. But it was too little too late. At first Topping objected to the schedule, complaining that Mara had kept all of the prime home dates for the Giants. Then he confirmed the speculation that had been rampant for months by announcing at the end of 1945 that the Dodgers/Tigers had become the New York Yankees of the All-America Football Conference and that they would begin play in 1946, with Yankee Stadium as their home.

Much as NFL owners recognized the move as a blow, the AAFC's owners saw the boost it would give their league. Not only would they have a foothold in New York, it would be an already existing organization that included nine Brooklyn players and four others whom the Yankees were able to sign away from other NFL teams. The other AAFC owners had sweetened the pot substantially for Topping by waiving the franchise fee and by giving him $100,000.

The Yankees were now free to select the choicest dates for home games. In addition, the AAFC would have a built-in rivalry between the Yankees and the new Brooklyn Dodgers franchise that would move into Ebbets Field. After years of frustration in which his team had been able to win only 35% of its games, Topping undoubtedly saw the possibility that the Yankees might be one of the new league's elite teams.

For Mara, on the other hand, perhaps the worst-case scenario had come to pass. Beginning in 1946, he would have to contend with a team of proven major league quality owned by Anaconda Copper Dan Topping playing just across the Harlem River, in a stadium that was newer and significantly larger than his team's home park. The fallout from the series of events involving Topping's franchise would fester for several years in NFL circles, leading to bitterness on the part of some owners (particularly Halas and Marshall) toward Mara for not agreeing to a compromise sooner as well as contributing to Commissioner Layden's 1946 firing.

The first of Cleveland's two wins over the Yankees was by 24–7 in the rain at Municipal Stadium on September 29. Despite the inclement weather, a crowd of 57,084 witnessed the game, one that was close throughout until the Browns pulled away with 10 fourth-quarter points. Afterward, frustrated Yankees head coach Red Flaherty berated his team for losing to a "Podunk team with a high school coach."

Like a number of his players, Flaherty had years of NFL experience prior to signing on as Yankees coach. He had been a very good end for the Giants for nine seasons, playing on New York's championship team of 1934. Immediately after retiring, he was hired as head coach of the Redskins at the age of 33. In seven seasons, Flaherty compiled a 54–21–3 record for a .720 winning percentage and guided his team to four Eastern Conference titles and two championships, a record that helped earn him a place in the Pro Football Hall of Fame.

With his team having been touted as the favorites in the AAFC's inaugural season—he said of the 1946 Yankees, "I have the best material I've ever had, and that goes for the fine Washington teams"—Flaherty's harsh postgame words reflected his disappointment at losing to the Browns. Paul Brown and his team did not take kindly to Flaherty's remarks, even if they were spoken in the heat of the moment. The remarks fueled a rivalry that would see the two teams play a total of six games in the AAFC's first two years, including twice in the league Championship Game.

Cleveland's second win over the Yankees was also played in a heavy rain, and the Browns prevailed 7–0 despite being outplayed. The last of Cleveland's seven consecutive wins to open the season was a 31–14 home win over the Dons, who entered the game at 3–1–1 in second place behind the Browns in the West. Not only was the game an important victory over a contending team, it marked the establishment of a new all-time pro football attendance mark with a crowd of 71,134.

Cleveland tasted defeat for the first time to a strong 49ers team on October 27, 34–21. San Francisco was led by an array of outstanding players including quarterback Frankie Albert, guard Bruno Banducci, end Alyn Beals, tackle John Mellus, and backs Len Eshmont, Norm Standlee, Earle Parsons, John "Strike" Strzykalski, Ken Casanega, and Joe Vetrano, who was also the team's placekicker. Albert threw three touchdown passes, and the 49ers built leads of 17–0 and 27–6 that proved too much for the Browns to overcome.

There were two bright notes for the Browns in defeat. Lavelli caught eight passes for 183 yards and a touchdown, and those reception and yardage totals were the most in the AAFC's first season. The game also attracted 70,385 fans, just 750 off another new record. That meant that in just five home games in a little more than half a season, the Browns had drawn crowds that at the time were the first, second, and fourth largest in the history of pro football.

The Browns flew to California for the first time and lost a second consecutive game, 17–16, to the Dons. Cleveland built a 16–7 halftime lead, but Groza's first miss on an extra point in twenty-four attempts proved to be the difference as the Dons scored 10 fourth-quarter points, including Joe Aguirre's 11-yard field goal with 0:20 seconds remaining. Although they were the AAFC's fourth best team and in contention in the Western Conference, Los Angeles continued to draw disappointing crowds. Only 24,800 fans were on hand for the game against the league's marquee team, and the Dons' average by season's end was just 19,899 (compared with the 42,382 per game drawn by a defending champion Rams team that was somewhat of a disappointment at 6–4–1).

With the loss to the Dons and a 27–14 San Francisco victory over Buffalo, Cleveland's lead in the West shrank to one game over the 6–3 49ers. The Browns stayed over for a week in preparation for a showdown with the 49ers in San Francisco. By beating the Browns, the Dons also kept their conference title hopes alive, moving to two games out at 4–3–1.

The Browns-49ers rematch on November 10 attracted 41,061 to Kezar Stadium, San Francisco's largest home crowd of its inaugural season. After Graham and Lavelli connected for the game's first score, a sequence of three plays near the end of the first half produced a second Cleveland touchdown that proved to be enough to win the game.

First, Mo Scarry stuffed a San Francisco drive when he recovered a fumble at the Browns 33. On the very next play, Motley took a screen pass from Graham and ran 64 yards to the 49ers 3-yard line. Gaylon Smith followed with a touchdown run that boosted the lead to 14–0, and the Browns were able to survive a late Albert touchdown and prevail 14–7.

The game was noteworthy for the play of some of Cleveland's second-line players. Backs Dippy Evans, Bob Steuber, and Bud Schwenk either played sparingly or not at all because of injuries. In their place, Bill Lund, Ray Terrell, and Smith filled in and played well.

At Municipal Stadium the following week, the Browns routed the Rockets 51–14 before 60,457, the fourth home crowd of more than 60,000. Graham threw two touchdown passes to both Lavelli and Speedie, and Cleveland took advantage of eight Chicago turnovers. Groza kicked the longest field goal of the season in either the AAFC or NFL from 51 yards, and the kick gave him ten field goals for the season, two shy of the all-time mark set by Paddy Driscoll in 1926. Frank Gatski capped the scoring with the only touchdown of his twelve-year career, a 36-yard interception return.

With the win and New York's 10–9 victory over the 49ers, the 9–2 Browns clinched no worse than a tie for first place in the West. The Dons were eliminated despite a 19–14 win in Brooklyn. In addition to helping Cleveland, the Yankees' win boosted their record to 8–2–1 and allowed them to clinch first place in the East.

The Browns clinched the West in impressive fashion the following week in the final home game of the season with a 42–17 victory over the Bisons. Cleveland piled up 455 total yards and reeled off 35 straight points after falling behind 10–7 in the first quarter. Edgar Jones had two touchdowns, Motley scored on a 76-yard run, and both Schwenk and Al Akins scored their only touchdowns of the season, Schwenk on a 1-yard keeper and Akins on a 50-yard run.

The crowd of 37,054 brought Cleveland's home attendance to 399,963 for the season, an average of 57,138 per game, which was an all-time record. That was far and away the best in football in 1946, besting the Giants 51,777 mark that established a new NFL record. The Browns' average of 43,783 for all games was just behind the Giants' new all-time record of 44,213.

Cleveland continued with its big scoring spree in their two final games. They defeated the Seahawks 34–0 behind an interception return for a touchdown by Graham and the only touchdown of fullback Gene Fekete's injury-shortened career. And they closed the season with a 66–14 rout of the Dodgers as nine different players scored touchdowns.

Groza equaled Driscoll's field goal record against Miami and then broke it in grand style with a 50-yarder against Brooklyn, his thirteenth. In the game against the Dodgers, Groza also set a new record with 45 extra points, breaking the record of 42 set in a ten-game schedule by Bob Snyder of the Bears (Driscoll's field goal record had been set in a sixteen-game schedule).

The Browns closed with 193 points in their final four games, an average of 48.3 per game, and finished the season with 423. They thus became only the fourth team in history to average 30 or more points in a season, joining the great Bears teams of 1941, 1942, and 1943. Cleveland's 137 points allowed led the AAFC by a wide margin, and by averaging fewer than 10 points per game allowed, the Browns became the first of only six teams to do that in the years since World War II. Cleveland's per-game point differential of 20.4 remains the third highest in history, behind only the 26.6 and 22.6 marks posted by the 1942 and 1941 Bears.

Miami's one-sided loss to the Browns and the events in the days leading up to the game in the Orange Bowl served as an appropriate farewell for the Seahawks franchise. After Motley received a letter threatening his life should he play in the game, Brown decided to play the game without the team's two black players. As the Seahawks were one of the worst teams in football and the conference title was already clinched, that was a luxury the Browns could afford.

What might have happened had the Seahawks been a more formidable foe, or had the Browns needed a win, or both, is a matter of speculation. As it is, the league would have faced a difficult situation had Brown taken Willis and Motley on the trip with the intention of playing them, as some officials in Miami made it known that they would have enforced laws barring the two black players. After it became known that Willis and Motley had not made the trip, several black newspapers and civil rights groups criticized Brown for giving in to racism.

There's a ring of truth to that. Brown made a point of refuting notions that he was a social reformer or pioneer, consistently referring to himself instead as a football coach interested in winning games and championships. In his defense, though, it's not clear that Willis and Motley would have been entirely safe had they arrived at the Orange Bowl intending to play. What Brown might have done had he wanted to strike a blow for social justice was to risk a forfeit by refusing to play the game without his team's two black players.

There is no evidence that Brown ever considered such an option, and that is probably at least in part because the Seahawks and the city of Miami were part of the AAFC project, warts and all. The attitudes of Hester and city officials in Miami were certainly racist, but Brown would likely have been reluctant to put them in the nation's spotlight as the forces of evil preventing blacks from playing football. It was, after all, the NFL and men like George Halas and Art Rooney who had kept blacks out of football for thirteen years, not Harvey Hester and the city of Miami.

As it was, the loss to the Browns was the last in the abbreviated history of the Seahawks. The team was transferred to Baltimore for 1947 and played under new ownership there as the Colts. It would take twenty more years and a civil rights movement that rocked the country to its foundations before another pro sports team took up residence in the Deep South.

The first season of the All-America Football Conference was capped by the Championship Game between the Browns and Yankees. Using the rotating system then also in use in the NFL, the AAFC had deemed before the start of the season that the Western champ would host the 1946 title game, the Eastern champ the 1947 title game, and so on. So it was that the Browns-Yankees game was played at Municipal Stadium on December 22.

Just a year earlier, Cleveland had hosted an exciting NFL Championship Game between the Rams and Redskins played in bitterly cold weather conditions with temperatures just above zero. The Rams won 15–14, and a month later they were off to Los Angeles and warmer climes. So for the second year in a row, Municipal Stadium would be the site of a pro football Championship Game.

Both teams had finished their regular season schedules by December 9, so each had almost two full weeks for practice and preparation. In Cleveland, there was some concern about slow ticket sales. Perhaps the images of Redskins and Rams players huddled around bales of hay the year before were still fresh in the minds of Clevelanders. Even with forecasts that indicated a repeat of those Arctic conditions for the Browns-Yankees game was unlikely, heavy snows fell in the days prior to the game, and ticket sales lagged.

The Browns' practice routine was dramatically interrupted on the weekend of December 14 and 15. Edgar Jones, Jim Daniell, Mac Speedie, and Lou Rymkus were out on the town in the early morning hours of Saturday the 14th drinking and killing time as they waited for Speedie's wife to arrive via airplane from Utah. Jones, Speedie, and Rymkus were among Cleveland's best players, and tackle Daniell had been a starter for most of the season. Daniell was also the team captain, for which he received an extra $1,000 on top of his $9,000 salary.

Daniell was one of many Browns who had played for Paul Brown at Ohio State. After graduating, he spent forty-five months in the Navy, where he participated in the battle of Okinawa. He was awarded a Silver Star, a presidential citation for valor, and nine battle stars. Daniell signed with the Bears just after being discharged in 1945, but he joined Cleveland the following year when his former college coach offered him almost three times what he had earned with the Bears. Of significance to the events of that December weekend, Daniell's playing time had steadily decreased over the course of the season as Ernie Blandin gradually took over the left tackle job.

With Daniell driving, he, Speedie, and Rymkus dropped Jones off and then became involved in a disagreement with several Cleveland police officers. After words were exchanged, the three players were arrested, held in custody for several hours, and then released. Stories of the arrests were prominently featured in Cleveland's newspapers.

There are different versions of what exactly happened in the moments before the three Cleveland players were arrested. Paul Brown claimed the police report indicated Daniell was the instigator and that Speedie and Rymkus acted as peacemakers. The version that Tony Adamle heard when he joined the Browns the following year is that

Daniell had played the role of peacekeeper in an effort to prevent Speedie and Rymkus from being arrested.

According to Otto Graham, eyewitness Edgar Jones told him that Daniell had initiated the disagreement by blasting his horn because the officer's police car was blocking the way. Lavelli claimed that the seeds of Daniell's ultimate release from the Browns were planted five years before at Ohio State when he angered Brown by skipping the team train back to Columbus after a big win in Los Angeles over the University of Southern California. The fact that Speedie and Rymkus were charged with creating a disturbance, while Daniell was charged with public intoxication, tends to support the notion that they and not he acted more aggressively once both parties got out of their cars.

There is no ambiguity about what happened at the team's next meeting, however. Brown confronted Daniell about newspaper accounts of the incident, ordered him off the premises, and cut him from the team. A week before the biggest game of the season, the team captain was gone, fired by a coach who apparently never once had second thoughts about his decision. In the same meeting, Brown told Speedie and Rymkus he would deal with them as well, but there is no indication that either was so much as fined.

Brown's explanation for firing Daniell is that as team captain, Daniell had "a special obligation to be exemplary in his behavior." There was no players association in 1946, no grievance procedure, no league body that Daniell could appeal to. His time with the Browns was simply at an end, and he left the team as ordered, never to play football again.

Any number of Browns in that meeting that day, perhaps all of them, believed the punishment excessive. But short of a revolt, they had no recourse to help their fallen teammate, either. Brown was the boss, and where personnel and business decisions were concerned, he neither countenanced democracy nor appreciated employee input. Daniell was through, and any player who had made his disagreement with the decision known to the coach knew, too, that he could very well have met the same fate.

What the Daniell incident represented to the Cleveland players was the absoluteness of Brown's authority over them. The details, but more important, the fallout, were passed on to generations of Browns as an example and a warning. It was crystal clear to some players at the time that Brown's decision had little to do with what was fair and everything to do with power—his power.

Daniell's termination did not hurt the team because, as Graham said, "His replacement was just as good as him." Daniell's captaincy and Brown's claims that he had been the most guilty of the three players were actually irrelevant. Speedie and Rymkus remained not because neither was team captain or because they were "innocent" but because both were among the best players in football at their positions and because firing them would have seriously jeopardized the team's chances against the Yankees.

The point of Brown's actions—and most of the players understood this, either at the time or soon thereafter—was that what the boss said, no matter any double standard or inconsistencies, was law. Drinking, carousing, and defying or talking back to the coach were all punishable offenses, but only when there was a player good enough to replace the one who committed the sin. As such they were not really sins at all, as the long careers of a number of outstanding Cleveland players who engaged in such activities, including some excessively, attest.

Although no snow fell after Friday the 20th and temperatures the day of the first AAFC Championship Game were in the 30s, the match drew a disappointing crowd of 41,181. True, that was almost 10,000 more people than had come out to the Rams-Redskins game the year before. But it was also fewer than all but one of Cleveland's regular season home games and a full 30,000 fewer than had attended the game with the Dons in October.

Still, the crowd was larger than all but three of the fourteen NFL Championship Games played up to that time, and the three games that had attracted more had all been played in the Polo Grounds. Those in attendance were excited about the prospects of the Browns capping a highly successful first season with a championship. The Musical Majorettes, female musicians and marchers that McBride had hired, added a bit of a festive note to the day as they entertained the fans with renditions of Christmas songs.

The Yankees went into the game having won seven of their last eight games, and they had overwhelmed the competition in the East, finishing first by seven games. New York's strength was its line play, and the defense was especially stingy against the run. Tackle Bruiser Kinard and a fine pair of ends, Jack Russell and Bruce Alford, were among the team's best players.

Unlike Cleveland, the Yankees used the single wing on offense. Quarterback Ace Parker had played six seasons in the NFL in the single wing, and it was a formation that, in addition to being coach Flaherty's preference, seemed better suited to Parker's skills. He was a good runner, and he threw well on the move. New York's other offensive standout was Orban "Spec" Sanders, a first-year halfback whose 709 rushing yards and twelve touchdowns were tops in the AAFC.

The game was a defensive struggle throughout, and points proved hard to come by. The Yankees scored first on a 21-yard field goal by Harvey Johnson, but only after the Browns defense pushed them back from a first and goal at the 7. The New York defense went one better a short time later as they allowed no points at all after the Browns had a first and goal at the 3. Brown's decision to go for the touchdown on fourth down may have been influenced by the fact that Groza was hobbled with a sprained left ankle. After his great season, Groza would miss three field goal attempts against the Yankees.

Cleveland took possession on its own 30 in the latter stages of the second quarter and proceeded to produce a touchdown that gave them the lead. Graham completed seven straight passes at one point, and Motley capped the drive by scoring from the 2. The half ended a short time later with the Browns leading 7–3.

Despite having the better of the play in the second half, Cleveland was unable to score in the third quarter or for most of the fourth. The Yankees, meanwhile, scored on a drive that started at their own 20, with Sanders running in for the score from 2 yards out for a 9–7 New York lead. The score remained 9–7 when Rymkus broke through and blocked Johnson's conversion attempt.

Late in the third quarter, the Browns drove deep into New York territory, largely on the strength of a 51-yard run by Motley, but the drive ended with Groza's third field goal miss from the 18. Lou Saban blocked a punt moments later to set the Browns up in great shape at the Yankees 32, but that possession also resulted in a missed field goal, this one by Chet Adams. Trailing by 2 points in the fourth quarter in the game that would make or break their season, the Browns found themselves stripped of one of their biggest weapons, Groza's field goal kicking.

Should they make it back to scoring position, the Browns would almost certainly have to go for a touchdown. There would not be many more changes of possession, and Cleveland could not risk having another scoring opportunity go unrewarded. With a defense as solid as New York's, of course, there was no guarantee the Browns would even get close enough for another chance at a score.

About half of the fourth quarter was gone when Cleveland forced a Parker punt and took possession at their own 25. The defense had done its job in preventing any further scoring after Sanders's touchdown, and now it was up to the offense. The Browns whose reputations as big-play players had not yet been established—Graham, Speedie, Lavelli, Motley, and Edgar Jones—took the field and collectively put together a dramatic drive that brought the Browns their first championship.

Jones made the first big play with the Browns facing third and 9 as he caught a Graham pass off his shoetops while running at full speed. The play was good for 24 yards and positioned the Browns in New York territory. Then on second and 10, Lavelli grabbed a Graham pass and alertly lateraled to Greenwood, who gained extra yards and put Jones in a position to make a crucial first down with a short run on third down.

With the ball on the 26, Colella gained 10 yards and another first down as the game clock moved inside of five minutes. From there it was Graham and Lavelli again, with Lavelli cleanly beating his man as he angled to the right flag. The Cleveland end hauled in Graham's pass and crossed over the goal line for the score that gave the Browns the lead. Groza's successful point after made the score 14–9 with 4:31 remaining.

The Browns were hardly home free, however, and their situation suddenly turned perilous when Sanders returned Adams's short kickoff 35 yards to the Cleveland 45. Then, just when it appeared the defense had saved the day by nailing halfback Eddie Prokop for a 14-yard loss on first down, the Yankees got all of those yards back on Parker's completion to Perry Schwartz. On third and 10, however, Graham intercepted at his own 30, and the Browns were able to run all but a few seconds of the remaining time off the clock. After a Colella punt to the New York 20 and a Parker to Prokop completion that gained only 5 yards, the gun sounded and the Browns were champions of the All-America Football Conference.

Graham was sixteen of twenty-seven for 213 yards on the day, with Lavelli and Speedie each catching six of his passes, Lavelli for 87 yards and

Speedie for 71. Motley rushed for 98 yards on thirteen carries, an eye-popping average of 7.5 yards per carry, which was actually below his amazing regular season figure of 8.2. And although Jones was shut down running the ball, he did contribute 45 yards on three catches.

As would be the case so often over the first ten years of Browns football, a great performance by the defense was overshadowed by the heroics of the offense. The 9 points allowed was almost exactly what the team had allowed per game during the season, and both Parker and Sanders were held in check. Parker was just eight of eighteen for 81 yards passing in what turned out to be the last game of his career, Sanders was held to 55 yards on fourteen carries, and the Yankees managed only 146 yards of offense.

"They were a wonderful team," Parker later said of the Browns.

For the season, Motley finished fourth in the AAFC in rushing with 601 yards, while Jones was fifth with 539. Cleveland's backfield mates finished second and third in yards per carry behind the 8.4 mark posted by Chuck Fenebock of the Dons, Motley at 8.2 and Jones at 7.0. Greenwood tied for the league lead with six rushing touchdowns.

Lavelli and San Francisco's Alyn Beals finished tied for first with forty receptions. Lavelli's 843 receiving yards was first by a wide margin, his eight touchdown catches was second to Beals's ten, and his 21.8 yards per catch was second only to Speedie's 23.5, the best among those who caught at least twelve passes. Among qualifiers, Speedie's mark was also the third best in history at the time. Speedie also had the highest touchdown to reception ratio, as seven of his twenty-four catches resulted in 6 points.

Colella finished first with ten interceptions, while Graham and Lewis finished sixth with five each and Saban added four. The team's forty-one interceptions was far and away the most in the league, and it was one of many defensive categories in which the Browns finished first. Although he was a largely unheralded player, Colella's value was further underscored by his 21.5-yard punt return average, which was the best of those with at least eight returns, as well as by the fact that his 40.3 punting average was one of the top marks among regular punters.

With records for both most field goals and extra points, Groza also established a new all-time single-season mark for points by kicking with 84. That points total was also the highest in the league. Groza also became the first kicker in history to make two field goals of 50 or more yards in the same season, and his kicks of 51, 50, and 49 yards were the three longest in both the AAFC and the NFL.

Of all the Browns who had outstanding seasons, however, none put up numbers as good as Otto Graham's. He threw the ball less frequently than in any of his ten seasons, but as he would throughout his career, Graham made those passes count with extraordinary marks in completion percentage, yards per pass, touchdowns per pass, and interceptions per pass. Most notable of these were a mark of 10.5 yards per pass, which was then the second best in history and remains the fourth best (Graham also owns the third highest mark), and a touchdowns per attempt ratio of 9.8.

Using the passer rating system in use today, Graham's season was the best in history until more than forty years later when overall ratings were dramatically higher. His 112.1 mark was not bested until Joe Montana posted a 112.4 rating in 1989. Graham's rating was an incredible 122% better than the combined rating of the rest of the AAFC's passers.

Not surprisingly, the Browns placed more players on the various all-AAFC and combined AAFC/NFL all-pro teams than any other team in the league. Motley was a unanimous all-league selection; Speedie and Graham were consensus selections; Lavelli, Willis, and Scarry were selected to one of the three all-AAFC teams; and Groza and Ulinski got second-team notice. Willis and Rymkus were selected to one of the two combined all-AAFC/NFL teams, while Motley and Lavelli were selected as second-teamers.

Off an excellent season punting and passing, Brooklyn's Glenn Dobbs was named the AAFC's Most Valuable Player. Dobbs, Sanders, Frankie Albert, guard Bill Radovich, and center Bob Nelson of the Dons; Yankees Kinard and Russell; and tackle Martin Ruby of Brooklyn were other AAFC players who received the most all-league and all-AAFC/NFL honors.

In every sense, the 1946 season had been a rousing success for the Browns. They won the league championship, they set a number of attendance records, they firmly established themselves among fans in Cleveland and much of the surrounding area, and they had a large nucleus of exceptional football players that figured to be good for a long time. For Mickey McBride, Paul Brown, the players, and the team's fans, there was every reason to believe that more success lay ahead.

Not even the most optimistic among them could have predicted how much success lay ahead, however. It would take just one year for many of the attendance records to fall, and the team would add outstanding players for years, sometimes two and three at a time.

As for championships, 1946's was just the first of many. It would not be until 1956, in fact, that the Browns and their fans would know what it was like to have a season end without a Championship Game. Along the way, they would do things that no other pro football team has ever done.

C H A **4** T E R

Two Championships in a Row

New in 1947: Tony Adamle (LB), Ermal Allen (QB), Bill Boedeker (HB), Bob Cowan (HB), Spiro Dellerba (FB), Jim Dewar (HB), Bob Gaudio (G), Horace Gillom (E), Weldon Humble (G), Lewis Mayne (HB), Ray Piskor (T), Marshall Shurnas (E), Len Simonetti (T)

Gone from 1946: Al Akins, George Cheroke, Alton Coppage, Jim Daniell, Dippy Evans, Gene Fekete, George Groves, John Harrington, Bob Kolesar, John Rokisky, Bud Schwenk, Gaylon Smith, Bob Steuber

T HE PRESENCE OF a championship flag hanging above Municipal Stadium was hardly cause for complacency in Cleveland. Over a third of the Browns roster turned over in 1947 as Paul Brown worked diligently to further improve his team. With a few notable exceptions, he again relied primarily on talent from Ohio State and other schools in the Great Lakes area to replenish the team's roster. In fact, Brown again incurred the wrath of some in the

Buckeye community by signing Ohio State players with college eligibility remaining for the second year in a row.

Most prominent among these was Tony Adamle, a fullback and linebacker who would excel at the latter position for six years with the Browns. Adamle's class had graduated in 1946, but because of military service he still had two years of eligibility remaining. However, even before hearing from Brown about playing for Cleveland he had decided not to return to Ohio State. In fact, Adamle was on the verge of signing with the Bears when Brown contacted him.

Adamle had been recruited to Columbus by Brown but left for the service before getting a chance to play for him there. At the time Adamle signed with Cleveland, Ohio State had had two head coaches since Brown's departure and was about to hire a third. That upheaval led, in part, to Adamle's decision to go pro.

Alex Agase played alongside Adamle at linebacker for four years. He remembered Adamle as "one of the best ever." Brown said Adamle was "perhaps as intelligent a player as I ever had." And Ara Parseghian recalled an incident that illustrated Adamle's legendary toughness.

"He dressed once with an ankle as big as a balloon," Parseghian said of Adamle. "I thought there was no way he'd play, but he did. There's nobody in the game today who's tougher than Tony Adamle."

Adamle also impressed his teammates and coach as a leader. Several Browns remembered that Adamle, like Edgar Jones, did not hesitate to talk back to Brown. Rather than being put off, the authoritarian Brown came to respect Adamle's candor to such an extent, in fact, that he named Adamle team captain in 1950 after Lou Saban retired. In that role Adamle made a valuable contribution to team harmony as a go-between between the players and their often cool and distant coach.

Despite Adamle's stated intention of turning pro before Brown contacted him, the Cleveland coach again came under heavy criticism from alumni and administrators at the school he once coached. As in the cases of Groza and Lavelli, Brown's reply was that Adamle's class had graduated, the player was a man of twenty-three looking to support himself and his family, and Brown would do everything in his power to induce Adamle to earn his degree. Since the dispute was not really about any of those things but about Ohio State's desire to have Adamle play for them,

Brown's explanations did no more to placate his critics than when he had made them the year before.

Guards Bob Gaudio and Weldon Humble joined the team and further bolstered an already strong group at that position. Like Adamle, Gaudio was a Buckeye with two years of eligibility remaining who forsook it to sign with the Browns. A Cleveland native, Gaudio was, according to Brown, "technically perfect" and had the speed and quickness Brown loved in his guards.

Originally drafted by the Colts, Humble so impressed Brown in an exhibition game that summer that the Cleveland coach traded five players to get him a short time later. Out of Rice University, Humble was also exceptionally fast for a guard, having been a sprinter in college. In addition to his outstanding guard play, Humble was sometimes called on to play linebacker, most notably in 1950, and he did an excellent job at that position as well.

Halfback Bill Boedeker came in a trade with the Chicago Rockets for John Harrington. He came out of DePaul University and did not play college football. Boedeker was recruited out of Fort Wayne, Indiana, as a basketball player, and he played on an outstanding DePaul team led by George Mikan. After serving in the Army for three years, he was granted a tryout with the Rockets at the recommendation of one of his DePaul coaches.

Boedeker moved into a starting job in the backfield alongside Motley and Edgar Jones, and he made a substantial contribution in his three years with Cleveland. Brown called Boedeker an "exceptional pass receiver" and "one of the most reckless runners who ever played for us and a terror when he ran back kicks." He scored thirteen touchdowns with the Browns on only 191 combined rushes and receptions and posted a glittering 33.7 yards per catch mark in 1949.

The player who was probably the biggest addition in 1947 was Horace Gillom, the third black player to play for Cleveland. Gillom would be a more than capable fill-in at end on both offense and defense, but it was as a punter that he really made his mark in ten years with the team. He was from Massillon and played high school football there for Brown, who recruited him to Ohio State. Gillom also excelled at basketball and other sports, and his reputation as one of Ohio's best schoolboy athletes preceded him to Columbus.

"I knew about Horace Gillom before I went down to Ohio State," Dante Lavelli said of his teammate on the Buckeyes' 1941 freshman team. "Man, when Brown changed me over to end and Horace was there, I said I didn't have much chance. So what happened, Horace ended up going over to the other side." Like another Buckeye, Lou Groza, Gillom entered the Army before he played a down of varsity football.

Upon being discharged from the Army, Gillom went not to Ohio State but to the University of Nevada-Reno in a deal arranged by Brown that, once it became known in Columbus, further angered the Buckeye faithful. The arrangement was the result of events the year before when Brown was attempting to sign Gillom to the Browns in the team's first season. When the Browns signed Motley just as he was about to return to Nevada, however, Brown backed off from signing Gillom. He instead arranged for Gillom to play for Nevada, whose coach Jimmy Aiken had been the coach at McKinley High School in Canton during the Cleveland coach's days at Massillon.

Gillom led the nation in punting with Nevada in 1946 and then played an outstanding game the following summer when the college all-stars defeated the NFL champion Bears 16–0. Brown called Gillom the best all-around athlete he coached in his nine years at Massillon. Gillom made an immediate impact with the Browns. His punting average of 44.6 in his rookie year was the second best in football, just 0.1 yards behind the leader.

"Gillom had such a powerful leg and kicked the ball so far; before that punters used to line up 10, 12 yards behind the center," said Sherman Howard, who played against Gillom and the Browns for three years before joining Cleveland in 1952. "He started the 15-yard drop. And with Horace, he would kick it so high that by the time the guys got down, the ball was coming down, so most guys had to fair catch."

Cleveland used its top draft choice in 1947 on future Dick Hoerner, a fullback from the University of Iowa who would sign with the Rams in the NFL. Of the other newcomers, none became a starter, and only halfback Bob Cowan played for the Browns for more than one year. However, another future selection, University of Michigan quarterback Bob Chappius, would be traded in 1948 for Dub Jones, and that trade proved to be one of the best of the team's dynasty years.

There were several coaching changes in Cleveland in 1947. Assistant

Bob Voigts left to take the head coaching job at Northwestern, and his spot was filled by Bill Edwards, who was named tackle coach. Center and end coach Red Conkright left for a similar job with the Bills, and he was replaced by Dick Gallagher. And one-time Notre Dame star halfback Creighton Miller left his job as one of Cleveland's backfield coaches when he finished law school and took up practice in Cleveland.

Several players who played with Miller at Notre Dame considered him the best back they had ever seen, but he did not play in the pros because of a heart condition. When the National Football League Players Association was founded in 1956, largely due to the work of Browns players, Miller became the union's first legal counsel. Because of his antipathy for the union, Paul Brown then had Miller's image blocked out of the Browns' 1946 team photo.

In addition to Gillom, AAFC teams featured six other new black players in 1947: halfback Bill Bass of the Rockets; halfback Elmore Harris of the Dodgers; halfback Buddy Young of the Yankees; and halfback Bert Piggott, center John Brown, and end Ezzert Anderson of the Los Angeles Dons. That brought the total of blacks in the league to nine. The signing of the three Dons players came a year after that team had violated their commitment to the city of Los Angeles to employ blacks as part of the agreement to use the Coliseum.

In the NFL, Woody Strode left the Rams to play in Canada and no other new black players were signed, leaving Kenny Washington as the only black in the NFL as the senior league continued to lag behind its new rival. Along with Gillom, Young was the best of the black newcomers in the AAFC. He would play nine years of pro ball and thrill fans in two leagues with his blazing speed and many great runs.

Among the other changes in the AAFC's second year, one of the minor ones was the changing of the Buffalo team's name from Bisons to Bills, while one of the major ones was the move of the Miami franchise to Baltimore. The team was purchased by a local ownership group, and it remained in the Eastern Conference. Roster limits were raised from thirty-three to thirty-five, and the league would again play a fourteen-game round robin schedule over fifteen weeks.

Among the veteran players who did not return for the AAFC's second season were Wee Willie Wilkin, future Hall of Famer Ace Parker, and one-time NFL MVP Parker Hall. Some of the best and most heralded of the newcomers, in addition to Young, Adamle, Gillom, and Humble, were halfback Billy Hillenbrand of the Colts, quarterback George Ratterman of the Bills, kicker Ben Agajanian of the Dons, halfback Ray Ramsey of the Rockets, and guard Dick Barwegan of the Yankees. The league also had a new commissioner, Admiral Jonas Ingram, who replaced James Crowley, and Mrs. Lou Gehrig's largely symbolic association with the league came to an end.

The Browns played just one exhibition game, a 28–0 win over the Colts in Akron before another sellout crowd at the Rubber Bowl in the game that Weldon Humble so impressed Paul Brown. The crowd of 35,106 and the one-sided win were both harbingers of what was to come during the regular season, as the Browns would more than live up to their success of the year before. And 1947 would also be the most successful of the All-America Football Conference's four seasons.

The Browns were idle the opening week as the AAFC season began on August 29, a full three weeks before the NFL. The three games that were played all drew good crowds: 41,182 in Chicago saw the Dons defeat the Rockets 24–21; 31,874 in San Francisco saw the 49ers defeat the Dodgers 23–7; and 32,385 in Buffalo saw the Bills win over the Yankees 24–21. In his debut, Buddy Young scored on a 50-yard pass from Spec Sanders for the Yankees.

Like the year before, however, it was in Cleveland that the biggest opening attendance splash was made: 63,263 fans attended the Browns opener against Buffalo on Friday night, September 5. And much as they had dominated the competition on opening night the year before, the Browns built a 27–0 halftime lead against the Bills and coasted to a 30–14 win.

Two days later, the Dodgers and Colts inaugurated pro football in Baltimore before 27,418 at Municipal Stadium. It would be a long first season for the Colts, but they began in spectacular fashion. Jim Castiglia recovered a Brooklyn fumble on the opening kickoff and ran for a touchdown on the first play in franchise history. Hillenbrand added a touchdown on a 96-yard kickoff return, and the Colts won 16–7.

A week after their opening win, the Browns traveled to Ebbets Field for another Friday night game and trounced the Dodgers 55–7. The

Browns' attack was diverse in its deadliness as they scored on the ground, through the air, on a kick return, and on defense. Motley scored on runs of 13 and 51 yards, Boedeker scored twice on runs, Graham threw a 53-yard touchdown pass to Lavelli and one of 19 yards to Speedie, Colella ran a punt back 82 yards, and Bill Lund scored on a 20-yard interception return. In Los Angeles, meanwhile, the Dons and Yankees broke Cleveland's all-time attendance record as 82,675 saw New York's 30–14 win.

The Browns continued to roll, with victories over the Colts and Rockets, and went into their October 5 game against the Yankees undefeated at 4–0. Rookie Gillom made his presence felt with a 74-yard punt in the 28–0 win over Baltimore, and Graham and Speedie connected for a 70-yard touchdown in the 41–21 win over Chicago. The Yankees, meanwhile, had rebounded from their opening defeat with four straight wins and came to Cleveland for the showdown with the Browns in first place in the East at 4–1.

A crowd of 80,067, second largest in pro football history, was on hand for the game, and the Browns and Yankees did not disappoint. After spotting New York a 3–0 lead on a 47-yard Johnson field goal, Cleveland scored 17 points in the second quarter for a 17–3 halftime lead. Cowan caught a 42-yard touchdown pass from Graham, Colella scored on a 29-yard run, and Groza kicked a 25-yard field goal for the points.

New York rallied to tie the game with two third-quarter touchdowns, but Cleveland took the lead again on a 10-yard Graham to Speedie touchdown pass. Although he missed the point after attempt, Groza kicked a 43-yard field goal in the fourth quarter that put the game out of reach. That concluded the scoring as the Browns prevailed 26–17.

The victory was Cleveland's tenth regular season win in a row and eleventh overall. Estimates were that 15,000 of those in attendance were black fans rooting on the home team, drawn by the great matchup, Cleveland's three black players, and Young of the Yankees. The Browns not only continued to reap the benefits of the talents of Willis, Motley, and Gillom, they also continued to benefit at the gate as their base of black fans grew ever larger.

The Browns came back to earth and suffered their first loss of the season the following week. Behind two second-half field goals by Ben Agajanian, the Dons rallied to win in Municipal Stadium 13–10 before 63,124. Agajanian's second field goal was from the 17 and came with just seconds left. On the previous play, he missed from the 22 but got a second chance when Lou Saban was unable to get off the field in time while the Browns were making a substitution, resulting in a penalty for too many men on the field.

The Browns bounced back with a win over Chicago, but it was a hard-fought game that saw Cleveland barely hold on, 31–28. Motley scored on a 22-yard run, Graham and Speedie hooked up on a 49-yard touchdown pass, and Jones scored on two short runs. The Rockets were led by Ray Ramsey, their outstanding first-year back. Ramsey scored three times in the fourth quarter as Chicago almost came all the way back after trailing 24–7.

Having tied the Colts and having lost only a close game to the Yankees, the 49ers were just a half game behind the 6–1 Browns in the West at 5–1–1. That set the stage for a showdown on October 26 at Kezar Stadium. As in 1946, the 49ers were led by an excellent core of players, a core that included Frankie Albert, Alyn Beals, Bruno Banducci, Norm Standlee, John Woudenberg, and John Strzykalski. Coach Buck Shaw was one of the game's best offensive innovators and was very popular with his players.

As they had the year before, the 49ers were enjoying success both on the field and at the gate in 1947. Their roster was made up of a number of players who had played their college ball on the West Coast, and they had established an intrastate rivalry with the Dons. Among their West Coast players were Albert, Banducci, and Standlee, teammates on an outstanding Stanford University team in 1940.

The best home crowd in San Francisco's year and a half of football was on hand, and they saw Cleveland boost its lead over the 49ers to a game and a half with a 14–7 win. In a game played in heavy fog, 54,483 fans watched as the Browns built an early lead on Graham touchdown passes of 22 yards to Lavelli and 42 yards to Speedie, and the defense limited San Francisco to Standlee's 1-yard touchdown run in the third quarter. For the day, Graham was nineteen of twenty-four for 278 yards, while Speedie proved too much for Strzykalski and the other 49ers trying to cover him. Speedie tied the AAFC record set three weeks earlier by Baltimore's Lamar "Racehorse" Davis with ten catches, good for 141 yards.

Speedie made his way into the record book again in Cleveland's next game, a 28–7 win at Buffalo. He and Graham hooked up on a screen pass that Speedie took 99 yards for a touchdown as the Browns duo equaled the mark set in 1939 by Frankie Filchock and Andy Farkas of the Redskins. Lavelli and Yonakor also caught Graham touchdown passes, and the Browns again played before an opponent's largest home crowd. In fact, the crowd of 43,167 at Civic Stadium was Buffalo's largest until the AFL Bills' championship season of 1965.

After the victories over the 49ers and Bills, the Browns returned home and managed to eke out a 13–12 win over the Dodgers. A 72-yard Graham to Lavelli touchdown pass was the game's big play, and Cleveland was aided by a bad day by Phil Martinovich, Brooklyn's placekicker. Martinovich missed four field goal attempts and two extra point attempts. With the win, the Browns expanded their lead to two and a half games over the 49ers, losers for a second time to the Yankees.

Cleveland settled matters in the West for good with a decisive 37–14 win over the 49ers before 76,504 at Municipal Stadium on November 16. Lavelli was the receiving star against San Francisco as he grabbed Graham passes for touchdowns of 23, 15, and 64 yards. The crowd was the Browns' eighth of over 60,000 in fourteen regular season home games, and it gave Cleveland nine of the nineteen largest crowds in pro football history in just two years.

Although they were 10–1 and the conference title was clinched, the Browns had no opportunity to let up. They traveled to Yankee Stadium for a game with the Yankees. At 9–2, the Yankees were in first place in the East, but their lead was only one and a half games over a tough Bills team. Looming a week down the road was a Yankees-Bills game that was likely to determine Cleveland's opponent in the Championship Game.

New York's Buddy Young was enjoying an outstanding first season. He was on his way to 712 yards rushing, which would place him fifth in the AAFC, and a stellar 6.1 yards per rush. Young also finished seventh in receptions with twenty-seven, good for an 11.2 average. And he was among the league leaders in punt returns, with a 15.9 average and a touchdown, and in kickoff returns at 27.7 and another touchdown.

Other Yankees having excellent seasons were guard Dick Barwegan, another rookie; the outstanding end tandem of Bruce Alford and Jack Russell; tackle Nate Johnson; and center/linebacker Lou Sossamon. New York's attendance was up over 1946, and the Yankees were more than holding their own at the gate in their competition with the Giants. Like the Browns, New York's attendance experienced a big boost from large numbers of black fans drawn to the exciting and excellent play of the team and to the presence of the electrifying Young.

Without question, however, the biggest reason for the Yankees' success was the outstanding play of Spec Sanders. Dubbed "Spectacular Spec" by Yankees fans and New York sportswriters, Sanders was on his way to a phenomenal season. With coach Flaherty still preferring the single wing, Sanders played the tailback position that Ace Parker had played for the Yankees the year before. He was a threat to run or pass on any play, was one of the league's better punters, and like Young was an excellent kickoff and punt returner.

By season's end, Sanders would have 1,432 rushing yards and a 6.2 average per carry. The yards were the most in a season by far, besting the record Beattie Feathers of the Bears set in 1934 by 428. Even accounting for the longer AAFC schedule, Sanders established a new high of yards per game, becoming the first player to ever average more than 100 yards rushing per game. That record of 102.3 and the yardage total were the best ever until Jim Brown topped both in 1958.

As a passer, Sanders added 1,442 yards, fourteen touchdowns, and an average of 8.4 yards through the air in 1947. He also averaged 27 yards per kickoff return, 27.3 per punt return, and 42.1 yards per punt. If that wasn't enough, Sanders also accumulated 63 return yards on three interceptions. His eighteen rushing touchdowns and nineteen overall were also new all-time highs that stood as records until the 1960s.

If anything, Sanders may have done *too much* for the Yankees that year. He was a fearless runner who took a pounding during the season, as his 231 rushing attempts also established a new all-time high. Although still very good, Sanders's numbers would drop significantly in 1948, and he would sit out the entire 1949 season because of injuries. In fact, he never played offense again after 1948, although he excelled on defense in 1950, his last season.

The matchup of the Browns and Yankees was one that may very well have featured the two best teams in football, and a variety of crosscurrents intersected to produce one of the most exciting and dramatic games of the season and of the short history of the All-America Football Conference. Among the crosscurrents was the presence of four outstanding black players in the game and the presence of 25,000 black fans at Yankee Stadium.

Just as the presence of Willis, Motley, and Gillom on the Browns galvanized thousands of black fans in Cleveland, so the presence of the exciting and talented Young on the Yankees galvanized thousands of black fans in New York. In fact, the black fans who came out to Yankees games provided the team a big boost in its attendance battle with the NFL Giants, who did not sign their first black player until 1948. And both black and white Yankees fans recognized that the addition of Young made New York a better team and improved their chances of winning the championship that had barely eluded them in 1946.

In all, 70,060 fans were on hand at Yankee Stadium on November 23. It was a new attendance high for a pro football game in the city of New York, a record that stood until 1958. For most of the first half, the game featured the potent duo of Sanders and Young. Sanders scored on runs of 1, 3, and 27 yards, and Young added a 5-yard touchdown run as the Yankees built a 28–0 lead. And as he had been in the 1946 Championship Game between the two teams, Lou Groza was injured, and this time he was unable to play altogether. That meant the Browns would have to try to make up the four-touchdown deficit without one of their biggest offensive weapons.

The Browns got one of the touchdowns back late in the half as Graham hit Boedeker with a 34-yard scoring pass. What many Cleveland players pointed to as the turning point of the game came a short while later as the two teams were leaving the field at halftime. Undoubtedly feeling a bit satisfied with their first-half performance and confident that a first win over the Browns after four defeats was at hand, some of the Yankees players had some derogatory things to say to the Browns for their poor play.

"[T]hey got us upset, got us angry," Graham recalled. "Finally we got mad as a team and we said, 'We'll show these guys,' and we started playing football."

The Browns dominated the second half as thoroughly as the Yankees dominated the first. A key sequence came after the Yankees took the second-half kickoff and drove inside the Cleveland 10. The Cleveland defense stiffened, New York came away with no points, and Graham and Speedie immediately hooked up on an 82-yard pass. In a matter of moments the Browns went from another possible score by the Yankees to being in position to pull within 28–14.

That's precisely what happened as Motley caught a 12-yard touchdown pass from Graham, and then he scored again later in the third quarter on a 10-yard run. Lou Saban, filling in for Groza, added his second and third extra points of the game. Then in the fourth quarter, rookie Jim Dewar scored the only touchdown of his career on a 5-yard run, and Saban's kick tied the game. Neither team scored after that, and the game ended 28–28.

Although it was only a tie, the game was a moral victory for the Browns because of the comeback. That was true not just because some of the Yankees had mouthed off, although that was certainly a reason. What the Browns also knew was that there was a good possibility they would be playing the same team on the same field three weeks later in an AAFC Championship Game rematch. Their comeback for a tie not only provided them with a boost that was likely to carry over, it also deflated a very good Yankees team that had again been unable to beat Cleveland.

It was on very rare occasions that Paul Brown allowed himself to get caught up in postgame good cheer, and almost unthinkable that he would do so after a game the Browns did not win. The fact that he did so after the game against the Yankees is further indication that it was more than just another tie. Brown went so far as to kid captain Saban about his tying extra point kick after Dewar's touchdown, saying, "It's the first time I ever saw a spiral kicked from placement," as other Browns players laughed and Saban smiled good-naturedly.

Tony Adamle recalled that Brown was also in an unusually generous mood monetarily after the game. "I made four tackles on the goal line," Adamle recalled of the key goal line stand. "Brown doubled my salary for that game."

The Browns closed the season with road wins over the Dons and Colts to up their record to 12–1–1, the best in football. With some starters resting and others such as Edgar Jones recovering from injuries, second-line players like Bill Lund and Lewis "Mickey" Mayne saw more action than usual. Each scored two touchdowns in the wins while Graham threw five touchdown passes to give him twenty-five for the season as he capped a second straight sensational year. In the East, meanwhile, the Yankees rode three more touchdowns by Sanders to a 35–13 victory in their showdown with Buffalo and finished first with an 11–2–1 record. Thus it was set that the Browns and Yankees would again tangle for the championship of the All-America Football Conference.

Although Championship Game play had been in effect for only fourteen years, the Browns-Yankees game in 1947 marked the fourth time that the same two teams met for the title in consecutive years. Another impressive crowd was on hand in the cold at Yankee Stadium on December 14. At 61,879, it was the largest ever to see a pro football Championship Game. By contrast, fewer than half as many attended the NFL Championship Game between the Eagles and Cardinals two weeks later in Comiskey Park.

The game was not quite the rousing affair that the 28–28 game had been, in part because an icy field made for less wide-open play. It was more like the previous year's Championship Game and the other games between the two teams in that it was a low-scoring defensive struggle. And just as they had the year before, the Browns showed they had both a bit more firepower and a bit more defense as they defeated the Yankees 14–3.

With 109 yards on just thirteen carries for an average of 8.4 yards per rush, Motley was the key performer for Cleveland. His 51-yard run up the middle in the first quarter set up the Browns' first touchdown and all the points they would need. After Motley's run, Graham converted a third down with a completion to Speedie at the 1-yard line and then scored on a sneak that made the score 7–0. Edgar Jones added a 4-yard touchdown run in the third quarter after New York had closed to 7–3 on Harvey Johnson's 12-yard field goal.

Relying mostly on short passes because of the unsure footing, Graham completed fourteen of twenty-one passes for 112 yards and had none intercepted. Speedie caught four for 25 yards, Lavelli three for 37, and Jones three for 31. Cleveland compiled seventeen first downs and 284 total yards.

For the second straight year, the Browns defense played superbly against the Yankees in the title game. They held New York to thirteen first downs and 212 total yards, and they came up with a big series just prior to Johnson's field goal when the score was 7–0. Sanders and Young led the Yankees down the field in a bid to tie the game, but the Cleveland defense stiffened at the 5 and kept the Yankees out of the end zone. A third-quarter interception by Colella was also a big play as it gave Cleveland the ball on the New York 41 and ultimately led to Jones's touchdown.

The Cleveland defense was successful in holding Sanders in check for the second year in a row. He finished with 40 yards rushing on twelve carries and was seven of seventeen passing, for 89 yards and one interception. Young did somewhat better with 69 yards rushing on sixteen carries and two receptions for 25 yards, but because of the icy field and Cleveland's strong defensive effort, he was unable to break free on any long runs, either from scrimmage or on kick returns.

Another factor in Cleveland's successful containment of Sanders and Young was Gillom's punting. Gillom's average of 45 yards on five punts was 9 yards better than that of New York's Bob Kennedy, and he effectively kicked away from the Yankees' two dangerous return men. For the day, New York had just 14 yards and a 4.7-yard average on punt returns. Gillom's punting also helped the Browns gain the advantage in field position, as the Yankees' best starting point during the game was from their own 41.

Brown was named the AAFC Coach of the Year by *Pro Football Illustrated*, and Graham led the AAFC in passing and was voted the league MVP. Speedie and Lavelli finished first and second in receptions and receiving yards, while Colella tied for the lead with six interceptions that he returned for 130 yards. Motley was third in rushing with 889 yards, good for a 6.0 average, while Jones added 443 yards despite missing five games and led the league with a 6.4 average.

Bothered by injuries, Groza's kicking was well off his record-setting 1946 season. Still, he finished sixth in the league with 60 points, and his seven field goals placed him in a tie for second behind Agajanian's new all-time mark of fifteen. Gillom, meanwhile, finished just a fraction behind the league-best 44.7-yard punting average of Buffalo's Mickey Colmer at 44.6.

Speedie, Rymkus, Graham, and Motley were unanimous all-AAFC choices, while Lavelli and Willis were each consensus choices. Speedie and Graham were both selected to the first team on the Associated Press's combined AAFC/NFL all-pro team, while Motley was selected to the second team. In all, exactly half of the players chosen to the AP's combined team were from the AAFC, five on the first team and six on the second.

Although all of the AAFC teams struggled financially because of competition with the NFL for players, attendance figures for the new league were very impressive in 1947. The 1,828,480 fans who attended games was 33% more than in 1946, and the 32,651 average per game was more than the NFL's 30,624. In the all-important New York market, the Yankees per-game mark of 37,773 bested the 31,428 posted by the Giants.

In Los Angeles, too, the balance of power at the gate shifted dramatically in favor of the AAFC. The 7–7 Dons drew 43,454 per home date, 10,103 more than the 33,351 average that came out to see the 6–6 Rams. In fact, the Dons' mark was second only to that of the Browns in all of football.

Due mainly to a disastrous 1–13 season, the Rockets' home attendance was off 31% to 19,325 per home date, and the Rockets fell further behind Chicago's two NFL teams, both of whom had excellent seasons. Likewise, a second consecutive poor season on the field in Brooklyn led to a drop of almost 3,000 per game as the 3–10–1 Dodgers played before an average of only 11,014 at home. A much-improved Buffalo team, on the other hand, attracted 14,249 more fans per home date than in 1946, while the first-year Colts drew almost four times what the Seahawks had drawn, with an average of 28,523 at home.

For all of its attendance accomplishments, Cleveland's per-game average at home was actually down 1,290 per game from 1946 to 55,848. That mark was still the best in the two leagues and second only to the Browns' mark the year before in pro football history. Home and away, the Browns played before 666,017 fans total and 47,573 per game, figures that were both all-time pro records.

The Cardinals won the NFL championship with a 28–21 win over the Eagles at Comiskey Park. Led by the Dream Backfield of Charlie Trippi, Pat Harder, Paul Christman, and Elmer Angsman, Chicago won its first title since 1925, one that remains the last in franchise history. It was the beginning of a brief run of excellence by the Cardinals. They made it back to the title game in 1948 with an 11–1 record but fell to 6–5–1 in 1949 and were a last-place team for much of the 1950s.

With a 24–3–1 regular season record and two championships in two seasons, it was natural enough for football fans and sportswriters to wonder what else the Browns could accomplish. When AAFC overtures for a "Super Bowl" between the Browns and the NFL champions went unheeded for a second year in a row, those fans and writers were left to look to 1948. In pro football Championship Game history, no team had ever won three times in a row, and only the Packers of 1929–1931 had finished atop their league three years in succession. Cleveland would go after those marks in 1948 and in doing so would have a season even better than their first two.

Jet Age Passing Attack

TTO GRAHAM'S great 1946 and 1947 seasons came just as pro football was embarking on a great upsurge in passing. With Graham, Dante Lavelli, and Mac Speedie leading the way, the Browns were at the forefront of that aerial revolution. From the very beginning, Cleveland established its deadly efficient passing game, and for a period of years it was either the best or among the best in football.

The Browns' passing game of the 1940s and 1950s combined the four features that are the most important for success, features that are very rarely seen in combination: accuracy (high completion percentage), distance (high in yards per attempt), low risk (low in interceptions per attempt), and points (a high ratio of touchdowns per attempt). Many were the times that Cleveland's marked superiority in passing was the difference over opponents in their ten years of greatness.

1947 marked a turning point in passing throughout pro football. Although there were no new playing rules then or immediately thereafter, there were other kinds of changes that partly explain the upsurge. The football itself had gradually gotten easier to throw as it became smaller and less round. Many of the best passers and receivers were back from military service and ready to resume or begin their playing careers. And the two-platoon system was slowly but inexorably taking hold, thus allowing players to devote themselves to the more specialized skills of either an offensive or defensive position.

Numerous passing records fell in 1947. Washington Redskins great Sammy Baugh shattered single-season marks with 354 attempts, 210 completions, and 2,938 yards (the previous marks were 295, 146, and 2,194). Baugh also became the first player to ever pass for 300 yards in three games in the same season. Washington's per-game team average of 278 yards also topped the previous high of 219 by a wide margin.

Throughout the NFL, 41% of all plays in 1947 were passes, up from 36% in 1946. The AAFC was just a step behind, as the new league reached the 41% mark in 1948. By 1953, the figure would be 47%, an increase of 31% in just seven years.

The shift was even more dramatic when the number of passes per game is examined. Where in 1946 the NFL and AAFC averaged 41.4 passes per game, just two years later the total had increased to 51. By 1953, the average per game was 59.3, an increase of 43% over seven years.

The numbers for passing yards per game were still more dramatic. While in 1946 there were 288 yards per game in the NFL, in 1947 there were 361, a one-year increase of 25%. By 1954, the figure was up to 422, an increase of 47% in eight years. For single-team marks, the postwar passing game explosion reached its apex with the 1950 Los Angeles Rams. That year the Rams set an all-time record with 309 passing yards per game, 34% higher than the best pre-1947 mark.

A major part of what fueled the dramatic upturn in passing in the late 1940s and early 1950s was the large number of great quarterbacks who were active then. Membership in the Pro Football Hall of Fame can sometimes be a tricky way to measure such things, but in this case the high proportion of quarterbacks who were later enshrined in the Hall is somewhat indicative of the greatness at the position in that era. The period of the late 1940s and early 1950s could, in fact, rightly be called the golden age of quarterbacks.

Several all-time greats, most notably Baugh and Sid Luckman of the Bears, were already well-established players as World War II came to an end. Then, six Hall of Famers came into the pro ranks in a period of four years: Bob Waterfield, Graham, Y.A. Tittle, Bobby Layne, Norm Van Brocklin, and George Blanda. In all, there were eight Hall of Fame quarterbacks active in the AAFC and NFL in 1949 and 1950. That figure for

1950 is particularly impressive given that there were only thirteen pro teams that year.

In Waterfield and Van Brocklin, the Rams had two future Hall of Famers sharing quarterbacking duties for four years beginning in 1949. The case of the Bears was perhaps even more dramatic. In 1949, Chicago had three Hall of Famers on its roster—Luckman, Layne, and Blanda—until Layne was traded away. And in 1949 and 1950, the Bears had two Hall of Famers, Luckman and Blanda, *sitting on the bench* behind Johnny Lujack. All Lujack did was gain all-pro honors both years. His potentially great career ended abruptly after the 1951 season, however, because of arm problems.

There were a number of other very good quarterbacks who played during most of those years besides the Hall of Famers. Among them, in addition to Lujack, were Charlie Conerly, Frankie Albert, and Tommy Thompson. George Ratterman eventually became Graham's backup in Cleveland, but he could be included in that group based on his first four seasons. The situation in San Francisco was somewhat like those in Los Angeles and Chicago after Tittle joined Albert in 1951, and it may have hastened Albert's retirement at thirty-two after a very good career.

In Otto Graham, the Browns had a quarterback who was arguably the best of the entire postwar group, one who may have been the best of all time. As great as his 1946 season was, Graham was even better in 1947. Despite throwing almost 100 more passes, his passer rating was down only slightly, he completed a higher percentage of his passes, and he made those passes count for twenty-five touchdowns, compared with seventeen in 1946.

The question of why the Browns threw the ball more often and for more yardage and touchdowns in 1947 is an interesting one. With Edgar Jones and especially Motley carrying the ball, it is easy to imagine the Browns achieving almost as much success on the scoreboard and in the standings had they continued with their 1946 ratio of passes and runs. In fact, one of the striking things about Motley's production throughout these years is that Cleveland did not take full advantage of his skills as a runner.

The biggest change in Cleveland and the best explanation for the shift to more passes is the emergence of Mac Speedie as a great receiver, as, in fact, the best receiver in football. Speedie had been very good in 1946, as he led the AAFC in several categories and was a first-team all-league selection. But what he did in 1947 catapulted Speedie to a status as the best in the game.

Some of Speedie's greatness that year is reflected in the numbers he put up. His sixty-seven receptions and 1,146 receiving yards were the best in both leagues, and both marks were then the second highest in history behind only those of seventy-four and 1,211 established in 1942 by Don Hutson. Even when the AAFC's longer schedule is factored in, Speedie was first in yards per game that year and second only to Jim Keane of the Bears in receptions per game. His six touchdown grabs were also among the best in both leagues, as was his mark of 17.1 yards per catch.

Lavelli also had a very good season in 1947 with forty-nine catches, 799 yards, and a 16.3 average, and his nine touchdowns and touchdown-to-reception ratio were both among the best marks in either league. Like Speedie, Lavelli was recognized as one of the game's best receivers for the second year in a row. He was selected to the first team on the AAFC's official all-league team, while Speedie was a unanimous all-AAFC choice and was chosen to the first team on the only combined AAFC/NFL all-pro team selected that year.

Like Speedie, Graham was a unanimous first-team all-AAFC choice and the combined AAFC/NFL first-team all-pro quarterback. Of Graham's numbers in 1947, the most impressive is his 10.2 yards per attempt. That was the third highest mark in history at the time, and it stands as the fifth highest to this day (three of the five top spots are held by Graham). Just slightly less impressive are his 60.6% completion percentage and 9.3% touchdown ratio.

Virtually all of those statistics compiled by Graham, Lavelli, and Speedie are impressive in their own right. Many are even far more impressive in context and stand as among the very best of their era. For a brief period in the 1950s, for example, Speedie and Lavelli ranked second and fourth on the career receptions list. It was only after several more seismic shifts in the passing game, in fact, that some of their numbers began to seem somewhat less impressive. And even with the many changes in the decades that followed, some of the things that Graham and Speedie in particular accomplished have been topped only a handful of times.

Graham, Lavelli, and Speedie may have been the key components of the Browns' passing attack, but they were not the only ones. There was the excellent play of the line protecting Graham in the cup, forerunner of the pass pocket. In every year of Graham's career, at least one, and very often more, Browns offensive lineman earned all-pro honors for offensive line play (a streak that actually ran for twenty-five years through 1970).

Whatever pass rushers got through the line inevitably had to deal with Motley. The extra time provided by the Cleveland protection both prevented sacks and allowed pass routes to develop to the fullest. Al Wistert, a perennial all-pro tackle with the Eagles, thought that was the single most important reason the Browns' passing attack was so much better than that of so many other teams. And Motley, Jones, and the team's other backs also provided rushing punch that made it impossible for defenses to overplay the pass.

But it *was* the immense collective talent of Graham, Lavelli, and Speedie that drove Cleveland's devastating passing game. Paul Brown recognized that talent where others did not, and he made a point of procuring all three players for his team at a time when only Graham was a well-known collegian. All three were among the first players Brown signed in the months after the formation of the franchise.

As was true of so many things, Brown was also attuned to the importance of the passing game before most other coaches and talent evaluators. Perhaps because he was a smallish man who had played quarterback and not tackle or guard, Brown understood that a dangerous passing game and its principle elements—speed, precision, dexterity—could trump the emphasis on line play that drove the game in the years before 1946. Cleveland's great pass and catch triumvirate did not fall from the sky, after all; it was Brown who threw them together, and he understood intuitively that in combination their skills would increase exponentially.

However, former quarterback or not, Brown was also smart enough to know what he didn't know. Graham later said that Brown played virtually no role in the intricate development of the patterns, timing, improvisation, and other aspects of the passing game. In Blanton Collier, though, Brown had an assistant who was a master technician and who worked closely with Graham, Lavelli, and Speedie.

More important, he had three players whose understanding of the game was such that, as a unit, they were able to do things that nobody had ever done before *and* do them as well as they have ever been done. Graham, Lavelli, and Speedie also put in the hours of work that were essential to making the whole thing go. They continually developed their skills, understood that adjustments made by opponents required that they also make adjustments, and accepted the fact that with so many great players the individual acclaim wouldn't be as great as it otherwise might. They also understood that all of those things required work, study, hours of practice, and a commitment to winning.

From such commitment and work come stories involving each of the three men. For Lavelli, it was many days spent alone practicing what he had seen Steve Bagarus do as he developed the down and out, sideline, and comeback patterns that became Cleveland hallmarks. For Speedie, who George Ratterman thought one of the smartest players he ever saw, it was the intense study of the footwork of defensive backs, study that enabled him to time his moves to maximum effect. And for Graham, it was the viewing of hours of film of unsuccessful plays in search of something he might be doing to tip the defense.

Together the trio worked to develop an assortment of pass routes. Cleveland was the first team to systematically run patterns where the receivers came back to the ball by design. Their patterns also utilized timing as never before. Where before a pattern was timed such that the quarterback threw after a receiver finished his last move and turned for the ball, Graham threw the ball at the beginning of the last move and before Lavelli or Speedie looked back.

Speedie cited an example of how a variation of an established pattern could create something new. "The pet pro pattern was the Z-out, where the receiver zee'd and went deep," he said. "In practice our defense men knew all the signs. When I made my first move, they automatically retreated deep to the final cut zone. We had to change things in order to have a good workout.

"I came back to the huddle one time and said, 'Otto, let's cut the pattern short just before the last break and you hit me at the side line.' We tried it some and Coach Brown put it in the offense."

In some sense, the work Graham, Lavelli, and Speedie did anticipated what later became known as "perfect practice." They added new moves and patterns to the offense's repertoire, polished ones that were consistently effective, and worked to improve those that had kinks. Little time was wasted.

Brown set the right atmosphere by keeping practice time brief and by eschewing scrimmages. No scrimmages allowed the players to work in as controlled an environment as possible, and the brevity made it possible for Graham, Lavelli, and Speedie to work on their own while still fresh.

Although it was not a regular part of their offense, the Browns also occasionally used screen passes to their ends. In 1965, the wide receiver screen resurfaced when Tom Landry put it in his offense after Dallas signed Bob Hayes. Two decades earlier, it had been yet another weapon in Cleveland's arsenal, and it worked most spectacularly in 1947 when Speedie took a screen at his own goal line and went for a 99-yard touchdown.

The attention to detail, the precision of the timing, and the exactness of the cuts and moves in no sense means that the Browns were not also expert practitioners of the long pass. They were, and that again is reflected in some of the numbers: The team's ratio of touchdowns per pass and the average yards per attempt were both consistently outstanding. Speedie and Lavelli were extremely fast and Graham had a very strong arm, after all, and they took advantage of those skills to develop what was probably the best long-ball team in football until 1950.

"Paul always said, 'Let them choose their weapons,'" Graham remembered, and early on the Browns established that they could win with long passes, short passes, and passes of any other distance.

It is interesting that Graham, Lavelli, and Speedie were all very good basketball players. Speedie had played college basketball, Graham starred for both Northwestern and the National Basketball League champion Rochester Royals, and Lavelli was good enough to be offered a contract to play professionally. The skills that make a good basketball player are generally not transferable to guard or tackle, but quarterbacks and ends use many of the very same skills.

Graham, for example, had excellent pivoting ability and the extraordinary peripheral vision that makes a good point guard. Lavelli's hands were both strong and sensitive in the manner of a good dribbler and outside shooter. And Speedie possessed excellent leaping ability and uncanny footwork that allowed him to cut sharply without sacrificing speed, skills that would serve a basketball player on a fast break. All possessed a range of other skills, of course, but those that were common to both sports were of greater value in the new passing age than they would have been in the kind of football that was played just a few years before.

In some ways, Speedie was the wild card in the Cleveland passing equation. Graham is recognized as one of the game's best ever players, and both he and Lavelli are in the Hall of Fame, but Speedie is largely forgotten. That is unfortunate because as pass receivers go, Speedie was one of the all-time greats, as can be demonstrated by comparing him with Hall of Famers who were his contemporaries and with greats from other eras.

The five best receivers in the decade after Don Hutson retired in 1945 were Speedie, Lavelli, Pete Pihos, Elroy Hirsch, and Tom Fears. All but Speedie are in the Hall of Fame. That Speedie is not can largely be explained by the fact that he played only seven years, with four of those in a league that is inaccurately perceived to be substandard.

Besides the obvious one that the AAFC was a major league almost as good as the NFL, such an explanation misses several important points. For example, in the context of the era in which he played, Speedie's career was not short. A number of Speedie's Hall of Fame contemporaries, including some whose Hall of Fame credentials are far less compelling than his, had careers that were shorter or of about equal length.

In his seven seasons, Speedie played in eighty-six games. By comparison, Doak Walker played six seasons and sixty-seven games, Arnie Weinmeister played six and seventy-one, Ace Parker seven and sixty-eight, George McAfee eight and seventy-five, Steve Van Buren eight and eighty-three, Jack Christiansen eight and eighty-nine, George Connor eight and ninety, and Bob Waterfield eight and ninety-one. All are in the Hall of Fame.

If we look at all Hall of Famers who played their entire careers before 1960, Speedie played more games than 30% of them. Well over half of those fifty-seven players played nine seasons or fewer. And the careers of the vast majority of them were not impacted by World War II.

Speedie's pro career, on the other hand, was delayed *four full years* because of military service during World War II. He was drafted by the Lions but instead went into the Army in early 1942 before his senior year of college even ended. He was discharged in time to join the Browns for training camp in 1946.

As a result, Speedie was four months shy of his *twenty-seventh* birthday when he played his first pro game, and he was already thirty-three and a half when he ended his NFL career by jumping to Canada. Of the many top-notch players who returned from military service to start or resume their playing careers, perhaps none was as impacted as severely as Speedie in time lost. Many who returned lost out on one, two, and even three seasons; very few lost out on four.

It is all the more remarkable, then, what Speedie accomplished as a player. Let's start with a comparison to his four Hall of Fame contemporaries. If we look at career receptions, Speedie, Lavelli, Fears, Hirsch, and Pihos rank fairly close together. The range extends from Fears's high of 400 to Speedie's 349. From 1954 until 1958, the five ranked second through sixth on the all-time list, behind only Hutson. Speedie was actually number two on the career list behind Hutson for almost three full seasons beginning on opening day 1952.

But suppose we look at how those five rank in a group of categories that tell us a bit more than career receptions:

	Catches per Game	Yards per Catch	Yards per Game	TD%	Catches per Season	Yards per Season
Fears	**4.6**	13.5	62.0	9.5	44.4	599.7
Hirsch	3.0	**18.2**	55.4	15.5	32.3	585.8
Lavelli	3.1	16.8	52.7	16.1	35.1	589.8
Pihos	3.5	15.1	52.5	**16.4**	41.4	624.3
Speedie	4.1	16.1	**65.1**	9.5	**49.9**	**800.3**

Speedie is tops in three of the six categories. Nobody else is tops in more than one. The difference between his yards per season and everybody else's is overwhelming. It's a bit of a generalization, but the numbers appear to indicate that Fears was the possession receiver of the group, while Hirsch, Lavelli, and Pihos were deep threats. More than any of the others, Speedie combines the best elements of both: He's high in catches per game like a possession receiver and fairly high in yards per catch like a deep threat.

If we award points based on how the five rank in each category (5 points for first, 4 points for second, and so forth) and then tally up the points, let's call them ranking points, this is how they rank:

Rank	Player	Ranking Points
1.	Speedie	23.5
2.	Fears	19.0
3.	Pihos	19.0
4.	Lavelli	16.0
5.	Hirsch	14.0

Speedie's margin over the others is considerable. The gap between him and Fears is about the same as the one between Fears and Hirsch. Suppose we take the five and compare them in the same way with Hutson and Jim Benton, the two best receivers who immediately preceded them. This is what the numbers look like:

	Catches per Game	Yards per Catch	Yards per Game	TD%	Catches per Season	Yards per Season
Benton	3.2	16.7	52.8	15.6	32.0	533.4
Fears	**4.6**	13.5	62.0	9.5	44.4	599.7
Hirsch	3.0	**18.2**	55.4	15.5	32.3	585.8
Hutson	4.2	16.4	**68.9**	**20.3**	44.4	726.5
Lavelli	3.1	16.8	52.7	16.1	35.1	589.8
Pihos	3.5	15.1	52.5	16.4	41.4	624.3
Speedie	4.1	16.1	65.1	9.5	**49.9**	**800.3**

Here's how they rank:

Rank	Player	Ranking Points
1.	Hutson	35.5
2.	Speedie	29.5
3.	Fears	24.0
4.	Pihos	22.0
5.	Lavelli	21.0
6.	Hirsch	19.0
7.	Benton	17.0

More than anything, the rankings serve to confirm Hutson's status as one of the two best of all time. Speedie is a solid second, and he ranks higher than even Hutson in both catches per season and receiving yards per season. Note, too, that the gap between Speedie and Fears is about the same as the one between him and Hutson.

How about if we group the five with outstanding receivers whose careers started after theirs, but not later than 1959. Raymond Berry and Tommy McDonald are the next Hall of Famers who come along, and Billy Wilson, Billy Howton, and Del Shofner are probably the best other receivers from that time frame. How do those ten compare?

	Catches per Game	Yards per Catch	Yards per Game	TD%	Catches per Season	Yards per Season
Berry	4.1	14.7	60.2	10.8	48.5	713.5
Fears	**4.6**	13.5	62.0	9.5	44.4	599.7
Hirsch	3.0	18.2	55.4	15.5	32.3	585.8
Howton	3.5	16.8	59.6	12.1	41.9	704.9
Lavelli	3.1	16.8	52.7	16.1	35.1	589.8
McDonald	3.3	17.0	55.3	**17.0**	45.0	764.5
Pihos	3.5	15.1	52.5	16.4	41.4	624.3
Shofner	3.1	**18.5**	57.3	14.6	34.9	647.0
Speedie	4.1	16.1	**65.1**	9.5	**49.9**	**800.3**
Wilson	4.1	14.5	59.0	12.0	40.7	590.2

Note: Shofner's one season as a defensive back is not included.

The rankings look like this:

Rank	Player	Ranking Points
1.	Speedie	44.5
2.	McDonald	40.0
3.	Berry	39.0
4.	Howton	38.0
5.	Fears	32.5
6.	Shofner	31.5
7.	Pihos	29.5
8.	Wilson	27.0
9.	Lavelli	25.0
10.	Hirsch	23.0

Again Speedie comes out on top. Perhaps most striking is the fact that because of longer schedules and a continued increase in passing, the later players do better—except none of them ranks higher than Speedie. Berry, Howton, and McDonald all rank higher than Speedie's four contemporaries and Benton, but not Speedie. In fact, Speedie's margin over those three is a comfortable one.

Now let's look at how the whole group of twelve stacks up by the numbers:

	Catches per Game	Yards per Catch	Yards per Game	TD%	Catches per Season	Yards per Season
Benton	3.2	16.7	52.8	15.6	32.0	533.4
Berry	4.1	14.7	60.2	10.8	48.5	713.5
Fears	**4.6**	13.5	62.0	9.5	44.4	599.7
Hirsch	3.0	18.2	55.4	15.5	32.3	585.8
Howton	3.5	16.8	59.6	12.1	41.9	704.9
Hutson	4.2	16.4	**68.9**	**20.3**	44.4	726.5
Lavelli	3.1	16.8	52.7	16.1	35.1	589.8
McDonald	3.3	17.0	55.3	17.0	41.3	700.8
Pihos	3.5	15.1	52.5	16.4	41.4	624.3
Shofner	3.1	**18.5**	57.3	14.6	34.9	647.0
Speedie	4.1	16.1	65.1	9.5	**49.9**	**800.3**
Wilson	4.1	14.5	59.0	12.0	40.7	590.2

The ranking points then give us:

Rank	Player	Ranking Points
1.	Hutson	61.5
2.	Speedie	50.5
3.	Berry	45.0
4.	Howton	45.0
5.	McDonald	44.0
6.	Fears	39.0
7.	Shofner	36.5
8.	Pihos	34.5
9.	Wilson	31.0
10.	Lavelli	29.0
11.	Hirsch	28.0
12.	Benton	24.0

Again Hutson is a decisive first and Speedie a decisive second. And again the latter-day players do better than the earlier group—except in the cases of Hutson and Speedie. And remember, six of the ten players after Speedie on this list are in the Hall of Fame.

In fairness to Hirsch, the old flanker back position that he played had him lining up mostly in the backfield for the first years of his career. It was only after he joined the Rams that he played exclusively outside. His numbers and his ranking here might have been a little higher otherwise. Benton's ranking would likewise be higher had he played more of his career during the postwar passing revolution, although that is somewhat balanced out by the fact that he had two of his three best seasons in 1944 and 1945 when playing talent was especially depleted by the war.

Excepting Hutson, Pihos was the best player of the entire group of twelve because of his skills on defense. Those skills were such that he earned all-pro honors as a defensive player. Had he played exclusively on offense after two-platoon football was established, his numbers would be higher.

The fact that Speedie left the Browns while still at the top of his game, and thus did not have a downside to his career, can be pointed to as partial explanation for his terrific showing in these comparisons. That explanation does not necessarily hold water, however, for while generally true, not all players have downsides at the end. Hutson and Pihos, for example, exactly duplicated the feat Speedie accomplished in his final season: league leader in receptions and first-team all-pro.

Benton and Howton are sometimes mentioned as Hall of Fame candidates. What separates Speedie from Benton by a wide margin, however, is how the two did in the all-pro teams. Speedie was a first-team all-league selection six times in seven seasons, plus he was first-team all-AAFC/NFL three times. By comparison, Benton made first-team all-NFL only twice in nine seasons and was a second-team all-league selection only two other times. Benton did very little in all-pro showings until 1944 when many players were in the military. And in five of the six years Speedie was first team, he gained those honors in the same single-platoon all-pro system in effect during Benton's career.

And while Benton's career overlaps the great Hutson's for all but two of his seasons, the overall competition at end even before the war was not as stiff as what Speedie faced. When Hutson reached the end of his career, Benton was the best receiver in football in both 1945 and 1946. That's an impressive accomplishment and is perhaps enough to warrant Hall of Fame consideration, but Benton did not play at the consistently high level that Speedie did.

Howton similarly lags far behind Speedie in all-pro honors despite playing almost twice as long. Howton earned first-team honors three times in a twelve-year career. And where Speedie was one of the best receivers in football throughout his seven seasons, Howton's career was much more erratic. Amid several excellent seasons were far more where Howton was a good but not great player.

Speedie was one of only a handful of players named on the joint all-AAFC/NFL teams in three different seasons. In fact, none of the other great receivers active in the late 1940s—not Pihos, Lavelli, Fears, Hirsch, Benton, or others like Ken Kavanaugh, Billy Dewell, Alyn Beals, and Mal Kutner—was named even twice. Of all the great players active in the late 1940s, only Graham, Steve Van Buren, Bulldog Turner, Al Wistert, and Speedie were named first-teamers on the joint all-AAFC/NFL and their all-league team in the same season three times.

Graham, Turner, Van Buren, Speedie, and Wistert were all-time greats; three are widely recognized as such, while Speedie and Wistert are not. Speedie is the best player of all time who is not in the Hall of Fame, and Wistert probably ranks right behind him at number two.

One huge difference between them, a difference that also distinguishes Speedie from all other Hall of Fame candidates as well, is the fifty-one months he lost to military service. Wistert, by contrast, did not serve in the military. And like Benton, Wistert also had some of his best seasons during World War II when many players were absent.

Perhaps the most impressive of all of Speedie's achievements was his being named to eight of the ten all-AAFC/NFL teams selected from 1946 to 1949. No player topped that mark and only Van Buren matched it. Graham, Turner, Motley, Willis, Hirsch, Lavelli, Wistert, Groza, Bob Waterfield, Sid Luckman, and Sammy Baugh are just some of the other great players active for the entire four-year period, and a much larger group was active for some portion of it. Yet it was Speedie and not any of those all-time greats who was one of the two most honored players of the period.

Another way of understanding Speedie's greatness is a system developed by the authors of *The Hidden Game of Football*. They came up with two statistical categories—adjusted yards per game (AYD/G) and adjusted yards per game relative to the league leader (AYD/L)—that are based on the assumption that receiving yards and touchdowns are more important than receptions. These measurements also adjust career totals by putting them on a per-game basis, thus eliminating the difference between the sixteen-game season in use since 1978 and the ten-, eleven-, twelve-, and fourteen-game seasons of earlier times.

Adjusted yards is determined by taking a receiver's yards in a given season, then adding 10 more for each receiving touchdown. Dividing by scheduled games gives us the AYD/G. AYD/L tells us how a receiver did compared with the league leader, both in a season and cumulatively over the course of a career.

Once the league leader is established, we can determine the AYD/L of any other player for that season by dividing his AYD/G by the league leader's. A player's career AYD/L is determined by dividing the cumulative AYD/G of the league leader in each of his seasons into that player's AYD/G.

A player's career AYD/L can then be compared fairly to players from other eras. In addition to negating the disparities resulting from the lengthening of the season, the system levels the playing field between the lower statistical totals of the 1930s, 1940s, 1950s, and 1970s, on the one hand, and the higher ones of the 1960s and the last quarter century, on the other.

The authors of *The Hidden Game of Football* compiled AYD/G and AYD/L data on about 100 of the best receivers ever in the second edition of the book, published in 1998. The following two lists are based on updated information on every receiver who played through the 2004 season but not after. That is, they're based on every Hall of Famer, every receiver currently eligible for the Hall of Fame including seniors, and recent retirees like Jerry Rice, Cris Carter, and Tim Brown. The lists also include a correction to a mistake in the calculation of Art Powell's AYD/L. Here is how Speedie ranks in career AYD/G and the more important AYD/L:

Player	AYD/G	Player	AYD/L
1. Sterling Sharpe	78.43	1. Don Hutson	96.77
2. Jerry Rice	77.74	2. Jerry Rice	83.86
3. Don Hutson	74.84	3. Lance Alworth	81.03
4. Charley Hennigan	74.83	4. Sterling Sharpe	80.80
5. Lance Alworth	72.18	5. Del Shofner	77.93
6. Steve Largent	66.45	6. Steve Largent	77.67
7. **Mac Speedie**	**65.91**	7. **Mac Speedie**	**77.33**

That's pretty exclusive company. Hutson, Rice, Alworth, and Largent may very well be the four best ever to play the position, and Sharpe may have been on his way to joining them until he suffered a career-ending injury at twenty-nine after seven seasons. Shofner had five great seasons but almost as many poor ones, including some in which he was injured and/or battling ulcers. Hennigan was an AFL original who never played in the NFL. He piled up big numbers when the AFL was significantly weaker than the NFL.

It's also important to note that Speedie was very definitely perceived to be the best receiver in football at the time he played. That is reflected in how he did in both the voting for all-league teams and the joint all-AAFC/NFL teams, as discussed above. Although his career was by far the shortest, Speedie was named to more of those teams as a receiver than Fears, Lavelli, Pihos, or Hirsch.

In 1948, for example, Fears and Pihos were first and second in receptions in the NFL, but neither was selected to the first team on any of the three all-AAFC/NFL teams that year. In fact, Fears wasn't even named as a first-teamer on any of the four all-NFL teams and was only a second-team choice on half. Speedie, on the other hand, was a unanimous all-league and all-AAFC/NFL choice.

The results also decisively favor Speedie in 1949 when Fears had a record-breaking season. Even with a new NFL-high seventy-seven receptions, Fears was named as a first-teamer to only one of the three all-AAFC/NFL teams selected that year. Speedie, by contrast, who had a record-breaking season of his own, was a first-team choice on all three AAFC/NFL teams.

One last startling fact about Speedie: As indicated on the previous tables, when he left for Canada after the 1952 season he did so as the all-time leader in catches per season and in receiving yards per season. His career average marks of 49.9 and 800.3 were higher than even Hutson's, although in fairness to Hutson the seasons he played were shorter.

No player retired with more receptions per year and receiving yards per year than Speedie until fifteen years later when a second passing revolution swept football. Then Charley Hennigan of the Houston Oilers from the early AFL years did it. Ironically, Speedie was Hennigan's receivers coach for four years in Houston.

Setting the early AFL aside for a moment, no player who played at least seven seasons topped Speedie's 800 yards per season for an entire career until Lance Alworth did so *twenty years later*. And no one surpassed Speedie's receptions per season over a whole career of at least that length until Charley Taylor retired *twenty-five years after Speedie's last game*. Even then Taylor, who like Hennigan and Alworth played his best years during the 1960s passing revolution and his entire career in the era of the fourteen-game season, just barely topped Speedie, 49.92 to 49.86.

Based on what he accomplished in all-pro voting, receiving titles, and championships won, plus in the especially meaningful statistical categories cited previously, Speedie was one of the best receivers of all time. In addition, Speedie was arguably the best player on the Browns in at least several seasons even though his teammates included some of the best players ever to play the game. He was also the top receiver in three of the six Championship Games in which he played, and his absence from the 1952 title game because of injury has been cited by a number of teammates as a key reason why Cleveland scored only a single touchdown in a 17–7 loss. In fact, when the Browns played against the Lions and their great secondary in the 1952 and 1953 title games without Speedie, they passed for only a combined 166 net yards and no touchdowns.

As to where Speedie ranks all-time, the evidence indicates several things. First, he was better than all four of his great contemporaries. Second, he was the best receiver in the two-decade period from Hutson's retirement to the emergence of Alworth, Charley Taylor, and Paul Warfield. And third, aside from the game's very best—Hutson, Rice, Alworth, Largent, Warfield, Taylor, and maybe a few others—Speedie was at least as good as and probably better than anybody who ever played. His absence from the Hall of Fame must then be seen not as just an unfortunate oversight but as big a mistake as any that the selectors have made.

Motley, Jones, and Cleveland's other backs were another important dimension in the passing game. Throwing to backs was not new, and the Browns did it with only somewhat more frequency than other teams. What passes to the backs did, however, was further increase the effectiveness of the overall attack. Because defenders had to respect the screen pass to Motley or the swing pass to Jones, they could not bunch up on the ends as they might have liked. Conversely, Motley and Jones were more effective running the ball because defenses simply could not single cover both Speedie and Lavelli for long.

A look at some of Motley's and Jones's receiving statistics bears this point out. Motley's 14.2 yards per catch in his five peak seasons was high for a back in that era, and his thirteen receptions in 1948 and fifteen in 1949 were especially high for a fullback. Jones's career 19.8 yards per catch was even more impressive, and that and his one touchdown for every three receptions is what made him an especially dangerous receiver.

Upon joining the team in 1947, halfback Bill Boedeker also became a valuable part of the passing game. Boedeker caught thirty-two passes in three years with the Browns, good for five touchdowns. Most impressively, he made those receptions good for 24.5 yards each.

But it was the arrival of Dub Jones in 1948 that added the most dangerous extra dimension to the Cleveland passing attack. Jones had been used primarily to run the ball in his first two seasons with the Seahawks and Dodgers. Although he had excellent speed and would make a valuable contribution with the Browns as a runner, Jones was not built to carry the ball on a regular basis. His six-foot-four, 200-pound frame made him ideally suited to play in the open field as a receiver, however.

It took several years before Jones blossomed in Cleveland, but when he did, he helped raise the Browns' passing game to even higher levels of excellence. By 1950, Cleveland had one of the first great three-receiver offenses in the game's history. Jones caught 104 passes from 1950 through 1952, the final three seasons that he was teamed with Lavelli and Speedie, and he made those catches good for an average of 16.1 yards and fourteen touchdowns. He continued as an important player in a somewhat reduced role after a 1952 injury, posting twenty-four receptions in 1953 and nineteen in 1954, good for an average of 16.7 yards.

Jones was especially effective with pass plays that began with him going in motion out of the backfield before the snap, yet another innovation the Browns used earlier and more often than most teams. Motion created confusion for defenses and better allowed Jones to get into his pattern without being jostled. Before opposing teams caught on, the motion also frequently allowed Jones a one-on-one matchup with a linebacker, usually a losing proposition for the defense.

It was the alignment of Speedie and Lavelli at ends and Jones at left halfback that took the NFL by storm in 1950. In fact, it was after Cleveland's very first NFL game that a stunned Russ Craft, defensive back for the two-time NFL champion Philadelphia Eagles, said of the trio that "it was like trying to cover three Don Hutsons . . . impossible . . . impossible." The highest praise that could be bestowed on a receiver in 1950 was comparison to Hutson.

The 1946 and 1947 seasons were just the beginning. The Browns' passing game remained a potent force through all the years of their ten-year dynasty. As players like Motley, Speedie, and Edgar Jones departed, new ones stepped in and played at a high level. Most notable among these were Pete Brewster and Ray Renfro, but others like Ken Carpenter and Sherman Howard also played well in less featured roles. The players who were backups also played a valuable role. Horace Gillom and George Ratterman, for example, were two who played very well virtually every time they were called on.

The diversity of Cleveland's attack is one of the things that links it to the great Rams passing game that emerged a few years later. Like the Browns, the Rams used their backs in the passing game more than was common. And also like Cleveland, Los Angeles utilized formations that were essentially three-receiver sets, first with Fears, Hirsch, and Bob Shaw and then with Fears, Hirsch, and Bob Boyd.

For all of its diversity, though, it was the big three of Graham, Lavelli, and Speedie who laid the foundation for the passing attack in Cleveland's early years. And they must specifically be included in any discussions of football's best passing tandems. In the seven years they played together, some combination of the three were among the statistical leaders and the all-pro teams every season.

In fact, they may have been the greatest passing and receiving trio in the game's history. They played at an extremely high level for a long time, and they changed the way teams passed the ball. Many of those changes—the timing and precision, some of the patterns themselves, coming back to the ball—have been standard wisdom ever since. All began with Graham, Lavelli, and Speedie in 1946 and 1947.

The depth of those roots can be measured in Bill Walsh's analysis of "the Catch," Joe Montana's famous pass to Dwight Clark. Listen to Walsh talk about that play, and invariably he'll say that he learned it as an assistant under Paul Brown and that its origins trace back to the early years of the Cleveland passing game.

Whether Graham, Lavelli, and Speedie were collectively the best ever at what they did, there is no doubt that they did so to the best effect. The Browns finished first in all seven years that they played together, and Graham and Lavelli played in all ten of Cleveland's dynasty years. The trio contributed enormously to the five consecutive championships from 1946 through 1950, years in which the Browns lost only six games.

The Browns were an extremely talented team in all facets of the game, and it would be inaccurate to say that they won *because* of the passing game. But it would be absolutely accurate to say that the team would not have won nearly as much as it did had they not excelled at that aspect of the game to the extent they did. That was true in 1946, it was true in 1947, and it was true right through 1955.

C H A P T E R

Perfect

New in 1948: Alex Agase (LB), Ollie Cline (FB/LB), Forrest "Chubby" Grigg (DT), Tommy James (DB), Dub Jones (HB), Frank Kosikowski (DE), Ara Parseghian (DB), Ben Pucci (T), Dean Sensanbaugher (HB), George Terlep (DB/QB)

Gone from 1947: Ermal Allen, Ernie Blandin, Spiro Dellerba, Jim Dewar, Don Greenwood, Alex Kapter, Bill Lund, Lewis Mayne, Ray Piskor, Mo Scarry, Marshall Shurnas, Ray Terrell

1948 WAS the most memorable year in Cleveland sports history. By the time the Browns began play in September, much had already happened that year in the city sports-wise. In April, the Cleveland Barons won the Calder Cup, emblematic of the championship of the American Hockey League. While it wasn't the National Hockey League, the AHL was one of the strongest of hockey's minor leagues at a time when the NHL consisted of only six teams. The Barons' 1948 championship was their fourth in ten years.

The Cleveland Indians, by contrast, had not won a championship since 1920. But things had begun to change at about the same time Paul

Brown was getting ready to open the Browns' first training camp in the early summer of 1946. It was around that time that Bill Veeck, the son of a former front-office official of the Chicago Cubs, purchased the Indians.

Veeck's genius at promotion and showmanship, combined with the same postwar boom at the gate that had also benefited the Browns, helped usher in the most successful era in Indians history. They drew over 1 million for the first time in 1946, drew 1.5 million in 1947, and were on their way to a new all-time baseball record of 2,620,627 in 1948. By season's end, the Indians would prevail in one of the greatest pennant races of all time and win the World Series.

Among the many outstanding players on the Indians were outfielder Larry Doby and pitcher Satchel Paige. Joining the team the year before, Doby became the first African American player in American League history three months after Jackie Robinson's first game. Thus in less than a year's time, Cleveland's two major league teams had played an instrumental role in integrating pro sports.

Even with consecutive championships, the Browns did not stand pat. A number of talented players joined the team in 1948, most notably on defense. Linebacker Alex Agase and defensive tackle Chubby Grigg arrived via a trade with the Rockets, while defensive back Tommy James jumped from the NFL. Warren Lahr from Cleveland's Western Reserve University signed with the team but broke a leg in the preseason and did not play at all until 1949. Lahr was one of the team's best defensive players until his retirement after the 1959 season.

Like Lin Houston and Horace Gillom, James played for Brown at Massillon and Ohio State. He was an outstanding two-way player in college and one of the fastest men of his era, fast enough to have caught the great Elroy Hirsch from behind four times in an Ohio State game against the University of Wisconsin. After a season with the NFL Lions, James ran into Brown in Massillon and agreed to join his old coach. Like Lahr, James would be a mainstay in the secondary for the rest of Cleveland's dynasty years.

In keeping with his innovation of putting fast and talented players on defense, Brown made cornerback James's full-time job. Year after year, the Browns would have the game's best pass defense. James's coverage skills and his ability to pursue and prevent breakaway plays were a big part of that success. Tony Adamle called him "a heck of a defensive back . . . one of those guys that people overlooked all the time."

Agase played for a University of Illinois team that won the Rose Bowl and was another player who played in the Big Ten against Brown. Brown said Agase was someone "who had great instincts, . . . consistently seemed to be in the right place at the right time [and] was the best I've ever seen at reading an offense." Brown thought Agase's diagnostic ability "so keen he could tell when a guard was going to pull out and in what direction he was going and would move toward the play before it ever got started."

Playing behind Agase, James echoed Brown's sentiments. "He had a knowledge of being where the ball was . . . when the ball carrier came through the line," James said. Agase and the rest of the linebacking corps prided themselves on their ability to prevent pass completions over the middle, an area they called Hump Back Ridge. It was an area few dared venture into and from which fewer still emerged unscathed. After his playing days, Agase had a long head-coaching career at Northwestern, Purdue, and other schools.

Among those added to the offense were halfback Ara Parseghian, an Akron native and Miami of Ohio graduate, and quarterback George Terlep, who came in a trade with Buffalo. Parseghian was a promising prospect whose career would be curtailed after just two seasons by a serious hip injury. He became a college head coach before he was thirty, starting at his alma mater, then Northwestern, and then guiding Notre Dame to some of its greatest seasons. After retiring from coaching, Parseghian became an outstanding college football television analyst.

Terlep had played on Notre Dame's 1943 national championship team, had been Buffalo's starting quarterback in 1946, and then lost his job to former Fighting Irish teammate George Ratterman. He would play mostly in the secondary in his one season with the Browns.

Cleveland's biggest catch that year was halfback Dub Jones, who came in a trade with the Dodgers for Michigan All-American Bob Chappius. It was one of the best trades in Browns history. Jones was a versatile player who ran the ball effectively but whose biggest contribution was as a receiver. With him in the lineup, Cleveland's already potent passing game became all the more dangerous.

Coming out of Tulane University, Jones had been a first-round draft choice of the Cardinals in 1946 but chose to sign instead with the AAFC Seahawks. He was traded to Brooklyn at midseason and languished for two years with one of the league's weakest teams. Jones ran the ball and threw an occasional pass but was not utilized at all as a receiver. He didn't catch a single pass in those two years. That would all change in Cleveland.

For the first time, Browns games would be broadcast on television. It was a development little noted, for at the time only a minuscule percentage of households had televisions. However small the beginning, though, in less than ten years' time the Browns had a national television presence of eighty-four stations stretching from Hartford to Seattle and down into Texas and Louisiana, where future Browns defensive back Ken Konz remembered watching them.

Only road games would be broadcast in northeastern Ohio, and they would be carried on the pioneering DuMont Network. Bob Neal and Stan Gee had been the announcers for Browns games on radio station WGAR-AM 1220 in 1946, with Neal continuing on in 1947. They also served as the first television announcing team.

At the same time that things remained difficult for the AAFC business-wise, teams continued to sign outstanding new players. Among them were Otto Schnellbacher, Joe Signaigo, and Arnie Weinmeister of the Yankees; Joe Perry, Verl Lillywhite, and Riley Matheson (who jumped from the Rams) of the 49ers; John Kissell of Buffalo; Dan Edwards and Hardy Brown of the Dodgers; and Len Ford of the Dons. The league also instituted a policy where players from the stronger teams were transferred to weaker teams without compensation in an effort to bolster competition.

One of Cleveland's prized rookies, Louisiana State University quarterback Y.A. Tittle, was lost in this way as the Browns were forced to relinquish Tittle to Baltimore. In a seventeen-year career with the Colts, 49ers, and Giants, Tittle was one of the game's best quarterbacks. As Graham was only twenty-six at the time, the best quarterback in the game, and an iron man who never missed a game, Cleveland's loss was less Tittle himself than what he might have brought in a trade.

The Browns played two preseason games, one in Akron and one in

Toledo. Parseghian got to open his career in his hometown, and Cleveland defeated the Bills at the Rubber Bowl, 35–21. Against Baltimore in the Glass Bowl, Cleveland lost, 21–17.

The game against Baltimore was hardly the typically uneventful preseason affair. Lavelli suffered a broken leg that kept him out of seven games and elevated Gillom to a starting end spot. Brown later said that the Browns didn't miss a beat with Gillom, high praise indeed given that Lavelli was a first-team all-league selection the year before and a future Hall of Famer.

On a lighter note, the game featured some hijinks by two Colts players. Baltimore end Hub Bechtol remembered that he and former Browns back Mickey Mayne successfully tapped into the phone line the Cleveland coaches were using to relay information from the press box to the field. Thus armed, the Colts were successfully able to adapt their play-calling and formations accordingly.

For the third time in three years, the Browns opened their season at home on the first Friday night of September. And for the third straight year the opening crowd topped 60,000. Their opponent, the Dons, had opened the previous week with a 7–0 win over the Rockets while the Browns had a bye.

For three quarters the game was almost as one-sided as the first two openers as the Browns built a 19–0 lead over the Dons. Parseghian made an immediate impact with a 17-yard reception from Graham for the game's first touchdown. A Los Angeles rally late in the fourth quarter made it close, but Cleveland prevailed 19–14. Groza kicked a 51-yard field goal, the third of his career of 50 or more yards, breaking the all-time record. He established the new record in just twenty-seven games.

1948 would be Marion Motley's greatest season, and he ran for 136 yards, an 8.0 average, and two touchdowns in the second game, a 42–13 win in Buffalo. The Browns totaled 508 yards, with Speedie catching an AAFC-record ten passes for 151 yards and a touchdown, while Graham threw for 197 yards and two touchdowns and ran for another.

The Browns then beat the Rockets on successive weekends. In the first game, a 28–7 win, Graham again scored a rushing touchdown and threw for three others. In the rematch in Cleveland, the Rockets had their way for a half and built a 10–0 lead. The Browns rallied and scored three times in the second half, however, to win 21–10. Boedeker and Dub Jones caught scoring passes from Graham that covered 37 and 43 yards, and Boedeker salted the game away with a 2-yard scoring run.

The game was a particularly rough one and included some dirty play. At one point a Rockets player threw dirt in Speedie's face, and the Cleveland end missed several plays until he could get his eyes cleared. More seriously, Elroy Hirsch suffered a fractured skull after being accidentally kicked in the head by a Cleveland defender.

The Browns were tested again the following week by the improved Colts and their rookie quarterback, Tittle. In a game played on a Tuesday night in a driving rainstorm and ankle-deep mud, Cleveland prevailed 14–10 on a second-half pass from Graham to Edgar Jones. It was Jones's second touchdown of the game, the first having come on a short run. Tittle had given Baltimore a 10–7 lead with a 77-yard touchdown pass to Billy Hillenbrand, but Motley again led Cleveland offensively with 130 yards rushing. That set the stage for one of the busiest days in Cleveland sports history.

After beating out the hated Yankees and besting the Red Sox in a playoff, the Indians had opened the World Series in midweek in Boston against the Braves. When the teams split two games there, it meant the Series would go at least five games, with Games 3, 4, and 5 scheduled for Municipal Stadium on Friday, Saturday, and Sunday afternoons. And as the Indians were the stadium's primary tenant, the Browns would not be able to play their game against the Dodgers on Sunday, October 10, as scheduled.

Among the options McBride and Brown considered in consultation with the league office were rescheduling the game for later in the week, rescheduling it to the open week between the end of the regular season and the Championship Game, and moving the game to Ebbets Field. None of those options had much appeal, especially to the Browns.

For one thing, the Browns were the attendance leaders of pro football, while the Dodgers were struggling badly at the gate. Moving the game to Brooklyn was thus ruled out. The open week existed in the event a first-place tie necessitated a playoff, so that option was likewise eliminated. And the Browns were concerned enough about their own attendance to make moving the game to a weeknight later in the week unappealing. So a decision was made to play on Sunday evening at 8:30. That would leave roughly four to five hours after the end of the Indians-Braves game for the stadium to be emptied and the field prepared.

When October 10 arrived, the Indians, on the strength of victories in Games 3 and 4, stood one win from their first Series triumph in twenty-eight years. A World Series record crowd of 86,288 came out hoping to see history, pushing the total for the three games in Cleveland to 238,491. They left disappointed, however, as the Braves stayed alive by bombing Bob Feller en route to an 11–5 win. That left matters to be decided back in Boston, where the Indians would win the Series in Game 6.

McBride, Brown, and the Browns were probably disappointed by the turnout on Sunday night, a subpar 31,187. True, there were extenuating circumstances, but throughout the AAFC and the NFL there were disturbing signs that pro football's attendance boom had already peaked. Attendance figures for a number of teams, the Browns included, were down, and it was clear that many of the people who had enthusiastically embraced a revitalized game in 1946 and 1947 were, by 1948, finding other things to do.

And for the fourth time that season and the third consecutive game, the Browns were severely tested before winning. Although they entered the game 0–5, the Dodgers took the Browns to the fourth quarter deadlocked at 17–17. But George Young recovered a fumble by Brooklyn's Ray Ramsey and ran for a touchdown, and Motley put the game away with a touchdown run as Cleveland prevailed 30–17.

Speedie again caught ten passes while Groza kicked a 53-yard field goal, the second longest in pro football history, the longest ever in the AAFC, and the longest of Groza's illustrious career. Later in the game, Groza attempted a field goal from 56 yards that would have bested Glen Presnell's all-time record 54-yarder in 1934. Groza's attempt just missed, as the ball hit the crossbar and bounced back. Despite that miss, Groza would kick four field goals from 50 yards or more during his first three years as he accounted for more than half the kicks from that distance in the NFL and AAFC combined in that period.

While not quite up to the standard of his great 1946 season, Groza's kicking was a vital weapon in the Browns' arsenal. In pro football in that era, and to an even greater extent in college, Parseghian recalled that field goals were only an occasional thing. Gordy Soltau, one of football's best placekickers and receivers in a nine-year career with the 49ers that began in 1950, recalled that his 1949 University of Minnesota team attempted only one field goal all season. But after looking on in disbelief as Groza nailed the 53-yarder and then just missed from 56, Parseghian remembered, "I was seeing a *new* game."

Although modest about his skills, Groza was candid enough to recognize the value of his kicking to his coach and team. "Paul Brown possessed an offensive weapon which no other team at that time (or before) had owned," he said.

Beginning in his first year with the team in 1948, Tommy James was Groza's holder for eight years. "Anywhere from 40 or 50 yards, he was a weapon," said James. Indeed, nobody had ever had a kicker like him. By 1948, just his third season, Groza was already among the greatest placekickers in the game's history.

Speedie was similarly making his mark in the game, specifically in the secondaries of AAFC opponents. He was enjoying his third straight outstanding season, and by year's end, despite missing two games with an injury, Speedie would again finish first in either league in receptions. Teammates and opponents alike marveled at his abilities.

Otto Schnellbacher had starred in basketball as well as football at the University of Kansas, and he would play a year of professional basketball after the 1948 football season was over. He recognized the basketball-influenced techniques Speedie used on the football field.

"He'd come out and hook and jump," said Schnellbacher, a rookie with the Yankees that season. "He was tough to handle." Even when injured in 1948 and 1951, Schnellbacher recalled, Speedie "was better at half speed than most guys were at full speed."

Soltau was another one-time college basketball player who similarly appreciated Speedie's basketball-influenced skills, remembering that Speedie "could really go up after the football. He was big and . . . could run like a deer."

Tommy James saw the football smarts Speedie employed both by watching him in games for five years and from playing against him every day in practice. "He would watch the defensive backs trying to guard him, and whenever they got their legs crossed, that's when he'd make his cut," James said. "He'd cut whenever he had the defensive back turning the wrong damn way. You never knew covering him when he was gonna do that so he got you twisted around."

"The premier receiver of that time," Sherman Howard said of Speedie. "The premier receiver of *any* time. Mac Speedie could turn you around. I don't care how good you were or how fast you were. He just had those kind of moves. You didn't realize how good he was until he started moving you around. And he could put a little speed on you, too, because he was tall and lanky and had a good stride."

The Browns began to play better as they rolled to wins over the Bills, Colts, and a disappointing Yankees team. Cleveland's 35–7 win dropped New York to 2–6 and third place in the East. That Yankees game also marked the return of Lavelli to the Cleveland lineup. Gillom had been an excellent replacement for seven games, but Lavelli showed that he was something else altogether, catching touchdowns of 29 and 18 yards. Graham had a great day in front of 46,912 fans at Municipal Stadium, with four touchdown passes and a 22-yard run for a score.

The Browns were 9–0, but, remarkably, they were in second place. Western rival San Francisco was 10–0, and the first of two matches between them was played on November 14. Never before had two pro teams with a combined record as good as 19–0 ever played each other, nor had two undefeated, untied teams played each other that late in a season. Something had to give, and Municipal Stadium was the site of the first showdown.

The 49ers were an offensive juggernaut in 1948. Rookie Perry was having a great season, as were quarterback Albert and end Beals. They were averaging 35.9 points per game and had put up 56 against the East-leading Colts. San Francisco was a big-play offense, with ten of their touchdowns having come on runs and passes of 40 yards or more. And the long touchdowns had been scored by eight different players, thus making the task of defending the multifaceted 49ers all the more difficult.

There were two areas where the 49ers did not match up to the Browns: defense and the kicking game. San Francisco's defense was strengthened by the addition of Riley Matheson, who jumped from the Rams, but it still had holes.

"Definitely, they were stronger," Perry said of the Browns. "Cleveland hurt us in both leagues. But we hurt ourselves more. We'd average thirty-five points and some teams would outscore us. You'd have to say that defense killed us. We didn't draft defensive players. We drafted for offense. Our drafting killed us."

In the kicking game, San Francisco placekicker Joe Vetrano was outstanding at extra-point conversions but was only serviceable when it came to field goals. He went into the first 49ers-Browns game with four and would finish the season with just five.

In fairness to Vetrano, that was in large part due to the potent nature of a 49ers offense that not only racked up lots of touchdowns but also made it worth going for a touchdown even from makable field goal range. Vetrano attempted only eight field goals all year and thus had a success rate of 62.5%, which was exceptional for that era.

But it was also due to something that underscores the advantage Groza gave the Browns: Vetrano did not have the range that Groza had. In San Francisco's first ten games, Vetrano had been good on only one kick from beyond 33 yards. That difference wasn't so important when the 49ers went up against a lesser opponent. But in head-to-head confrontations with the Browns, Groza's powerful leg was an important difference indeed.

"We had a great rivalry with the Browns," Verl Lillywhite said. "Groza would beat us . . . on a field goal. Just killed me. Groza probably kicked more big game winners. Groza was a great one."

On defense, the Browns, as they were in 1946 and 1947, were first in the AAFC in fewest points allowed. Cliff Lewis especially was having an outstanding season in the secondary, and Willis and Saban were also having great years. San Francisco's defense was a very good unit, the second best in the league, but it was not on the same level as Cleveland's.

Pro football's attendance problems were nowhere in evidence when the 49ers and Browns took the field in Cleveland. 82,769 fans filled Municipal Stadium to near capacity as the Browns again set an all-time record for a pro game. And what a game that record crowd saw, as both teams battled all out in a game in which defense predominated in a 14–7 Browns victory.

Perhaps unnerved by the weight of the clash of unbeatens or the size of the crowd, the 49ers fumbled the opening kickoff. Saban recovered and Cleveland moved to an early lead when Graham scored on a 14-yard run several plays later. Perry scored later in the quarter to tie things up, but Edgar Jones scored on a 4-yard run in the third quarter for the winning margin.

The Cleveland defense was up to the task of stopping the mighty 49ers. In addition to holding San Francisco to just the one score, the Browns limited them to 185 yards of total offense. Cleveland didn't do much more than the 49ers on offense, but they capitalized on the game's biggest break.

It was the fourth straight time San Francisco had lost to the Browns. In contrast, they had lost just six games to the league's other teams in three years. More important, in their valiant struggle to dethrone the Browns atop the AAFC, the 49ers had lost the upper hand. In spite of the 10–0 start, they found themselves a half game out of first place after the loss. They would have another chance at the Browns at Kezar, however, before season's end.

There was no time for the Browns to relax after the big win. They were about to set out on a trek that would see them play three games in three different cities, all on the road, in a span of eight days. The busy week would begin with a game in Yankee Stadium on Sunday, November 21, followed by a cross-country flight to Los Angeles for a Thanksgiving Day game against the Dons, and would conclude with the rematch in San Francisco on the 28th. With the 49ers playing so well and his own team clinging to a threadbare division lead, Paul Brown probably wondered at some point during the eight days how he had allowed Branch Rickey to talk him into agreeing to such scheduling.

Rickey was part of a new ownership group that had purchased the football Dodgers in the offseason. Rickey drew on his many years in baseball, arguing that three games on the road would be a new football novelty that would draw attention to the AAFC. He likened it to the road trips of baseball teams, and in Rickey's eyes what worked for the national pastime would work for football. Probably because they were the league's best team, the Browns were the sacrificial lambs for the experiment. "The toughest thing," Groza said about the three games, "was to make three game plans in one week."

* * *

New York was the first stop. Whatever the Yankees' woes on the field and at the gate, a game with the Browns was good for a large crowd, and 52,518 were on hand to see Cleveland raise its record to 11–0 with a 34–21 victory. Motley scored twice on a 78-yard pass from Graham and on a 12-yard run. Then it was off to Los Angeles, a trip that took sixteen hours and included stops in Chicago and Denver.

The Dons were again having a decent season, but for the third straight year they were not quite up to the same level as Cleveland and San Francisco in the Western Division. Glenn Dobbs had regained his form of two years before and was having an excellent season, while Bob Reinhard and Bob Nelson were firmly established as two of the best linemen in the league. And the Dons were more than holding their own attendance-wise in their competition with the Rams.

That was clear on Thanksgiving when 60,031 were on hand at the Los Angeles Coliseum. And just as they had the first time around, the Dons played the Browns tough. They took a 14–7 lead in the second quarter and were even at 14–14 into the third quarter until the Browns reeled off 17 points to win 31–14. Cleveland's last score came on a 19-yard run by Adamle, who was filling in on offense. It was the second and final touchdown Adamle scored as a pro.

Afterward, Los Angeles coach Don Phelan said, "The Browns are unquestionably the best team in pro football, and probably the greatest team ever assembled." It was a minority opinion at the time but one that many more people would come to share.

Next it was up to San Francisco and two days of preparation before the rematch on Sunday, November 28. The 49ers had beaten the Dodgers 63–40 the week before to improve to 11–1 and stay right on the heels of the 12–0 Browns. The San Francisco-Brooklyn affair was the highest scoring game in history and stood as such for eighteen years. Fifty-eight years later, it still ranks as the third highest scoring game of all time.

A 49ers win in the rematch with Cleveland would knot things up in the West and in all likelihood set up a third meeting between the two teams in a playoff. For the Browns, a win would wrap up a third straight Western title. Almost exactly a year after their great comeback in the

28–28 tie with the Yankees, the Browns took on the 49ers in what was another of the best games in the history of the AAFC.

The combined 23–1 record of the two combatants added to the backdrop of the game. Just as in the initial contest when the teams became the first two undefeated and untied teams to ever play with as many as nineteen combined wins, so it was in the second game that the Browns and 49ers played with a best-ever combined record of 23–1, a mark that has never been duplicated. Not only was first place at stake, there was good reason to think that the matchup was one between the two best teams in football.

The 49ers and San Francisco fans knew that the team had to win or their great season would be for naught. That and all the other drama surrounding the game resulted in a Kezar Stadium crowd of 59,785, the largest that would ever see a game in San Francisco until 1957. But there was more drama involved than even the record crowd knew, drama involving Otto Graham.

Graham was enjoying a third straight marvelous season and was established as the best quarterback in all of football. Among other things, he was on his way to a second straight season of twenty-five touchdown passes and over 2,700 passing yards. Graham had also established himself as one of the best rushing T-formation quarterbacks. By season's end, he would have six rushing touchdowns.

But there was so much more that Graham meant to the Browns. Leadership was the biggest thing. Graham demanded the best of himself at all times and inspired his teammates to do likewise. In addition, he had shown the uncanny ability again and again to rally his team when defeat seemed a distinct possibility. The Browns weren't often in that position, but any time they were they knew there was a very good chance Graham would either lead them to victory or come very close. What was later said about Bobby Layne—that he never lost a game, he only ran out of time—was true first of Graham.

Graham had suffered a knee injury against the Dons, and in the two days between games it looked doubtful that he would play against the 49ers. It wasn't until a short time before kickoff that, after consultations with Brown and trainer Wally Bock, it was decided Graham would start. In the San Francisco locker room, meanwhile, head coach Buck Shaw made it clear that he would not tolerate any efforts by his defense to knock Graham out of the game by going after his knee.

Played before San Francisco fans that in just three years had proven themselves as passionate and knowledgeable as any, the game between the two powerhouses lived up to all of its advance billing. The Browns built an early 10–0 lead on a 41-yard Graham to Lavelli touchdown pass and a Groza field goal. In contrast to the first game between the two clubs, meanwhile, the Browns defense did not have much success containing the San Francisco offense. The 49ers reeled off three straight touchdowns and took a 21–10 lead. Two of the scores came on Albert to Beals passes.

The game swung dramatically in the third quarter as Cleveland put up three straight touchdowns. Playing like a man possessed rather than like one with a bad knee, Graham accounted for the three scores with passes to Motley and each of the Jones boys. The 49ers countered with an Albert to Perry pass to close to within 31–28, but they could get no closer. The Browns improved to 13–0 and clinched the AAFC West for the third consecutive year. At the time Brown said of the game that it was Graham's "greatest performance."

Frankie Albert had played magnificently all season, and in a matter of weeks he and Graham would be named co-MVPs of the AAFC. Against Cleveland, he had done all he could with three touchdown passes. With the loss, however, despite a final 12–2 record and 35.4 points per game, the most that could be said about the 49ers was that they were one of the best second place teams ever.

Albert was as fiery a competitor as ever played pro football. The loss stung him as much as it stung any of his teammates. In spite of the frustration he felt at having his team come so close, Albert made his way to the visitors locker room to congratulate the Browns. He had some special words for Graham, and it was then that the Cleveland quarterback learned of Shaw's pregame instructions to his team.

"Throughout the entire game nobody on the 49ers tried to hurt me once," Graham said. "In fact, the few times they did get to me it seemed like they eased me to the ground. I don't think there are enough Buck Shaws around in football, or in any professional sport for that matter."

A week later, the Browns wrapped up an undefeated, untied season by building a 31–0 lead and defeating Brooklyn, 31–21. The unstoppable

Graham threw two more touchdown passes and added a score on a run as the Browns became the third team in pro history to go through an entire regular season with a perfect record. The Bears had previously accomplished the feat in 1934 and 1942. Only 9,821 fans were on hand for what turned out to be the last major league football game ever played at Ebbets Field and in the borough of Brooklyn.

The game epitomized the disparity in the fortunes of the AAFC's teams as the league's third season came to a close. Attendance-wise, the league continued to be a big hit at the gate in Cleveland, San Francisco, and Los Angeles and a moderate success in Buffalo, New York, and Baltimore. Overall, the AAFC again outdrew the NFL: 28,904 per game to 25,421.

The Browns again led all of football with 45,517 per game, although that figure was more than 10,000 per game lower than in 1947. In their brief history, the Browns had drawn eleven of the twenty-three largest crowds in pro football history to games at Municipal Stadium. Factoring in their two games in New York against the Yankees in 1947, the Browns had played in front of more than half of the twenty-five largest crowds in history in only three years.

The Dons again outdrew the Rams in Los Angeles, this time by 41,097 to 32,401. Because of their fall to 6–8, on the other hand, the Yankees were off 15,000 per game at home to 22,793, and the Giants just edged them out at 23,261. The Dodgers and Rockets were the weakest AAFC teams on the field and at the gate, so weak, in fact, that doubts began to surface about whether either would be back in 1949.

The future was cloudy even for the franchises that were fielding decent teams and drawing fairly well. The bidding war with the NFL for players had driven salaries up three years in a row. One result was that the 49ers were the only team in the AAFC to show a profit in 1948. But more important, attendance had not remained at the levels of 1946 and 1947. Despite the league's moves to help the weaker teams by transferring players, talent was nowhere near evenly distributed, and as the Dodgers and Rockets floundered on the field, so they floundered at the gate and financially.

The situation was almost as bad in the NFL, where nine of the ten teams lost money. And it wasn't just because of rising salaries and declining attendance. Even had the 1946–1947 rise in attendance continued, it is doubtful that either Chicago or New York could have sustained three teams for much longer. Where in 1948 there were a combined six teams in those cities, by 1952 there were three. And there has never been more than three in all the years since.

In the midst of the bad economic news, merger talks grew more serious. Actually they were less merger talks than negotiations on how many AAFC teams the NFL was willing to take in. The AAFC at different times proposed that as many as four teams survive in an expanded NFL. A majority of the NFL's owners were prepared to take in Cleveland, San Francisco, and Baltimore, but New York's Tim Mara and Washington's George Preston Marshall, pushing to allow in just Cleveland and San Francisco, were able to scuttle an agreement.

The talks served as a backdrop as the Browns prepared for the league Championship Game scheduled for Cleveland on December 19. The Colts had beaten the Bills at Baltimore's Municipal Stadium on the last day of the season to gain a tie for first in the East, and the two teams played again in the same stadium a week later in a playoff. The Bills won that game 28–17 and earned the right to play the Browns.

Although the 1929–1931 Packers were NFL champions three years in a row, no team had ever won three years in a row since Championship Game play was first instituted in pro football in the NFL in 1933. The Browns were thus attempting to become the first team to do so. The Browns were also attempting to become the first team to go an entire season undefeated and untied. Most of them were aware, no doubt, that those undefeated Bears teams of 1934 and 1942 had both had their seasons spoiled by losses in the Championship Game. And although the Browns were a stronger team than the Bills, having beaten them by a combined 46 points in their two meetings, they were also aware of the adage that claimed beating a team a third time in the same season is rarely easy.

In this case, however, it was. The Browns overwhelmed Buffalo with 35 second-half points and won 49–7. It was as good a game as the Browns had ever played. James set the offense up at the Bills 20 with an interception on the first play from scrimmage, and Cleveland took a 7–0 lead a few plays later. The lead grew to 28–0 before Buffalo scored for the only time in the third quarter.

For the third straight Championship Game, Motley led the way with 133 yards, 9.5 yards per carry, and touchdown runs of 29, 31, and 5 yards.

Graham played unspectacularly as the running game carried the day with 215 yards, but he did throw a touchdown pass. Edgar Jones scored twice, and the Browns defense intercepted five passes (including two by James), held Buffalo to 167 yards, and scored two touchdowns on a fumble return by George Young and an interception by Saban.

The Browns were perfect. Afterward Paul Brown called them "the best team I've ever coached," an opinion he stuck to for the rest of his life. In just their third season, Cleveland became the first pro team to win three straight Championship Games and the first to go start to finish winning every game. They also tied a record established by the Bears on two separate occasions by winning their eighteenth consecutive game, including the postseason, a record that stood until 2004.

The 1972 Miami Dolphins are the only other team in history to have a perfect season. That the NFL chooses not to recognize their accomplishment cannot obscure the fact that the 1948 Cleveland Browns were one of the greatest teams in the history of pro football.

Graham, Speedie, and Motley were the AAFC's passing, receiving, and rushing leaders, respectively, although if the passer rating system used today were in effect, Albert would have beaten out Graham rather handily. Graham and Albert shared the AAFC Most Valuable Player, Brown was named AAFC Coach of the Year by the *New York Daily News*, and Groza led in field goals for the second time in three years. Speedie was tops in receptions in both the AAFC and NFL for the second year in a row and also led both leagues in catches per game.

Cleveland players were again prominent when the various all-pro teams were announced. On the AP's combined AAFC/NFL all-pro team, Speedie was selected to the first team for a second straight year while Graham and Motley were also picked, and Rymkus and Willis were selected to the second team. The *Sporting News* also selected a combined all-pro team, and Speedie and Motley made that first team as well, while Willis and Graham made second team. Both quarterbacks on the *Sporting News* team were from the AAFC, as Albert was named to the first team.

The *New York Daily News*, United Press International, and the AAFC all selected all-league teams. Motley, Willis, and Speedie were first team on all three while Graham, Saban, and Rymkus were selected first team on two of the three and second team on the third. Lavelli was a unanimous second-team pick, and Ulinski and Humble were consensus second-team picks.

The 1948 NFL season ended with a fifth different champion in five seasons. The Eagles defeated the Cardinals in a title-game rematch, avenging their loss the year before with a 7–0 win. The game was played in Philadelphia's Shibe Park in a blizzard, and the only score of the game came on a Steve Van Buren run after a Chicago fumble deep in its own territory.

Unlike in the previous two years, at least one NFL voice publicly expressed support for a Championship Game between the winners of the two leagues. Steel tycoon Alexis Thompson was the owner of the Eagles, and he was not happy that his franchise was again losing money despite a two-year run of success on the field that included the team's first ever championship.

Among NFL owners, Thompson was one of the biggest advocates of peace with the AAFC on the new league's terms (the four-team proposal). Around the same time the possibility of such an agreement was defeated, Thompson's call for an AAFC-NFL Super Bowl was also shot down. Things had apparently progressed to the point where Thompson and McBride had both agreed to a playoff. One plan was for the Eagles and Browns to meet in a game at Yankee Stadium; another had the teams playing a best two of three format, with games in Philadelphia and Cleveland and a third on a neutral field (presumably Yankee Stadium).

Thompson not only saw such a playoff as a way to recoup some of the money he was losing, he was one of the few on the NFL side who saw that it would be a boon to the game. How isolated he was in NFL circles became apparent when Thompson was reprimanded by Commissioner Bert Bell for even suggesting that the NFL meet the AAFC on the field. Disenchanted with what he saw as the intransigence of his NFL colleagues and tired of losing money, Thompson sold the Eagles just a month after the team's Championship Game victory.

Last Hurrah for the AAFC

New in 1949: Les Horvath (HB), Warren Lahr (DB), Bill O'Connor (E), Derrell Palmer (T), Joe Spencer (T), Ed Sustersic (FB/LB), Tommy Thompson (LB)

Gone from 1948: Chet Adams, Ollie Cline, Tom Colella, Bob Cowan, Frank Kosikowski, Mel Maceau, Ben Pucci, Dean Sensanbaugher, Len Simonetti, George Terlep

L es Horvath was the best known of the players the Browns added in 1949. He had won the Heisman Trophy in 1944 and jumped to the Browns after two seasons with the Rams. Horvath would play only sparingly in his one season with Cleveland before retiring. According to backfield mate Bill Boedeker, at 170 pounds Horvath was just too small to take the weekly physical punishment of pro football.

The additions who proved to be the most valuable were three excellent players who stepped in and bolstered the great Cleveland defense: tackle Derrell Palmer, defensive back Warren Lahr, and linebacker Tommy Thompson. Palmer and Thompson would be standouts for the next five seasons, while Lahr would be a key member of the secondary for eleven.

Palmer came in a trade from the Yankees. A graduate of Texas Christian University, he had combined with the likes of Bruce Alford, Jack Russell, Nate Johnson, Bruiser Kinard, Arnie Weinmeister, Dick Barwegan, and Joe Signaigo to give the Yankees one of the best lines in all of football during his three years with the team. He would play a fair amount of offense in his years with the Browns, but it was on defense that he made his biggest contribution. Future linemate Jerry Helluin called Palmer "wiry and very quick."

Thompson was a rookie out of William and Mary University who in a short time became a terror in the middle of the Cleveland defense. Particularly adept at stopping the run, Thompson was known for his hard hitting. He fit in very well with Agase, Adamle, and Saban and improved an already strong linebacking corps.

Recovered from his broken leg, Lahr helped the Browns withstand the loss of Colella. He was a starter that first year and had the first four of his team-record forty-four interceptions. He also returned punts and occasionally played on offense in the last days before the two-platoon system was solidified.

In all, Lahr was a standout on Cleveland's great defense through 1959. He played the first ten of those years at cornerback and then played safety in his final season. He and James were the mainstays of the defensive backfield. While their secondary mates changed frequently because of trades, retirement, and players lost to military obligations, Lahr and James played through the rest of the dynasty years, intercepting a total of sixty-seven passes between them in the seven years from 1949 through 1955.

The All-America Football Conference struggled through the 1949 off-season. The Brooklyn franchise was no longer a viable one and ceased functioning as an independent entity. A partial merger was worked out with the Yankees, and the team was even called the New York/Brooklyn Yankees for a while. But the franchise was essentially the Yankees with some of Brooklyn's personnel tacked on. All of the 1949 home games were played in Yankee Stadium, and after a short time the New

York/Brooklyn tag was dropped, and the team continued as simply the New York Yankees. When the Dodgers players that did not join the Yankees were made available to the rest of the league's teams, the Browns signed tackle Joe Spencer.

No franchise was added to replace the Dodgers. The league decided instead to go with seven teams. The division format was dropped and the schedule reduced from fourteen games to twelve, with each team again playing every other team twice. The top four teams would then play in an expanded postseason, with the top team hosting the fourth-place team, the second-place team hosting the third, and the two winners playing a week later for the league championship. It would be the first time in pro football that home field advantage in postseason play would be determined by a team's regular season finish.

One event that would have an impact on the fate of the AAFC, specifically its New York franchise, occurred during the offseason. In a move that was little noted by most football fans because it involved the newest and by far the weakest of the NFL's franchises, the Boston Yanks were granted permission to move to New York. Owner Ted Collins was drowning in red ink after five seasons in which the Yanks compiled a 14–38–3 record. The Yanks had been a strange operation from the start, indicative of the still unstable nature of pro football in the 1940s.

The Boston Yanks franchise began play in 1944 when wartime restrictions were at their apex. Where just a year or two earlier serious thought had been given to shutting football and other pro sports down altogether, Collins decided the war years were a good time for the NFL to expand. Just the year before, the Rams had suspended operations for a year and the Steelers and Eagles had combined into one team. At the same time Collins was granted a team in Boston, the Steelers were working out an agreement that would see them join forces with the Cardinals for the 1944 season.

Things got off to such a rocky start for Collins in Boston that his franchise was forced to merge operations in 1945 with Topping's Brooklyn team the year before Topping threw in his lot with the AAFC. Nothing Collins tried worked. The team's best record while in Boston was 4–7–1. Attendance was not bad considering the Yanks' consistently bad play. They averaged over 20,000 per game the first four years but by 1948 were below 12,000. As it turned out, things were far worse in New York.

Failure in Boston notwithstanding, it is not clear why Collins thought a weak team that had garnered only fair support in that city, where it had no pro competition, could make a go of it in New York, a city that already had two teams that were both far better than his and despite that were still losing money. He was obsessed with setting down stakes in New York, convinced despite all the evidence to the contrary that magic would rub off on his franchise there.

When Collins made his original pitch in 1943, he had wanted to play in New York. But just as Tim Mara successfully stonewalled Topping several years later, so he kept Collins out of the Bronx in 1944. The Yanks did play one of their games there during the season they merged operations with Brooklyn, and they drew 30,988, more than they drew in all but one of the games they played in five years in Boston. However, that game was against the Giants and was thus not a true test of the Yanks' potential appeal in New York.

Renamed the Bulldogs, the franchise did not move into ideal circumstances upon arriving in New York in 1949. First, they had to make yearly payments of $25,000 to the Giants for infringing on Mara's territory. Second, Topping-controlled Yankee Stadium was unavailable, so the Bulldogs played at the Polo Grounds, where they were third-class citizens after the baseball and football Giants. And third, with the Giants able to pick the best dates, the Bulldogs were relegated to playing half their home games on Thursday and Friday nights. And on two of their three Sunday home dates, the Bulldogs were scheduled against a far stronger Yankees team playing less than a mile away across the Harlem River.

Perhaps Collins believed that if he established a toehold in New York, his team and not the AAFC Yankees would survive a merger. He knew that he wasn't the only one operating in the red: Sixteen of pro football's eighteen teams had lost money in 1948. He also knew how close the two leagues had come to consummating an agreement the year before. So while there's little to support the notion that Collins was much of a football business man, he did succeed in getting an NFL franchise in the city where he so desperately wanted to be.

Tim Mara did not fear the presence of Collins's Bulldogs the same way he feared Topping's Yankees. Still, if events had unfolded differently, it's possible a deal could have been worked out where Topping would have made territorial payments and other concessions to the Giants for the right to be included in a merger. But the Bulldogs' presence complicated that possibility; after the financial bloodletting of the previous three years, absolutely no one was willing to argue for three pro teams in New York.

So before they even took the field for the start of the season, the future of the Yankees was suddenly far more precarious. It mattered not how well the team might do—and they did, in fact, rebound to have a solid season in 1949. The move of a second NFL franchise to New York meant that merger negotiations, negotiations in which Mara was certain to do everything he could to ensure his franchise remained as top dog in New York, would make it only a minimal possibility that the Yankees would survive to play in a post-AAFC NFL.

In the end, that is exactly how things went at year's end. That is unfortunate for several reasons. First, although he had achieved major success as a manager of show business entertainers, it was apparent through his entire tenure as an owner that Ted Collins knew next to nothing about running a football team. The Yankees, on the other hand, were both a well-run organization and a success on the field.

The trio of Topping, Del Webb, and Rickey, who had come over from the Dodgers in the New York-Brooklyn amalgamation, had a track record of success in baseball. In addition, Anaconda Copper was among Topping's other holdings, and he was far wealthier than not only Collins but probably every other pro football owner as well. In theory anyway, he was in a much better position to withstand short-term financial losses than Collins, not an insignificant factor at a time when football was still a shaky financial proposition. One result of the Bulldogs' financial problems was that the team traded away both Bobby Layne and Doak Walker, leaders of Detroit's great teams of 1952–1954 and future Hall of Famers, at the end of 1949.

It is not Monday-morning quarterbacking, therefore, to say that a second post-AAFC NFL franchise in New York with Topping, Webb, and Rickey at the helm would have done far better than with Collins. Tim Mara undoubtedly suspected and feared the same thing. The presence of Collins's franchise meant competition, but it was competition of a clearly inferior sort. Once the saga of Collins's franchise ran its course with the team's collapse after the 1951 season, Mara's Giants remained as New York's only pro football team.

This is by no means to suggest that Mara's agreeing to the transfer of the Yanks was advance planning to prevent the inclusion of the Yankees in a merger. His franchise was hurting both on the field and at the gate, and he was more than likely simply hoping to alleviate that situation. Mara knew all too well that successful teams such as his own suffered when the league's weaker teams struggled. Even if the relocated Yanks cut into the Giants' attendance somewhat, that still had its advantages over Giants games in Boston against the Yanks like the one in 1948 that drew only 7,428 fans.

Plus, whatever his concerns about a second NFL franchise in New York, Mara also understood that two healthy franchises in the city could be a good thing for the Giants and the league. The greatest rivalry in the history of sports, the one between the baseball Dodgers and Giants, then at its peak, was proof of that. If peace could be reached with the AAFC, the possibility of two teams succeeding in New York would be greatly enhanced. The events in New York football that would unfold over the next several years underscored more than anything how bitter things had become between the two leagues.

As training camp commenced, Paul Brown was acutely aware that the AAFC was not likely to continue much past 1949. Although that awareness did lead him to pause and consider for a moment the possibility of a return to Ohio State, once that matter was resolved he went about the business of preparing for a fourth championship. Brown was already famous for his absolute dedication to football—one of his defining characteristics.

"Football is war," he once said. "Wars are won by the army that's fit and ready." Battles already won meant little with so many still to be fought.

"[T]he singleness of purpose is what Paul Brown brought to coaching—that football wasn't just a job, but something you gave your life to," recalled future coaching great Parseghian. Winning required organization and preparation. Son Mike Brown, who succeeded him atop the Cincinnati Bengals, said that his father "changed the way teams had gone about their business. He made it a more serious undertaking."

"Organization and work effort; we were schooled to the nth degree," remembered Boedeker. "Keep your nose to the grind, keep out of trouble, and play as hard as you can." On one level, that sounds like something any coach would say. What was unique about the Browns, however, was an extraordinary confidence that emanated down from the coach, a confidence that came from preparation. When the Browns went on the field, they knew both what to expect from the other team and what they were going to do in response, as well as what they were going to do to the other team and why it would likely succeed.

"Brown scripted the first six or nine plays," defensive back Ken Gorgal remembered of Cleveland's preparation for the first preseason game of Gorgal's rookie year. "'We're gonna do this and then we're gonna do this and then we're gonna do this and do this and I think by then we'll have a touchdown.' And I'm in the back of the room, and I'm thinking, 'Holy Christ, what the hell's this guy talking about?'

"Well, we got the ball," Gorgal continued, "and Otto Graham did this and they did that and they did this and they did that and we had a touchdown. It made a believer out of me real quick."

Some players remembered that when they hit the playing field for the first time every summer, the lessons began with calisthenics: how to do calisthenics properly and why it was important to do them. Bob Schnelker spent only the 1953 preseason with the Browns before getting cut. He was impressed by Brown's organization, his thoroughness, and how he began at the most basic level of instruction.

"I'd been through some good organizations in high school and college, and, geez, the minute you walked into a classroom with Paul Brown you knew it was entirely different," Schnelker recalled. "I mean the first day he even taught you how to run, the perfect way to run. Not that he wanted to change you, but if you could get any thoughts out of it, to help you."

"He stressed repetition all the time," Graham said. "We ran the same plays over and over and over again until we ran them perfectly."

"[T]he key thing that made Paul Brown stand out was his confidence," Mike McCormack said. "He was so absolutely sure. You just believed that the way he told you to do something was the final, the best way to do it. Now what this means to a team is considerable. It means you go out on the field to play a game supremely confident that you're prepared. Confident all the time that you're going to win."

"There wasn't any of this, 'If this, if that, if the other,'" defensive tackle Jerry Helluin said. "It was, 'Here's what we're gonna do.' He was one of these people who built confidence in people. And it just radiated all down the line. These are the type of people he had. That was his coaches. He expected his coaches to export it to the players, and he expected the players to absorb it."

Many thought Brown inflexible. Inflexibility on the field and in his relationship with Art Modell contributed to his eventually being ousted from his job with the Browns. However, Bob Gain remembers Brown being quite willing to make adjustments during games at the suggestion of players.

"He would listen to you on the sidelines," Gain said. "You'd come out, you had a suggestion, some idea of what to run because somebody's hurt, or pick on somebody, go after somebody. If you told him, he would listen, he would do it." Gain recalled a game where a linemate was blocked effectively on play after play by a superior opponent. Gain spoke with Brown about the need to make an adjustment, and "I moved to the outside and we put somebody else at tackle," and the defense was more effective.

There was something else new that Paul Brown brought to football, an innovation that has been confirmed by the vast majority of studies of how people learn most effectively. Cleveland's practices lasted only seventy-five to ninety minutes. Most coaches, in the 1940s and to this day, believe in practices of up to three hours. The more work you put in, the thinking goes, the more likely you are to develop your team's collective abilities to the fullest.

Perhaps because he'd been a teacher or perhaps just coincidentally, Brown did things differently. His practices were not only short, they were also light—including no scrimmaging and no heavy hitting—and they were incredibly efficient. It is not that Cleveland's players did not put as much time in as those on other teams, it's just that that time was spent differently. In classrooms and in the film room, for example.

It is far more widely known now than it was in Brown's time that ninety minutes is about the maximum time in which people learn effectively. And it is not only a question of diminishing returns after that. People develop bad habits on a practice field or in a classroom if they continue while tired, bored, or otherwise spent.

This is especially true when physical exertion is involved. When compensating because of fatigue, for example, a football player begins to do things that undo the very techniques the coach is trying to instill. That was rarely if ever true with the Browns, and it is just one more way that the coach gave the team a leg up.

It was evident to most Browns players during their dynasty years that Brown gave them a distinct advantage over opponents. They got the jump early and the rest of the AAFC never caught up. NFL teams, convinced of their superiority, refused to take seriously the revolutionary changes the "high school coach with a team from Podunk" had brought to football. Similarly, they spent most of the 1950s desperately trying to catch up.

So the shakiness of their league notwithstanding, it was a supremely confident group of Browns who kicked off 1949. They had the game's best coach, many of the best players in either league, and, many of them were convinced, the best football team on the planet. All they had done from day one was win. They could not control whether they would get a shot at the NFL, to prove on the field that they were the best. And to some degree that didn't matter. They were a great football team, and as a group they were determined to keep on winning no matter who the competition was.

The AAFC continued to attract almost as much good, new playing talent as the NFL. Although the total number of players was still very small, the new league continued to sign blacks at a much faster rate than the NFL. Where only three NFL teams had integrated by 1949 (the Rams, Lions, and Giants), employing a total of seven blacks, six of the AAFC teams had integrated (all but the Colts and Bills), and they had employed a total of twenty blacks.

The Browns opened play on Monday night, September 5, in Buffalo in a rematch of the previous year's Championship Game. Buffalo continued to do well both on the field and attendance-wise. 31,839 fans were on hand, and for most of the game they saw the Bills stick it to the Browns. Behind four rushing touchdowns including two by Ratterman, Buffalo built a 28–7 lead after three quarters.

But as on so many occasions, Graham led the Browns back in a furious rally, and Cleveland was able to gain a 28–28 tie. Graham threw three touchdown passes in the fourth quarter and four for the game. Edgar Jones caught three of them, and Speedie caught the final one that tied the game, a sensational shoestring grab with two minutes left. Graham was fourteen of sixteen in the fourth quarter and finished with 330 yards in all as Cleveland outgained Buffalo 507–175. Speedie finished with ten catches in the game.

The tie brought Cleveland's eighteen-game winning streak to an end, but the Browns got back on the winning track with a 21–0 win over the Colts in the home opener. Edgar Jones scored two more touchdowns, while the defense recorded its seventh shutout in the forty-six regular season game history of the franchise. It was some cause for concern, however, that the game was witnessed by only 21,621, the smallest home crowd in team history.

The presence of a revitalized 1–0 Yankees team in Municipal Stadium the following week didn't improve matters much. That crowd of 26,312 was the second smallest in Browns history and gave credence to the increasingly popular notion that Cleveland fans had grown bored with winning. In winning 14–3 in the rain, the Browns defense bent but did not break. New York penetrated inside the Cleveland 20 on six different possessions, including three times in the first quarter, but did not get a touchdown. On three of those drives the Yankees reached the 4-, 8-, and 1-yard lines.

The defense not only held the Yankees to a field goal, they also accounted for all of Cleveland's points on touchdowns by Horvath on an 84-yard return of a Buddy Young fumble and by James on a 27-yard interception return. New York's defense was superb. The Browns were able to muster only five first downs, 36 yards passing, and 125 yards from scrimmage and never got deeper than the New York 47.

Edgar Jones returned to his scoring ways in Baltimore with two touchdowns in a 28–20 win. That gave Jones seven touchdowns in four games. The following week Motley rushed for 139 yards and two touchdowns, Graham and Boedeker connected on a spectacular 74-yard touchdown pass, and the Browns piled up 550 yards to beat the Dons 42–7. That put the Browns at 4–0–1 as they prepared to fly to San Francisco. The 49ers were 4–1, having lost only to the tough Bills in Buffalo.

Playing under the slogan "The 49ers in '49," the high-powered San Francisco offense had picked up right where it left off in 1948. They went into the Cleveland game having scored 174 points for an average of 34.8 per game in their five games. Again it was a balanced, multifaceted attack, with Albert, Standlee, Beals, Perry, Strzykalski, Lillywhite, and Visco Grgich all having outstanding seasons.

For all of their firepower, the 49ers had really been able to put it together offensively only twice in six games against the Browns. In those two games, San Francisco had scored 34 points in a win and 28 in a loss in the last meeting between the teams. The other four times the teams had squared off, Cleveland held them to 7, 7, 14, and 7 points, all games the Browns had won.

But on October 9 at Kezar Stadium, the 49ers put it together and then some. And then some more. They bombed the Browns for eight touchdowns and won 56–28. 59,720 delighted San Francisco fans witnessed the barrage that included 511 total yards, five touchdown passes by Albert, and two touchdowns each by Strzykalski and Perry. Each of Albert's scoring tosses was to a different receiver.

San Francisco bolted out to a 21–0 lead and withstood Cleveland rallies that closed the gap to 28–21 and 42–28. Graham threw for three touchdowns, but the Browns defense was unable to stop San Francisco and give Cleveland a fighting chance. After five straight losses, the 49ers had beaten the team that always stood in the way of first place. With the win, the 49ers moved into the top spot at 5–1, with Cleveland second at 4–1–1.

"I think that was about the first time that anybody shot a linebacker," Verl Lillywhite said of the success he had pressuring Graham. "I had Otto Graham on his back eight, nine times in the first half." Although the 49ers pulled away and won by a big margin, the rest of the game did not go so well for Lillywhite.

"The second half I came out there, old Paul Brown, being as smart as he was, he trapped me," Lillywhite said. "I mean, every time I shot that gap, they just trapped me. Boy, they buried me right down on the ground. But the first half we really got to them."

The game brought to an end the Browns' twenty-nine-game winning streak, a record that still stands fifty-seven years later. The streak covered parts of three seasons and included two Championship Games. Cleveland's streaks of nineteen consecutive road games without a loss and of twenty including the postseason (the 1947 title game) are also records that still stand.

Paul Brown was not exactly reflecting on his team's remarkable streaks as the Browns flew south to prepare for their next game with the Dons in Los Angeles, though; far from it. He let his players know he was not happy with their play against the 49ers, and he threatened to get rid of anyone and everyone who did not play to a higher standard. It was vintage Paul Brown, a part of his personality that earned him the tag "master psychologist" from some of his players. It was all well and good to go two years and not lose a game, but lose one, no matter that it was to what may have been the second best team in pro football, and there was hell to pay.

Cleveland players recalled that week in Los Angeles as one in which the entire team and coaching staff were even more focused and determined than usual. The ghost of Jim Daniell hovered over their practices. None of them got cut, but to a man the players knew that Brown was serious. Plus, they were professionals who were as committed to winning as their coach was. They had not only just suffered the worst loss in team history, they were also out of first place that late in a season for the first time.

The poor Dons never had a chance. Graham and Lavelli led the charge as the Browns built a 34–7 halftime lead and romped 61–14. The Cleveland aerial show was never better. Graham threw six touchdown passes and Lavelli caught four of them, covering 46, 31, 67, and 2 yards. Lavelli accounted for 209 receiving yards, while Speedie added two touchdown receptions. Lavelli's yardage was the most in league history, and his four touchdowns equaled the all-time record set by Don Hutson. In all, Cleveland threw for 423 yards, and Cliff Lewis added a seventh touchdown pass to tie the record for the most by one team in a game. And when the 49ers lost to the Yankees nine days later during Cleveland's bye week, the Browns were back in first place.

One sour note in the Dons game was a broken collarbone suffered by Edgar Jones. Although he played his entire career in the shadow of Motley, Graham, Lavelli, and Speedie, Jones was an important cog in the Cleveland machine. He had a knack for the end zone, scoring eighteen times on the ground on just 289 career rushes. Jones scored ten additional touchdowns on thirty-two pass receptions and averaged 19.8 yards per catch. His twenty-eight touchdowns from scrimmage on 221 touches ranks with the best ratios in history for running backs.

"Jones wasn't particularly fast, but he was a great money player, always good for short yardage," Graham said. Lavelli likewise remembered him as "always good for yards in a close situation." And Brown considered Jones "one of the finest clutch players we ever had."

Jones missed Cleveland's remaining regular season games because of his injury but returned and made a valuable contribution in the postseason. His shoulder never really healed properly, however, and rather than risk further damage by reinjuring it, he retired after the season. With Parseghian having suffered a career-ending hip injury the month before, the Browns went into the home stretch somewhat depleted at halfback. The responsibility of picking up the slack fell to Motley, Boedeker, and Dub Jones.

The Yankees' win over the 49ers catapulted them into the thick of the AAFC race. With a 5–1 record, they were tied for first with Cleveland (5–1–1), just ahead of San Francisco (6–2). After an off season in 1948, New York was playing as they had in 1946 and 1947. Led by Schnellbacher, Weinmeister, and rookie defensive back Tom Landry, the defense was second only to Cleveland's.

The offense, however, was a far cry from the franchise's first two years. Buddy Young had bounced back from an off year and was again one of the most dangerous backs in football, but injuries kept Spec Sanders out for the entire season. The Yankees were particularly lacking at quarterback. They had tried unsuccessfully to trade for George Ratterman, and they missed out on several players who played for the Dodgers in 1948 who were not included in the Brooklyn-New York organizational marriage.

Games between the Browns and the 49ers had become pro football's marquee matchup, and the game between them on October 30 in Cleveland was as good as any of their previous encounters. 72,189 fans, the largest pro crowd of the season, were on hand, and once again the two teams played an exciting game that wasn't decided until the final moments. After a scoreless first quarter, the 49ers again got the jump on Cleveland and built a 14–7 lead. But Dub Jones, Graham, and Speedie all scored touchdowns; Jones returned a kickoff 64 yards to set up a touchdown; and Groza kicked a fourth-quarter field goal that proved to be the winning points.

Albert and the 49ers offense played well but met a lot more resistance than the first time around. And as was often the case in the big matchups, their defense proved too leaky, and the 49ers again experienced frustration at the hands of the Browns. The 49ers fought to the very end as Albert scored on a short run in the dying moments of the game to draw them to within 30–28, but they did not get the ball back again.

San Francisco rebounded with a 28–10 win over the Colts, the first of three straight wins to close the season. But the 49ers couldn't help but feel that whatever they did wouldn't be good enough. For two years they had the best offense in football—one of the most explosive units of all time, in fact—but still they continued to come up short. As impressive as their win over Cleveland in Kezar had been, losing in the rematch pushed them two games behind the Browns, a margin they must have known was impossible to make up with less than a month left.

"The only difference between us was that they had so highly developed the sideline pass pattern to Dante Lavelli and Mac Speedie" is how Visco Grgich, an outstanding guard for the 49ers from 1946 to 1952, put it. "We'd hold them, it would be third-and-10, and Otto Graham would complete that damn sideline pass for a first down."

Still, the 49ers were assured of a playoff spot and a possible rubber game with the Browns in the postseason. That was better than the situation they had found themselves in the three previous years. Despite a 29–11–2 record, the 49ers had been bridesmaids each time. This time they could get another crack at the Browns without having to finish first. That's all the 49ers could ask for. The road to a championship was a perilous one, though, and not the least because if there was to be a third game with the Browns, it would have to be in Cleveland in December.

Attendance continued to plummet in Cleveland when the renamed Chicago Hornets came to town a week after the 49ers game. A crowd of only 16,506 saw the Browns win, 35–2. Motley and Horvath scored two touchdowns, and Dub Jones added his third in three games as the Browns racked up 542 yards, 246 rushing and 296 passing.

On one of his touchdown runs, a 49-yarder, Motley fumbled the ball and then recovered it on the dead run when it bounced right back up to him. The defense completely shut down the Hornets, allowing only 46 yards rushing, 230 total, and no points. And when the Bills rallied to beat the Yankees, the Browns were alone in first place.

At the gate it had become apparent that the Browns could expect good-sized crowds only when they played the 49ers. Teams like Chicago and Baltimore had proven themselves to be no match on the field, and Cleveland fans were no longer as interested in seeing games with those teams as they had been. More disappointing was the fact that the Browns were no longer drawing for games against strong competition. That is reflected in the poor turnout for the Yankees game in September and by the fact that only 22,511 were on hand on November 13 against Buffalo.

As they had in their first meeting, the Browns and Bills played to a tie. Graham scored first, but Buffalo's outstanding back Chet Mutryn countered in the second quarter, and that was all the scoring as the game ended 7–7. Attendance woes continued to plague other AAFC teams. Most baffling was the situation in New York where for three years the Yankees had battled the Giants on better than even terms.

New York's win over the Hornets on the same day as the Browns-Bills tie improved their record to 7–2, yet only 9,091 fans were on hand. And that game was no aberration. Except for a crowd of 38,187 for their game with San Francisco (a turnout that, all things considered, was still a disappointment), the Yankees were drawing terribly. Excluding the 49ers game, New York was averaging fewer than 13,000 per home game. Their average to that point of 17,833 was down from 42,059 in 1947. The only thing that made the overall numbers in 1948 and 1949 somewhat respectable were the games with San Francisco and Cleveland.

It was like old times at Yankee Stadium when the Browns came to town in a showdown for first place on November 20, however. 50,711 were on hand as the Yankees began the same Thanksgiving-week adventure the Browns had gone through the year before, with three games in eight days. Apparently satisfied that his innovation was a sound one, especially since the Browns had won all three of their games the year before, Rickey scheduled his own team for a Sunday game with the Browns, a Thanksgiving game in Los Angeles, and a Sunday game in San Francisco.

Unlike some of their storied matchups, this Browns-Yankees game was one-sided early and Cleveland romped, 31–0. The Browns scored all of their points in the first half and completely shut down the Yankees throughout. Having come hoping that this would be the game where the home team would finally beat the Browns, the big crowd filtered out steadily in the second half as the outcome became increasingly obvious. Boedeker scored on a pass from Graham, Motley scored on a run, and Dub Jones added two rushing touchdowns, his fourth and fifth in five games.

Although the passing attack did not account for any touchdowns, it was spectacular. Graham threw for 382 yards, and Speedie again had a great game, setting AAFC standards with eleven catches and 228 yards. The receptions topped his own mark of ten, while the yardage figure surpassed that set by teammate Lavelli five weeks earlier. To date, 228 receiving yards in a game remains the most ever in Browns history.

Speedie's performance made a lasting impression on New York rookie cornerback Tom Landry, assigned the unenviable task of covering the great Cleveland end. "Mac Speedie turned me inside out and hung me out to dry," Landry said. "That game was the most embarrassing athletic performance of my entire life." Landry was neither the first nor the last to have that experience. Things would take an interesting turn the following year, however, when Landry was wearing the uniform of the New York Giants.

In the stands at Yankee Stadium that day was a sixteen-year-old high school senior named Chet Hanulak. Speedie, Graham, and company also made a lasting impression on him. Hanulak's high school team in neighboring Hackensack, New Jersey, had just won their league championship, and Hanulak's older brother treated him to a day at the stadium. Describing his reaction fifty-four years later to seeing the Browns easily handle the home team that day, Hanulak remembered thinking, "Jeez, what a great team they are."

"What impressed me . . . was the way Cleveland went about winning the game," Hanulak said. "I mean, they had such a balanced offense. They could run the ball with Marion Motley running up the middle and also could throw with Otto, and Lavelli and Mac Speedie catching it . . . their offense was just outstanding." Little did Hanulak know that less than five years later he would be a member of that offensive steamroller.

With the win over New York, the Browns moved to 8–1–2 and

clinched the top spot in the AAFC. The battle to settle second and third places went down to a season-ending game between the Yankees and 49ers at Kezar. Going into Thanksgiving, the Bills, Rockets, and Dons were all still alive in the battle for fourth place. The Browns prepared for a Thanksgiving game in Chicago knowing they would have home field advantage throughout the playoffs.

Chicago was the AAFC team that was in the worst shape as it staggered to the season's finish line. Bleeding money and playing in front of miniscule crowds, there appeared to be no way the Hornets could go on for another season. The two teams that took the field that Thanksgiving thus represented the very best and the very worst of the All-America Football Conference.

While recognizing that the success of the powerful Browns hurt the competitive balance and thus the long-term prospects of his league, Arch Ward couldn't help but also be proud of the AAFC's beacon franchise. In just four years they had done things that no other team had done in the history of pro football. Ward was one of those convinced that the Browns were not only the best team in either league but perhaps the best team ever.

The team in Ward's adopted city, on the other hand, was an unmitigated disaster. After a fantastic beginning in front of over 50,000 at Soldier Field in their first ever game against these same Browns, things had gone all wrong in Chicago. The team was poorly run, was poorly coached, and never made a lasting impact with fans after the initial solid beginning in 1946.

The Bears were the city's undisputed number one football team, but Ward and the Rockets/Hornets owners thought the odds of them overtaking the long downtrodden Cardinals for the number two spot were pretty good back when the new league was formed. But the years after World War II marked the best era of a Cardinals franchise that for most of the rest of its time in Chicago was a perennial doormat.

Talk circulated in those years that the Bears' George Halas was helping the Cardinals by steering players to the South Side in an NFL-united front designed to quell the AAFC challenge. Perhaps it was true, perhaps it was just AAFC sour grapes, but either way the Rockets/Hornets couldn't compete. As it turned out, ironically, by 1949 the Cardinals had already begun a downward slide that would soon land them the dubious distinction as the worst franchise in football. They were gone from the city a decade after the demise of the Rockets/Hornets.

Although the Hornets were probably the franchise in either league that was in the worst shape, they were by no means the only one with severe financial problems. The situation of a number of teams in both leagues could only be described as desperate. Another season of competition between the two leagues would have permanently jeopardized some of them.

The AAFC season was scheduled to end on November 27, followed by the first round of playoffs on December 4 and the Championship Game on December 11. The NFL season would end on the 11th with the league championship game on the 18th. Groups from both leagues contacted each other about meeting during that time to once again talk about peace terms. McBride and others from the AAFC talked boldly about carrying on in 1950, but the situation was too far gone, and circumstances were moving toward a resolution.

It was perhaps fitting that there were only 5,031 on hand to see the Browns beat the Hornets 14–6. Not many people could have been surprised by the turnout. As funereal as it may have been in the vast, empty expanses of Soldier Field, however, the Browns had a mission to accomplish. The game was both a tune-up and one in which Cleveland tried to keep everyone healthy. Motley and Boedeker had touchdown runs, and Chicago's hopes for the fourth playoff spot vanished. The Browns finished 9–1–2 and raised their all-time regular season record to 47–4–3.

The 49ers bested the Yankees in the battle for second place with a come-from-behind 35–14 victory at Kezar Stadium. That meant the two teams would play again in the playoffs in the same stadium a week later. Buffalo, meanwhile, clinched fourth place. That meant the Browns would host the Bills, the team they had managed only two ties against during the season.

The Bills again played the Browns tough and led as late as the final moments of the third quarter in the first-round playoff game. After spotting Cleveland a 10–0 lead on a 51-yard Graham to Lavelli pass and a Groza field goal, the Bills rallied behind two Ratterman touchdown passes and led 14–10 at halftime. Back in action, Edgar Jones put Cleveland ahead again, but Chet Mutryn caught his second touchdown pass from Ratterman, and Buffalo retook the lead at 21–17. Saban set up Jones's score with an interception. He almost duplicated his feat in the Championship Game the year before against the same team by bringing it back for a touchdown, but he was tackled 2 yards short.

Graham next hit Dub Jones with a 49-yard touchdown pass to give the Browns the lead for good, and Warren Lahr put the game out of reach with a 52-yard interception return in the fourth for the last score of the game as Cleveland won 31–21. Graham and Ratterman filled the air with footballs, Graham going twenty-two of forty-three for 326 yards while Ratterman was twenty-one of thirty-nine for 293 yards. Each was intercepted twice. Speedie finished the day with seven catches. Despite the stakes, the game was played before only 17,270 spectators.

A much better turnout of 41,393 was in attendance to see the 49ers defeat the Yankees in San Francisco, 17–7. The Yankees' great defense didn't yield much to the high-powered crew led by Frankie Albert, but the weak New York offense did even less against a San Francisco defense not known for its stinginess. It was the third straight postseason game in which the Yankees offense was shut down. A great punting day by Landry helped keep the game closer than it might have been.

So it would be the two best teams and the league's two strongest franchises in the Championship Game. That was only fitting as the game turned out to be the last in AAFC history. Meeting while Cleveland and San Francisco were preparing for the game, NFL and AAFC owners reached a peace agreement. The Browns, 49ers, and Colts would play in an enlarged NFL beginning in 1950, while the other AAFC teams would go out of business.

There were other terms involving the inclusion of some of the AAFC owners in NFL franchises and the dispersement of the leftover AAFC players, but the agreement on the three teams was the same one Mara and Marshall had vetoed the year before. For a brief time into 1950, the new entity was known as the National American Football League, but eventually American was dropped and the traditional NFL name reinstituted.

The possibility of the Yankees being a part of the merger was still on the table until Topping himself decided against it. For several years in the beginning, the combined football/baseball Yankees organization had been run by Topping, Webb, and Larry MacPhail. MacPhail was the hands-on member of the trio, and he served as general manager of both teams. However, he parted company with the organization after a drunken confrontation with Topping and several other people after the baseball Yankees won the 1947 World Series.

As a result, Topping was forced to step in and take up the slack on the baseball side. With MacPhail on hand, it had been possible for Topping "to devote enough of my time to the running of the football enterprise." By the end of 1949, however, Topping had had enough of trying to run both teams and decided that "baseball is the primary interest of the New York Yankees," by which he meant the corporation overseeing the two teams.

Thus the two survivors in New York were the Giants and the Bulldogs. Part of the peace agreement was that most of the Yankees players became the property of Collins and the Bulldogs (soon to be renamed the Yanks). With the infusion of talent, the Bulldogs/Yanks would experience a remarkable turnaround and become one of the better teams in the NFL in 1950 after winning just one game in 1949.

Not all of the Yankees were destined for Collins's franchise, however; Tim Mara saw to that. As compensation for the hardships he had endured in four years of competition, Mara extracted the rights to six Yankees. Five of them would sign with and play for the Giants in 1950, as would two other AAFC players, and *that* infusion of talent helped turn a Giants team that had been lousy from 1947 to 1949 into one of the NFL's best in 1950.

Most on the AAFC side were content to cut their losses, recognizing that the three-team deal and the minority ownership offers were about the best they could do. Paul Brown did not feel that way, however. Still clinging to Ward's original idea of two separate leagues playing in one unified organization, Brown criticized the deal. He still believed that a setup like the National and American Leagues in baseball was possible.

Perhaps Brown was simply striking a hard pose in the hopes of getting a better deal when the final touches were put on the agreement. If that was the case, he succeeded. The terms in which Cleveland would get several players from the Bills, for example, because, as Brown put it, "we have given away players to help the league," were included in the final agreement that was signed in January.

Or perhaps Brown really believed that the two leagues could survive as long as they weren't competing for players and if several franchises relocated out of the places where football was stretched too thin. That seems somewhat unlikely in that Brown, one of the greatest organization builders in sports history, knew better than anyone that too many of the franchises in the AAFC, not to mention the NFL, were poorly run and destined for further failure.

It is more likely that Brown's criticisms of the agreement simply reflected his disappointment that the AAFC project that had begun so promisingly, one that had served as his introduction to the pro game, had ended with only three teams surviving. He was also undoubtedly disappointed that despite all that had been invested, in both work and money, the AAFC wasn't able to cut a better deal. And Brown's disappointment was probably exacerbated by the decisions of Topping and Buffalo owner James Breuil not to go on, as well as the absence from the negotiations of Dons owner Ben Lindheimer.

Lindheimer was the AAFC's staunchest hawk. He had not only absorbed much of the Dons' financial losses, Lindheimer had also made money available to other AAFC teams to help keep them afloat. He was one of the few in the AAFC camp still sympathetic to the two-league idea. And Rams or no Rams, agreement or no agreement, he wanted the Dons to continue. But Lindheimer was seriously ill and unable to attend the merger negotiations.

Given the level of NFL intransigence, it would have taken some hard bargaining for the Dons, Bills, or Yankees to have been included in the merger. In the case of the Yankees, the Bulldogs would have had to have been dispersed and Collins compensated and/or taken in as a minority partner. Topping, however, made the point moot with his decision to withdraw from football. He and Webb chose not to hire someone to fill MacPhail's shoes, someone to do on the football side what George Weiss did on the baseball side.

Breuil similarly decided that he had had enough. Had he not been able to cut a deal that allowed him to become a part owner of the Browns, which he did in exchange for the rights to three of Buffalo's players, Breuil might have fought to include the Bills in the merger. Although Breuil's decision ultimately benefited Cleveland, the decision left Brown disappointed. The Bills were not only a solid franchise, they were also an improving one.

In addition, unlike the Yankees, Dons, and Hornets, the Bills had their city to themselves. But Breuil wanted out, and although there was an uproar among the Buffalo citizenry that included a petition drive demanding the inclusion of their city in the merger and a commitment from thousands of fans to purchase season tickets, no one stepped forward to take his place. The NFL, preferring to keep the number of new teams to a minimum, was not about to go recruiting for new Buffalo ownership. Thus Buffalo fans would have to wait until 1960 for the chance to again show that they were and are among the best in all of football.

The decisions by Breuil and the NFL were unfortunate for the NFL, and even more so for fans in Buffalo. While it was the Browns and, to a lesser extent, the 49ers, Dons, and Yankees who attracted the big AAFC attendance numbers, in its own way Buffalo may have been the most successful attendance story of the late 1940s. Considering Buffalo's relatively small population (less than all of the cities with AAFC or NFL teams except for Green Bay) and the fact that Civic Stadium was one of the smallest stadiums, the Buffalo attendance story is nothing short of remarkable. In fact, when calculated on the basis of tickets sold as a percentage of capacity, the Bills' attendance performance was better than even Cleveland's.

The other unfortunate aspect of the Bills' demise is that it curtailed the possibility of rivalries developing between Buffalo, Cleveland, and Pittsburgh, for rivalries are one of the lifebloods of pro football. The three cities lie in very close geographical proximity in an area that is one of the nation's real football hotbeds. It is possible to imagine a Buffalo team in the NFL establishing rivalries with Cleveland and Pittsburgh akin to the one that developed between the Browns and Steelers. But because of a combination of shortsightedness and vindictiveness, it was not to be.

So it would be the AAFC's two crown jewels in the league's last ever game. The 49ers would have one more chance at the Browns, the team that always seemed to be a little bit better. News of the settlement took away from the game somewhat, but AAFC partisans who chose to view the game not as a sad ending but as a rubber match between the two best teams in football wouldn't have been that far off.

Over four years, the 49ers had compiled a 38–14–2 record for a .731 winning percentage and had played some of the most exciting football anybody had ever seen. Their four second-place finishes had come behind what was arguably the best team in football each of those years. Together with the Dons and Rams, the 49ers had proven that pro football belonged on the West Coast and, absent an interleague war, could prosper there.

The natural rivalry between northern and southern California, only hinted at in the games with the Dons, would soon flourish and become one of football's best with outstanding Rams and 49ers teams playing under the same banner. In 1949, in fact, the 49ers wrested the AAFC attendance championship away from the Browns, averaging 39,032 to Cleveland's 31,491. Whether San Francisco could also supplant the Browns as the league's champion, however, remained to be seen.

The Browns had put together a four-year run unmatched in pro football annals: a 47–4–3 regular season record, a .922 winning percentage, three (and soon to be four) championships, a core of exceptional players, and a coach whom championships followed everywhere he went. The ridicule premised in the notion that the AAFC was a minor league could not negate the Browns' magnificent accomplishments.

Additionally, beginning in 1950, the Browns now knew, that same ridicule could be put to the test on the field. That is all the Browns had wanted all along. The question of Cleveland's AAFC legacy was still an open one at the end of 1949. If they flopped in the NFL, the ridicule would be proven justified. If they performed as well as the team collectively believed they could—and to a man they seem to have believed that they could have prevailed against the NFL from day one, whether in a single "Super Bowl" or over the course of a season—then the four championships would be validated and the doubters forced to admit that they had been wrong and the Browns partisans right all along.

Legacies and speculation about how either team would do against the NFL were not likely to have been much on the minds of the players who took to the Municipal Stadium field on December 11. Although they knew by then the terms of the merger, both teams were focused in pursuit of what they most wanted: the 1949 AAFC championship. Only 22,550 were on hand for the last AAFC game, a far cry from the 60,000-plus who had been on hand for the league's first ever game in the same stadium.

That attendance woes were not just an AAFC problem was underscored when a crowd not much larger than the one in cold, wet Cleveland attended the NFL Championship Game a week later in rainy Los Angeles. For the third time in four years, the AAFC's average attendance was higher than the NFL's. Over its history, the AAFC outdrew the NFL by about 700 per game.

For the fourth consecutive year, the Browns defense was outstanding in Championship Game play. They held the vaunted San Francisco attack to one touchdown and 230 total yards in winning, 21–7. A 49ers offense that averaged just under 35 points and 400 yards per game could not get going, either through the air or on the ground. Albert was just nine of twenty-four for 108 yards, and league rushing leader Joe Perry gained only 36 yards, while the team's 3.4 yards per rush was well below their regular season mark of 5.5.

While not overwhelming, Cleveland's offense seized the early lead and provided the game's biggest play. Edgar Jones special-delivered one last time to the end zone and finished with 63 yards rushing. It was Jones's fourth touchdown in four AAFC Championship Games.

Graham, meanwhile, led an efficient passing game and added 62 yards rushing. Motley again made his presence felt in Championship Game play on a 63-yard burst up the middle for Cleveland's second touchdown. And Dub Jones clinched things with a fourth-quarter touchdown after San Francisco had closed to 14–7. In the AAFC's four championship games, Motley rushed for 415 yards, five touchdowns, and a mind-boggling 8.7 yards per carry.

The Eagles beat the Rams 14–0 behind a record 196 yards rushing by Steve Van Buren for their second straight NFL championship. It was also the second straight title-game shutout for Philadelphia, something no other team has ever done, although both had been accomplished in terrible weather conditions. Afterward head coach Greasy Neale said of his Eagles, "This is the best team ever put together."

There was, as a year earlier, at least one NFL owner who publicly supported the AAFC's proposal to play one more game and find out if the Eagles were even the best team then extant in pro football. Pittsburgh's Art Rooney endorsed Mickey McBride's call for such a game.

For the fourth and final time, however, the majority of NFL owners nixed the idea.

Content at having outlasted the upstart league and beaten them at the negotiating table, NFL owners were acutely aware of the embarrassment they would expose themselves to in the event of a Browns victory. In addition, they probably couldn't be bothered, convinced beyond all doubt that a Cleveland victory was an impossibility. Whatever the reasons, it would be nine more months before the Browns would destroy the Eagles and begin a season that would help prove their own, if not exactly the AAFC's, superiority—and that they and only they were the rightful claimants to the title "the best team ever put together."

There was one more game for the Browns and the AAFC before the final curtain fell. A Texas oilman named Glen McCarthy had been angling for a pro team for Houston for several years. To establish his and his city's worthiness, he organized a game in Houston between the AAFC's champions and a league all-star team.

Although with the league's demise an AAFC expansion team was now an impossibility, McCarthy was not deterred. A good showing at the gate and an enthusiastic reception in Houston would certainly not go unnoticed by the NFL, McCarthy reasoned, and it would put him on the right track to eventually being granted a team.

McCarthy was wrong on virtually all counts. Dubbed the Shamrock Bowl, the game was played in the rain and was a disaster at the gate as only 10,000 were on hand to see the AAFC All-Stars defeat the Browns, 12–7. There was also some initial uncertainty about whether black players would be allowed to play and whether black fans would be allowed to attend. In part because of national pressure exerted from the black community, Willis, Motley, and Gillom of the Browns and Joe Perry and Buddy Young of the All-Stars were allowed to play, and tickets were sold to black fans.

Still the game was surrounded by racial controversy. Years later, Motley angrily recalled being forced to wait outside Rice Stadium in the pouring rain at length after he was denied entrance by stadium employees. In addition, the five black players were not allowed to stay at the hotel where the white players stayed (a hotel that was owned by McCarthy), a situation that, Parseghian recalled, angered white and black players alike. Although there was some sentiment at the time to consider Houston as a possible NFL expansion site, nothing ever came of it. The circumstances around the Shamrock Bowl, especially the hostile racial atmosphere, were undoubtedly a factor to an NFL that was integrating at a snail's pace, but integrating nonetheless.

For the third straight year, Graham was the AAFC's leading passer. Speedie was the league's leader in catches for the third straight time and in receiving yardage for the second. Speedie also became the first receiver ever to twice surpass 1,000 yards, and he tied Hutson's record of three seasons of fifty or more catches. In just his fourth season, he also joined Hutson as the only players to lead their league in receptions three times. Speedie added a fourth title in 1952, and fifty-four years after his last game, he remains one of only three players in history with four or more receiving titles.

Speedie, Graham, and Saban were named to all of the various all-AAFC teams. Motley and Rymkus were named to one of the all-AAFC first teams and to the second team on others, while Lavelli and Willis were unanimous second-teamers. Brown was named AAFC Coach of the Year by the *Sporting News*.

Both the AP and the International News Service selected a combined AAFC/NFL all-pro team in 1949 (the *Sporting News* and the *Chicago Herald-American* did not after having done so in the past). While the AP again selected one team of eleven players, the INS selected complete offensive and defensive units.

Ten of the twenty-two players chosen by the INS were AAFCers: Graham, Speedie, Rymkus, Beals, Signaigo, and Mutryn to the offense and Saban, Buffalo tackle John Kissell, 49ers cornerback Jim Cason, and Baltimore cornerback Herman Wedemeyer to the defense. Al Wistert, Wash Serini, Vince Banonis, Steve Van Buren, and Tony Canadeo from the NFL made the offense, while Pete Pihos, Ed Sprinkle, Dick Huffman, Darrell Hogan, Milan Lazetich, Don Doll, and Emlen Tunnell made the defensive team.

Five of the eleven players chosen to the AP's combined team were from the AAFC: Graham, Speedie, Mutryn, the Yankees' Weinmeister, and Baltimore's outstanding guard Dick Barwegan. The NFL players on the team were Van Buren, Pihos, Huffman, Buster Ramsey, Fred Naumetz, and Bob Waterfield (two quarterbacks and no fullback were chosen). Graham and Speedie joined Van Buren, Wistert, and Bulldog Turner as the only players named as all-league and to the AAFC/NFL team in the same year three times.

No all-time all-AAFC team was picked, either by the league or by any of the wire services, major newspapers, or magazines, or later by the Pro Football Hall of Fame. The Browns would have been well represented on such a team. If separate offensive and defensive squads were picked, Graham, Speedie, Motley, Willis, and probably Rymkus, Yonakor, and Saban would have been selected as first-teamers. Lavelli, Houston, Adamle, Lewis, and possibly Ulinski would have been likely second-teamers.

There was no such thing as kicking or return specialists then, but Groza would have been the likely choice as the league's best placekicker. Tom Colella spent three years with the Browns and one with Buffalo and ranked as the league's best ever punt returner among players who played more than two years. And although he never so much as cracked the second all-league team in four years, Cliff Lewis would have rated strong consideration for the secondary given that he was the AAFC's all-time interception leader. Colella, second in career interceptions, might also have been selected.

The Browns dominated the league's all-time leaders. In addition to Lewis in the interception department, Motley led in rushing yards and was second to Perry in yards per carry, Graham led in passing, Groza led in field goals and was second to Beals in total points, and Speedie was first in catches and receiving yards by wide margins, with Lavelli fourth and second in those two categories and first in yards per catch.

Years later the Hall of Fame sought to honor the game's history by selecting all-decade teams going back to the 1920s. Although flawed in a number of ways, these teams serve as some measure of the best playing talent in different eras. Willis, Motley, Speedie, and Lavelli were all chosen for the 1940s team. Graham's absence is explained in part by the fact that he was selected to the 1950s team, although there were some players chosen in more than one decade, and he could easily have been one of them.

There can be little doubt now, with the benefit of knowing what came in 1950 and after, that Graham was the best quarterback in football in

1949 and had been for some time. In all, the fact that four Browns were chosen to the 1940s team is quite impressive given that the AAFC is wrongly thought to have been a minor league by some. Those selections are all the more impressive given that the Browns existed for less than half the decade. Given an honest assessment of the relative strengths of the AAFC and NFL, Graham and Rymkus, and perhaps Saban, would have joined Willis, Motley, Speedie, and Lavelli on an all-1940s team.

In all, sixty-five men played at least one game for the Browns during their four AAFC seasons. Fifteen played in all four seasons, and the same fifteen played in both the first ever game against the Seahawks and the last game against the 49ers—Frank Gatski, Otto Graham, Lou Groza, Lin Houston, Edgar Jones, Dante Lavelli, Cliff Lewis, Marion Motley, Lou Rymkus, Lou Saban, Mac Speedie, Ed Ulinski, Bill Willis, John Yonakor, and George Young. Of the fifteen, eleven would play for the Browns in the NFL.

The Browns had accomplished a great deal in their brief history. By the end of 1949, Paul Brown and his players were probably as confident a team as has ever existed in the history of sports. It is unlikely that any of them, however—not Brown, not Graham, not Mickey McBride—would have been willing to predict the kind of success they would enjoy in 1950 and in the years through 1955. By the end of that time, their legacy would be such that the Browns and only the Browns could be considered the greatest dynasty in the history of pro football.

C H A P T E R

Taking the NFL by Storm

New in 1950: Rex Bumgardner (HB), Ken Carpenter (HB), Emerson Cole (FB), Len Ford (DE), Abe Gibron (G), Ken Gorgal (DB), Hal Herring (LB), John Kissell (DT), Jim Martin (DE/LB), Dom Moselle (DB), Don Phelps (DB), John Sandusky (T)

Gone from 1949: Bill Boedeker, Bob Gaudio, Les Horvath, Edgar Jones, Bill O'Connor, Ara Parseghian, Lou Saban, Joe Spencer, Ed Sustersic, Ed Ulinski, John Yonakor

Remaining from 1946 (11): Gatski, Graham, Groza, Houston, Lavelli, Lewis, Motley, Rymkus, Speedie, Willis, Young

HE YEAR 1950 was one of the greatest in the history of pro football. The first year of the new decade ushered in what has accurately been called the game's golden age. The 1940s were marked first by world war and then a war between two competing leagues. Both had an adverse impact on the quality of play, as well as on the game's financial well-being.

There had been eighteen pro teams from 1946 to 1948 and seventeen in 1949, but by 1950 there were only thirteen. That meant there were approximately 20–25% fewer players on pro rosters that year. And although imperceptible to all but the keenest observers, television was becoming a social force, one that would become an inseparable part of pro football by decade's end.

Where the games and players were concerned, there was a sense of anticipation in 1950 in a lot of places. Not the least of that anticipation was in Baltimore, San Francisco, and Cleveland as fans looked forward to a first season in the NFL. But there was a lot of anticipation in the old NFL cities as well. For one thing, it would finally be determined if the AAFC teams, especially the powerhouse Browns and 49ers, were the real thing.

Of more immediate interest was the influx of a large number of new and talented players. Once the players involved in the special deals between the Dons and Rams; the Giants, Yankees, and Bulldogs/Yanks; and the Browns and Bills were finalized, the NFL held a special disbursement draft of the players remaining from the defunct teams.

Dozens of the AAFC's best would now be playing in the NFL. Among them were Spec Sanders, Buddy Young, Bob Hoernschmeyer, Bob Reinhard, Otto Schnellbacher, Dick Barwegan, Arnie Weinmeister, Julie Rykovich, Alex Wizbicki, Harmon Rowe, Bill Boedeker, Johnny Rapacz, Hardy Brown, and most of the rosters of the Browns, 49ers, Colts, and Yanks. Not coincidentally, the NFL teams that added the fewest AAFC players finished toward the bottom of the standings in 1950. The NFL's best teams in 1950 besides the Browns—the Rams, Bears, Yanks, and Giants—were all helped immensely by playing talent added from the AAFC.

Given his track record since signing with Cleveland in 1945, it was no surprise that Paul Brown secured some excellent players from other AAFC teams for the Browns. Three came in the deal that was made with Bills owner James Breuil. In addition, Paul Brown took advantage of a degree of ignorance on the part of the NFL about AAFC playing talent to secure several other players in the dispersement draft.

In the deal with Buffalo, the Browns added guard Abe Gibron, defensive tackle John Kissell, and halfback Rex Bumgardner. Gibron would have an excellent ten-year NFL career and be one of the best guards of the 1950s, while Kissell was a starter for most of his six years. Each would be valuable contributors to the NFL part of the Browns dynasty. Bumgardner was a capable player who played three years and made his biggest contribution in the fourth quarter of the 1950 NFL Championship Game.

Although he was a hard-liner in the negotiations with the AAFC, Giants owner Tim Mara knew football talent when he saw it. Unlike George Preston Marshall, a loose-mouthed braggart thoroughly convinced the AAFC was a minor league (the Redskins could only bring themselves to sign one AAFCer), Mara secured the rights to some of the Yankees' best players in the negotiations. Five of those players—Weinmeister, Schnellbacher, Rowe, Tom Landry, and John Mastrangelo, plus Rapacz of the Hornets and Dick Woodard of the Dons, who New York selected in the dispersement draft—helped transform a Giants team that had gone 12–22–2 in 1947 through 1949 into one of the NFL's best teams of the early 1950s.

In the dispersement draft, the Browns selected defensive end Len Ford from the Dons and linebacker Hal Herring from the Bills. Ford had been an All-American at the University of Michigan, where he helped lead the Wolverines to the 1947 NCAA national championship. He was an exceptional athlete of rare size and agility who was also a good enough basketball player to play professionally. In what may have been a case of NFL arrogance regarding the capabilities of AAFC players, every other team passed on Ford before the Browns selected him.

Ford was six foot five and 230 pounds when he joined the Browns. He had been an excellent two-way player for two years with the Dons. In addition to catching sixty-seven passes for a 17.5 average and eight touchdowns, Ford was also one of the best pass rushers in the AAFC.

But two-platoon football was increasingly the norm by 1950, and Brown made Ford a full-time defensive player. That enabled him to get bigger and stronger. Ford soon bulked up to 260 pounds and became a dominating defensive end who was a perennial all-pro and was elected to the Pro Football Hall of Fame in 1976.

"Lenny was a great pass rusher," Walt Michaels said. "A lot of times he would just crank it up and run over the tackle." Michaels credited Ford and Gino Marchetti, who came along several years later, with inventing the modern era pass rush. Longtime NFL defensive coordinator and head coach George Allen seconded Michaels, saying that "Ford was the first great pass-rushing defensive end."

"He was a fierce player, and something to behold when he uncoiled and went after a passer," Brown said of Ford. After joining the Browns, Ford became "one of the greatest to ever play in the NFL." Lou Groza, one of the game's best offensive tackles in the 1950s, said that practicing against Ford for eight years made him a better blocker.

Ford's skills were such that Brown soon changed the defensive alignment to maximize his opportunities to rush the passer. Instead of five- or six-man fronts, Cleveland could play more frequently with a four-man line and get just as much pressure on the quarterback. Willis and the team's linebackers were thus better able to pursue laterally to stop running plays and short- to medium-range passes. The fact that offenses often had to deploy more than one player to block Ford also created more openings for other defenders to exploit.

"We started with the line and built from there," Brown said of the team's defense, and the addition of Kissell further strengthened the line. Kissell combined first with Grigg and Palmer and later with Bob Gain and Don Colo to give the Browns pocket-crushing and run-stopping strength at tackle. His strong play alongside Ford for six years also provided Ford the leeway to pass rush with greater abandon.

"Oh boy, he was a good one," Agase said of Kissell. "Oh, Kissell was as mean and tough as they come. He was some kind of player. He was tough. And mean. And good."

Dom Moselle joined the Browns the same time as Kissell. "Brown liked him because he was so strong. And he was mean," Moselle said. "I remember those blocking sleds they have. He broke one of those one day. Kind of like a wild man."

"He was different," John Sandusky said of Kissell. "He was a guy who would try to knock your head off and stuff like that. And he could do it. He was a guy who was a little bit rowdy."

Like Ford, guard Gibron weighed about 260 pounds, only he was seven inches shorter. Gibron was incredibly quick and fast, though, and strong. "His shoulder width [fifty-four inches across] made him a fine pass protector, but his greatest attribute was the explosive speed with which he came off the ball," Brown said of Gibron. "No guard was ever faster for the first five yards, and when he pulled out to lead our sweeps, he could stay in front of our fastest backs until he threw his first block."

"He was really a tough guy," Lavelli said about Gibron who, like

Lavelli and other Browns, was a World War II veteran. "He would go down to the last inch with you."

Like Speedie, Adamle, and Edgar Jones, Gibron could also be a bit of a thorn in Paul Brown's side. Several players remembered him as a carouser, while others recalled Gibron talking back to Brown on more than one occasion. Sometimes Gibron's individualism surfaced on the playing field. He once nailed Emlen Tunnell, one of the era's best punt and kickoff returners, after Tunnell signaled for a fair catch on a punt. As the referee marched off a 15-yard penalty against Gibron, Brown demanded an explanation for what he thought was a bonehead play.

"[Y]ou won't have to worry about Tunnell anymore today," was Gibron's reply, an explanation that must have held a certain logic even for the discipline-conscious coach. Gibron made all-pro twice, played in four Pro Bowls, and later had an unsuccessful run as head coach of the Bears.

Linebacker Hal Herring also came to the Browns in the dispersement draft after one season with the Bills. He had the football smarts, the intelligence, and the diagnostic skills that Brown liked so much, especially in his linebacking corps. Herring was a sometimes starter for three years who went to graduate school after his playing career, authoring a doctoral dissertation titled "Defensive Tactics and Techniques in Professional Football."

Of the rookies, first-round choice Ken Carpenter and Jim Martin, the second of two choices in round two, were the most heralded. Martin came from Notre Dame and was drafted at the suggestion of fellow Golden Domer Lou Rymkus, who, while scouting Heisman Trophy winner Leon Hart, came away more impressed by Martin, the Fighting Irish's other end. Carpenter had an outstanding career at Oregon State University and played for the Browns for four years, earning a spot in the Pro Bowl in 1951.

With the loss of Edgar Jones, Boedeker, Horvath, and Parseghian, Brown used the draft in an effort to shore up the backfield. In addition to Carpenter, Cleveland selected Emerson Cole from the University of Toledo, Don "Dopey" Phelps from Kentucky, and Moselle from little Superior State Teachers College. Cole backed up Motley for three years, Phelps was primarily a kick returner in his two years in Cleveland, and Moselle played as a backup in the secondary and returned kicks for a year.

Tackle John Sandusky of Villanova University was selected in the second round. Like Palmer, Sandusky proved valuable because he could play tackle on both defense and offense. He played mostly on defense at first but eventually moved to offense after Rymkus retired. In short yardage and goal line situations, though, Sandusky was used on defense throughout his career. He played six years with the Browns, finished up in 1956 with the Packers, and then went on to a long career as an assistant coach.

As much as Sandusky contributed over six years, getting him was the result of a lost opportunity by the Browns to get Doak Walker, the great Heisman Trophy–winning back from Southern Methodist University. Cleveland had selected Walker as a future in the 1949 AAFC draft, while the Lions acquired his NFL rights from the Bulldogs. About the time the AAFC and NFL reached peace, Walker's playing career at SMU was ending, and both Detroit and Cleveland asserted their rights to him.

Although the Browns were not happy about it, matters were resolved with the Lions getting Walker while the Browns got Detroit's second-round pick, which they used to select Sandusky. Walker played only six seasons, but he was all-pro four times, made it to the Hall of Fame, and was a cog on a Lions team that won two championships and became a Cleveland nemesis.

Rookie Ken Gorgal from Purdue won a starting spot in the secondary, relegating Cliff Lewis to the second string. At six foot two, Gorgal was unusually tall for a defensive back. He intercepted six passes his rookie year, second best on the team behind James's nine, and also did some punt returning. Gorgal missed two complete seasons to military service but still intercepted eleven passes in his three years with the Browns. He played two additional years with the Bears and Packers in 1955 and 1956.

Another rookie who was in camp but never played for the Browns was end Gordy Soltau from Minnesota. Drafted by the Packers and acquired by Cleveland early in training camp, Soltau impressed Brown and earned a spot on the roster. However, Brown traded Soltau to the 49ers, where he played for nine years and was one of the NFL's better receivers and placekickers in the 1950s.

As much as Soltau impressed Brown, the Cleveland coach made an even greater impression on Soltau. "In the two weeks that I spent with him, I learned more about playing football and playing your position and understanding . . . many of the subtleties of the game that I never had the opportunity to learn prior to that," Soltau said of his brief stint with the Browns. "It certainly was helpful the rest of my career."

Because of his placekicking skills, Soltau thought another reason the Browns acquired him may have been to motivate Lou Groza. Groza had slumped badly in the field goal department in 1949, and Brown made it known that he expected more from the kicking game. Jim Martin, another rookie, was also an accomplished placekicker who joined the team that summer. In the end, Brown's nudging worked; Soltau was traded, Martin never did any kicking for the Browns, and 1950 marked the first of Groza's many great seasons in the NFL.

While it was understandable that Brown would have better information than his NFL counterparts about players from the AAFC, his selection of Moselle underscored how he found talent in places where others did not. Moselle was an outstanding back at tiny Superior State Teachers College, now the University of Wisconsin-Superior. Recommended to Brown by a coach of a school Superior State had played in 1949, Moselle was drafted in the twenty-third round. He played just the 1950 season with the Browns but remembered his stay in Cleveland fondly.

"He gave me an honor," Moselle recalled of something Brown said in a meeting of all of Cleveland's players. "He said that if I'd gone to Ohio State or Notre Dame, I would've been an All-American." After playing with the Browns in 1950, Moselle went on to play with the Packers, Eagles, and Calgary Stampeders.

In all, it was a dramatic turnover from 1949, with twelve new players including seven rookies. In addition to being quickly indoctrinated into the Cleveland Browns system, the new players also learned early on of the team's collective determination and self-assurance as they approached their first NFL season.

"The guys who played before 1950 on the team certainly wanted to prove that they were a pretty damn good football team," Gorgal said. "They were confident, and there was a determination that they had something to prove and they were going to get the job done."

"It was awesome for me being a rookie," Carpenter said. The Browns, Carpenter remembered, "were very confident we could win."

Where the signing of black players was concerned, the Browns continued to be far out in front of other teams. Ford and Cole joined Willis, Motley, and Gillom to bring the total of black players on the team to five. On opening day 1950, about one third of the blacks in the NFL were on Cleveland's roster. Four years after the debuts of Willis, Motley, Washington, and Strode, the Packers, Bears, Cardinals, Eagles, Steelers, Colts, and Redskins had still not employed a single black player, although Bob Mann joined the Packers later in the season.

And in the same way that the fact that they signed Willis and Motley a year before Jackie Robinson joined the Dodgers is oftentimes obscured, so too is the fact that the Browns continued to set the pace for all of the pro sports world. Although they were already firmly established as black America's favorite team, the baseball Dodgers had two fewer black players in 1950 than the Browns. And professional basketball remained all white until later that year when Chuck Cooper joined the Boston Celtics.

Beyond the fact that Cleveland had one third of the NFL's black players was the quality of those players. Of their five black players, Willis, Motley, Ford, and Gillom were among the very best ever at their positions, and three of them eventually made it to the Hall of Fame. Talent of that magnitude could accurately be cited as one of the key differences between the Browns and some of their NFL competitors.

The Bears, for example, did not sign a black player until 1952 and did not sign an impact black player until 1956 when J. C. Caroline joined the team. After winning the NFL championship in Willis's and Motley's first year with Cleveland, the Bears were among the NFL's best teams for more than a decade. In a thirteen-year span beginning in 1947, Chicago made it to the title game once, finished second eight times, won 63% of its games, and finished with a .667 or better winning percentage nine times. Yet the Bears were unable to win another title during that span.

It would be simplistic to say that the Bears were unable to get over the top solely because they were slow to sign black players, but clearly it was a factor. Similarly, the Eagles and 49ers had some good seasons in the 1950s but were nowhere near as successful as the Browns, in part because they signed blacks at a slower pace. At the other end of the spectrum from the Browns were the Redskins. The last football holdouts for segregation, Washington went from perennial championship contenders before the integration of 1946 to perpetual doormats thereafter.

The Rams, on the other hand, made four Championship Game appearances in the decade after they signed Washington and Strode. Although both were gone by 1950, the Rams continued to roll in part because they had added such talented black players as Woodley Lewis, Deacon Dan Towler, Bob Boyd, and Tank Younger to their roster. The great Lions teams of the early 1950s were the only notable exception to the correlative relationship between a team's success and the pace at which it signed black players. Although the Lions were the second NFL team and the eighth football team of the postwar era to integrate, their 1952 and 1953 champion teams were all white, the last all-white teams to win a pro football championship.

The failure of teams to keep pace with the Browns in signing black players was not simply a matter of nearsighted decisions made by management, although it certainly was partly that. Black players continued to face extra obstacles both on the field and off that made playing in the often unforgiving world of pro football that much more difficult. Who knows how many of the blacks signed or scouted in the decade or so after 1946 would have emerged as great players in less hostile surroundings.

Ken Carpenter and Emerson Cole became teammates of Marion Motley's in 1950, Motley's fifth season. In the years they played with Motley, Carpenter and Cole recalled that he was still forced to confront much of the same hostility he had faced earlier in his career.

"Everybody was taking a lot of cheap shots at him," Carpenter said. "But it didn't bother him, he just played his own game and did one hell of a job." Carpenter's admiration for his backfield mate was all the greater because of the obstacles Motley faced. "He was a tough one and a great football player."

"They stomped on his hands, kicked him in the head," Cole said. "That stuff went on constantly."

For black players who possessed less talent and perhaps less inner strength than Motley, careers often ended before they had a chance to begin. Baltimore Colts great Lenny Moore was every bit as talented and every bit as tough as Motley, yet he could not escape the fact that he, and other black players, might have been even better in different circumstances.

"[I]f I could just play football without this pressure and tension and constant thing on me, what a joy it would be" is how Moore expressed that sense of what might have been.

Although the AAFC's survivors and their one-time rivals were now joined in one merged league, bad blood continued to fester in the nine months between the merger announcement and opening day. As he had for four years, George Preston Marshall publicly and emphatically belittled the Browns and the insurgent league. At one function in Washington, Marshall exchanged harsh words with fellow speaker Otto Graham.

One-time AAFC commissioner O. O. Kessing preceded Graham on the dais and referred to the AAFC as "defunct." The Browns quarterback took exception to that characterization.

"The AAFC is not defunct," Graham said when it was his turn to speak. "We simply absorbed the NFL."

Sitting in the audience, Marshall was visibly upset. Graham continued with some remarks directed to the Washington owner. "Mr. Marshall, maybe you better buy back a piece of that laundry business if we play the Redskins."

"You probably won't even have a job next winter," Marshall retorted. "Maybe you'd like to drive one of my laundry trucks." Marshall was also on record as having said, "Our weakest team could toy with the Browns." On the other hand, Ray Flaherty, the man who coached Marshall's Redskins in their glory years and against the Browns for the Yankees, was among those who was certain that the Browns could beat the best the older league had to offer.

Cognizant of the drama that the 1950 season possessed, Bert Bell shrewdly scheduled the Browns to play the NFL's two-time defending champion Eagles in Philadelphia in their first ever NFL game. To add further to the drama, the game was scheduled for Saturday night, September 16, the night before the rest of the league's teams began play. Furthermore, with a seating capacity of just over 30,000, Shibe Park, the Eagles' home stadium, was determined to be too small for the anticipated crowd for the showdown. The game was moved to the much larger Municipal Stadium in Philadelphia, which seated more than twice as many and was best known as the site of most of the Army-Navy games.

Before their game with the Eagles, however, the Browns had a grueling preseason schedule to navigate. In the AAFC they had never played more than three such games, but in 1950 they were scheduled for five. In part the Browns used those games as they had in the AAFC—as a local road show designed to firm up support for the team in areas that were just a bit too far from Cleveland for most people to travel to see the team play.

In addition to a game against the Bears in Cleveland, the Browns played the Colts in Cincinnati, the Packers in Toledo's Glass Bowl, and the Lions in Akron's Rubber Bowl. They also actively courted jilted Buffalo fans by scheduling a game with the Steelers in Civic Stadium. Although the crowd was a modest 15,259, the move was a wise and fruitful one; for the next ten years, Buffalo (and much of western New York) was a Browns stronghold.

To some extent, what the Browns did in the NFL during the 1950 season was foreshadowed by what they did in the summer. After some momentary doubts when Green Bay kicked off Cleveland's preseason debut by scoring on their first possession, the Browns rebounded and shut the Packers out for the rest of the game, winning 38–7.

Cleveland won similarly one-sided games against the Colts and Lions, and then finished up with closer victories over Chicago and Pittsburgh. Although it was only the preseason, some of those games were played with the intensity of regular season affairs. None of the NFL teams, least of all the proud and mighty Bears, wanted to give an inch to the AAFC upstarts. But when training camp ended, the Browns had yet to lose.

The hard-fought 27–23 win over the Bears before 51,076 fans in Cleveland was especially satisfying for several other reasons. First, the Bears were the most storied franchise in pro football history, one whose seven championships were the most by any team. And second, Chicago's George Halas was the game's most prominent figure, one who had been there when the NFL was formed as the APFA and who was still going strong three decades later. Few in the Browns organization were unaware that Halas had also been one of the most vociferous opponents of the AAFC, critical of the league's quality of play and resentful of its intrusion into Chicago.

Perhaps that string of five preseason victories should have raised some eyebrows in Philadelphia. Cleveland's win over the Bears was especially noteworthy as Chicago had come within a hair of winning the NFL's Western Conference the previous year. In addition, the Bears had been the only team to defeat the champion Eagles in 1949.

According to the accounts of a number of Eagles players, however, head coach Greasy Neale did not take the Browns very seriously. Convinced of his team's invincibility, Neale did not even send scouts to Cleveland's preseason games, choosing instead to rely on films of several Browns games from 1949. Tackle Al Wistert, one of the very best Eagles players, remembered that Neale dismissed much of the information he did get about the Browns.

"I went to see them play," Wistert said, "because I hurt my knee, and while my knee was injured, I went to Cleveland and watched the Browns. Then when you'd come back and tell [Neale] some things that they were doing, he would say, 'Well they can't do that against us. They'll never do that against us. They can't do that,' because he was very proud of his football team."

In the preseason, perhaps the biggest thing the Browns learned, besides the confidence-instilling fact that they could dominate NFL teams much as they had AAFC foes, was how they might exploit Philadelphia's defense. Nicknamed the Eagles Defense, Philadelphia's alignments had been widely copied throughout the NFL because of the team's great success the previous three years. Among the teams that employed it regularly were the Lions.

One of the things that Paul Brown discovered against the Lions was that the defensive backs were left without help against Cleveland's ends whenever the Browns sent a back in motion out of the backfield. The Browns offense was far more innovative than most in the NFL, and they loved to put Dub Jones and their other backs in motion. Were they to do that on a regular basis against the Eagles, Brown realized, Philadelphia's cornerbacks would be left with the impossible task of covering both Speedie and Lavelli one on one.

Philadelphia also relied on its linebackers to provide help to its somewhat undersized secondary by holding receivers up at the line of scrimmage. But few of the NFL receivers that the Philadelphia defense had been so successful against were as big, elusive, and athletic as Speedie and Lavelli. The more room Cleveland's ends had to operate, the bigger the advantage they would have. None of the Eagles' four starting defensive backs was anywhere near as tall, broad, or strong as Speedie, Lavelli, or Jones.

In addition to the physical and strategic preparation was a psychological buildup that grew ever larger as opening night approached. Marion Motley recalled that the *Philadelphia Inquirer* had sent sports reporter Moe Berry to cover Cleveland's practices, and copies of the newspaper were sent to camp every day. While Berry's stories spoke glowingly of the Browns, other articles on the sports page contained quotes from Neale and Eagles players to the effect that Cleveland was inferior.

"Reading this paper for two weeks," Motley said, "we were just ready to hit anything the Eagles had."

Not that the Browns needed much more in the way of motivation; four years of ridicule had provided quite enough. Paul Brown later said that he had to curtail practice sessions in the week before the game for fear that in their eagerness, the players might leave their best game on the practice field. But Ken Carpenter recalled that the coaches, including Brown himself, were also caught up in the anticipation.

"I think the coaching staff was up higher than the players," Carpenter said. "Paul Brown said it in a meeting there that that game meant so much, even the coaches were nervous about it, the pressure was so great."

Brown knew better than anyone that far more than one game or even NFL supremacy was on the line. "There's not only this season at stake," Brown told his players, "but four years of achievements. I'm asking you to dedicate yourselves to preserving the reputation the Browns have made."

7 1,237 fans were on hand for the game. It was the largest crowd ever to see an NFL game in Philadelphia and the seventh largest ever in pro football history, topped only by four AAFC games in Cleveland and two Dons games and a Rams game in the Los Angeles Coliseum. The game came amid a baseball pennant race that culminated several weeks later with the Phillies winning their first National League flag in thirty-five years.

In fact, it was a great time in Philadelphia sports, and the future looked equally bright. After decades of ineptitude, the Phillies had assembled the young and talented Whiz Kids team that looked capable of remaining among baseball's elite for years to come. And many Philadel-phians were certain that nobody anytime or anywhere was better than an Eagles team that had won two straight titles and looked still to be the best in the NFL.

The Browns quickly went to work to show that there was indeed a better team—and they were it. After Cleveland's defense held the Eagles on the first series of the game, Don Phelps returned a punt 70 yards for an apparent touchdown. Ford was called for clipping, however, and the return was nullified. Afterward Brown said that Ford's block had not only been perfectly legal, it was "one of the greatest blocks ever thrown on a punt return—Len Ford had wiped out three Eagles' players in one move." Later in the game, another Browns touchdown and another long Phelps punt return were negated by penalty calls that Brown called phantom and "that never showed on the films."

Undaunted, the Browns soon showed that the lost touchdown by Phelps was just a temporary setback. Philadelphia took an early 3–0 lead, but before the first half was over, Cleveland had burned Philadelphia's secondary beyond anything even Paul Brown had hoped for. After set-ting up his man by running a series of short patterns to the outside, Jones broke long and caught a Graham pass over the middle for a 59-yard touchdown. No one was within 7 yards of Jones when he caught the ball.

Cleveland boosted its lead to 14–3 when Graham threw his second touchdown pass of the game in the second quarter, a 26-yarder to Lavelli. Perhaps the turning point of the game came early in the second half when Motley, with the score still 14–3, provided the NFL a glimpse of his tremendous all-around talents. Inserted at linebacker with the Eagles inside the Cleveland 5-yard line, Motley made four straight tackles and the Eagles were rebuffed. Cleveland proceeded to up its lead on Graham's third touchdown pass, this one to Speedie from 13 yards.

Philadelphia finally cracked the Cleveland end zone in the fourth quarter on a Bill Mackrides to Pete Pihos touchdown pass to close to 21–10, but Graham and Bumgardner scored on short runs, and Cleve-land won 35–10. It was a dominating performance. Cleveland totaled 487 yards from scrimmage against the vaunted Philadelphia defense, with Graham leading the way.

In as fine a game as he had ever played in the AAFC, the Cleveland quarterback completed twenty-one of thirty-eight passes for 346 yards and three touchdowns. In an unprecedented move that was yet another measure of the magnitude of the game, Bell had announced beforehand that there would be an MVP award for the game, complete with trophy. Graham was the recipient.

No award or piece of hardware could capture the satisfaction Graham and the other Browns felt at their collective achievement, however. Against the Eagles, Brown said, "we were the best football team I have ever seen."

"I had never seen perfection until that game, or after that game," Lin Houston said. "But in that game, it was perfection." Echoing Houston, Jones gave much of the credit to the coach. "It was a great coaching game," Jones said. "What a game plan Paul Brown put together. It worked to perfection."

Bell similarly sang Cleveland's praises. An adversary for four years, he had realized more than most people in the NFL that the Browns were both an excellent team and an asset to the league. Having encouraged the Browns on beforehand, Bell proclaimed afterward that they were "the greatest team to ever play the game."

Shell-shocked and perhaps a bit disbelieving, most of the Eagles players gave Cleveland credit. With the mistake of his dismissive attitude now glaringly obvious, Neale said, "Geez, they've got a lot of guns, haven't they? A lot of guns . . . they're a fine football team."

In remarks similar to those made by many others before and after, defensive back Russ Craft spoke in glowing terms of the Browns' passing game. "We never played against a team that threw to a spot as well as Cleveland. We would be on top of their receivers but they caught the ball anyway because it was so well-timed."

"They dominated us, there's no question about it," Chuck Bednarik said years later. "I was impressed."

Neale also made a point of quashing the notion that having the injured Steve Van Buren in the lineup would have produced a different result. "We'd probably have had another touchdown if Steve had been in there . . . maybe two more. But as for winning the game, well . . . that's something else." In addition, though, Neale uttered some not so complimentary words deriding the Browns as little more than a basketball team for their penchant for throwing the ball. He would come to regret those words when the teams met a second time eleven weeks later.

The last word on the opening-night confrontation belonged to Pete Pihos, the greatest Eagle of them all, when he said what many AAFC and Browns partisans may have been thinking in the game's aftermath. When asked by his incredulous wife after the game what had gone wrong, Pihos replied, "Honey, we met a team from the big league."

Just as many American Football League players celebrated and felt vindicated when teams from their league won Super Bowls against NFL teams in 1968 and 1969, veterans of the AAFC celebrated and felt vindicated when the Browns defeated the Eagles. "By all means, I felt very good," one-time Yankee Lou Sossamon said. "Cleveland proved that our conference was pretty strong."

"Look at what the Browns did to 'em," former Bill and Brown George Terlep said. "I think the NFL found out in a hurry that that All-America Conference was a pretty tough league."

Ara Parseghian was back in Ohio in September 1950, less than a year removed from his playing career with the Browns and about to begin his long and distinguished college coaching career.

"I remember vividly because I would've loved to have been a part of that," Parseghian said of Cleveland's smashing NFL debut. "I felt I was missing something." At the same time, "I felt elated about it, that I had been a part of a team that had not been in the minor leagues," Parseghian added with a laugh.

Cleveland's demolition of the Eagles reverberated throughout the NFL. If an undefeated preseason had not been enough to do so, the win in Philadelphia ensured that the Browns would not catch anybody else off guard. Greasy Neale and New York Giants head coach Steve Owen had been bitter Eastern Conference rivals for ten years, but that did not prevent Neale from sharing a detailed analysis of the Browns with Owen.

The Colts were already very familiar with the Browns' prowess, and still it didn't help. Baltimore succumbed rather meekly in Cleveland's second game, 31–0. Baltimore was playing that season as a kind of floater. Placed in the National Conference, the Colts were scheduled to play the other twelve teams once rather than the usual home and away matches against conference foes combined with several games against teams from the other conference.

It would be a long season for the Colts. The loss to the Browns came a week after a 38–14 opening-day loss to Washington. Having fallen on hard times in 1949, the Colts struggled throughout 1950. Their 1–11 record was the same as in 1949, and they set a record by allowing 38.5 points per game.

In the game against Baltimore, Graham completed his first seven passes and the Browns shot out to a 17–0 first quarter lead. Jones scored on runs of 11 and 60 yards, and Carpenter rushed for 100 yards on just three carries, largely on the strength of a 61-yard touchdown, the first of his career.

The following week the Browns hosted the Giants before 37,647 in their NFL home debut. The game marked the beginning of a heated rivalry that would last twenty years, one that ranks as one of the best in football history. In contrast to the Eagles, the Giants, who had an open date the week before, thoroughly prepared for Cleveland. Otto Schnellbacher recalled that the Giants' attitude toward the Browns and the AAFC players changed diametrically after opening night.

"Everybody wanted to know about the Cleveland Browns," Schnellbacher said of the two weeks after the Browns' win over the Eagles. Schnellbacher and four of New York's other starters on defense had played against the Browns in the AAFC. Based on what he heard from those players and on what the Browns did in Philadelphia, Steve Owen decided that a defensive innovation was necessary to contain Cleveland's passing game.

According to Schnellbacher, what became known as the Umbrella Defense evolved out of formations the Yankees used in 1949 because of their weakness at linebacker. It didn't work then, but when Schnellbacher, Landry, Weinmeister, Rowe, and Rapacz joined with outstanding holdovers Emlen Tunnell, Al DeRogatis, John Cannady, and Ray Poole, the Giants had one of the best defenses in football. In that first meeting with Cleveland, New York did something to the Browns in a regular season game that no team had done before and none would do again until 1971: They shut them out.

The key component of the Umbrella Defense was the utilization of both defensive ends in pass coverage. The Giants lined up in a six-man line and had the ends drop diagonally toward each sideline any time Graham went back to pass. In so doing, the ends cut off Cleveland's medium-range sideline passes and freed the linebacker and the safeties to cover the middle of the field. The great push the Giants got from Weinmeister and DeRogatis on passing downs was also an immeasurable help in making the Umbrella effective, Schnellbacher thought.

And effective it was. Cleveland did not have a single completion in the first half, and the Giants intercepted four passes. With all of that, the Browns still had several chances to win the game in the fourth quarter because of the superb play of their own defense. The first and best opportunity was set up by a good punt return by Moselle to midfield. After Graham completed four straight passes, however, that bid was foiled when Graham and Motley got their signals crossed and collided in the backfield, with New York recovering the resulting fumble.

Later, a Graham pass to an open Speedie in the end zone sailed just out of reach. And on Cleveland's last possession, a fourth-down Graham to Gillom pass in the end zone likewise just missed. Eddie Price's first-quarter touchdown thus stood up, and New York won 6–0.

Playing again on a Saturday night, the Browns rebounded with a 30–17 win over Pittsburgh at Forbes Field. The Browns picked up 191 yards and four touchdowns on the ground as Cleveland began a twenty-year domination of the Steelers. Jones scored his fourth and fifth touchdowns of the season, while Graham also scored twice.

A week later against the Cardinals, the Browns had to battle back from a 24–10 third-quarter deficit to win 34–24. Graham threw for 369 yards and touchdowns of 29 and 26 yards to Lavelli. Late in the victory, however, Ford was seriously injured on a dirty hit by Pat Harder, and he lost several teeth and suffered a broken jaw. Incredibly, Ford was the one penalized on the play. He would not return to the lineup for ten weeks.

The Browns ran into the Giants again at the Polo Grounds the following week and lost for a second time, 17–13. New York rushed for 200 yards and again held Cleveland's offense completely in check. The Browns had only 12 yards on the ground and 130 in all, and Graham threw three interceptions. Their only touchdown came after Carpenter recovered a kickoff that was misplayed by Jim Ostendarp at the 1-yard line. As in the first New York game, Graham and Speedie barely missed connecting on a potential game-winning pass late in the game, and

Schnellbacher intercepted. At the halfway point of the season, the 4–2 Browns trailed the Giants and Eagles, who were tied atop the American Conference at 4–1.

Motley broke out for the first time in 1950 the following week as the Steelers again fell, 45–7. The Browns established an all-time team mark that still stands with 338 yards rushing. Motley led the way with 188 yards on just eleven carries for an all-time pro football mark of 17.1 yards per carry. That record stood for over fifty years. He scored on a 69-yard run and on a 33-yard pass from Graham. On defense, Tommy James intercepted two passes, and Cleveland intercepted six in all.

When the Browns edged the Cardinals 10–7 on November 5, they moved into sole possession of first place with a 6–2 record. Jones scored his seventh touchdown on a 33-yard run in the first quarter to give Cleveland an early lead they never relinquished. Having lost to the Cardinals the week before, the Giants fell a half game back at 5–2, tied for second with Philadelphia, 9–7 losers to the Steelers.

Motley led the way again as Cleveland defeated their old rival San Francisco, 34–14. The 49ers were struggling badly in their first NFL campaign. The loss dropped them to 2–7 and sixth place in the National Conference. Still, they hung tough with the Browns for three quarters until Cleveland scored 17 fourth-quarter points to pull away. Motley gained 114 yards including a 22-yard touchdown run.

Motley was the best back in football in 1950. His game was the same as it had been in the AAFC—devastating power, great inside running, an important last line of blocking defense for Graham, and a part of the team's strong passing game. By season's end, Motley would win the NFL rushing crown and be a unanimous first-team all-pro selection.

For all of that, former teammate Saban later said that NFL fans had not seen Motley at his best. "The people who are talking about Motley are talking about the Motley who played in the NFL—on two bad knees. The Motley they saw was just a shadow of the old Motley, even when he made all-pro in '50 and led the league in running. Don't forget, he was twenty-six years old in his rookie year."

While Saban is right at least to the extent that Motley had several better AAFC years than his 1950 season, the big fullback's play was a tremendous part of Cleveland's success that year. He also made the same lasting impression on NFL opponents that he had made in his first four years.

"[H]e was as close as anyone has ever come to being a human wave," Jack Christiansen said.

"Marion Motley just bowled you over," said Vince Banonis. "I got to know him later in life . . . I would say, 'Marion, you know, you'd come around that end and I'd try to tackle you. You'd knock me over and I'd look up, and all I would see was blackbirds.'"

Because of the Browns' great passing attack, Motley did not carry the ball anywhere near as often as backs in more recent times. His 1950 rushing title, for example, came on just 11.7 carries per game. Remarkably, that was the highest mark of his career. But Motley made each of those runs count. He averaged 5.8 yards per carry, the fifth of sixth times he would average 5 yards or better in a season.

What separated Motley from just about every other back was his ability to make a valuable contribution even when he didn't touch the ball. Many was the time he helped open holes for Jones and the other backs as Cleveland led the league with a team 4.6 rushing average and Jones finished second in the league in touchdowns with eleven. But it was in pass protection that Motley really showed his skill as a blocker.

"Well, you rush Graham and put a move and beat your man, and there's Motley waiting for you," said Gail Bruce, a 49ers defensive end. "Next play, you beat your man with a different move, and there's Motley waiting again. Pretty soon you say, 'The hell with it. I'd rather stay on the line and battle the first guy.'"

"Old Marion Motley, he was one of the best pass blockers I ever saw," Colts end Hub Bechtol said. "He was tough to get by to get to Otto Graham. I never could get to him."

"Marion took the romance out of the blitz" is how Browns assistant coach Weeb Ewbank put it.

The AAFC-NFL merger may have brought peace to pro football, but it hadn't resulted in greater prosperity at the gate. Attendance continued to lag far behind the high water marks of 1946 and 1947, and despite the excitement of their success against new competition, the Browns were no exception. Where in four previous regular season home games against the 49ers the Browns had averaged over 75,000, for example, the 1950 game attracted only 28,786.

The 40,714 Cleveland drew against the Steelers turned out to be the largest home crowd of the season. In all, the Browns averaged 33,386 per home game and drew an additional 62,805 for two postseason home games, both of which were played in cold temperatures. The NFL's newest power did turn out to be a successful road act, however. Bolstered by the record crowd in Philadelphia, the Browns played before more fans away than they did at Municipal Stadium for one of the few times in their history, averaging 38,727 per road game.

Although they had their hands full throughout, the Browns ultimately prevailed in their first ever meeting with George Preston Marshall's Redskins on November 19. Motley had another big day with 178 yards, but it took an 8-yard Don Phelps touchdown run with four minutes left in the game for Cleveland to eke out a 20–14 victory. Two Lou Groza field goals provided the margin of victory.

While the Browns took a week off with a bye, the Giants tied them for first place with a 7–3 win over the Eagles. Cleveland and New York both stood at 8–2 while the slumping Eagles, losers of two in a row and three of four, were 6–4. Those same Eagles came to Cleveland December 3 looking to avenge their humiliating opening-night loss and stay alive in the conference race. For Paul Brown, the game was an opportunity to do a little score settling of his own.

Although Greasy Neale had spoken of the Browns in mostly complimentary terms after his team's 35–10 opening-night loss, Brown had not forgotten the many unflattering things the Philadelphia coach had also said. Neale's remarks likening the Browns to a basketball team especially stuck in Brown's craw for weeks. Having devised a brilliant game plan for the first encounter that emphasized the pass, Brown came up with an approach that was as different as could be for the second game.

"Coach Brown said, 'As long as the score is tied or we're ahead, we're not gonna throw a pass,'" Alex Agase recalled of the rematch with Philadelphia. "And we didn't."

Agase and his defensive mates were superb in the game, played on a sloppy field. The defense, in fact, staked the Browns to the early lead Brown wanted when Lahr returned an interception 30 yards for a first-quarter touchdown. They also held Van Buren to –2 yards rushing on ten carries. That allowed Brown to stick it to Neale and the Eagles. The Browns did not attempt a single pass yet were able to position Groza for field goals in the second and third quarters to boost the lead to 13–0.

Their season on the line, the Eagles finally broke through for a touchdown with just over a minute to play, but they were unable to get the ball back. Despite only 68 yards of offense, Cleveland won 13–7. No team since has gone an entire game without throwing a single pass.

It is a remarkable testament to the Browns' overall greatness that they could do so and *actually win the game*, especially against an opponent as strong as the Eagles. The first time around, they had run circles around the Eagles defense. In the second game, despite huge disadvantages in field position and time of possession, they had shown Philadelphia some real defense.

Brown later referred to his decision to show up Neale and his team as "a silly grandstand play," but he knew exactly what he was doing. The ridicule directed toward Cleveland by Neale and the rest of the NFL is something Brown never forgot. The cool, thick-skinned appearance he presented to the world was real enough, but so too were the passions that burned inside.

To have beaten the two-time defending NFL champions, the mighty Eagles that Brown and his team had been hearing so much about for two years and that were supposedly so much better than the Browns, must have been extremely satisfying to the coach and players beyond the importance the games had in the standings. To have won the two games in such disparate fashion—"choose your weapon"—first with an aerial assault as good as any ever seen and then with a game plan out of football's stone age, is all the more remarkable.

Understandably, Greasy Neale found it difficult to live with the humiliation. Fired at the end of the season after a falling out with the Eagles owners, years later Neale disingenuously remembered the second Browns game as one where the Eagles "didn't allow a single completion." Of course, he left out the two most important parts of the story: First, that his statements ridiculing the Browns as pass-happy were the backdrop to the rematch; and second, that the Browns had not attempted a single pass, which went a long way toward explaining why they didn't complete any.

While not exactly a "silly grandstand play," Brown's decision not to throw the ball even once was a risky one, coming as it did in the midst of an extremely close conference race. A mishap here, a turnover there, and the game could have gone the Eagles' way. Here again, however, in addition to the greatness with which they played, is the hallmark of the Browns dynasty teams that struck 1950 rookies like Gorgal and Carpenter so forcefully: confidence.

The players were extremely confident that they could prevail in any circumstances, and their coach was equally confident they could do so, too. And Brown's confidence in them made them more confident in themselves. Perhaps never was that more evident than in the second Eagles game.

The same day the Browns eliminated the Eagles, the Giants defeated the Yanks. That meant Cleveland and New York went to the final week of the season deadlocked at the top of the American Conference at 9–2. The Browns had won five in a row and had defeated all comers except the Giants.

The Browns finished with a 45–21 win over the Redskins at snowy Griffith Stadium. As in a number of games that season, it was a close battle for a while until the Browns asserted themselves and wore down an inferior opponent.

Washington led 21–14 in the third quarter, and Motley was done for the day, ejected after gaining forty-eight first-half yards on just four carries. But Cleveland got touchdowns from all three units on another Lahr interception return, a Phelps punt return, and two Graham touchdown passes, including one to Groza on a tackle-eligible play. It was the only touchdown of Groza's twenty-one-year career.

Groza also added his thirteenth field goal of the year. That broke the twenty-four-year-old NFL record set by the Bears' Paddy Driscoll and at the time was second only to Ben Agajanian's fifteen in 1947 with the AAFC Dons. Graham also had a superb day, with twenty-three completions on thirty-two attempts for 321 yards and four touchdowns. He thus joined Sammy Baugh as the second NFL quarterback to ever have three 300-yard passing games in one season.

The Giants won a fight-filled game over the Eagles at Shibe Park, 9–7, to force a playoff. The Browns won the coin toss to determine home field advantage, and the game was scheduled for Sunday, December 17, in Cleveland. The Bears and Rams also finished tied atop the National Conference and would square off the same day at the Los Angeles Coliseum. It was the only time of the 1933–1966 era that that ever happened.

Temperatures were in the teens, and the Municipal Stadium turf was frozen solid for the game between the Browns and Giants. The teams had scored only 36 points between them in their two games, and with the slick field, gusting winds, and biting cold compounding matters for both offenses, the playoff game was more of the same.

Cleveland drove to the New York 5 early in the game but was forced to settle for a Groza field goal and a 3–0 lead. Those points held up until the Giants drove into Cleveland territory in the fourth quarter. It was there that Bill Willis made what was probably the biggest defensive play in all of the long history of the Cleveland Browns.

With the ball at the 36, New York back Choo Choo Roberts broke free around right end and seemed headed for a sure go-ahead touchdown. But Willis angled over from his middle guard position and took off in pursuit. Making up almost 5 yards, Willis brought Roberts down at the 4. "All I could think of was that number on Roberts's back represented the championship running away from me," Willis said later.

Even with Willis's great play, the Browns were not out of the woods. Over the next few minutes the Giants repeatedly took cracks at the end zone. With both teams' seasons on the line, it was an incredibly dramatic sequence. On third down from the 3, it appeared that New York had taken the lead on a Charlie Conerly completion to Bob McChesney in the end zone. New York's other end was offside, however, and the play was nullified.

On the very next play it appeared that the Browns had emerged entirely unscathed when Tommy James intercepted a pass in the end zone. But that play was negated by a Cleveland penalty for holding, and the Giants found themselves back where the sequence began, with a first and goal at the 4. At that point the Cleveland defense really stiffened. Three stops and a New York penalty brought about fourth down at the 13.

From there, Randy Clay kicked a field goal that tied the score. If not for the heroics of the defense, things could have been much worse for the Browns. Willis's play was the biggest, but rookie Jim Martin, one of the players who had filled in at end in Ford's absence, also came up big when the defense was backed up to its goal line.

When Cleveland got the ball after the kickoff, Brown made an important strategic decision. To that point, the Giants defense and the playing conditions had ground Graham, Motley, Lavelli, Jones, Speedie, and the Browns offense to a complete halt. But here Graham's athleticism came into play. Concerned that victory that had seemed within grasp might be slipping away, Brown tapped that athleticism and went on the offensive.

Brown figured that quarterback draws and bootlegs would be effective maneuvers on a frozen field. The New York defense not only might be caught off guard by those plays but also would have a more difficult time on a frozen field, making up for the momentary indecision and confusion that is a crucial aspect of such plays. In addition, the slippery footing had thrown off the delicate coordination between Cleveland's blockers and running backs. Quarterback keepers would bypass that problem.

The key ingredient to the success of the strategy was Graham. Not many quarterbacks would have been able to make it work. But Graham was bigger, stronger, faster, quicker, and had a greater awareness of what was going on around him than just about anybody else who had ever played the position. Plus there were the intangible qualities Graham possessed: leadership, unbelievable determination, and a killer instinct for making the big play in the big spot. Here Brown's likening of his team to the baseball Yankees was never more appropriate. Having Graham at quarterback late in a close game was like having Tommy Henrich up with the go-ahead run in scoring position or Allie Reynolds protecting a lead in the ninth inning.

Brown's strategy worked to perfection as Cleveland drove to the New York 22 almost exclusively on the strength of Graham's running. He gained 45 yards in all, and with 0:58 seconds remaining, Groza kicked a 28-yard field goal to give the Browns a 6–3 lead. And then in what was a fitting ending, the defense iced the game in the final seconds when Martin sacked Conerly for a safety to make the final score 8–3. Willis was credited with the safety, but in the film footage of the play it is clearly number 50 Martin who makes an unassisted tackle on the play.

The primitive nature of the game is reflected in the fact that the two teams combined for only six pass completions in twenty-four attempts for a combined 91 yards. The weather and field conditions were undoubtedly factors, but so too were the two great defenses.

Although he did not garner headlines for his effort the way that kicking mate Groza did, Horace Gillom also played a key role in the victory. With the Browns unable to move the ball, he was called on repeatedly to either punt the ball out of danger or pin New York deep in its own territory. Gillom did both superbly, and his high positional kicking kept the outstanding Tunnell-Schnellbacher return tandem at bay.

Gillom also made a crucial play in the first quarter. He was awaiting the snap from center in punt formation in Cleveland's end of the field when Gatski hiked the ball over his head. Considering the weather and the quality of the two defenses, it was precisely the kind of play that could have given the Giants an important early advantage. But while eluding pursuing Giants, Gillom was able to scoop the loose ball up on the dead run and get off a kick that carried all the way to the Giants 15-yard line.

A week later on Christmas Eve day, snow ringed the Municipal Stadium field as the Browns hosted the Rams, 24–14 winners over the Bears, in the eighteenth NFL Championship Game. Los Angeles was making its second straight title-game appearance and had a terrific array of talent, particularly on offense. In fact, the Rams offense that year was probably the greatest in pro football history. They scored 466 points, an average of 38.8 per game, a record that still stands.

Most of that firepower came from the passing game. The Rams had taken the baton from the Browns and developed the game's most explosive aerial attack. Led by quarterbacks Bob Waterfield and Norm Van Brocklin, ends Tom Fears and Bob Boyd, and flanker Elroy Hirsch, the Rams had passed for 3,709 yards, an average of an incredible 309 per game. That, too, was an all-time record at the time, one that stood until 1984.

Fears joined Speedie as the only players to ever record 1,000 receiving yards twice. His eighty-four receptions and seven catches per game were also all-time records that stood until Lionel Taylor broke them in the early years of the AFL. No NFL player topped eighty-four receptions until 1964, and Fears's seven catches per game stood as an NFL record until 1994.

Football was Paul Brown's life. He played quarterback at Miami University in Ohio in the 1920s and was the owner of the Cincinnati Bengals at the time of his death more than sixty years later. Courtesy of Special Collections, Cleveland State University Library.

Paul Brown (right) with Browns' owner Leo "Mickey" McBride after Cleveland's third consecutive All-America Football Conference Championship Game victory in 1948. After an unsuccessful attempt to purchase the NFL Cleveland Rams, McBride helped found the All-America Football Conference. Courtesy of Special Collections, Cleveland State University Library.

Otto Graham (14, eluding Norm Willey in a 1955 game against the Philadelphia Eagles) was the first player signed by the Browns. He earned more all-pro honors and MVP awards and led his team to more championships than any quarterback in history. Courtesy of Special Collections, Cleveland State University Library.

Bill Willis anchored Cleveland's defense for eight years. When he took the field at the start of Cleveland's first game in 1946, Willis became the first African-American to play major league football since 1933. Courtesy of Special Collections, Cleveland State University Library.

Known more for his record-shattering placekicking feats, Lou Groza (76) was also an outstanding offensive tackle, garnering all-pro honors six times. Here he leads Ken Carpenter (20) around end against the Chicago Bears. Courtesy of Special Collections, Cleveland State University Library.

No sight was quite so troubling to defenses as that of Marion Motley carrying the ball, as he is here in Cleveland's 8–3 win in the 1950 conference playoff versus Emlen Tunnell and the Giants. Motley was also a great blocker and linebacker, and he was the second black player elected to the Hall of Fame (Tunnell was the first). Courtesy of the Cleveland Public Library.

Although almost twenty-seven by the time he played his first game due to military service, Mac Speedie (catching a pass against Tunnell of the Giants) was the best receiver of the post-war era. He won four receiving titles and established career marks for most catches (50) and receiving yards (800) per season. Courtesy of Special Collections, Cleveland State University Library.

The best of the players to jump from the NFL to the Browns in 1946, tackle Lou Rymkus was Cleveland's top offensive lineman during his six years with the team. He also guided the Houston Oilers to the 1960 AFL championship in his only full season as a head coach. Courtesy of the Cleveland Public Library.

The Browns' assistant coaches included (left to right) Weeb Ewbank, Howard Brinker, Blanton Collier, and Fritz Heisler. Heisler coached Cleveland's many outstanding offensive linemen over twenty-five years, Collier posted a .675 winning percentage and won an NFL championship as Paul Brown's successor, and Ewbank won two titles in the NFL and one in the AFL. Courtesy of Special Collections, Cleveland State University Library.

Dante Lavelli catching a touchdown pass in 1954 against Bob Hudson of the Philadelphia Eagles. Nicknamed "Gluefingers," Lavelli was elected to the Pro Football Hall of Fame in 1975. Herschel Forester (62) is in the background. Courtesy of Special Collections, Cleveland State University Library.

Linebacker Lou Saban, with Paul Brown in 1949, was Cleveland's captain for three seasons. Saban was one of many Cleveland players who went on to have successful coaching careers as he guided the Buffalo Bills to consecutive AFL championships in 1964–65. Courtesy of Special Collections, Cleveland State University Library.

The Browns regularly played in front of the largest crowds in football both at home and on the road, as is evidenced by the turnout for this 1946 game against the 49ers in San Francisco's Kezar Stadium. Some of the players pictured are Alex Kapter (tackling Norm Standlee), Lou Saban (66), John Yonakor (50), and Ernie Blandin (48) of the Browns and Bruno Banducci (33), Pete Franceschi (82), and Frankie Albert (63) of the 49ers. Courtesy of Special Collections, Cleveland State University Library.

Halfback Edgar "Special Delivery" Jones gets ready to take a snap from center Frank Gatski. Like a number of early Browns, University of Pittsburgh graduate Jones first attracted Paul Brown's attention as an opponent during Brown's days at Ohio State. Gatski never missed a game in his twelve-year career, and he and Lou Groza share the all-time mark of having played on seven championship teams. Courtesy of Special Collections, Cleveland State University Library.

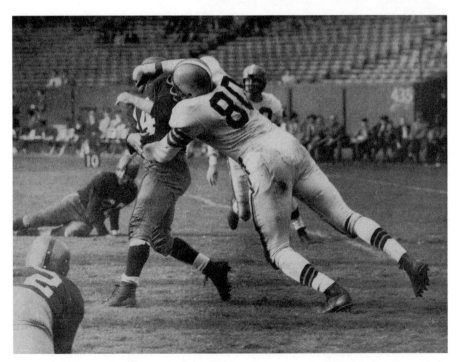

At six-foot-five and 260 pounds, Len Ford was a terror at defensive end in his eight seasons with the Browns. Quick and agile as well as incredibly strong, Ford also played for the New York Rens, an all-black professional basketball team. Courtesy of Special Collections, Cleveland State University Library.

Cleveland's finest hour came when Lou Groza kicked this game-winning field goal in the 1950 NFL Championship Game against the Los Angeles Rams in what may have been the greatest game in pro football history. The Browns are the only team in any sport to win a championship in their first year in an already-existing league. Courtesy of Special Collections, Cleveland State University Library.

Halfback Ara Parseghian played two years for the Browns before a serious hip injury ended his career. A college head coach by age twenty-eight, Parseghian was one of Notre Dame's greatest coaches, guiding the Irish to two national championships. Courtesy of Special Collections, Cleveland State University Library.

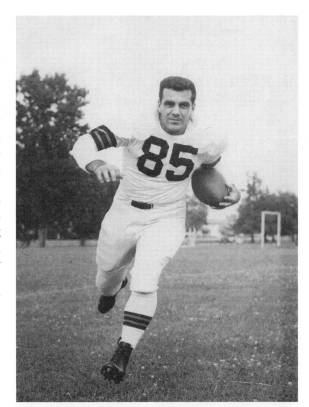

The best punter of his and perhaps any era, Horace Gillom kicks against Visco Grgich (34) and Hal Shoener of the San Francisco 49ers in 1950. Gillom also played offensive and defensive end during his ten seasons with the Browns. Courtesy of Special Collections, Cleveland State University Library.

Tommy James (42) tackling Ollie Matson in a 1952 game against the Chicago Cardinals. A mainstay in the secondary for eight years, James played for Paul Brown in high school and college as well as with the Browns. Courtesy of Special Collections, Cleveland State University Library.

Cleveland's solid quartet of linebackers in the early 1950s: left to right, Hal Herring, Tommy Thompson, Alex Agase, and Tony Adamle. Courtesy of Special Collections, Cleveland State University Library.

Dub Jones holds six footballs, one for each of the record-tying six touchdowns he scored in 1951 against the Bears. Jones scored twenty-three touchdowns in 1950–51. His son Bert was an MVP quarterback and one of numerous Browns' offspring who made their mark in pro football, others being Mike Renfro, Mike Adamle, Nick Saban, Scott Palmer, and David Shula. Courtesy of Corbis / Bettmann Archives.

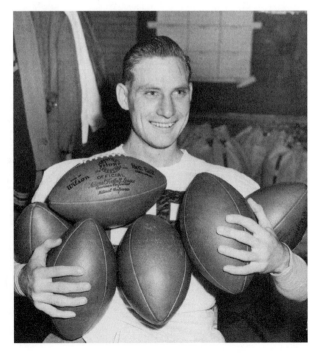

Cornerback Warren Lahr breaks up a pass intended for Ray Poole in a 1952 game against the New York Giants while safety Ken Gorgal (15) looks on. In eleven seasons in Cleveland, Lahr had forty-four interceptions and once held the NFL record with five returned for touchdowns. Courtesy of Special Collections, Cleveland State University Library.

The Browns acquired rugged Bob Gain from the Green Bay Packers in one of the best trades in team history. The 1950 Outland Trophy winner excelled at four defensive positions in his twelve-year career. Courtesy of Special Collections, Cleveland State University Library.

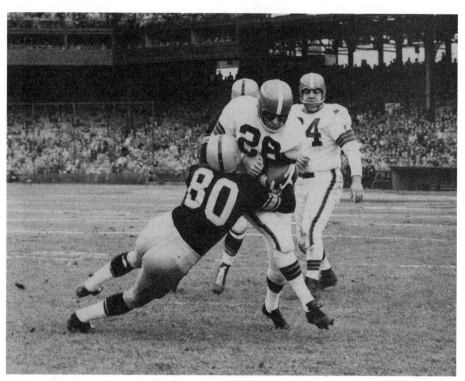

Speedy Ray Renfro (here catching a pass against Jack Butler of the Pittsburgh Steelers) averaged 19.6 yards per reception in his career. In the background is Abe Gibron, who came to the Browns from the Buffalo Bills and was one of the NFL's best offensive guards of the 1950s. Courtesy of Special Collections, Cleveland State University Library.

Mike McCormack came to Cleveland in a trade involving fifteen players and took over the middle guard position in 1954 when Bill Willis retired. He moved to offensive tackle the following season and was a standout for eight years. Courtesy of the Cleveland Public Library.

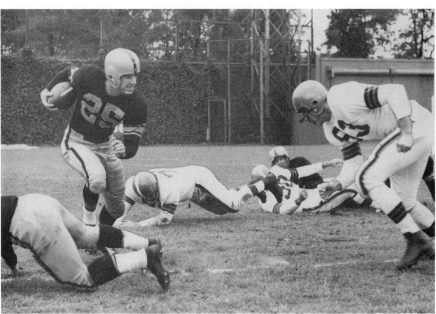

Doug Atkins was six-foot-eight, 275 pounds, and could high jump seven feet, but after just two years with the Browns he was traded to the Bears in one of the worst deals in team history. Too individualistic for Paul Brown, Atkins played seventeen years in all and was elected to the Pro Football Hall of Fame in 1982. Courtesy of Special Collections, Cleveland State University Library.

Members of the great Cleveland defense in action against the Detroit Lions in 1954: end Carlton Massey (82), tackle Don Colo (70), linebacker Tom Catlin (50), middle guard Mike McCormack (74), and cornerback Ken Konz (22). For Detroit, Bob Hoernschmeyer is the ball-carrier and Andy Miketa (52) is at left. Courtesy of Special Collections, Cleveland State University Library.

Joining Cleveland in 1952, end Pete Brewster (88) led the team in receptions three times. Here he catches a pass in a 1954 game against Paul Cameron (34) of the Pittsburgh Steelers. The Browns clinched their ninth straight conference title with a 42–7 victory in this game as Chet Hanulak (44, foreground) scored three touchdowns. Courtesy of Special Collections, Cleveland State University Library.

Los Angeles had a strong running game, too. Led by Dick Hoerner, Vitamin Smith, Deacon Dan Towler, and former Army great Glenn Davis, the Rams averaged over 140 yards rushing per game. All told, Los Angeles had put up an amazing 451.7 yards of offense per game in 1950, another record that has never been equaled. The Rams also scored 70 points against the Colts (the most in a regular season game at the time), 41 points in one quarter against the Lions, and 135 points in back to back games, two more marks that still stand.

If the Rams had an advantage on offense, Cleveland had a decided edge on defense and a smaller but very real advantage in the kicking game. Los Angeles gave up more than twice as many points as the Browns, an average of 25.8 per game to Cleveland's 12. Only four teams had allowed more points than the Rams. However, Los Angeles's low ranking can be explained in part by the fact that opponents were often airing things out to make up big deficits. The team's best defenders were rookie defensive back Woodley Lewis, linebacker Fred Naumetz, and former Dons tackle Bob Reinhard.

Like Otto Graham, Rams quarterback Waterfield was one of the best all-around athletes in the NFL in 1950. He was not only an outstanding passer but also a good runner. Waterfield also handled both the team's punting and placekicking and did both very well.

Waterfield was a notch below Cleveland's two kickers, however. Beginning a six-year stretch in which he was the NFL's best punter, Cleveland's Gillom had missed the punting title by an eyelash, and his 43.2 average was more than 3 yards better than Waterfield's.

Cleveland's advantage in placekicking was just as marked. Waterfield made seven of fourteen field goals on the season and was one of the few kickers of his era with a career success rate of over 50%. Groza, however, had really come into his own in 1950. His thirteen field goals set a new NFL record, and his 68.4% success rate was one of the best ever, just one more successful kick away from a new all-time record. Cleveland also figured to be more likely to convert from long distance as Groza had four successful kicks from 50 yards or longer at that point in his career, while Waterfield had never kicked one from that distance.

The news on the Cleveland injury front was mixed. Len Ford declared himself sufficiently recovered and ready for his first action since October, but his mouth had been wired shut for ten weeks and he had lost a substantial amount of weight. Brown decided to start Martin and use Ford as needed.

Speedie suffered a leg injury in the week before the Championship Game and was still hobbled on game day. That did not prevent Brown from announcing that Speedie was fully recovered, however. Wary of the damage the great Cleveland end could do and uncertain of his health status, the Rams took no chances and spent much of the game double teaming him. That would prove an important factor as Lavelli had a record-breaking day.

Ken Gorgal remembered one other bit of Cleveland intrigue in the week before the game. All too aware of the success the Giants had had against his team's passing game with the Umbrella Defense, Brown announced that his team would use a similar formation against the explosive Los Angeles offense. Although Cleveland practiced the Umbrella and even deployed it at the beginning of the game, Gorgal said it was all a ruse.

"He planned to get Los Angeles thinking about it, show it to them for a few plays, and then go back to our regular defense," Gorgal said. When the Rams topped even themselves by scoring on the game's first play from scrimmage on an 82-yard Waterfield to Davis pass, however, Cleveland immediately shifted gears.

"End Jim Martin, who was supposed to cover Davis, lost his footing on the slick field and that was it for the Umbrella Defense," Gorgal said. Although the play provided the Rams with an early 7–0 lead, it may also have hastened Ford's entry into the game. Martin had done a decent job in Ford's place, but Ford showed he was a special kind of player with his inspired play against the Rams. The pass rush that he spearheaded was a major factor in Cleveland's disruption of the Los Angeles passing game. And on three consecutive plays at one point, Ford tackled Smith for a loss of 14, sacked Waterfield for a loss of 11, and trapped Davis for a loss of 13.

Unfazed by the early deficit, the Browns offense went to work on the Los Angeles secondary. Graham scoring passes of 27 yards to Jones and 37 yards to Lavelli were sandwiched around a Hoerner touchdown, and Cleveland was within 14–13. The 1-point difference was the result of a high snap from center on the extra-point try after Cleveland's second touchdown. More telling than that miscue, however, was Waterfield's miss on a 15-yard field goal attempt right before the end of the half.

Cleveland took the lead in the third quarter as Graham again hooked up with Lavelli for a 39-yard touchdown, but the Rams responded with two touchdowns in a matter of seconds. Hoerner scored his second touchdown of the game, and then Larry Brink ran 6 yards to score after recovering a Motley fumble. Suddenly, as the fourth quarter began, Cleveland trailed 28–20.

It had been a great season of football and the Browns had been a big part of it, but they were a quarter of play away from losing the biggest game of all. As Brown had said at the beginning of training camp five months before, more than a season was on the line. Four years of achievements in the AAFC were also at stake. A game but losing effort against the Rams would be nowhere near enough. The gap between being a champion and a runner-up, after all, is the largest gap of all.

Playing in the shadow of the two great offenses, the Browns defense helped turn the game Cleveland's way. Timely interceptions by Lahr and Thompson both halted the Rams' momentum and consistently set the offense up in good field position. Shortly after Lahr's interception, Cleveland was confronted with the first of a series of do or die plays.

The Browns faced a fourth and 1 at the Los Angeles 43. In need of two scores with ten minutes remaining against the highest scoring team in football history, the Browns' chances for victory would diminish drastically if they failed to convert and gave up the ball in that part of the field. Although Groza had proven himself capable of making field goals from such a distance, Brown chose to go for it, and Graham picked up a first down with a 3-yard run.

Twice more as the Browns moved goalward they faced fourth-down situations. Both times Brown went for it rather than call on Groza, and both times the offense came through. The first was a 7-yard completion to Lavelli on fourth and 4, while on the second Graham barely made it past the first-down marker on a run on fourth and 3.

A short time later from the 14, Graham connected with Bumgardner in the far corner of the end zone for his fourth touchdown pass of the game. Bumgardner made a sensational diving catch on the play, and Cleveland was within 1 at 28–27. The defense stood firm through several exchanges, and soon Cleveland was again moving down the field against the Los Angeles defense.

With the Browns well within Groza's range, Graham lost a fumble at the 19 after scrambling out of the pocket. A golden opportunity had gone by the boards, but with more than three minutes remaining, there was still time if the defense could make a stand. Preferring to keep the clock moving with running plays and avoid the possibility of another interception in their own territory, Los Angeles kept the ball on the ground. Even when it was third and 10, Waterfield eschewed the pass and ran Davis up the middle, and the Cleveland defense stopped him 4 yards short.

With two minutes left, Waterfield had to kick the ball away from his own 25. He boomed a 59-yard kick, which Lewis returned 15 yards to the Cleveland 31. Graham and the offense came on the field with 1:49 remaining. In contrast to their final drive against the Giants the week before, the Browns' game plan was to move the ball downfield by throwing it.

"Nobody knew about sideline passes, how to stop them, because this was our first year in the league and we had perfected it," Graham said. The sideline pass was the same play San Francisco's Visco Grgich had cited as the difference between the Browns and the 49ers in the days of the All-America Football Conference. As the final drive began, Cleveland had already piled up 250 yards passing.

But that did not mean that Graham could not also hurt the Rams the same way he had hurt the Giants and so many other teams—with his legs. In that era, "when a quarterback ran," Graham said, "there was no one to cover him, and you could pick up a few yards without anyone touching you." It was further proof of Graham's mettle that he did not allow the fumble on the previous series to alter his style of play. On the first play of Cleveland's last possession, he scrambled for 16 yards to the 47.

Next came four passes, all to the outside, three completions and one miss. Lavelli was having a great day, and he and Speedie were two of the best receivers in football. But in that situation they were primarily decoys used to tie up as much of the Los Angeles defense as possible. The underneath pass to backs, particularly to Jones, was one of the things that made the Browns' passing game so especially dangerous.

The first of the completions was good to Bumgardner for 13. After an incompletion, Graham hit Jones for 17 to the 23 with less than a minute remaining. Playing the game of his life, Bumgardner made another outstanding catch of Graham's next pass and slid out of bounds at the 11 after picking up 12 more yards. Graham's sneak on the next play gained 2 yards, but more important, it positioned the ball near the middle of the field. After a time-out, Groza came on to attempt a 16-yard field goal.

It was almost the same situation as Groza had been in the week before: closing seconds of the game, short field goal attempt toward the open end of Municipal Stadium, Cleveland's season on the line. It was not exactly the same, however. There was one big difference, one huge difference: Groza's winning kick against the Giants had been with the score tied. His attempt against the Rams was with Cleveland down a point and nowhere near enough time left to get the ball back again.

"I never thought I would miss," Groza later said of his approach to kicking. Maybe so, but if that was true it made him a very rare human being. Tommy James, the Cleveland holder, also remembered that the wind was strong enough at the open end of the stadium to have an impact, and not just on the flight of the ball after Groza kicked it.

The wind was actually strong enough to throw the ball off course when it was snapped from center, James knew. And if that sounds too freakish to be possible, James claimed that the wind was a factor in Gatski's errant snap on Cleveland's missed extra point. And a similarly strong wind helped spoil a snap from center on a botched Baltimore Colts field goal attempt in the 1964 NFL Championship Game at the same open end of Municipal Stadium.

There were no mishaps on Groza's attempt, however. The kick sailed true through the middle of the uprights, and Cleveland was ahead 30–28 with 0:28 seconds left on the clock.

There were still several exciting moments remaining in this great game, though. The first came on the ensuing kickoff when the Browns appeared to have finalized victory by recovering a fumble. However, the officials ruled that Groza had kicked the ball off prematurely. The play was negated, and Cleveland was made to kick again. On the rekick, the Rams returned the ball well within striking distance to their own 46. They were a sizable completion and a field goal of their own from victory.

Off the bench came Norm Van Brocklin to take his first snap of the game. Rams head coach Hamp Pool reasoned that Van Brocklin had a stronger arm than Waterfield and thus had a better chance of completing a long pass deep into Cleveland territory. It was a move that surprised no one who had seen Van Brocklin play. Joining the Rams in 1949, he was not the least bit cowed by the presence of one of the best quarterbacks in football on the Los Angeles roster.

In fact, although nominally a second stringer, Van Brocklin had actually outperformed Waterfield in 1950, at least statistically. He would do the same in 1951 and 1952, Waterfield's last two years, as the Rams successfully navigated a situation that has undone many other teams over the years. Like Waterfield, Van Brocklin would gain recognition as one of the game's greatest quarterbacks, and both would eventually gain induction into the Pro Football Hall of Fame.

But one last time the Browns were able to turn back the great Los Angeles passing attack. Lahr intercepted Van Brocklin's sideline pass to Davis at the 10-yard line, apparently ending the game once and for all. According to Otto Graham, however, there were still a few more seconds of drama. Immediately after Lahr caught the ball, Davis wrapped him up in a desperate attempt at gaining a simultaneous possession call, which would result in the offensive team being awarded the ball.

"It was terrible," Graham said. "We didn't know what the referee was going to call." Even once it was clear that Lahr had possession, Graham worried that the play might be called a safety, as Lahr's momentum had carried him into the end zone. But the worry was for nothing. Cleveland was awarded the ball at the spot of Lahr's interception, and seconds later the game was indeed over.

Superlatives abounded, both in the game's immediate aftermath and years later when any of the major participants reminisced. In the winning locker room, Commissioner Bell said the Browns were "the greatest team ever to play football" and the game was the best and most exciting game ever played.

Looking back from a distance of about thirty years, Brown said that "it was the greatest game I ever saw," pinpointing "the tremendous exhibition of passing both teams put on. Both of us were the leaders in a modern-day revolution of switching the emphasis from running to passing."

The game was full of superlative individual performances. Lavelli set a Championship Game record that stood for eight years with eleven receptions, good for 128 yards and two touchdowns. Fears was just as

good with nine catches for 136 yards, while Hirsch, Jones, and Bumgardner all caught four passes. Three of Bumgardner's receptions came in the
crucial fourth quarter and were good for a total of 40 yards.

The Waterfield to Davis first-play touchdown was the longest scoring play in title-game history, and Waterfield had a good day even with
the four interceptions as he completed eighteen of thirty-one passes for
312 yards and a touchdown. Groza's game-winning kick certainly cannot be overlooked and is all the more remarkable considering it came at
the end of a grueling game in which he went all the way at his offensive
tackle spot.

And both defenses played better than the 58 points might indicate.
The Rams completely stifled Motley and the other Cleveland backs and
also produced a touchdown. The Browns, meanwhile, consistently made
big plays, especially the five interceptions, and shut Los Angeles down in
the fourth quarter when doing so was of the utmost importance. Ford's
inspired play and Lahr's two interceptions were especially noteworthy.

In the end, though, the player who had the biggest individual day
was Graham. He was superb both passing the ball and running it. With
Motley and the other Cleveland backs completely shut down, Graham
picked up the slack with 99 yards rushing and an 8.3 average, both tops
in the game. But it was with his right arm that he did the most damage.

Graham finished the day with twenty-two completions on thirty-
two attempts for 298 yards and four touchdowns. That's a one-game
passer rating of 124.7. Beyond any statistics, though, was Graham's great
play with the game on the line in the fourth quarter. Three times he led
the Browns on drives into Rams territory; two of the drives produced the
10 points essential to victory. It was a comeback the magnitude of which
was matched only once in championship play.

In the television decades that followed, John Unitas, Bart Starr, and
Joe Montana would thrill football fans by leading their teams on sterling
late-game comebacks in Championship Games/Super Bowls. Images of
Unitas waving Raymond Berry to an open spot, of Starr diving into the
end zone over Jerry Kramer, and of Montana whistling a last-minute
touchdown pass to John Taylor are indelibly etched in the collective football mind. Even millions of fans not even born to witness the heroics of
Unitas and Starr have repeatedly seen highlights of the last minutes of
the Greatest Game Ever Played and the Ice Bowl. Entire books have been

written about both games; in fact, *two* whole books have been written about the Ice Bowl.

Far, far fewer fans know of Graham's heroics against the Rams. Television was a negligible force in sports in 1950, and Cleveland's 30–28 win over Los Angeles, while arguably a greater game than the 1958 Colts-Giants matchup, rarely ever shows up on the various television channels that broadcast historical moments from the world of sports. It is therefore worth noting what Graham and the Browns did in comparison to those who came after.

Like Graham and the Browns, Unitas, Starr, Montana, and their mates all turned defeat into victory at the very end of their respective games. Unlike the others, however, Cleveland came from two scores down in the fourth quarter to win. Only the 1934 Giants did that before 1950, and no team has done it in a Championship Game or Super Bowl since.

Graham also became the first quarterback in pro football history to twice engineer winning fourth-quarter comebacks in Championship Games/Super Bowls, a feat that only Unitas has matched in the more than fifty years since. Graham previously had done it in 1946 with a late touchdown pass to Lavelli in Cleveland's 14–9 victory over the Yankees. Cleveland's win over the Rams marked only the fourth time in history that a team made up a fourth-quarter Championship Game deficit. 1950 also marked the first of three occasions in his six NFL seasons that Graham played a game for the ages in a Championship Game.

"We felt that as long as we had a quarterback like Otto," Lavelli said, "even if we were 10 or 14 points behind, we could always catch up by throwing the ball."

"[Y]ou know that at some point in time, he's going to make that play to get you back in the game," Dub Jones said of Graham. "Another team might get behind by a few points, and they're broken. That seldom happened to us."

The individual honors that accrued for a number of Browns players closed the book on Cleveland's great season. Motley led the NFL in rushing with 810 yards, and his 5.8 average was the highest among running backs. Gillom finished second in punting by 0.1 yard with a 43.2 average, and his net of 38.4 was the best mark in the league. In addition to establishing a new NFL record with thirteen field goals, Groza also finished first with a .684 field goal percentage and converted 29 extra points without a miss.

1950 was the last year that the AP and UPI selected single-platoon all-pro teams. The *New York Daily News*, on the other hand, began selecting separate teams for offense and defense that year. Rushing champion Motley was a unanimous first-team selection, and Speedie and Willis were consensus first-teamers. Graham, Rymkus, Houston, Adamle, and James (nine interceptions) were all second-team picks on one of the three teams.

Former AAFCers Barwegan and Weinmeister were also unanimous first-team all-pros (three of the five unanimous first-team picks were former AAFC players). Eleven other former AAFC players were selected to at least one first or second all-pro team: ends Dan Edwards and Jack Russell; tackle Bob Reinhard; guards John Mastrangelo and Joe Signaigo; center John Rapacz; quarterback George Ratterman; and backs Spec Sanders, Otto Schnellbacher, John Strzykalski, and Buddy Young. In all, twenty-one former AAFCers were named.

Adamle, Graham, Speedie, Motley, Willis, Groza, and Weldon Humble were named to play in the first ever Pro Bowl and the first NFL All-Star Game in eight years. As if his season-long heroics had not been enough, Graham led the American Conference back from a 27–14 deficit to a 28–27 victory over the National Conference with a touchdown pass and two touchdown runs in the Pro Bowl. He was named the player of the game.

There was more greatness to come for the Browns in the next five years. The game against the Rams was but the first of a record six straight NFL Championship Game appearances. In those seasons, the Browns would accumulate a six-year regular season winning percentage that no team has matched in the five decades since.

It is the 1950 season that many of the Browns players point to as the pinnacle, however, even those players who played in a number of the team's great seasons before and after.

"That was a great year," Dub Jones said simply. Jones scored eleven touchdowns that year on just 114 touches and would score twelve more the following year. "Coming into the National Football League was the most exciting thing you could imagine."

"The highlight of my career would be that entire 1950 season," Graham said. In just five seasons as a pro, Graham had already won more championships than any quarterback in history. Although Graham's statistics were more impressive in each of his other nine seasons, he was never better than in 1950. He had engineered winning drives in the final minutes on consecutive weeks against the Giants and Rams, and in Cleveland's two biggest games, the opener in Philadelphia and the Championship Game (arguably the two biggest games of Cleveland's ten-year dynasty), Graham compiled a combined passer rating of 119.0.

Paul Brown refrained from calling the team or season Cleveland's greatest. Undoubtedly in part because of the tremendous pride he had in the team's years in the upstart AAFC and the refusal of the NFL to ever fully recognize the accomplishments of those years, Brown always insisted that the 1948 team was the Browns' greatest. Still, when he considered all that his team accomplished in the face of so many doubts and naysayers, Brown conceded that "1950 was the most satisfying football experience of my life."

The AAFC, the NFL, and the 1946–1949 Browns: Comparison and Evaluation

W ITH A YEAR in the NFL under their collective belts, an analysis of the Browns and of the AAFC as represented by the league's players who continued on in 1950 is called for. The end of the 1950 season, then, is the best time to address several questions that are central to the legacy of the Cleveland dynasty. How good was the AAFC? More peripherally, how do the 1950 Browns compare with the franchise's earlier teams? And most important, how do the Browns of the AAFC compare with the best NFL teams of the 1946–1949 period?

The striking thing about the AAFC is how strong a league it was right from the beginning. It was far stronger in its first year than any of the NFL's other rivals, and that includes the AFL of the 1960s. Relative to the NFL, in fact, the AAFC was stronger throughout its existence than the AFL was until at least 1968 and possibly for that other league's entire ten-year history.

The AAFC and the NFL never met on the field, so can we compare them? Not easily, but there are ways. Much of the most useful information became clear after 1949; additional information that helps clarify continues to unfold to this day.

One fact that goes back to the summer before the AAFC began play is that 44 of the 60 men (73%) who played for the collegians in the 1946 College All-Star Game were bound for the new league. In the first season after peace was declared, 40% of the nonrookies who played in the NFL in 1950 were veterans of the upstart league (rookies in 1950 would not have had a chance to play in the AAFC). Considering that 41% of the players active in the two leagues in 1949 were in the AAFC, that number indicates almost precise equality.

How many of the NFL's best players in 1950 had played in the AAFC? There were three major all-pro teams selected that year: one by the AP, one by UPI, and one by the *New York Daily News*. The AP and UPI selected single platoons, while the *Daily News* picked separate offensive and defensive units. All three also included a second team. Of the players named to the three teams, excluding rookies, 21 of 51 (41%) were former AAFCers. More impressive, 20 of the 40 first-team spots, exactly half, went to players who had played in the AAFC.

How many of the very best players of the late 1940s were in the AAFC, and how many were in the NFL? Of the Hall of Famers active in 1946, 45% (9 of 20) played in the AAFC that season. Since the AAFC had fewer teams and fewer roster spots, the percentage of its players that year who were Hall of Famers is actually higher than the NFL's. Similarly, the AAFC averaged more Hall of Famers per team than the older league. The numbers swing slightly in the NFL's favor for the rest of the decade, but the difference is small.

By comparison, only 8.5% of the Hall of Famers (4 of 48) active in 1960 played in the AFL. As late as 1966 the NFL's advantage over the AFL was still 44 to 14, or 76% to 24%. Even when the much larger size of the NFL is factored in, the AFL's numbers are nowhere near as good as the AAFC's. The NFL had twice as many Hall of Famers per team as the AFL in 1966, and the percentage of NFL players who were Hall of Famers was similarly about twice as high. In 1968 and 1969, these last two measurements were about equal, further proof that relative to the NFL, the AFL in its last two years—the same years AFL teams won the Super Bowl—was about as strong as the AAFC, but not until then.

Of the 33 Hall of Famers active at some point from 1946 through 1949, 13, or roughly 40%, played in the AAFC. That and all the numbers mentioned already are impressive enough. What narrows the gap to a point where the AAFC is about even with the NFL is the fact that the AAFC was always at least 20% smaller, both in number of teams and players, than the NFL. In 1949 it was 30% smaller.

How about if we look at AAFC players and how they impacted the NFL teams they joined? Of the nonrookies on the NFL's five best teams in 1950—the Browns, Rams, Giants, Bears, and Yanks—*52%* (68 of 131 players) were former AAFCers. Where the league's very best team was concerned, the Browns, only 2 of the 33 players who played for Cleveland in 1950, Lou Rymkus and Tommy James, had ever played in the NFL before, with a grand total of twelve NFL games between them. Put another way, not one member of 1950's best team had played only in the NFL before that, while 24 of Cleveland's 26 nonrookies had played exclusively in the AAFC.

The 1950 records of teams compared with 1949 records provide more striking evidence of the strength of the AAFC. In fact, the correlation between signing or not signing AAFC players and a better or worse record for the ten teams that played in the NFL in 1949 couldn't be clearer. The four teams that had the fewest AAFC players on their rosters in 1950—the Steelers, Redskins, Eagles, and Cardinals—all had worse records than the year before. With only two AAFCers, the Eagles' record dropped off by *five* games, from 11–1 to 6–6.

The six holdover NFL teams that had the most AAFC players on their 1950 rosters—the Yanks, Lions, Packers, Rams, Bears, and Giants—all improved or stayed at a high level. With seven AAFCers, the Giants went from 6–6 to 10–2 and a tie for first place. The Bears and the Rams, two of the NFL's best teams in 1949, remained so in 1950 with added AAFC talent. The Bears went from 9–3 and second place to 9–3 and a tie for first, while the Rams went from 8–2–2 to 9–3 and repeated as Western champs. With more AAFCers than any of the NFL teams from 1949, the Yanks experienced one of the biggest turnarounds ever, going from 1–10–1 doormats as the Bulldogs to 7–5 contenders. The Yanks were in first place through eight weeks until they lost four of their last five games.

The Yanks had so many veterans of the AAFC that they might more accurately be called the fourth merged AAFC team. Had they also had some combination of the five outstanding Yankees players who instead wound up with the Giants, they would have done even better than 7–5. In fact, the NFL might have faced the double embarrassment of a Browns-Yanks Championship Game matchup in 1950 had the Yanks had Weinmeister, Schnellbacher, Mastrangelo (all three of whom made all-pro), Landry, and/or Rowe. As it was, New York finished third, the same place the Yankees finished in the AAFC the year before—with more talent.

The Colts were as bad in the NFL as they'd been in the AAFC in 1949. They posted the same 1–11 record both years. The surprise team of the bunch was San Francisco, who fell to 3–9. That can be explained in part by the massive roster turnover that saw the team lose thirteen players from the year before including Len Eshmont, Joe Vetrano, John Woudenberg, and Bob Mike.

Of perhaps greater relevance is San Francisco's long-term success beginning in 1951. The 49ers rebounded to 7–4–1 and a half game out of first place that year and remained one of the NFL's best teams for a decade. In the seven seasons after 1950 in the very competitive Western Conference, San Francisco finished lower than third only once. The team added a number of excellent players during those years, but Frankie Albert, Joe Perry, Bruno Banducci, Verl Lillywhite, Lowell Wagner, Norm Standlee, John Strzykalski, and others who played for the team in the AAFC were a big part of that success (as were other AAFC veterans like Y. A. Tittle and Hardy Brown).

The cost of football's racial discrimination, although obvious to many at the time, has become even clearer as the sport has evolved to where the vast majority of players are African American. The AAFC's willingness to sign blacks in greater numbers and sooner than their NFL rivals is an important reason it was so close talent-wise to the older league. Perhaps more telling than the vast discrepancy in the total number of black players in the two leagues is the even wider gap in the number who were outstanding.

From 1946 through 1949, the only blacks in the NFL who were among the league's best players were Bob Mann and Emlen Tunnell, and not until 1948. Kenny Washington could be added to that list, but because of injuries and the Rams' underutilization of him, he averaged only forty-seven carries in his three seasons. Mann was a top receiver with the Lions, and Tunnell was an all-pro defensive back and kick returner with the Giants at the beginning of a Hall of Fame career.

By contrast, the AAFC had eight blacks who were among that league's best players: Willis, Motley, and Gillom of the Browns; Buddy Young and Sherman Howard of the Yankees; Len Ford and George Taliaferro of the Dons; and Joe Perry of the 49ers. All would continue at a high level in the NFL well into the 1950s (Perry played until 1963), and four would join Tunnell in the Hall of Fame.

It is no surprise, however, that the biggest piece of evidence that indicates that the AAFC was about as good as the NFL is the post-1949 success of the Browns. In the six years from 1950 through 1955, Cleveland's record was 58–13–1. Their .817 winning percentage is the best posted over six years by any team in the last sixty years and is topped only by the Monsters of the Midway Bears. To put that in perspective, if a present-day team went 13–3 every year for six consecutive years, they *still* wouldn't equal that Cleveland winning percentage. Cleveland's six straight NFL Championship Game/Super Bowl appearances is an all-time best, with the second best 1940–1943 Bears and 1990–1993 Bills trailing well behind.

Look at how the Browns did against NFL teams that were assumed to have been so superior to them before 1950. In their first six NFL years, Cleveland went 12–0 against the Cardinals, 11–1 against the Steelers, 10–1 against the Redskins, 8–4 against the Eagles ("the best team ever put together"), 8–4–1 against the Giants, 2–0 against the Bears, 2–0 against the Packers, and 2–0 against the Rams. Cleveland's cumulative average score in those six years against the mighty NFL was 28–16. That domination is comparable to Cleveland's domination of the AAFC Dodgers, Rockets, Seahawks, and Colts.

There are some other noteworthy similarities in how the teams of the two leagues fared against Cleveland. While it's true the Browns dominated the AAFC, the 49ers hung tough with them in the battle for first place every year but 1946. The 49ers were second to the Browns all four years, and San Francisco's cumulative winning percentage was better than the second-place teams in Cleveland's first six NFL seasons by .731 to .707.

In 1953 the Browns finished first by three and a half games, equal to their biggest margin in the AAFC. From 1951 through 1955, Cleveland finished first by an average of almost two full games. And on four occasions in the six years, Cleveland had first place wrapped up with at least one game remaining.

Three of the four AAFC Championship Games were close, as were the first four NFL title games the Browns played in, although they did lose three of the four. Their 1954 and 1955 title-game victories, on the other hand, were about as close as their 49–7 win over Buffalo in 1948.

The Browns added talented players in 1950 and beyond from the AAFC, from trades, and from the college draft. What is striking, though, is how many excellent players—the nucleus of the dynasty—were with the team in the AAFC as well as the NFL. Graham, Motley, Groza, Lavelli, Willis, Speedie, Rymkus, Young, Gatski, Adamle, Houston, James, Dub Jones, Thompson, Lahr, Palmer, Gillom, Agase, Grigg, and Humble all played with the team in both leagues, and without exception all played about as well against NFL competition as they had against the AAFC.

One way of measuring that is by looking at the various individual honors the Cleveland players received. Graham won two MVP awards in four AAFC seasons, including one in which he shared the award with Albert, and he won three in six NFL seasons. Conceivably, he could have won four or even five NFL MVPs, but none was awarded in either 1950 or 1952. Groza never won an MVP award in the AAFC, but he won one of the two awarded in the NFL in 1954.

Marion Motley was the best running back in the AAFC, and he won a league rushing title in 1948. NFL elitists figured he'd get his when he tried running against their superior defenses. What happened? Motley matched that rushing title in his very first NFL season.

Horace Gillom was an excellent punter in the AAFC, but he never won a punting title. In his first three years in the NFL, he won two and finished second by 0.1 yard. His NFL average was more than 3 yards better than his AAFC average, and by the time he retired he was second all-time behind only Sammy Baugh, who remains first five decades later. Groza may already have been the best kicker ever after four AAFC seasons (although not in the eyes of many from the NFL), but what he did before 1950 pales in comparison with what he did in his first five NFL seasons.

Groza set, reset, and reset the all-time NFL record for field goals in a season in a four-year span. At the end of that time, the new record he established was almost double what it had been before he came along.

Groza also set new NFL career marks in a number of kicking categories in half the time it had taken the previous record holders to accumulate their record totals. What was perhaps his most eye-opening record, the 88.5% field goal percentage of 1953, shattered the old mark and was so far off the charts that almost thirty years passed before it was broken.

Look at what Groza did in demolishing the NFL single-season record for field goals from another perspective. The record at the end of the 2005 season was forty. To replicate what Groza did from 1950 through 1953, a player today would have to have seasons of 43, 63, and 76 field goals in a four-year span.

After the 1950 season, 10 Browns were selected for either the Pro Bowl or as first- or second-team all-pros. All played for the team in the AAFC. Seven of the 10 had been with the team going back to 1946. During the NFL portion of their dynasty covering six seasons, Cleveland earned 42 spots in the Pro Bowl. Of those, 26 went to players who played for the team in the AAFC, while another 9 went to players with AAFC experience with teams other than the Browns. Only 7 (16.7%) went to players who did not play in the AAFC.

Look at how Cleveland did on the all-pro teams in their second NFL season, 1951. An almost unbelievable 14 Browns received all-pro mention that year, out of 59 players selected (24% of the total). Of those 14, 11 were with the team in the AAFC, and the other 3 also played in the AAFC but not with the Browns.

From 1950 through 1955, the Browns garnered 151 spots on either the first or second team of the five major all-pro teams (the *Sporting News* joined the AP, UPI, and the *Daily News* in 1954, and the Newspaper Enterprise Association followed suit in 1955). Of those 151, 107 (71%) went to players who had been with the team before 1950. Three others who played exclusively in the supposedly inferior AAFC before joining the team in 1950—Ford, Abe Gibron, and John Kissell—captured many of the additional honors. As late as 1955, 4 Browns who had been with the team in the AAFC got all-pro recognition, including 3 who went back to 1946.

The post-1949 performance of AAFC Browns is even more impressive if we look only at first-team all-pro spots. Of the 99 first-team all-pro spots earned by Browns players in the team's first six years in the NFL, 78% went to men who played for the team in the AAFC. Had some of their best AAFC players not retired at relatively young ages (Saban, Rymkus, Willis, Adamle, Ulinski), suffered career-ending injuries (Thompson), or gone to Canada (Speedie), those numbers would be higher still.

As to how the 1950 Browns compare with the Browns teams in the AAFC, no football team is ever exactly the same from one year to the next. That's true even if the personnel remain precisely the same. Players are always getting better or worse, and they never play at exactly the same level in any two years. In addition there are subtle vagaries, like team chemistry, that change with the addition and subtraction of players or if certain players get more or less playing time.

Comparing the 1950 Browns with their predecessors in the AAFC, specifically the 1948 and 1949 teams, is thus problematic in a number of ways. Not the least of these is the fact that the roster turnover was so great. Twelve players who were not with the team in 1949 joined the Browns in 1950.

In addition, few teams had as much to play for in 1950 as the Browns. For four years, they had heard from NFL partisans that they were champions of an inferior league and that they were nowhere near as good as the best teams in the NFL (or even the worst). Their chance to prove otherwise came in 1950. All that they had achieved in the AAFC—the four championships, the perfect season, the right to claim that they were the best team anywhere during that time—was at stake. If they failed, or even if they had a good season but fell short of a championship, their AAFC accomplishments would have been regarded as exactly what the naysayers said they were.

Does that mean the team was more motivated, more determined, in 1950 than it was in, say, 1946, 1948, 1951, or 1954? Maybe, but probably not. Collective motivation and determination are qualities as difficult to measure as team chemistry. Cleveland had a lot to play for in 1950, but they also had a lot to play for in every other one of their dynasty years. The circumstances changed, but not necessarily the degree of determination and motivation.

More important, all the motivation in the world is not very useful if it is not connected to talent. George Preston Marshall had derided the

AAFC since its formation in 1944, and it is safe to assume that the Redskins were super-motivated to defend his and their league's honor against the Browns. What happened? The super-motivated Redskins lost twice to Cleveland in 1950 by a combined score of 65–35.

All the motivation in the world plus drastically insufficient talent and that's what will happen 99% of the time. Washington's motivation stayed high over the next five years, but their talent also stayed about the same. And their success against Cleveland was about the same, too: a 1–10 record and a 371–149 points disadvantage, an average score of 34–14.

Even having said that, it is no surprise that a number of Browns players have said over the years that the 1950 season was the team's apex, and that season was more satisfying than any other. Their legitimacy as champions and their legacy weren't *primary* in the Browns' collective approach to 1950, however. What they wanted more than anything else was what all great teams want, to win football games and yet another championship. They wanted to beat all comers as they had done for four years.

Their legacy and the legitimacy of their four AAFC seasons were factors, but first and foremost the task at hand in 1950 was to be the best. Many is the team that has gone into a game or a season on a mission, with tremendous collective determination, only to get blown out or finish in last place. Talent is what carried the Browns, and that was no more or less true in 1950 than it was in 1946, 1949, 1951, or 1955.

What is also important to remember is that whatever role collective motivation may have played on the Browns' behalf was more than matched by the collective determination of every single NFL team on Cleveland's 1950 schedule. Beginning with the very first preseason game, nobody wanted to lose to the new kid on the block from the minor leagues. And that attitude made league-wide partners out of teams that normally hated each other. It was no secret that other NFL teams shared game films and scouting reports about the Browns with each other. The Eagles and Giants were bitter Eastern Conference rivals, but no sooner was Cleveland's opening game in Philadelphia over than Greasy Neale was in touch with New York coach Steve Owen to give him a scouting report and film.

As Len Ford said, "Every team we played we brought out the best in them. Nobody wanted us to win. Every team was a bunch of wildcats."

But even saying that what the Browns accomplished in 1950 was unmatched by anything they did before or after (and possibly unmatched by *any* team before or after) is not the same as saying that that was the best team of their dynasty years. That, however, is a popular opinion. John Steadman, longtime Baltimore sportswriter who covered football for over fifty years and first saw the Browns in 1947, for example, said the 1950 Cleveland team was the best football team he'd ever seen, period.

Certainly the fact that the Browns played on a bigger stage in 1950 than they had previously is a factor. But significantly, that has more to do with how they were perceived than what they were. It's quite possible that every one of Cleveland's AAFC teams was better than the 1950 team. But because they were not (and are not) widely *perceived* to have been on the same level as the NFL from 1946 to 1949, people believed, and continue to believe, in many cases simply because they want to believe, that those AAFC championships didn't count for as much.

Incredibly, even when the Browns dominated the NFL almost as thoroughly as they had the AAFC, people like Neale and Eagles lineman Bucko Kilroy continued to deny what they were seeing with their own eyes. Years after the Browns began their march to NFL supremacy by thrashing the two-time defending NFL champion Eagles on opening night of 1950, Kilroy said, "The team we played in Philadelphia and the one we had studied were not one and the same. What we faced was an all-star team from the All-America Conference, and we just weren't up to beating any all-star team."

Kilroy's statement is ludicrous no matter how it is looked at. What makes it all the more ridiculous is the fact that it was not spoken immediately afterward in frustration. Neale said some rather unflattering things about the Browns in the pall of the losers' locker room, things he later came to regret. But Kilroy's comments were not said out of frustration at the time but years later and are therefore something else altogether because they are so contrary to the historical record that was clear at the time he said them.

What Kilroy obviously meant was that the 1950 Browns were not the same as the 1949 team because they had added five players from defunct AAFC teams to their roster. Len Ford had come to Cleveland from the Los Angeles Dons, and Gibron, Kissell, Rex Bumgardner, and Hal Herring had come from the Buffalo Bills. Further compounding matters perhaps (at least enough to have possibly confused Kilroy, anyway), although irrelevant as far as the AAFC is concerned, is that Cleveland's 1950 roster also included seven rookies.

Perhaps Kilroy's remarks were so amiss because he was speaking at a time when it was known that Ford, Gibron, and, to a lesser extent, Kissell had gone on to have outstanding NFL careers. But Kilroy misspoke two times, first in that of the five players only Kissell had received any kind of AAFC all-star recognition. In 1949, Kissell had been named to the *New York Daily News* first all-AAFC team and to the first team of the International News Service's joint AAFC/NFL team. Neither Ford nor Gibron, not to mention Bumgardner and Herring, was so much as a second-team all-league selection in the AAFC.

More important was the error in the implication behind Kilroy's remarks. While it is true that Ford went on to have a Hall of Fame career and Gibron was one of the outstanding guards of the 1950s, that tells us nothing about how they played in 1950. Neither was an all-star that year, either. Far from it. Ford played only five games in 1950 and Gibron's first mention as a first-team all-pro wasn't until 1953.

There were, however, a number of Browns who were all-stars in 1950, and their names were quite familiar to followers of the All-America Football Conference. Mac Speedie, Lou Rymkus, Lin Houston, Bill Willis, Tony Adamle, Otto Graham, Tommy James, and Marion Motley were all named first- or second-team selections on at least one all-pro team that first NFL season, an accomplishment all the more impressive in that two of the three all-pro teams were still single platoon. Seven Browns, meanwhile, were named to play in the Pro Bowl: Adamle, Graham, Motley, Speedie, Willis, Lou Groza, and Weldon Humble. All ten Browns who received either all-pro mention or a spot in the Pro Bowl in 1950 had played at least two years in the AAFC, and seven were original Browns.

Kilroy's remarks are so contrary to the factual record that they beg a question: What would have been sufficient evidence to convince the likes of Kilroy (and to a lesser extent Neale) that the Browns were simply the best team in football in 1950 and earlier? Ten straight NFL championships? Ten straight undefeated championship seasons? Ten straight undefeated championship seasons without allowing a single point?

If 35–10 in their first game and a championship in their first season was not evidence enough; if six years of manhandling the Redskins, Steelers, Cardinals, and other NFL teams as thoroughly as they ever dominated the Dodgers and the Rockets was not evidence enough; and if more Championship Game appearances in their first six years in the league than all NFL teams but the Bears, Redskins, and Giants and more than the Steelers, Rams, Cardinals, Dodgers, Lions, and Yanks/Bulldogs before 1950 combined was not evidence enough, then the only conclusion is that nothing could have ever been enough.

If it were simply a matter of a lunatic fringe embodied by Kilroy, that would be enough said on the matter. But the NFL has pretended for more than fifty years that what the Browns did in the AAFC came against substandard competition. Their championships are not recognized, their won-loss record is not recognized, their perfect season and eighteen-game winning streak and twenty-nine-game unbeaten streak are not recognized, and the statistics of individual players are not recognized.

The most egregious of these omissions is the four championships. Overwhelming evidence points to the Browns being the best team in all of football in all four of their AAFC seasons, yet the official NFL policy continues the fiction that those championships are tainted because they came against supposedly minor league competition. Meanwhile, championships won by the Houston Oilers, Dallas Texans, and San Diego Chargers in the early years of the American Football League, years in which the AFL was nowhere near as strong as the AAFC relative to the NFL, are recognized as legitimate major league accomplishments.

A closer look reveals that Cleveland's championship in 1950 and what the team did through 1955 validates the four championships they won from 1946 through 1949. It doesn't necessarily mean that the Browns were the best team in football those four years (although it may mean precisely that). What 1950 does at minimum is make it impossible for any reasonable person to ignore or even downplay what the team did in the AAFC.

In attempting to determine how the 1950 Browns stacked up to their predecessors on a factual basis, from the evidence and not from fantasy like Kilroy or a need to protect its status like the NFL office, it is instructive to evaluate how the new players did in comparison to those whom they replaced. This is an inexact science to be sure, but it is central to even the most general of conclusions. Surprisingly, at least as far as the popular opinion is concerned, the weight of the evidence does not favor the 1950 team in such a comparison.

The player who turned out to be Cleveland's biggest addition, Len Ford, played only four games and part of a fifth in the 1950 season before he was seriously injured by a cheap shot by Pat Harder. He missed the rest of the regular season and the playoff game against the Giants. Ford returned for the title game when he came off the bench and played very well against the Rams. Ford's predecessor, John Yonakor, meanwhile, was the second best defensive end in the history of the AAFC behind Jack Russell.

In an era when the single-platoon all-league selections were overwhelmingly dominated by offensive players (especially at the end position), Yonakor never got so much as a mention on any all-AAFC team. But there is little doubt that had separate offensive and defensive teams been selected, Yonakor would have been picked at least several and perhaps four times. And he and Russell would have been picked on the first unit of an all-time all-AAFC team. Paul Brown said Yonakor was the third best defensive end he ever coached, behind only Ford and Paul Wiggin and ahead of George Young and Bill Glass, a four-time Pro Bowler in the 1960s.

Were Ford's four-plus games and his substitutes an upgrade over Yonakor? No. After 1950, and perhaps even for five games in 1950, Ford was one of the best defensive ends of all time. But what he and Jim Martin, Horace Gillom, and his other replacements did at defensive end in 1950 was not as good as what Yonakor did at that position before them.

Graham, Motley, and Dub Jones were the continuum in the offensive backfield in the years 1948 through 1950. Edgar Jones and Ara Parseghian had both retired at the end of 1949, and Billy Boedeker had been cut loose and played in 1950 with the Packers and Eagles. Bumgardner, Ken Carpenter, and Emerson Cole were added, Bumgardner from the Bills and Carpenter and Cole from the draft, and each contributed in 1950. Cole was a backup for Motley, while Bumgardner and Carpenter split time at the other halfback spot alongside Dub Jones.

None of the new backs was as good in 1950 as Edgar Jones had been. In addition, with Edgar Jones gone, Dub Jones and Motley carried the ball slightly more times per game than they had before 1950. Obviously, Paul Brown decided to rely more on his established tandem than on the three newcomers.

Still, Bumgardner, Cole, and Carpenter made a contribution in both the running game and as receivers. Although none was as good in 1950 as Edgar Jones or even Boedeker in 1948–1949, their collective contribution prevented a drop-off from the losses of Jones, Boedeker, and Parseghian. In the end, though, the performance of the newcomers was not up to that of their predecessors. Dub Jones had his best season up to that time in 1950, especially as a receiver, and that more than anything accounts for the backs performing at about the same level as the previous years.

Rookie Ken Gorgal took a starting safety job from Cliff Lewis in 1950. Gorgal had an excellent season with six interceptions, but Lewis had been one of the best defensive backs in all four years of the AAFC. He also played well off the bench in 1950. Whether Gorgal was a better player in 1950 than Lewis had been in previous years is difficult to say; it's more likely that he was better than Lewis as Lewis began the downside of his career. Still, Gorgal's presence strengthened the secondary, so a slight edge should be given to the 1950 secondary over its predecessors.

Lou Saban was the best linebacker in the history of the AAFC. He retired after the 1949 season to pursue a coaching career and not because of any diminishment in his skills. 1949, in fact, was probably his best season. The two players who picked up most of the slack in Saban's place were Herring and Humble.

Humble was one of the few Browns to play a substantial amount on both offense and defense in 1950. With guard Ed Ulinski having retired, Humble played more at left guard, sharing time there with Gibron, but he also played a lot at linebacker. Gibron's addition to the team was valuable both because he played a lot as a backup to Humble and because his presence allowed Humble to help plug the hole created by Saban's retirement. However, Gibron did not become a full-time player until 1951.

So the moves Brown made in adding Herring and Gibron helped fill holes created by retirements. But it's not at all clear that the performances of the new players were superior to those of their predecessors. Humble made it to the Pro Bowl in 1950, but he was not as good a linebacker as Saban had been in 1948 and 1949, and it would be a real stretch to say he was as good a guard as Ulinski had been.

Gibron eventually became one of the best guards in football, but he was clearly not yet that in 1950. Ulinski, meanwhile, had been one of the top guards in the AAFC, while Bob Gaudio, another guard gone from 1949, had been a decent player. As with Ford, Gibron eventually became a better player than the man he replaced, but that was not the case in 1950. The issue, then, comes down to a comparison of the play at the left guard spot of Humble/Gibron in 1950 and Ulinski/Humble/Gaudio in 1948–1949 and the linebacking of Humble/Herring in 1950 compared with Saban in 1948–1949. And again the advantages lie with the pre-1950 group.

Where the new players are concerned, the final major piece in the puzzle is John Kissell. One of the best defensive tackles in the AAFC in 1949 while with Buffalo, Kissell became part of a triad at the position with Chubby Grigg and Derrell Palmer after joining the Browns. Joe Spencer, a backup tackle in 1949, had been let go and signed with the Packers. Kissell was definitely an upgrade over Spencer, but he was not a starter in 1950.

There was no noteworthy drop-off in the play of any of Cleveland's starters in 1950. Of those who returned from 1949, only Lewis lost his starting job, and even he still saw significant playing time. Speedie, Graham, Motley, Willis, Rymkus, Adamle, and James were among the very best at their positions in the NFL in the same way they had been in the AAFC. While not all-pros or Pro Bowlers, others like Agase, Young, Thompson, Lahr, Grigg, and Palmer continued to play at the same solid level that enabled the team to continue as a champion. Groza, Gillom, Gatski, Houston, and Dub Jones were actually better than they had been in the AAFC, a fact that boosts the case for the 1950 team a bit (or perhaps it means that competition in the NFL was not as good as in the AAFC).

But the cutting-edge question, the one that goes both to the heart of Kilroy's remarks and, more important, to the question of whether the 1950 Browns were better than their predecessors, involves the new players. The large influx of new players in 1950 included some who were absolutely crucial in the continuation of the Cleveland dynasty. But in the vast majority of cases, those players were not better in 1950 than the men they replaced, and in a majority of cases the earlier players were better.

Thus, the only conclusion that can be drawn with any degree of certainty, provided we are not using the logic employed by Kilroy and, sadly, three successive NFL commissioners, is that the AAFC Browns of at least

1948 and 1949 were probably better than the 1950 team. They were not *decisively* better; the difference is not great. But there is more evidence on the side of the earlier teams than on the side of the 1950 team.

A thorough analysis of the 1946 and 1947 teams compared with 1950 will not be attempted. Going back even three years is too dubious a proposition, especially considering that almost two thirds of the roster turned over in that time. However, although the Browns had a perfect season in 1948, their first two teams were about as good and possibly better. There were more quality teams in the AAFC in 1946 and 1947, and that partly accounts for the fact that the Browns lost three games, compared with none in 1948.

But if it's possible for a near-perfect team to be better than a perfect one (and it is; just consider that the 1972 Dolphins are generally not considered the best single-season team in history), then the 1946 and 1947 Browns may warrant a slight edge over the 1948 team. They scored more points and allowed fewer those two years, and their per-game point differentials were better, although the 1948 point differential, like the other two years', is one of the best ever.

What the 1950 team accomplished in coming into a new league and winning it all in its first year is unprecedented. It is certainly one of the greatest team achievements in sports history. All the more remarkable, then, that at least two and possibly more of the Cleveland teams that preceded it were probably better.

Finally and most importantly as far as Cleveland's legacy is concerned is the question of how the Browns of the AAFC compare with the best NFL teams of those years. Even a conclusion that the AAFC was not quite as good as the NFL does not negate the possibility that the Browns were the best team in either league in some or all of those years. And although there are, unfortunately, no pre-1950 head-to-head games we can draw from, there is, as for the two questions addressed previously, evidence we can sift through.

Let's start with this: Imagine if the NFL-AFL merger had occurred two years earlier and the third and fourth Super Bowls, the final ones played between the NFL and the AFL champions, had taken place after the realignment that created the NFC and AFC. Whatever the reason, think about a pro football past without those games between the Colts and Jets and the Vikings and Chiefs. Now think about what the AFL's legacy would be absent those games. It's quite different, isn't it? It's not only different, it's dramatically different.

After the Chiefs and Raiders lost the first two Super Bowls, the victories by the Jets and Chiefs the next two years brought about an enormous change in the collective assessment of the AFL, both then and to this day. Those two wins changed the entire equation. Whether they prove that the AFL was superior to the NFL in 1968 and 1969 is not the point.

What those two games definitely did was establish that, at minimum, the AFL in its later years was a major league close to the same level as the NFL. Whether it was as strong, stronger, or almost as strong as the NFL doesn't really matter. What is important is that those two games drastically lay waste to the overwhelming perception, held by probably 90% of football fans and experts at the time, that the NFL was vastly superior to the AFL.

The AAFC never got that chance. Yet the AAFC *began* at about the level that the AFL was at when the Jets and Chiefs triumphed. Absent an AAFC-NFL title game, however, the AAFC's legacy is stuck about where the AFL's would be without the third and fourth Super Bowls.

As in the discussion of the two previous questions, some of the evidence comes from how matters played out after 1949. Besides the Browns' great six-year run through the NFL, there are the many individual accomplishments of the many players who played for the team in both the AAFC and NFL. Can we explain Cleveland's dominance of the NFL by the fantastic notion that the Browns collectively improved after four years of playing beneath their capabilities? The absurdity of the notion is obvious, yet it or something close to it is essentially the foundation of the argument that the Browns would not have won against the NFL champions: the Bears in 1946, the Cardinals in 1947, and the Eagles in 1948 and 1949.

Perhaps experience has something to do with it. A majority of Cleveland's players had no pro experience before 1946, such an argument might go, and the 1946-1949 period was a sort of apprenticeship period. Once their apprenticeship was finished, the Browns became the best team in football in 1950. Prior to that, they would have made the mistakes typical of the inexperienced that would have cost them games against teams like the Bears, Cardinals, and Eagles.

Such an argument explains nothing. A team that wins with players who have been around is said to be experienced; one that loses with such players is said to be over the hill, in decline, or in need of rebuilding. A younger, less experienced team wins just as often when it goes up against an older, more experienced team. The early Browns were a youngish, superbly talented team that jelled and dominated. That Paul Brown was head and shoulders above his coaching contemporaries was also a big reason for their success.

In 1946, every single NFL team was older and had more experience than the Browns. Anybody think the Boston Yanks or the 1–10 Lions were better than Cleveland that year? That's because the real issue is talent, not experience, and the Browns had it in abundance from the very beginning (six Hall of Fame players in their very first year, compared with four for the NFL-best Bears).

For every team that won partly because they'd been there before like, say, the 1967 Packers, there are as many or more like the Browns who vanquished all of the more experienced foes that they played. The 1992 Cowboys' wins over the 49ers and Bills, the 1937 Redskins' defeats of the Giants and Bears, the 1972 Dolphins' conquest of the Raiders and Redskins, the Patriots' 2001 victories over the Steelers and Rams—from every era in the game's history, superior talent and coaching trumps experience more often than not. Generally, experience comes into play only when it is connected to great talent.

Cleveland's dominance of the Yankees in the AAFC provides some specific evidence. Far more experienced than the greenhorn Browns, the Yankees numbers in 1946 included an organization that had been transferred over wholesale from the NFL, more than a dozen players with NFL experience, six players who had been NFL all-pros (Ace Parker, Bruiser Kinard, Pug Manders, Frank Sinkwich, Perry Schwartz, and Bob Masterson), two seasoned veterans who were on their way to the Hall of Fame (Parker and Kinard), two NFL MVPs (Parker and Sinkwich), and a coach who was one of the best ever and was also headed for the Hall of Fame. Before Pearl Harbor, they were one of the NFL's best teams as the Brooklyn Dodgers.

Add to that the sensational Spec Sanders and other outstanding newcomers like Bruce Alford, Jack Russell, Derrell Palmer, Nate Johnson, and Lou Sossamon, and the experience factor would lead one to assume that the Yankees would best the Browns head to head. As we know, though, the Yankees were never able to beat the team from Podunk with a high school coach even once in ten tries. One cannot help but ask whether they and many that came after them over the next ten years who were similarly dominated by Cleveland would have been better off with less NFL experience.

There's another way of looking at the relative strengths of the Browns of the AAFC and their NFL contemporaries. It would not have been difficult to find a lot of football fans who believed that Philadelphia's Tommy Thompson was a better quarterback than Otto Graham in 1949. Among NFL fans, that might even have been a majority view; Philadelphia fans would have thought so overwhelmingly. Based on what people found out about Graham once the Browns joined the NFL, that opinion changed a bit, probably to a point where shortly after 1949 not one single person even vaguely familiar with football would have expressed it.

Anybody think Cliff Patton of the Eagles was a better placekicker than Lou Groza in 1948? That was a popular opinion once, also held by perhaps a majority of football fans. That one, too, could be said to be slightly less popular in the years since. Anybody think Billy Dewell of the Cardinals was a better receiver in 1947 than Dante Lavelli? Huge numbers of football fans would have laughed at you if you had suggested otherwise in the late 1940s.

How about Marion Motley? The man now considered to be the best fullback between Bronko Nagurski and Jim Brown was not thought to be that by NFL partisans when he was playing exclusively on AAFC fields. Anybody willing to stand up in public today and proclaim that Joe Osmanski of the Bears was a better fullback than Motley in 1946? A whole lot of people would have done so then—and as with all of these other examples, they would have been no more right then than they would be today.

Sure, Graham, Groza, Lavelli, and Motley got plenty of recognition at the time—all we have to do is look at the joint AAFC/NFL all-pro teams to understand that. But the NFL was much better known, and in the NFL community—players, owners, the league office, and most definitely fans—AAFC teams were minor league and would not stand a chance against their own. The all-pro accomplishments and Cleveland's championships were looked upon as dubious until, beginning in 1950, they were replicated against NFL competition. And those post-1949 accomplishments, already discussed at some length and accomplished by so many of the same players, are among the best arguments in favor of the Browns being the best team in either league in the AAFC years.

The exact same sense of assumed inferiority that was held about Cleveland's players in the AAFC era was held for the Browns as a team in the NFL community. The stature of the Cleveland players changed pretty quickly once the NFL saw firsthand what they could do, and with some noteworthy exceptions, they have generally gotten their due, to a point where the laughable nature of the earlier views is manifestly clear. Why hasn't the view of the 1946–1949 Browns teams as a whole gone through the same metamorphosis?

The NFL champions of the AAFC era did not include a single black player. That puts all of them at an immediate disadvantage going up against a Browns team that included two blacks who are among the greatest players of all time and a third who was the best punter in that era (some say of any era). What about other comparisons?

The Browns' passing game is one area where they have a decisive advantage over the Bears, Cardinals, and Eagles. Sid Luckman was a great quarterback, but his best years were behind him in 1946 and he was at best the equal of Graham that season. Where the Browns have a huge edge is at end. The Bears had a nice combination in Ken Kavanaugh and Jim Keane, but it was one that was nowhere near as good as Speedie and Lavelli, who right from the beginning established themselves as football's best receiving duo.

It's the same story with Mal Kutner and Dewell of the Cardinals. Both were very good players, especially Kutner, but not in the same class as a receiving tandem as Cleveland's. Pete Pihos of the Eagles was a better all-around football player than either Speedie or Lavelli because he also excelled on defense (with standouts George Young and John Yonakor at defensive end, the Browns did not need either Speedie or Lavelli to go both ways on a full-time basis). Looked at just as receivers, Pihos and Lavelli are about in the same class, while Speedie ranks ahead of both.

The Eagles' two other ends, Jack Ferrante and Neill Armstrong, like those from the Bears and Cardinals, were above average receivers. Even taken as a trio, however, Pihos, Ferrante, and Armstrong come up a bit short compared with Cleveland. The disparity in the passing game is all the more pronounced when Cleveland's other receiving threats—Dub and Edgar Jones, Motley, and Boedeker—are added to the equation. Few if any NFL teams had integrated their backs into the passing game to the same degree.

Paul Christman of the Cardinals was a decent quarterback who had several good seasons as a pro. He was not in the same class as Graham, however—not in 1947, and not on the best day of his career. Philadelphia's Thompson had a monster year in 1948; maybe on his best day he was in the same class throwing the ball as Graham.

But there are lots of factors that go into playing quarterback besides throwing the ball. Graham did all of those things as well as or better than anybody who ever played the position and for that reason stands above his NFL contemporaries. Look at one: running with the ball. In 1948 and 1949 (Thompson's two best seasons), Thompson rushed twenty-seven times for 63 yards, three touchdowns, and a 2.3 average. In those same seasons, Graham rushed fifty times for 253 yards, nine touchdowns, and a 5.1 average.

In a comparison of the number of Hall of Famers each team had, the Browns again have a decisive advantage on all counts. The 1946 Bears had four Hall of Famers (Luckman, Bulldog Turner, George McAfee, and Joe Stydahar), the 1947 Cardinals had one (Charlie Trippi), and the 1948 Eagles had three (Pihos, Steve Van Buren, and Alex Wojciechowicz) and then added Chuck Bednarik in 1949 to bring their total to four. The Browns, on the other hand, had six in each of those four seasons: Graham, Lavelli, Motley, Groza, Willis, and Gatski.

The greater number of Hall of Famers is an important argument in favor of the Browns, for obvious reasons. The number of Hall-worthy players a team has certainly is some indication of how good that team was. Dominant teams from just about any era tend to have more Hall of Famers than every one of their contemporaries. The greater the disparity, the greater the degree of dominance. Disparities of six to four and six to three are quite large; one of six to one is off the charts.

Could it be that players from these teams have been unjustly passed over by Hall of Fame voters? Absolutely. And wouldn't you know it, the Browns have an advantage there, too. There are four players from these teams who are not in the Hall but should be: Pat Harder of the Cardinals, Philadelphia's Al Wistert, and Speedie and Rymkus. No Bears, one Cardinal, one Eagle, and two Browns. Are there players on any of these teams who perhaps don't belong in the Hall? Yes, one—and he's not a Brown. Wojciechowicz is generally thought to be one of the two or three worst selections in Hall of Fame history.

It's also worth noting the case of Charlie Trippi of the Cardinals. Based just on his credentials, Trippi did not have a Hall of Fame career. However, selectors rightly factored in the two years he lost to World War II and inducted him. But Speedie (four years) and Rymkus and Harder (two years each) also lost time to military service and all are more Hall-worthy than Trippi, yet all remain outside looking in. Speedie's Hall of Fame credentials in particular are vastly superior to Trippi's.

So the Hall of Fame argument favors Cleveland from all angles. They have more Hall of Famers than any of the four NFL champions by a wide margin, they have more players who should be in the Hall but aren't than any of those teams, and no Brown is a questionable choice, while one of the Eagles is at the top of the list of biggest Hall of Fame mistakes. In addition, had electors been fairer in their application of time lost to military service during World War II, two more Browns would have gone in ahead of Trippi, the Cardinals' only Hall of Famer.

Aside from Cleveland's 1950–1955 NFL dominance and the sterling individual accomplishments in those same years, the lopsided Hall of Fame advantage the Browns hold is perhaps the most compelling piece of evidence that points to them being better than all NFL comers from 1946 through 1949.

The 1946 Bears had the kind of experience that matters—the kind that's connected to superb talent. A number of players were still on hand from Chicago's four great years of 1940–1943. Still, important players like George Musso, Lee Artoe, Danny Fortmann, and others were gone by 1946, and the team was not as good as the earlier ones. Chicago's 1946 championship turned out to be a sort of last hurrah. They remained an excellent team for years thereafter but did not win another title until 1963.

The Browns were erroneously thought by some to be strictly a finesse team. However, their line was tough and it was very good. It wasn't Monsters of the Midway good, but by 1946 neither was the Bears'. It's difficult to say what advantage Bulldog Turner, Ray Bray, and the others would have had going up against Cleveland. Rymkus and Scarry had more than held their own against the Bears and other NFL competition, and the additional likes of Willis, Ulinski, Houston, Yonakor, and Young might actually have given the Browns an advantage.

And as in the early 1940s, it was the Bears' line play that made the team go. In 1946, McAfee didn't have much of a year but Luckman was very good, and overall the offense was the best in the NFL. There was nothing special about Chicago's kicking game, while Groza had his first big year. Cleveland had a definite advantage in that part of the game.

Perhaps the two biggest questions concerning such a game, the keys to determining a winner even, follow: Would the Bears' line have outplayed the Browns the way it did so many NFL opponents? And would the Bears have been able to contain the Cleveland passing game? The answer to the first question is likely not, but the answer to the second—definitely not—tips the balance Cleveland's way. With the exception of two games against the Umbrella Defense and the 1953 Championship Game, nobody stopped the Browns' passing game for ten years. The Bears had never seen anything like it, and there's no reason to believe they would have been able to stop it either.

Where the 1947 Cardinals are concerned, there's every reason to believe the Browns would have beaten them rather handily. Playing in an NFL weakened by competition from the AAFC for players, the Cardinals posted a regular season record that is in the lowest 25% of pro football's ninety-five champions. Cleveland's advantages at quarterback and at end have been discussed. The Cardinals had good linemen and linebackers like Buster Ramsey, Vince Banonis, and Chet Bulger, but for each the Browns had one and more just as good. And the Browns had Willis, who was both the best middle guard in the game and the best player from these two teams at these positions. Cleveland also had an advantage in the kicking game.

The other side of the kicking game is the return game. McAfee was the NFL's top kickoff returner in 1946 and Trippi one of the NFL's best punt returners in 1947. From 1946 through 1948, however, the Browns had Tom Colella, perhaps the best punt returner in football. In 1946 Colella was first among AAFC punt returners with at least eight returns, with an outstanding 21.5-yard average. And among players who played more than two seasons, he was the AAFC's all-time punt return leader, with a 17.3-yard average. The advantage the Browns had in the return game may only be slight, but taken together with all of their other advantages, its importance grows.

With their Dream Backfield, the Cardinals might be assumed to have had an advantage in the running game, but that's not at all clear from the evidence. Motley was better than any of Chicago's backs in 1947. He rushed for almost twice as many yards per game as any Cardinal, and his 6.1 yards per carry was likewise much higher. Edgar Jones was steady if not flashy, and his 6.4 average, like Motley's, was one of the best in either league. Bill Boedeker was an effective runner and receiver on those occasions when he got the ball.

Collectively, the Dream Backfield was actually quite a bit better in 1948 than in 1947. Their yardage totals were substantially better, they did better on the all-NFL and all-AAFC/NFL teams, and the team improved from 9–3 to 11–1. If we were looking at the backfields in that year, the comparison might favor the Cardinals.

In 1947, the advantage is slight either way. If we take the running backs and the quarterback together, the Browns have an advantage. Otherwise, the backfields are about even. Even if Chicago is deemed to be stronger, it is not by much and the advantage does not come anywhere close to balancing out Cleveland's advantages elsewhere.

Jimmy Conzelman was a very good coach for Chicago, but Paul Brown he was not. Once the Browns began kicking NFL butt, Brown was accorded full recognition as a genius and one of a handful of the game's greatest innovators, something that remains true more than fifty years later. However, all of the innovations that earned him that rarefied status were in place beginning in 1946. As in so many other areas, Cleveland's advantage over the Cardinals in coaching is substantial.

Finally, there are the two-time champion Eagles. A more lengthy discussion of Philadelphia's teams is necessary for several reasons. For one, unlike either the 1946 Bears or the 1947 Cardinals, the Eagles were popularly thought to be one of the best NFL teams ever after they repeated in 1949. There are very good reasons that opinion was popular. Philadelphia was only the second NFL team ever to win consecutive Championship Games, they remain the only team to ever win consecutive Championship Games/Super Bowls by shutout, and they ran roughshod over opponents to a degree that few have, before or since. Philadelphia's 18.3 and 19.1 per-game point differentials, for example, are the twelfth and fifth best ever going back to 1921 in the NFL, AAFC, and AFL.

Injuries and sudden aging were factors in why the Eagles fell so dramatically from their championship perch in 1950. Steve Van Buren, Bosh Pritchard, and others did miss time because of injuries, and the Eagles may have aged more quickly than is common. In no sense are those the major reasons they fell from 11–1 champions to 6–6, however. There is, on the other hand, an avalanche of evidence that indicates the Eagles were *almost exactly as good in 1950 as they were in 1949.*

What changed was the competition they had to play against. First and foremost, they had to deal with the Cleveland Browns. As we know from what happened in 1950, just the presence of the Browns in the same conference was enough to end Philadelphia's run as a champion. And lest anybody argue that Cleveland's 13–7 victory over the Eagles more accurately reflects the relative strengths of the two teams than the 35–10 blowout, the second game was not as close as the score. Cleveland controlled the game after they took an early lead, and the Eagles did not get their only points until about a minute remained.

More important, though, the Browns won the game without attempting a single pass. For that reason, *Cleveland's second victory over Philadelphia may be more impressive than the opening-night thrashing they administered.* What the Browns did in essence was play the second game with one hand tied behind their collective backs. They had one of the best passing attacks in the game's history, one that had helped usher in the postwar passing revolution, yet they were able to beat a very good team without utilizing that part of their arsenal for even a single play.

That they accomplished this against the Eagles and not, say, the Redskins or Colts is something. It is all the more impressive considering that it happened not in football's early years but at the apex of the passing-est era in the game's history up to that time. From Pearl Harbor until today, no other team has duplicated it.

But the tougher competition Philadelphia faced took other forms in 1950 than just the Browns. There was a massive infusion of good players from the AAFC and a huge increase in the black talent in the NFL (also mostly from the AAFC). Significantly, except for one player who played only three seasons in Philadelphia, the Eagles were left behind because they declined to pursue either of those avenues of talent.

Did the Eagles age suddenly, and was that the reason they fell so far in 1950? They may have collectively aged more than is common in one year, but if so that is only one minor reason. For one thing, at the same time some players were aging, second-year man Chuck Bednarik was emerging as one of the game's best players, and Norm Willey made an immediate impact as a rookie.

Injuries were also likewise a factor, but only a minor one. All teams experience injuries. Take the 1950 Browns. As has been mentioned, Ford played four games and part of a fifth for Cleveland. Had he played an entire season, he might have established himself as the game's best defensive end in 1950 rather than in 1951, and the Browns might have had an even better season than they did.

And Ford was not the only key player who missed time for Cleveland. Most notable among the others was Groza, who missed two games and fifty-nine minutes of a third. Significantly, Groza and Ford were each absent for one of Cleveland's losses in 1950. Groza missed the first Giants game, one Cleveland lost by only six points, and Ford missed the rematch with New York, a game that was even closer at 17–13.

Still, the Eagles were hurt more by injuries than Cleveland was. But there's something else about Philadelphia's injuries in 1950, something curious. More Eagles missed games to injury in 1949 than in 1950, yet the team in 1949 was able to steamroll through the Eastern Conference, finish first by four and a half games, and shut out the Rams in the title game.

And they weren't insignificant players or amounts of time, either. Frank Reagan missed eight games in 1949; Vic Lindskog missed seven; John Green missed five; Jay MacDowell missed four; and Bednarik, Russ Craft, Mario Giannelli, and Frank Ziegler all missed two. And remember, that's in a twelve-game season.

Why were the Eagles able to so thoroughly dominate despite such injuries in 1949 but not in 1950? Because the level of competition they were playing against improved dramatically. In 1949, Philadelphia dominated Eastern Conference lightweights Pittsburgh, Washington, the Bulldogs, and the Giants despite all of their injuries. In 1949, those four teams were 0–8 against the Eagles. Even their combined record in games against teams other than the Eagles was below .500. And Philadelphia outscored those teams head to head 255 points to 65, an average score of 32–8.

As far as AAFC talent is concerned, the Eagles signed only one player in the offseason after the merger, defensive back Joe Sutton. Although he had played only one season with the 5–5–2 Bills, Sutton won a starting job and led the Eagles with eight interceptions in 1950 despite playing only nine games. In the last weeks of the season, Philadelphia acquired AAFC veteran Bill Boedeker from Green Bay, but he played only one game with the team after they had already been eliminated.

As two-time defending NFL champs, the Eagles probably figured they didn't need players from what they considered a minor league. On some level, that's a valid point, for the Eagles had a lot of very good players. One cannot help but think there was a degree of arrogance at work as well, however. Such an attitude toward their one-time rival lingered on many NFL teams, and as the NFL's best, Philadelphia undoubtedly thought that AAFC players would have a difficult time making the team, let alone starting and contributing.

As a result, like every other NFL team, the Eagles passed on Len Ford in the dispersement draft. They then passed on everybody else available as well except for Sutton. Better they should have done like other teams and gone after players like Dick Barwegan, John Rapacz, Billy Grimes, Hardy Brown, Bob Hoernschmeyer, and dozens of others.

Perhaps even more telling than a lack of AAFC players was Philadelphia's lack of black players. In the fifth season of modern football integration, the Eagles remained all white and would remain so until 1952. On the other hand, 15% of the players on the roster of the Browns team that took the field against them in September of 1950 were black.

Of Cleveland's five blacks, only Cole had a minor role. Gillom was the best punter in the game and a skilled enough player to fill in on both defense and offense. The Browns' three other blacks were on a fast track to the Hall of Fame. In completely ignoring such an important source of talent, the Eagles ceded other teams an important advantage. When they went head to head with the Browns, that advantage was massive. It is no coincidence that the two teams with the most black players, the Browns and the Rams, played in the first two postmerger NFL Championship Games.

The issue of black players is relevant because not only Philadelphia lagged behind in signing them. The vast majority of the NFL teams the Eagles so thoroughly dominated in 1949 were also all white. Tunnell was the only black player on the five Eastern Conference teams that year. With the drastically increased competition in 1950 from a huge influx of black talent and a massive infusion of AAFC players, the Eagles went from "the greatest team ever" to a 6–6 record and third place in one season.

The striking thing about Philadelphia's 1950 season is that that drastically increased competition *was not across the board*. It came almost entirely from the Browns, the new bully on the block, and a Giants team that had substantially pumped itself up with AAFC talent. The Eagles dominated the rest of their opponents almost as completely as they had in 1949. A good part of that domination came against the very teams that also continued to both have no blacks and the fewest number of AAFC players.

Let's look at the Eagles' 1950 season in more detail. After getting blown out by the Browns, Philadelphia rebounded nicely to win five straight and six out of seven. Two thirds of the way through the season, they were 6–2 and tied for second place with—guess who—the pumped-up Giants, just a half game behind—guess who—the 7–2 Browns. Up to that point, the Eagles had outscored their opponents 227 to 98, or by an average score of 28–12.

All of those numbers are impressive enough, but consider this. Take away their loss to the Browns and the Eagles are 6–1 and in first place, and they've outscored their opponents 217 to 63, an average score of 31–9. Not only does that record closely parallel what they did in 1949, but that per-game point differential is substantially better than Philadelphia's great 1948 and 1949 seasons. In fact, had they recorded such a differential over the whole season, it would have been the third best in the entire history of pro football.

In their ninth game, the Eagles built a 10–0 third-quarter lead over the Cardinals. From that point on, however, their offense utterly collapsed, and they finished the season with four straight losses. In their final three and a half games, the Eagles scored 17 points, an average of 4.9 per game. And, surprise, surprise, three of those losses came at the hands of the Browns (13–7) and the Giants (7–3 and 9–7).

In those four losses, the Eagles allowed fewer than 11 points a game, so clearly their defense was still playing at an exceptional level. For the season the Eagles edged out the Browns in fewest points allowed, 141 to 144. When their points allowed per game is compared with the average for the rest of the league, the 1950 Eagles turned in one of the best defensive performances ever (again topping their 1948 and 1949 teams).

Let's look at something else about Philadelphia's 1950 season, something that brings us still closer to the heart of the matter, which is that the Browns were better than the Eagles in 1948 and 1949 just as surely as they were in 1950. It should also dispel once and for all the notion that Cleveland overtook the Eagles because of age and injuries. It's fairly simple and is supported by a ton of evidence: If there was no merger between the AAFC and NFL at the end of 1949, the Eagles would have run roughshod over the NFL about the way they did the previous year and won a third straight NFL championship.

Suppose there had been no merger. Who would the Eagles have played in 1950? They wouldn't have played the Browns, to whom they lost twice, and the Giants team that they would have played would not have been the pumped-up one that likewise beat them twice but rather a much weaker version similar to New York's 1949 team. It has already been mentioned, but because of its importance it's worth repeating: In contrast to the stand-pat Eagles, the Giants aggressively pursued AAFC talent. All seven of the AAFC players the Giants signed became starters in 1950, and four of those were named all-pro.

With no merger, Ted Collins's New York Bulldogs would have remained in the Eastern Conference. They also would have remained about the same as they were in 1949 when they won exactly one game. Without the merger, there would have been no radical influx of AAFC players to the Bulldogs/Yanks; no turning over the majority of the roster with much better talent; and no all-pros Spec Sanders, Dan Edwards, Jack Russell, Buddy Young, George Ratterman, and Joe Signaigo. Most important, there would have been no turning 1–10–1 into 7–5.

Guess what: That's who the Eagles would have played two games against in 1950 in place of their two games against the Browns—the New York Bulldogs. The same Bulldogs the Eagles beat twice in 1949 by a combined score of 49–0. Then there are the Giants, the same Giants who prior to 1950 had been in a tailspin, winning just twelve games in three years. Without the added AAFC talent—Hall of Famer and all-pro Weinmeister; all-pros Schnellbacher, Rapacz, and Mastrangelo; and starters Landry, Rowe, and Woodard—the Giants would have been the same pushovers for the Eagles they were in 1949 (New York's two losses to Philadelphia that year were by a combined 41–6 score).

Without the merger, the smart money says those four 1950 Philadelphia losses turn into victories. Instead of playing four games against the two best regular season teams of 1950, the Browns and Giants, they would have played those four against the very worst NFL team and a Giants team that was, at best, in the middle of the pack. Against the other two Eastern weaklings, the Steelers and Redskins (the Cardinals were in the West until the merger), the Eagles won three of four in 1950 and outscored them 92–22. That's not very different from 1949. There's no reason to think they wouldn't have dominated the Bulldogs and unimproved Giants the same way.

The Eagles did lose two other games in 1950, to the Steelers 9–7 and the Cardinals 14–10. In one sense, those games are just the kind of bumps in the road that all first-place teams hit along the way during a long season. But here's the funny thing about one of those losses: Although the Cardinals did not sign as many AAFCers as most other teams, they did have three times as many as the Eagles. It's very possible those players were just enough difference in a very close game.

Take the Browns and the AAFC talent added by the Giants and even the Cardinals out of the equation, and the 1950 Eagles are a runaway conference champ at 10–2, maybe 11–1, 9–3 at worst. The Giants and Steelers battle for second place with .500 records, while the Bulldogs and Redskins contend for nothing but the rights to the first-overall draft pick in 1951. That's an almost exact replication of 1949. Excluding the games against Cleveland and the Giants, the average per-game score of Philadelphia's eight other games in 1950 was 25–8. That is not only a dominant level exactly like 1949, but like their 1948 and 1949 marks it would have been one of the best in history, NFL, AAFC, and AFL.

Believe it or not, there's still more: The Eagles would have been odds-on favorites to beat the Rams in a title-game rematch and claim their third straight NFL championship. Doubt it? Take all the previous information and add three more things. First, during the 1950 regular season, the Eagles routed Los Angeles 56–20. The game was even more one-sided than the score indicates, as the Rams scored all their points in the second half, well after the outcome had been decided.

Second, although Los Angeles emerged in the mid-1940s as one of the NFL's best teams and remained so well into the 1950s, they did not beat the Eagles once in eight tries from 1944 through 1950. Only twice in those eight games were the high-powered Rams able to score more than 14 points against Philadelphia. The average score of those games was 29–14, which is very lopsided considering how good the Rams were during those years.

Finally, the Eastern Conference winner was slated to host the title game in 1950. The implication of *that* is clear enough. A warm-weather Rams team whose offense was the most pass-oriented in history up to that point, one that the Eagles had shut out in Los Angeles the year before, a team that could not beat the Eagles even during their 9–1 championship season of 1945, that team would have had to play the 1950 NFL Championship Game in wintry Philadelphia. Anybody want to bet that the two-time defending NFL champs wouldn't have been solid favorites to win such a matchup?

Undoubtedly there will continue to be some who cling to the fiction that in 1950 the Browns improved themselves over 1949 while the Eagles were undone by age and injuries. Many such people will continue to believe, to a great extent because they want to believe, irrespective of the inconvenience of facts. The great preponderance of the evidence says otherwise, however. It indicates that the Browns were simply a better team than the Eagles in all three of the years under discussion. If anything, the evidence points not to there being doubt or a slight Cleveland advantage but to the Browns being *decisively* better in 1948 and 1949, as well as in 1950.

A Super Bowl in 1947 between the Browns and Cardinals would have been like a lot of Super Bowls: one-sided. Super Bowls between the Browns and Eagles in 1948 and 1949 would have been better. They would have been compelling games with lots of drama and anticipation because of the stakes, but also ones in which Cleveland had a clear edge.

A Super Bowl in 1946 between the Browns and Bears would have been a terrific game, and over time it could have developed into a great story: a great dynasty in its first year against another great dynasty that was about at the end of the line. George Halas, the single most important figure in the history of the pro game, would have been pitted against Paul Brown, soon to be the most successful pro coach of them all. But the NFL refused to play, so we are left, alas, with the kind of analysis and sifting of evidence contained herein.

Although a game with the Bears is probably the most difficult for Cleveland of these four hypothetical matchups, it is likely they would have won such a game for a clean four-year sweep. Had such a game been played not in Wrigley Field, where Halas was notorious for getting his way with officials and everybody else, but on a neutral field, with an officiating crew drawn evenly from the AAFC and the NFL, then you've got to think Cleveland's chances would have been better than even. So the ultimate conclusion, based on the evidence and not emotion or bias, is that the Browns were the best team in football every year from 1946 through 1949.

Continued Greatness and a Championship Game Loss

New in 1951: Harry "Chick" Jagade (FB), Bob Oristaglio (E), Don Shula (DB), Carl Taseff (DB)

Gone from 1950: Weldon Humble, Jim Martin, Dom Moselle

Remaining from 1946 (11): Gatski, Graham, Groza, Houston, Lavelli, Lewis, Motley, Rymkus, Speedie, Willis, Young

IN MARKED CONTRAST to 1950 when Cleveland turned over more than one third of its roster, only three players who were with the team the previous year did not return in 1951. Dom Moselle was traded to Green Bay but left with no regrets. He had beaten long odds in even making the Browns the previous year and had played for the team during the season of its greatest accomplishments.

Like Moselle, Jim Martin was traded after just one season with the team. He went to the Lions for a first-round draft choice in 1952 that the

Browns would use to select defensive back Bert Rechichar. Martin would play thirteen more seasons, mostly with the Lions, as a linebacker and sometime placekicker. Weldon Humble retired after four seasons of stellar play, although he would come out of retirement to play in 1952 for the short-lived Dallas Texans franchise in his home state.

Among those new to the squad were two Ohioans who were both defensive backs out of Cleveland's John Carroll University, Don Shula and Carl Taseff. Neither would play long for the Browns, but Taseff would play into the 1960s, including with the Colts in their glory years of 1958 and 1959, before embarking on a long career as an assistant coach. Shula would play two seasons with the Browns and seven in all and then make his mark as the winningest head coach in history in a thirty-three-year career with the Colts and Miami Dolphins.

After playing with the Colts in the AAFC in 1949, fullback Harry "Chick" Jagade came to Cleveland as a free agent after missing the 1950 season because of an injury. Brown liked Jagade because of the determination he displayed when he ran with the football. The Cleveland coach called Jagade "the most reckless football player I've ever seen." Jagade would play sparingly in 1951, then more for several years as Motley's knee problems reduced the great fullback's playing time. Bob Oristaglio was another newcomer who was an AAFC veteran and who served as a backup end on both offense and defense in his one season with the team.

Going with Moselle in the trade with Green Bay were several newcomers, including linebacker Walt Michaels, whom the Browns would soon reacquire. In exchange the Browns got the NFL rights to Bob Gain. A six-foot-three-inch, 255-pound tackle out of Kentucky, Gain won the 1950 Outland Trophy as college football's top lineman. Unable to come to terms with the Packers, he played the 1951 season in Canada.

After Gain's team won the Canadian championship, Brown contacted him about joining the Browns for the last weeks of the 1951 season. Having played in the College All-Star Game, training camp, and the Canadian regular season and postseason, Gain declined. Although he did not join the Browns until 1952, the Gain trade ranks with the one for Dub Jones as one of the best of Cleveland's dynasty era.

Defensive back Ken Konz and tackle Jerry Helluin were draft choices who did not join the team because of military obligations, Helluin until 1952, Konz until 1953. Bob Gaudio came out of retirement and played one more year, and Brown continued in his efforts to obtain Doak Walker. When Lions head coach Buddy Parker inquired about the availability of second-year fullback Emerson Cole, Brown was amenable. He pointed out that Detroit was weak at tackle and offered Cole and any one of Cleveland's tackles for Walker.

"We're not interested in trading a layer cake for two doughnuts," Parker replied, and Walker remained a Lion.

One other personnel move that went largely unnoticed at the time was the trade of defensive tackle Art Donovan. Cleveland selected Donovan in the dispersement draft of Colts players when the Baltimore franchise went under. Unable to beat out Grigg for the third tackle spot behind Palmer and Kissell, Donovan was sent to the Yanks for two draft choices. He played for the Yanks and Texans, then went on to have a Hall of Fame career with the new Colts franchise that began in 1953.

Ohio State rumors again circulated around Brown when Buckeyes head coach Wesley Felser resigned. Brown did not immediately refute the rumors but instead expressed frustration at the Browns being number two in Cleveland behind the Indians, as well as at the Browns' disappointing attendance of the previous season. Although up from 1949, Cleveland's 1950 home attendance was only 33,387 per game, and the two postseason games averaged even less. That was just over half the 56,623 per game that the team had drawn in 1946 and 1947.

In the end, Brown stayed. And although the Browns did not overtake the Indians during their dynasty years (a period that was, oddly enough, also precisely the greatest in Indians' history), within a few short years the balance in popularity and gate appeal had shifted dramatically in favor of the Browns.

With the unfortunate death of the Colts, the NFL was made up of twelve teams in 1951. The league would remain that size until 1960 when it would expand in the face of a challenge from another rival. Even with the AAFC war in the past, franchises continued to struggle. By season's end, in fact, the Yanks would go the way of the Colts, and the NFL would make an ill-fated foray into Texas.

Winning the NFL championship meant the Browns would play the college all-stars. For Paul Brown and his team, it was one more peak to scale. And quite a peak it was. In an era before sporting events such as championship poker and arena football being pitched at high volume as spectacles of great proportions, the College All-Star Game was truly one of the biggest sporting events each year.

With the game played on such a large stage, no one, least of all Arch Ward, should have been surprised that the Browns went into Soldier Field and buried the all-stars, 33–0. Playing all out was the only way that Brown knew how to play the game. He never liked to lose or have his team play poorly in any circumstances, but certainly not to a team of collegians in front of 92,180 spectators and sportswriters from every major newspaper in the country.

Although he was the catalyst behind the All-America Football Conference, Ward was first and foremost a college football man, and he did not like the pasting the Browns administered to the all-stars. He confronted the Cleveland coach on the sidelines as the teams left the field at halftime with Cleveland holding a 12–0 lead that in no way reflected the one-sided nature of the game.

"Young man," Ward reportedly said to Brown, "don't ever hurt this game of ours."

What Brown said in response is not known. But one backdrop to the game goes back to something Ward had written in late 1946 shortly after the conclusion of the AAFC's first season. Although the new league had gotten off to an excellent start, Ward was not as impressed by the Browns' first championship and the Bears' title in the NFL as he had been by what he had seen at West Point and South Bend that season. In his *Chicago Tribune* column, Ward asserted that Army and Notre Dame were better than both the Browns and the Bears.

Ward may not have meant any harm, but Brown could only have been stung by the words, especially as they came from someone with whom he had such a close relationship. For that reason, there may have been some payback involved at the College All-Star Game. Brown, after all, was a veritable elephant. He never forgot anything having to do with football, especially when someone, friend or not, denigrated or so much as cast a question mark over the accomplishments of his team.

So in the same way that Brown took Greasy Neale behind the woodshed and taught him a lesson in the mud of Municipal Stadium the previous November for Neale's ill-advised remarks, so Brown and his team stuck it to Ward with a 33–0 victory. Brown no longer had a professional relationship with Ward, after all (not that that would have mattered). More important, the 1950 season had provided substantial evidence that for five years the Browns had been the greatest of all football teams and that they could continue to be so indefinitely. A loss to college players in an exhibition game might not have much bothered other coaches, but to Paul Brown it could only have tarnished his team's status.

"We destroyed the popular belief that a good team of college players always had a chance to beat an established professional team," Brown said. In addition, however, Brown settled a score and added just a small bit to his team's legacy. *Chicago Daily News* writer Bob Russell joined an already large chorus that would grow larger still in the years to come when he wrote that "it will be hard to convince anyone that Paul Brown's 'old pros' aren't one of the great football teams of all time."

One of the tackles for the college all-stars was Mike McCormack from the University of Kansas. McCormack would spend nine of his ten NFL seasons with the Browns, but on this night he was on the losing end against Cleveland. A few days later he began his professional career with the New York Yanks.

"We lose to the Browns in the College All-Star Game 33–0," McCormack remembered, "and then I go to training camp with the Yanks. Less than a week later we play our first preseason game against, who else, the Browns. And they beat us 52–0.

"So both of my first two games against professional competition come against the Browns in a matter of less than a week, and they win both by a combined score of 85–0," McCormack said with a laugh. "I said to myself, 'I hope I don't ever see this team again.' They were a great team, definitely the best football team I had ever seen."

Counting the College All-Star Game, the Browns won four of five preseason games and then opened against old rival San Francisco at Kezar Stadium on September 30. One of the early plans for NFL realignment after the three AAFC teams had been absorbed had the Browns in the National (or Western) Conference with the 49ers, which would have meant the two teams would continue to play each other twice a year. That plan was changed in part because of complaints by the Browns, thus leaving the teams to play each other only every third year or so. The teams did play an annual preseason game for the next twenty-five years.

The 49ers were looking to bounce back from a disappointing first season in the NFL. In 1951, San Francisco began to retool, adding Y. A. Tittle and end Billy Wilson on offense and linebacker Hardy Brown and back Rex Berry on defense. The season would mark the beginning of a decade-long run in which the 49ers were in the running most years but, as in the AAFC, always a little bit short.

The defending champion Browns got off the mark in a big way as Graham hit Dub Jones with an 81-yard touchdown pass less than three minutes into the new season. But the 49ers took control of the game a short time later and scored 17 straight points en route to a 24–10 win. The 49ers defense pressured Graham all day and intercepted two of his passes. On offense, San Francisco piled up 236 yards rushing including 145 on seventeen carries by Verl Lillywhite. After a 17–0–1 record the previous five years, the loss was Cleveland's first ever in the month of September.

After a week of practice in California, the Browns won a rematch of the Championship Game with a 38–23 win over the Rams in Los Angeles. Motley and Jones both rushed for over 100 yards as the team compiled 293 yards on the ground and over 500 total. Second-year man Ken Carpenter scored three touchdowns.

The Cleveland defense and running game were the keys as the Browns rang up consecutive shutouts on the Redskins and Steelers. With Motley sidelined by an injury, the rushing attack was a group effort that totaled 192 yards in a 45–0 whitewashing of Washington, while Emerson Cole led the way with 126 yards in a 17–0 win over Pittsburgh. The Browns defense and special teams contributed three touchdowns in the two games, including an interception return by Warren Lahr against the Steelers. Incredibly, in doing so, Lahr tied the all-time NFL record of four interceptions returned for scores in just one and a third seasons.

The Browns took over first place in the American Conference with an October 28 win against the Giants, 14–13, New York's first loss of the season. Played before 59,942, the largest home crowd in Cleveland's time in the NFL, the game between the two rivals was another defensive battle that was decided by a missed extra point. Kissell led a defensive charge highlighted by a goal line stand in the game's final minutes. Disdaining a short field goal attempt, the Giants were rebuffed from up close, including on fourth down from the 1-yard line, and fell a half game behind the 4–1 Browns at 3–1–1.

The Cleveland running game again came through with a big day, totaling 238 yards in a win over the Cardinals. Carpenter led the way with 118 yards, while Jones added 78 and a touchdown in a 34–17 victory. The following week against the Eagles, Lahr again came up with a big play as the Browns prevailed 20–17. Lahr intercepted a fourth-quarter pass and then lateraled to Adamle, who returned the ball to the Philadelphia 22. Groza kicked a short field goal a few plays later for the winning points.

The defense continued to dominate a week later, registering another shutout in a 10–0 win over the Giants in front of 52,215 at the Polo Grounds. A Groza field goal and a 68-yard Graham to Jones touchdown pass in the game's first eight minutes stood up as Cleveland won its seventh straight and increased its first-place lead over the Giants to one and a half games. Afterward Steve Owen, New York head coach since 1930 and one of the game's greatest defensive innovators and a future Hall of Famer, called the Browns defense one of the greatest in NFL history.

The Graham to Jones touchdown pass against the Giants was a fitting prelude to the Browns' next game against the Bears on the Sunday after Thanksgiving at Municipal Stadium. The Bears were 6–2 and in a first-place tie with the Rams and Lions in a wild four-team race in the National Conference that also included the 49ers. The 7–1 Browns, meanwhile, had a Giants team that had not lost to anybody else right on their heels and thus could not afford a loss. The game also marked the first regular season meeting between pro football's most legendary coach, George Halas, and Brown, the legendary coach in the making.

Uncharacteristically for that era, Chicago assistant coach Hunk Anderson, a former Bears player from the 1920s, added fuel to the fire by publicly questioning whether the Browns were a tough enough football team in the manner of the old NFL he had played in.

"I don't get all this calculus stuff," Anderson said. "If the boys hit with a little more enthusiasm than usual and get fined, we have a jackpot ready to take care of that for them. Trouble with our boys is that they've been worried about fines. They don't need to worry Sunday."

Although no longer the Monsters of the Midway, the Bears were still one of the NFL's elite teams. Bulldog Turner and Ray Bray were the only players remaining from the team's glory years, but Chicago had added outstanding players like George Connor, Johnny Lujack, and former AAFCers Dick Barwegan and Julie Rykovich in recent years. Although respectful of the Bears, the Browns were not impressed by Anderson's remarks or by the notion that Chicago would out-tough them.

"They thought if they pushed us a little bit we'd quit," Gatski said. The "calculus stuff" proved to be more than a match for Chicago's rugged style of play. "They spent all their time trying to beat us up," Adamle said, "and they weren't watching Dub."

Through eight games, Dub Jones was already having a fine season. What he did against the Bears before a crowd of 40,969, however, was something else again. Jones scored six touchdowns in a 42–21 Cleveland romp, a feat previously accomplished only by Ernie Nevers and matched since only by Gale Sayers. Jones's feat is all the more remarkable in that he touched the ball only twelve times in the game and scored the last five times he touched the ball.

Jones made every one of those touches count as he rushed for 116 yards on nine carries, for a 12.9 average and four of his touchdowns, and caught three passes for 80 yards, a 26.7 average, and his other two touchdowns. Jones scored twice in the second quarter on a 2-yard run and a 34-yard catch, twice in the third quarter on runs of 12 and 27 yards, and twice in the fourth quarter on a 43-yard run and a 43-yard reception. The sixth and final touchdown came when Graham changed the play sent in by Brown after being exhorted to do so by teammates who wanted Jones to have a shot at Nevers's record.

That sixth touchdown made the score 42–7, after which Chicago scored twice late to make the final score more respectable. The game, in fact, could have been an even bigger blowout as the Browns turned the ball over four times and were assessed 209 yards in penalties, a record that still stands. That somewhat negated Cleveland's 550 to 256 advantage in total yards, although the Bears were penalized sixteen times for 165 yards of their own. Overshadowed by Jones's great day were outstanding performances by Graham, who threw for 277 yards, and Speedie, who caught six passes for 144 yards and a 24.0 average.

Cleveland's twenty-one penalties and penalty yardage were highly uncharacteristic of a Paul Brown team, but it's unlikely the coach was entirely displeased. His team had been challenged, after all, by an old-school player and coach representing the game's most prestigious franchise. It is likely that Halas and his players, like Anderson, refused to believe that the Browns were really as good as their six-year record indicated.

Behind Sid Luckman and later Lujack at quarterback and Ken Kavanaugh and Jim Keane at end, the Bears had kept up with the changes that swept football during the late 1940s and developed a decent passing game. Primarily, though, they remained in 1951 what they had been before and during World War II: a team that won with a good running game and great line play.

In that sense, the game against the Bears was like Cleveland's NFL opener in 1950 in that it pitted the face of the game's recent past and the face of its present and future. Jones's magnificent day and the Browns' thorough domination in such a symbolically significant matchup makes the Browns' first encounter with the Bears one of the greatest regular season games in team history.

Having been an important contributor since joining the Browns in 1948, Jones had his best year in 1951. Aside from touchdowns, Jones never put up the kinds of numbers that Graham, Motley, Lavelli, and Speedie did. But like his namesake Edgar, Dub had a knack for making a high percentage of his rushes and receptions big ones.

Brown called Jones "the most underrated player in the league," sentiments echoed by Ken Konz. "He never got the recognition he deserved," Konz said.

"Dub has the speed, the guts, and the know-how of a great player," Brown said. Jones was also six-foot-four and fast, a combination of attributes that led his coach to say that "no defensive back could cover him man-for-man."

Joining the team as a rookie in 1950 at the same position as Jones, Dom Moselle said that Jones couldn't have been a better teammate. "He was right there to help me all the time," Moselle said. "And I needed it because I came from a small school, and there were a lot of things I didn't do in college that they did in the big time."

In his relationship with Moselle, Jones displayed the commitment to collective success that is one of the distinguishing hallmarks of teams that are great over many years. The continuation of that success requires that established players support and tutor new players even if a newcomer is in direct competition with the veteran for a job. "You owe it" is the way players from championship teams have characterized the sense of obligation that permeates such teams. Jones was not its only practitioner on the Browns, but he was as generous as any in passing on what he knew.

"That was one thing that most of that whole team did," Sandusky said, recalling that Lou Rymkus, the man who tutored him, did so knowing that Sandusky might take his job and hasten the end of his career. "They helped each other. They were a team, really a team."

Cleveland's high-powered passing game asserted itself in a big way the following week in the team's rematch with Chicago's South Side team. Graham threw three touchdowns to Speedie and one to Lavelli in the first half as the Browns built a 42–0 lead en route to a 49–28 pasting of the Cardinals. Graham completed fourteen of twenty passes for 217 yards and also ran for a score, and Cleveland pulled to within one win of a second straight NFL conference championship and sixth straight overall.

They got that win the next week at Forbes Field with a second shutout of the Steelers, 28–0. It was the Browns' fourth shutout of the season and raised their record to 10–1. Carpenter continued to show the kind of form the Browns had been looking for when they made him their top draft choice the year before by scoring the game's first touchdown on a 24-yard run. It was the sixth touchdown of a season that would be the best of Carpenter's career, one that would land him a spot in the Pro Bowl. For the second year in a row, the Giants finished with the second best record in football but again finished behind Cleveland.

Next it was on to Shibe Park for the finale and a waiting game to see who the opponent would be in the Championship Game. There was no sign of any letup as the Browns again dominated on both sides of the ball in besting the Eagles for a fourth consecutive time, 24–9. Graham threw scoring passes to Lavelli and Bumgardner, while rookie Taseff scored on a run for the second week in a row. The defense was again magnificent, holding Philadelphia to nine first downs, 65 yards rushing, and 96 yards passing.

Philadelphia's great fullback Steve Van Buren, football's all-time rushing leader, didn't play much in the final game of his career. The Eagles' only points came on a safety and a late touchdown that came after the Browns had built a 24–2 lead. The game marked the end of a ten-game stretch in which the Browns allowed just 10.5 points per game.

Philadelphia fell still further from their lofty perch atop the NFL in 1948 and 1949. After going 6–6 in 1950, the Eagles finished 4–8 and in fifth place in the American Conference in 1951. Combined with their four straight losses to close the 1950 season, they had lost twelve of their last sixteen. Age, injuries, and the aftermath of the upheaval in 1950—the team's new owners had fired Greasy Neale at the end of that season—were all contributing factors. There can be no doubt, though, that the arrival of the Browns was the main factor in the fall of a team that just two years before had been so powerful.

That was true in several ways, one of which was Philadelphia's four straight losses to the Browns. Those losses included two humiliations in 1950 and a one-sided game to close 1951. No series of games better encapsulated how Cleveland represented something altogether new and dangerous upon entering the NFL. While it was no small feat to roll over the likes of the Steelers, Cardinals, Redskins, and even the Bears the way they did, it was all the more impressive how the Browns handled a proud championship Eagles team that had run roughshod over the NFL with a 22–3–1 record in 1948 and 1949.

The Browns had passed the Eagles silly, they had run the ball down their throats, they had trumped their excellent kicking game, and they had defensed them to death, allowing only 43 points in the four games. "Choose your weapon," and the Eagles had found the Browns superior in every area. The demoralization that resulted from being so over-matched by a team they had scoffed at prior to September 16, 1950, could only have hastened the Eagles' fall.

The Eagles still had the two championships to be proud of, but even that glory was somewhat diminished by 1951. The claim that those champions had been one of the best teams of all time looked rather dubious in the face of mounting evidence that they had not even been the best team in football in either of those years. None of that could be explained away by injuries or age or even by the firing of the best coach in franchise history. The Browns were not only clearly superior to the Eagles and the NFL, they had been superior for a lot longer than most NFLers cared to admit.

* * *

Several hours after the Browns defeated the Eagles, the Rams prevailed in one of the wildest conference races in history and thus earned a third straight berth in the title game. The Rams were in second place as the day began, a day that started with a four-way tie still a possibility. The Bears needed help but played host to the last-place Cardinals; had they won, the Bears would have faced the Rams in a playoff for the second straight year. When the Cardinals pulled an upset, however, the Bears were eliminated.

Also needing help, the host Rams stumbled through a 14–14 first half against a weak Packers team. The Rams' fearsome passing game was at its best in the second half, however, and they buried Green Bay, 42–14. The Rams' win knocked out the 49ers, who were hosting the first-place Lions. Despite being eliminated, San Francisco rallied gamely from 10–0 and 17–14 deficits against a Detroit team that could have clinched with a win or tie. Y. A. Tittle's touchdown run with three minutes left settled matters, catapulting the 49ers to a 21–17 win and the Rams to a title-game rematch with the Browns. Los Angeles finished 8–4, San Francisco and Detroit 7–4–1, and the Bears 7–5.

Unlike the year before, the Championship Game was scheduled just one week from the end of the regular season. 1951 would, in fact, be the second to last time that format was used in the pre-1967 era. Having only one week would not much affect either team's preparation. It was, after all, the fourth time in a year the Browns and Rams played each other. The Browns had won all three of the previous encounters: the title game the year before, a September preseason game, and a 38–23 win the second week of the season.

Where the layoff of only one week may have come into play, however, was in the Browns' travel problems in the week leading up to the game. Those problems began even before Cleveland knew that the Rams would be their opponent. A blizzard that hit much of the East Coast wreaked havoc on the team's efforts to get back to Cleveland after their win in Philadelphia. In addition to the weather, those efforts were further hampered by airline travel restrictions in place because of the Korean War.

After finally returning to Cleveland, the team's travel woes continued on their second trip to the West Coast that season, something that teams rarely did at that time. The plane with the team's equipment and uniforms was delayed, thus disrupting practice for several days. Eventually order was restored, but the week's mishaps left Brown strangely apprehensive about his team's chances against the Rams.

The Rams would not have been at all sympathetic to Cleveland's travel problems. Since moving to Los Angeles they logged far more travel miles than any other NFL team until the AAFC merger brought in San Francisco. Even though they played only five of their twelve games on the road in 1951, the Rams still logged about 20,000 travel miles, more than twice as many as the Browns.

The crowd of 57,522 barely filled half of the Los Angeles Memorial Coliseum and was thus a bit of a disappointment. Still, it was the third largest crowd ever to see a championship football game, bested only by the Bears-Giants game at the Polo Grounds in 1946 and the Browns-Yankees game in 1947 at Yankee Stadium. The game figured to be an explosive one. If the same two teams could account for 58 points and over 500 passing yards in Cleveland's cold a year earlier, the thinking went, they would be good for more than that playing in the warm temperatures of Southern California.

Although still nowhere near as good as Cleveland's, the Rams defense was better than the year before. Rookie end Andy Robustelli from Arnold College in Milford, Connecticut, was the most noteworthy addition. Cornerback Herb Rich, tackle Charlie Toogood, and linebacker Don Paul, who switched from center, also bolstered the unit. Still, the Rams had allowed 21.8 points per game compared with Cleveland's 12.7. That difference, Cleveland's five consecutive championships, and their overall seven-game postseason winning streak made the Browns the consensus favorites.

Although not quite up to their record-breaking level of 1950, the Rams offense was still a deadly one. Waterfield, Van Brocklin, Hirsch, and Fears were still the fulcrum of that attack. Hirsch in particular enjoyed one of the best seasons ever by a wide receiver, with sixty-six catches for 1,495 yards, seventeen touchdowns, and 22.7 yards per catch. Prorated to a sixteen-game season, those figures translate to 1,993 yards and twenty-three touchdowns. Most astounding is the fact that Hirsch's yards were almost double Gordy Soltau's, the player with the second highest total.

"I had always considered myself a pretty good offensive player until I saw Crazylegs Hirsch, Tom Fears, and Bob Boyd," Robustelli said. "Crazylegs was probably the premier end in the league, along with Fears, and Boyd was just about the fastest. I knew I wasn't going to beat them out, so I decided to go all out and try to make the defense."

Along with the team's two receivers and two quarterbacks, Robustelli became a Hall of Famer. In addition, second-year back Deacon Dan Towler set a franchise record with 854 rushing yards on a 6.8 average and added an important dimension to the offense.

Because of the rotating home field advantage system in use for the Championship Game, the game was played in Los Angeles despite the fact that the Browns' 11–1 record was a full three games better than Los Angeles's. On top of that, Cleveland had beaten the Rams handily in week two of the regular season. Needless to say, the weather was a bit different in Cleveland than it was in Los Angeles on the day the Championship Game was played.

Like the previous year, it was a hard-fought game throughout that wasn't decided until the final minutes. After a scoreless first period, the Rams scored first to take a 7–0 lead. But Jones and Groza continued to spin their magic as the Browns rebounded to assume a 10–7 halftime lead. Jones caught a 17-yard touchdown pass from Graham, while Groza kicked a 52-yard field goal, a record for an NFL Championship Game/Super Bowl that stood for an incredible forty-two years.

In the third quarter, the Los Angeles defense, as it had the year before, forced a turnover that produced a touchdown. Larry Brink leveled Graham, forcing a fumble, and Robustelli picked up the loose ball and ran 24 yards to the Cleveland 2 to set up a Towler touchdown that gave the Rams a 14–10 lead. Later in the period, it appeared that Cleveland had taken the lead back on a 49-yard Graham to Speedie scoring toss, but the play was called back because of a holding penalty, and Cleveland was forced to punt.

Then on consecutive possessions, the Cleveland defense halted drives by the Rams inside their own 5-yard line. All the Rams could get out of the two thrusts was a Waterfield field goal that boosted their lead to 17–10. It was a clutch performance by the defense; had those possessions resulted in any more than 3 points, Cleveland would have been in a position of needing two scores.

Perhaps inspired by the defense, the Cleveland offense put together a ten-play, 65-yard drive a short time later in a touchdown run by Carpenter. It was a situation that must have been eerily familiar to the Rams and their fans. A year earlier, Los Angeles had built a 28–20 fourth-quarter lead, only to lose when the Browns mounted two clutch drives that netted 10 game-winning points. In 1951, the Rams were again less than a quarter from victory when the Browns tied the game. Suddenly a field goal from the powerful leg of Groza might again be enough to beat them.

But the late-game heroics were on the Los Angeles side this time. Backed up in their own territory halfway through the fourth quarter, the Rams' big-play offense struck. Fears had been the league's leader in receptions the previous three years, but in 1951 he had been hit with injuries that kept him out of five games and held his numbers down. The slack had been more than picked up by Hirsch, but in this crucial moment it was Fears who broke free just behind the Cleveland secondary. He caught a perfectly thrown Van Brocklin pass for a 73-yard touchdown that gave the Rams a 24–17 lead.

After blocking a Waterfield field goal attempt that would have iced the game, the Browns responded by doing what everyone expected them to do. They moved the ball to the Los Angeles 42 in search of the tying touchdown, their methodical style in contrast to the big strike the Rams deployed so often and so successfully. But the drive stalled, and with about three minutes remaining the Browns were confronted with a fourth down.

Jones was more often than not good for the short yardage that was needed, but the Rams knew that and anticipated the call. Jones was tackled almost immediately after taking the handoff, and he was not even able to get back to the line of scrimmage. The Rams kept the ball for all but the final 0:15 seconds and became football's new champions.

The statistical ledger slightly favored the Browns. Cleveland compiled a 22–20 edge in first downs and a 372–334 edge in total yards. The Rams had the edge in takeaways, 4–3. Aside from Graham, who averaged 8.6 yards on five carries and was the game's leading rusher, neither team's running game did much. Towler, Motley, Carpenter, Jones, Tank Younger, Dick Hoerner, Vitamin Smith, and Glenn Davis were all held in check; the

Rams rushed for just 1.9 yards per carry, while the Browns other than Graham totaled only 49 yards and a 2.7 average.

The teams combined for 553 passing yards, but those yards did not come easily, either. Graham was nineteen of forty for 280 yards, three interceptions, and one touchdown. Speedie caught seven for 81, Lavelli four for 66, Jones four for 62, and Carpenter three for 48. Waterfield and Van Brocklin were a combined thirteen of thirty, good for 253 yards with two interceptions, with Fears catching four for 146 and Hirsch four for 66. It was the big play that turned the tide in the Rams' favor: the Van Brocklin to Fears touchdown pass and the forced fumble by Brink. Cleveland's biggest play, on the other hand—Speedie's long touchdown catch—was negated by a penalty.

"It was a very disappointing loss," Agase said. "We weren't quite as sharp as we normally were on offense." That assessment squares with most of the pertinent facts. The Cleveland defense held the high-powered Rams to almost 9 fewer points than their season average. Cleveland, meanwhile, scored 10 fewer points than its season average against a team that was only in the middle of the pack in scoring defense.

It was therefore understandable that linebacker and defensive captain Tony Adamle resented Paul Brown's postgame remarks that put the onus for the defeat on the defense. Adamle took the remarks so hard that they contributed to his decision to retire. If anything, the loss underscored problems with the running game, particularly the decline of the injured and aging Motley.

Motley was approaching thirty-two and was never able to round into form after hurting his knee in training camp. All of his 1951 rushing statistics—273 yards, 4.5 average, and one touchdown—were well below his five previous seasons. Similarly, Motley's 23 yards on five carries against the Rams was a far cry from the many big Championship Game performances of his career.

For the sixth straight season, the defense was outstanding. The Browns posted four shutouts and led the NFL in fewest points allowed. The unit proved itself especially opportunistic with fifty-one takeaways, an average of better than four per game. Twenty-nine of those takeaways were fumble recoveries, an NFL record that stood until the advent of the fourteen-game season.

Gillom was the league's leading punter with a 45.5 average, Lavelli was fifth in receptions, Groza was second in placekicking behind Waterfield, Graham was third in passing, and Jones's twelve touchdowns placed him second behind Hirsch. Adamle, Carpenter, Graham, Lavelli, Groza, Jones, Willis, and Len Ford all played in the Pro Bowl.

Graham, Ford, Willis, and Jones were unanimous all-pro selections. Lavelli, Groza, Gatski, Adamle, and Lahr were consensus first-team choices, and Rymkus, Gibron, Houston, Kissell, and Thompson got second-team notice. Graham received the third MVP award of his career, and Brown was named Coach of the Year by the *Sporting News* and the *New York Daily News*.

Despite the many accolades and awards, the season was a bittersweet one. On the one hand, Cleveland's regular season record equaled the best in the NFL since 1942, and many of the team's core players were at or near their peaks. There was, therefore, no reason to believe that the team's great success would not continue. Opponents were already all too aware, too, that the Browns had an uncanny knack of coming up with new players who were often as good or better whenever someone departed.

Still, the Championship Game loss to the Rams was a big disappointment. The franchise's tremendous success in so short a time had pushed the bar to the highest rung on the expectations ladder. The Browns had truly fulfilled their coach's 1946 goal for them; they had become the Yankees of football. As with their baseball counterpart, that meant anything less than a championship was unacceptable. So while they looked with pride at what they had accomplished, the Browns also looked to 1952 facing the new challenge of whether they could reclaim their place atop the football world.

11

Lake Erie Rivalry

New in 1952: Darrell Brewster (E), Bob Gain (DT), Jerry Helluin (DT), Sherman Howard (HB), Walt Michaels (LB), George Ratterman (QB), Bert Rechichar (DB), Ray Renfro (HB), Ed Sharkey (G), Joe Skibinski (G)

Gone from 1951: Tony Adamle, Alex Agase, Bob Gaudio, Chubby Grigg, Cliff Lewis, Bob Oristaglio, Don Phelps, Lou Rymkus, Carl Taseff

Remaining from 1946 (9): Gatski, Graham, Groza, Houston, Lavelli, Motley, Speedie, Willis, Young

With the retirement of Cliff Lewis, who in addition to playing safety was Cleveland's second quarterback, Paul Brown acquired several players through trades and the draft as possible backups behind Graham. Graham would turn thirty-one before the year was out. In the back of his mind, Brown was also thinking ahead to the day when someone would have to step into Graham's shoes.

There was little doubt that, barring injury, Graham had a number of good years left. But Brown had not earned a reputation as someone who left little to chance for nothing. He also lived by the maxim coined by Branch Rickey: Better to get rid of a player a year too soon than a year too late. That way, your team would not suffer from that player's declining performance, and you could still get about maximum return in exchange.

Brown played that game well. In the short time since he had built the first Browns team, a number of outstanding players had been traded or encouraged to retire, including some of Brown's personal favorites. Edgar Jones, Saban, Yonakor, Colella, Ulinski, and Humble had all come and gone by 1952. In addition, mainstays Lewis, Adamle, Rymkus, Gaudio, Agase, and Grigg were all gone just since the previous season. Brown once called trading or releasing players the most difficult part of his job. But he had not yet let the difficulty of doing so get in the way of strengthening the team if he believed that that would be the end result.

Graham was different. For one thing, he was the first player Brown ever signed, and the coach held a special regard for his quarterback. For another, he was an extension of Brown on the field. An unassuming, no-nonsense leader, Graham very quietly gained the respect of his teammates through dedication and by consistently playing his best at the most difficult moments. And he was a tremendous football player. His best was a level rarely seen before or since.

Graham, to some degree, may also have been the player Brown, an old Miami of Ohio quarterback, wished he could have been. He was brilliant right from the start of his career at all aspects of the game's most demanding position. By 1952 Graham had already accomplished more than all of the quarterbacks in the game's history by whatever measures one chooses to use—winning percentage, passing titles, MVP awards, or championships.

Brown thus knew better than anyone that Graham would be virtually impossible to replace. Even more difficult would have been deciding to get rid of the man he would consistently refer to as the greatest player ever to play the game. 1952 was not the time when Brown would have to face the prospect of the Cleveland Browns without Graham; but that day would come eventually, and Brown began preparing accordingly.

To that effect, Cleveland added several quarterbacks in 1952. One,

George Ratterman, was an old rival from the All-America Football Conference. He had a special clause in his contract that stipulated that he did not have to accompany the Yanks in the event the team moved from New York. When owner Ted Collins sold the franchise back to the league and the Dallas Texans were organized to take its place, Ratterman became a free agent and signed with the Browns.

When Ratterman joined the Browns, he had five years of pro experience under his belt but was still only twenty-five. He was good enough that he could have stepped into a starting job with several teams, yet Cleveland was the only team he contacted. Ratterman was that impressed with Paul Brown and the Browns organization, and he wanted to be a part of their dynasty. He thought them the best football team he'd ever seen.

After his playing career, Ratterman was a football broadcaster for many years. That career spanned the Packers dynasty of the 1960s and the Steelers dynasty of the 1970s. Almost six decades after seeing the Browns for the first time, Ratterman still considers them the best team he's ever seen.

Ratterman was a practical joker who even played jokes on Paul Brown, a man not known for his sense of humor and one who did not consider anything concerning football to be at all funny. One of Ratterman's best stunts was in 1949 while he was with the Bills. He was a member of the AAFC all-star team that played against the Browns in Houston that December.

Several days before the game, he called the front desk of the hotel where the Browns were staying, identified himself as Paul Brown, and instructed the hotel operator to call all of Cleveland's players and notify them that the team's practice scheduled for that day was cancelled. Brown soon remedied matters but apparently never knew that Ratterman was the perpetrator of the joke.

Ratterman's reputation as a joker should not obscure the fact that he was a good quarterback. He had four good seasons with the Bills and Yanks and was a second-team all-league selection in 1947 and 1950. He was a more than adequate backup for four years behind Graham. Although he didn't play often, the Browns barely missed a beat when he did. His numbers during those four years—89 for 147, good for 1,290 yards and fourteen touchdowns with only eight interceptions—work out to a passer rating of 98.2 That's very good for any era and superlative for the 1950s.

When Graham retired, Ratterman stepped in and became the starting quarterback. His tenure as the starter was short-lived, however. In just the fourth game of the 1956 season, he suffered a serious knee injury and never played again.

The Browns also drafted quarterbacks Harry Agganis from Boston University with the second of two first-round picks and Don Klosterman of Loyola University in Los Angeles in the third round. Ratterman held off the rookie challengers, however, and won the backup spot. Klosterman played briefly with the Rams and then began a long front-office career. A great all-around athlete, Agganis showed great promise in parts of two seasons with the Boston Red Sox, but he died tragically at twenty-six of a pulmonary embolism in 1955. He and Klosterman were among the first of many young quarterbacks Brown would bring to the Browns in the hopes of catching lightning in a bottle.

With Gorgal, Konz, and Taseff unavailable because of military obligations, Cleveland used its first draft choice to select Bert Rechichar, a tough-as-nails defensive back from the University of Tennessee who won a starting job. End Darrell "Pete" Brewster, who was acquired from the Cardinals shortly after the draft; back Ray Renfro; defensive tackle Jerry Helluin; and guard Joe Skibinski were rookies who made the team as backups. In trades the Browns reacquired Walt Michaels, who won one of the starting linebacking openings created by the departures of Adamle and Agase. Also in trades came back Sherman Howard and guard Ed Sharkey, AAFC veterans with the Yankees who had also played for the NFL Yanks.

Although neither would play much in 1952 (Brown hated to play rookies unless absolutely necessary), Brewster and Renfro would make the biggest long-term impact of the new players, along with Gain. Renfro had the kind of speed Brown craved. Where prior to his arrival Lahr and James were probably the fastest players on the team, Renfro gained that honor in his first training camp.

In his rookie year, Renfro did little more than return punts. Eventually, he played well both out of the backfield and as a wide receiver. Renfro was never a consistent threat like Speedie or Lavelli, but he was dangerous nonetheless. His career mark of 19.6 yards per catch is the second best in team history behind Paul Warfield, and he made his receptions count, scoring a touchdown every 5.4 catches. Brown said of Renfro that he "was a great competitor and an inspiration to his teammates," in part because of a willingness to play with injuries.

Brewster, too, eventually blossomed after playing behind Speedie and Lavelli in his rookie season. At mid-decade he would lead the team in receptions three straight years and be selected to the Pro Bowl twice. Playing opposite Brewster in practice for four years, James was impressed by his teammate's willingness to listen to suggestions and utilize them in making himself a better player. In his nine-year career, Brewster averaged 17.9 yards per catch.

Gain was the newcomer who was the most heralded and who contributed the most despite missing half the season with a broken jaw. Together with Kissell, Palmer, and Helluin, Gain gave Cleveland the power in the middle of the line that Brown considered so important to a good defense. But over his twelve-season career, Gain proved to be far more than just an outstanding tackle. He also played middle guard, middle linebacker, and end, excelling at all of them.

Likening him to Agase, Brown said Gain "was someone who had great instincts" and "consistently seemed to be in the right place at the right time." Teammate Chuck Noll cited Gain's ability to "parallel and read" (diagnose a play while fighting off blocks and moving laterally along the line of scrimmage) as part of the reason for his success. And Jim Brown and Gain himself have both noted that Gain brought an aggressive, even thuggish dimension to the Browns.

"He was right in front of me," said longtime opponent Dick Stanfel, a guard who played against Gain with the Lions and Redskins, "and we went at it pretty good. Good player. Strong, tough guy. I wished it was somebody else playing in front of me at that time. He was an aggressive, hard-nosed player."

Among the impressive group of veterans who did not return in 1952, offensive tackle Lou Rymkus was the most noteworthy. An original Brown like Lewis, Rymkus had been one of the team's best players for six years. Together with Groza, Rymkus formed one of the best tackle tandems in football, and he was one of the anchors of an outstanding offensive line that itself was the anchor of the Cleveland offense.

Brown called Rymkus "the best pass protector I've ever seen." Walt Michaels said Rymkus was the standard the Cleveland coaches used to teach pass blocking. "Pass protection as it's taught started with Lou

Rymkus," said Michaels, who, in addition to his fine ten-year playing career, was a longtime college and pro coach.

"He was a great tackle," Joe Signaigo said of Rymkus, "one of the best blocking tackles in the business." Signaigo played with Rymkus at Notre Dame and then against him in both the AAFC and the NFL. "When he threw those arms up, those elbows up, it looked like it covered about six feet. You couldn't get around him."

"One great ballplayer," Ken Carpenter said of Rymkus. "Nobody got by him."

As is often the case with offensive linemen, Rymkus has been overlooked somewhat because of the many other extraordinary players that were on the team at more glamorous positions. However, his teammates were very aware of how good Rymkus was. Some mention him as someone who belongs in the Hall of Fame. Rymkus was a senior nominee one year but failed to gain induction.

The evidence in support of Rymkus is certainly compelling. He was named as at least a second-team all-pro in every one of the seven seasons he played, garnering first-team honors five times, including in his rookie season with the Redskins. In both 1946 and 1949 he was named to the first team of the joint AAFC/NFL all-pro team, and he was all-AAFC/NFL second team in 1948.

Rymkus's teams were similarly successful every year that he played. His teams were a perfect seven for seven in making it to their league Championship Game, winning five times. And to top it off, Rymkus was also perfect as a head coach: In his first and only full season, Rymkus coached the Houston Oilers to the 1960 AFL championship.

It's also worth pointing out that the radically different nature of pro football's economics partly explains the fact that Rymkus played only seven seasons. Although by 1951 he was bothered by pain in his elbow that was sometimes quite severe, Rymkus said he could have played several more years, and it's clear from the record that this is true. However, he retired when he did because he wanted a career in coaching, and he was offered a coaching job that paid him about what he had earned as a player in 1951.

That a player who was an all-pro every year could earn as much working as an assistant coach or in any other job is almost unfathomable today. In the 1950s and before, however, it was quite common. Great contemporaries of Rymkus's like Stanfel, Lou Creekmur, and Doak Walker retired early in part for the same reason, as did many other less accomplished players. Yet when Rymkus was rejected for the Hall of Fame as a senior finalist, one of the main stumbling blocks was the brevity of his career. That was also likely the case when Stanfel failed to gain induction, and it is probably the main reason Creekmur was not inducted until almost forty years after he retired.

As with Speedie, perhaps one of the other reasons Rymkus is not in the Hall of Fame is that he played four of his seven seasons in the AAFC. The argument that the AAFC was a major league about as good as the NFL has already been made and will not be repeated. However, it's noteworthy that Rymkus was named as a first-team all-pro in the NFL in 1943 and then as a second-teamer in 1950 and 1951 after the Browns joined the league. To say that he was an elite player in 1943 and then again in 1950 and 1951 but not for four years in between when he was playing in a supposedly inferior league—the illogical nature of the proposition is obvious just in the stating of it.

Again like Speedie, Rymkus also missed prime seasons of his career to military service. The loss of the 1944 and 1945 seasons is additional explanation for why his career was comparatively short, at least by more recent standards. Rymkus was already thirty-two when he played his last game. More important, it reflects an uneven attitude on the part of Hall of Fame voters toward outstanding players who lost time from their pro careers because of World War II.

Time lost to military service was factored in fairly when Hall voters did the right thing and elected Ace Parker, Bill Dudley, Tony Canadeo, George McAfee, and Charlie Trippi, but it was not in the cases of Rymkus and Speedie. And that's even though the credentials of the two Browns are stronger than those five players, as are those of several players from other teams, including Stanfel, who lost time to the military in the 1940s and also remain outside looking in.

One other newcomer in 1952 was announcer Ken Coleman, the man who could accurately be called "the Voice of the Browns." He worked radio his first two years and then switched to television in 1954, where he remained through 1965. Coleman did the national television broadcasts of many of the team's postseason games in those years before shifting strictly to baseball and college basketball in 1966.

After splitting four preseason games, the Browns thrashed the Rams at Municipal Stadium in the season opener, 37–7, in a rematch of the Championship Game. Cleveland's running game and the defense were the keys. As he had in 1951, Carpenter showed the kind of form the Browns hoped would make him the team's next great runner. He rushed for 145 yards and 9.1 per carry, while Motley added 69 and Jones 53 as the team piled up a total of 291 yards on the ground.

Van Brocklin, Waterfield, Hirsch, Fears, and Boyd were completely stifled as the Rams completed only six of twenty-seven passes for 65 yards. The Browns intercepted three and kept Los Angeles off the scoreboard until the fourth quarter. The 7 points was by far a season low for the Rams, who averaged 31 in the rest of their games and led the league in scoring for the third straight year.

The following week Cleveland played the Steelers on a Saturday night for the second time in three years. The Saturday-night game between the two teams was an on-and-off thing for a dozen years before becoming a yearly tradition in 1963. Playing one of their games under the lights added a little zest to a rivalry that in the 1950s was still in its infancy. The Saturday night tradition was discontinued after 1970.

Graham led the way as Cleveland rallied to win at Forbes Field, 21–20, as he passed for a career-high 401 yards and connected on touchdowns of 68 yards to Motley, 17 yards to Jones, and 57 yards to Howard. A missed Steelers extra point after their first touchdown was Cleveland's margin of victory. Howard's scoring catch was his second in two games.

The Browns and Giants continued their series of defensive struggles the following week as New York took sole possession of first place in the American Conference with a 17–9 win in Cleveland. Speedie had a big day with eight catches for 161 yards, but it was Tom Landry who had the last word against his old nemesis with a 30-yard interception return for the touchdown that clinched the game for the Giants. Cleveland's points came on three Groza field goals, including one of 52 yards.

The injury bug that would plague the Browns all season hit the team hard as Carpenter and Lavelli were sidelined against the Giants. Each would miss four entire games and parts of others throughout the season.

In the six games they had played against each other, New York and Cleveland had combined to score just 110 points.

Graham next threw for 290 yards and four touchdowns, and Ratterman added a touchdown pass as Cleveland destroyed the Eagles, 49–7. The Browns outgained Philadelphia 507 yards to 162, and as it had against the Rams, the defense came within a few minutes of a shutout. Jagade ran for 98 yards on just eleven carries, and Groza had another milestone day as he broke the all-time record of eighty-four consecutive conversions without a miss. This, however, was the game in which Gain suffered a broken jaw. He did not return until December.

Groza kicked the Browns into sole possession of first place with four field goals in a 19–15 win against the Redskins as Cleveland rallied from a 13–6 deficit. Graham's go-ahead touchdown run was set up by another long connection to Howard of 57 yards. Gillom got in on the kicking action with an excellent punting day that included one kick of 73 yards.

In victory, however, the Browns suffered a setback as Howard's season ended when he suffered a shoulder injury. Although a backup, Howard had provided an important spark with a series of long plays in the season's first five games. His 219 receiving yards came on just eleven catches, good for a 19.9-yard average and three touchdowns. His absence would prove especially telling late in the season when Cleveland's running game bogged down and a number of front-line offensive players were lost to injuries.

The following week Cleveland slipped back into a tie with the Giants at 4–2 with a 17–6 loss in Detroit. The Lions pressured Graham all day and limited the Browns to 214 yards from scrimmage. For the second time in four games, Groza scored all of Cleveland's points. His two field goals raised his season total to twelve. Just halfway through the season, he was one away from the NFL record he had set in 1950 and that Waterfield equaled in 1951, and just three away from Agajanian's all-time record.

The win boosted the Lions to 6–2 and kept them in a first-place tie with the 49ers in the National Conference. Behind the leadership of head coach Buddy Parker and quarterback Bobby Layne, the Lions had gone from perennial weaklings to one of the NFL's best teams. In just three years, Detroit had added outstanding young players like Layne, Creekmur, Stanfel, Walker, end Leon Hart, and a trio of defensive backs that were the heart of a secondary known as Chris's Crew that was soon the league's best: Yale Lary, Jim David, and Jack Christiansen.

That core of young players was fortified by a group of recently acquired veterans. Center Vince Banonis and fullback Pat Harder were former teammates of Parker's with the Cardinals and had played for Chicago's 1947 championship team. Two of Detroit's other veterans, standout halfback Bob Hoernschmeyer and fullback Ollie Cline, had played in the AAFC, Hoernschmeyer with the Rockets, Dodgers, and Hornets and Cline with the Browns and Bills.

"I think the 4–3 defense originated with him [Parker] and his coaches," Dub Jones said of the Detroit team that so stifled Cleveland in that first ever meeting between the two teams. "They threw that in our face in '52 and it was tough for us to cope with, having not played it."

While Layne and Walker garnered most of the headlines, the Lions defense was as big a key to their success as any. They allowed the fewest points in 1952, unseating the Browns atop the NFL. It was one of only two times Cleveland would not finish first in that department in the twelve-year span from 1946 to 1957. The Lions also established a new NFL record with fifty-seven takeaways, an average of almost five per game.

The Browns continued their mastery of teams from Chicago with a 28–13 win over the Cardinals on November 9. The win improved their record against the Cardinals, Bears, and Rockets/Hornets to 14–0. Speedie, Motley, Graham, and Carpenter all had big days as the team piled up 423 yards and held Chicago to 15 yards passing.

Another 1-point win over the Steelers a week later put the 6–2 Browns in sole possession of first place again as the Giants lost to the Packers. The Browns built a 22–0 lead against Pittsburgh and held on to win, 29–28, behind 201 yards rushing, two touchdown grabs by a healthy Lavelli, and a first-quarter safety by Young that proved to be the decisive points. Groza added two field goals.

The Eagles catapulted themselves into the American race by beating the Browns, 28–20, in the season's ninth week. By day's end, Philadelphia, New York, and Cleveland were all tied for first at 6–3. Graham, Speedie, and Groza all continued their great play in the loss, Graham with 227 passing yards, Speedie with seven catches for 156 yards and touchdown grabs of 28 and 48 yards, and Groza with two more field goals that gave him sixteen and the all-time single-season record.

With a quarter of the season still remaining, the Browns' three losses were already the most in franchise history. Although any number of other teams would have traded places with them without a moment's hesitation, it was clear that 1952 was a little bit of a different kind of a season for the Browns. Years later Brown said that "a festering mood of selfishness had infected our team," led by players near the end of their careers who "wanted to get as much as they could for themselves and supported by others who put money ahead of their team."

Maybe that was an exaggeration, maybe not. Perhaps those words were the reflections of a great coach looking back with some degree of frustration at a comparatively disappointing season. Or perhaps the Browns were, in fact, undermined by selfishness. What seems more accurate is that the team, because of players lost to the military, numerous injuries, and premature retirements like Rymkus's, just did not have as many good players available in 1952. The drop-off is reflected by a number of key statistics.

As good as the Browns defense remained, the unit gave up more points than in any of its first nine seasons, an average of 17.8 per game. That was more than 7 points higher than the best of the dynasty seasons, 1946, and 5.5 higher than in the first two NFL seasons. The personnel changes in just one year were great, what with Lewis, Adamle, and Agase gone; Gorgal, Taseff, and first-round pick Konz completely unavailable; and Gain the best newcomer out with an injury for half the season. Such upheaval was more than the substantial talents of the rest of the unit could overcome. Shula and Herring were pressed into full-time starting roles for the first time, as was rookie Rechichar; all would be gone the following year.

But the offense was also playing at a level somewhat below the usual Browns standard, a fact disguised somewhat by some gaudy numbers. Graham and Speedie were again having seasons worthy of their status as the best in the game at their positions. Speedie was on his way to yet another receptions crown, Graham threw for a career-high 2,816 yards, and the team's 2,839 passing yards were the most in the league.

However, at thirty attempts per game, Graham was throwing the ball far more frequently than at any time in his career. His twenty-four interceptions and 49.7% completion percentage were also the worst figures of his ten seasons. In the symmetrical way that offense and defense are intertwined, weaknesses in one area can create weaknesses in other areas. Graham, for example, was pressed into throwing more because of some of the deficiencies of the defense, as the team found itself having to battle for points in a way they never had to before.

At the same time, turnovers and other offensive problems created more opportunities for opponents and put more pressure on the defense. While the defense allowed more points at any time during the dynasty years, the team's 310 points scored (25.7 per game) was also equal to the team's lowest mark of those years. Groza's great year, a year that saw him attempt a career-high thirty-three field goals, was both a reflection of his greatness as a kicker and of the offense's problems. Among those problems was a frequent inability to finish drives with touchdowns. Nine of Groza's field goals were from 24 yards or closer, and five were from 14 yards or less.

What ailed the Browns more than anything were problems in the running game. Motley showed occasional signs of his great form of 1946–1950, but he was no longer a dominant runner. He finished 1952 with 444 yards and a career-low 4.3 yards per carry (although in an increasingly pass-oriented league, the 444 yards was good enough for sixth place). Jones was steady, but he was not someone who could carry a heavy load in the running game, as his 5.4 carries per game in 1952 indicate.

More telling was the fact that none of the other runners who had taken a turn in the backfield since the departures of Boedeker, Parseghian, and Edgar Jones—Carpenter, Bumgardner, Cole, Moselle, Phelps, and Jagade—had become a top-notch NFL runner. Carpenter and, to a lesser extent, Cole and Jagade had shown flashes of what the team was looking and hoping for, but something was missing. Motley had always been good for more than a fair share of long runs, big yardage totals on not many carries, and tremendous performances in the biggest games. When he was no longer able to do so to anywhere near the same degree, the team suffered. Perhaps what the dip in the running game revealed more than anything was Motley's greatness.

Still, even without Motley at his best, the Browns had gone 11–1 in 1951 and were on their way to another conference championship in 1952. In fact, the Browns continued their dynasty run despite an ever-changing cast of running backs. After Motley led the team in rushing in each of its first five seasons, no player did so more than once in the next five years. And where for five years Motley had been football's best player at his position, only Dub Jones in 1951 could make that claim among the team's backs in the next five seasons (and in Jones's case, that was as much for his achievements as a receiver as for what he did as a runner).

And yet other teams longed to have Cleveland's problems. The team's strength was evident as first the offense and then the defense performed in dominant fashion as the season entered the home stretch. First the offense piled up 448 yards of total offense as the Browns manhandled Washington 48–24. Jagade had 127 yards rushing and a touchdown, Carpenter showed his versatility with a big day returning punts including one for a 54-yard backbreaking touchdown, Jones caught a touchdown pass and threw for another, and Graham passed for two scores and ran for two others.

Next the defense completely shut down the Cardinals in a 10–0 victory. Cleveland forced five turnovers and held Chicago to 152 yards. The Browns didn't do much on offense, but a 56-yard Graham to Jones touchdown pass on the third play of the game staked them to an early lead, and a Groza field goal in the third quarter put the game out of reach.

While the Browns were winning two in a row, the Giants lost to the Steelers and Redskins and were eliminated. Philadelphia lost to the Cardinals, beat the Texans, and went to the final week one game behind the Browns. The Eagles would close at Washington, while Cleveland's last game was in New York.

In contrast to all of their previous meetings, the Browns and Giants game was a wild shootout. New York broke the game open with three third-quarter touchdowns and held on to win, 37–34, to sweep the season series. As they had all year, Graham, Speedie, and Groza led the Browns on offense. Graham threw two touchdown passes; Groza added two field goals and finished with nineteen; and Speedie won his fourth receiving crown, finishing with sixty-two catches. Jagade also scored twice. The loss was Cleveland's first ever in a regular season game in December after ten straight wins.

Throughout the afternoon, the Polo Grounds scoreboard showed that the Eagles-Redskins game was close. As they fought desperately for a comeback win that would eliminate any need for a playoff in the event Philadelphia won, Cleveland's casualties mounted. Perhaps the injuries would have occurred irrespective of the team needing to win the game. As it was, Groza, Speedie, Jones, Kissell, and James all sustained serious injuries against the Giants.

However, the Browns clinched first place despite the loss when the Redskins scored two fourth-quarter touchdowns to turn a 21–14 deficit into a 27–21 victory over the Eagles in the last game of Sammy Baugh's great career. Bobby Walston missed three field goals for Philadelphia. Washington's last score broke a 21–21 tie with 0:18 seconds left, and the Eagles could do nothing in their final desperate possession.

After losing to the Browns and twice to the Lions in their first four games, the defending champion Rams won eight in a row, gained a tie for first place in week nine, and finished tied atop the National at 9–3 with the Lions. The Lions proved to be too much in the playoff, however. Having won the coin toss for home field advantage, Detroit built a 24–7 lead behind two touchdowns and a field goal by Harder and beat Los Angeles for a third time that season. The Rams closed to 24–21 with two fourth-quarter touchdowns and got the ball back deep in their own territory in the final minute, but a Waterfield pass was intercepted and the Lions scored again and prevailed 31–21.

Despite an extra week off brought about because of the playoff, Speedie, Kissell, and Jones were unable to play in the Championship Game because of their injuries. James and Groza did play, but Groza in particular was hampered against the Lions. The drop-off in talent was most marked in the cases of Speedie and Jones and their replacements, Brewster and Renfro.

Brewster and Renfro both had solid careers ahead of them, but they were both rookies and neither had played much during the season. Where Speedie had been football's best end for six years and had led the league in receptions in 1952, Brewster caught just four passes that year. Jones caught forty-three passes, good for 651 yards, rushed for 270 more, and scored six touchdowns, while his replacement Renfro caught only one pass for 8 yards, rushed for just 26, and did not score any touchdowns.

Still, the Browns had reason to be confident. They were playing in their seventh straight Championship Game, while the Lions were making their first title-game appearance in seventeen years. Only Harder, Banonis, and Jim Martin among the Lions had previous Championship Game experience. The Browns also caught a break in that it was the American Conference's turn to host the game, which meant it would be in Cleveland despite Detroit's superior record, 9–3 to 8–4. Plus the Lions had had to play an extra game, while Cleveland had two weeks to rest, heal, and prepare.

The Lions were a bit of an unknown quantity in 1952. They had had a very good year in 1951, losing out on first place only in the dying moments of the season. They bounced back and prevailed in 1952 in the annual multiteam dogfight that was the National/Western Conference in that era. But the Detroit players who are now legendary heroes of the team's golden age of the 1950s were not yet that in the days leading up to their meeting with the Browns.

In a strange twist, the Lions were the young upstarts while the Browns, who had been cast in that role just two years before, were the entrenched power of pro football. The people who doubted that Cleveland was a great football team were far fewer in number by 1952. But while Layne, Walker, Hart, Lary, and Christiansen had all been great players in college, their collective greatness with the Lions had yet to be established. The Championship Game against the Browns would be a big step in that direction.

The 1952 title game was the most frustrating game in the long history of the Cleveland Browns. The Browns had distinct statistical advantages on both sides of the ball. They outgained Detroit 384 yards to 258, had a twenty-two to ten advantage in first downs, and ran seventy plays to Detroit's forty-four. But they also turned the ball over twice in crucial spots, first on an interception that bounced off Renfro's hands and into Jim David's arms deep in Detroit territory and then on a fumbled punt by Carpenter that set up Detroit's final 3 points. The Lions, meanwhile, played turnover-free football.

Most striking was Cleveland's inability to score more than 7 points despite numerous opportunities. Time and again they drove deep into Detroit territory; time and again they were rebuffed by the Detroit defense and went away empty-handed. In all, the Browns made seven forays deep into Detroit territory but were rebuffed on all but one.

The first three of those forays—to the Detroit 17, 31, and 32—came in the first half and resulted in missed field goal attempts by Groza. In the third quarter, David's interception thwarted a drive that reached the 24, and in the fourth Cleveland turned the ball over on downs on one drive that reached the 5 and on another that reached the 8.

Despite its generally lethargic play, meanwhile, the Lions offense was able to break a big play as Walker ran 67 yards in the third quarter for a 14–0 Detroit lead. Layne had scored the first touchdown on a 2-yard run in the first quarter. After Jagade scored on a 7-yard run to cut the lead to 14–7, Cleveland set out on a drive that seemed to have them well positioned to tie the game. But in the biggest sequence of the game, they were turned away by the best of Detroit's defensive stands.

The sequence began when Motley broke loose from midfield and raced toward the end zone. It was the kind of play Motley had broken in Championship Game wins over the Yankees, Bills, and 49ers, the kind of play Cleveland so often came up with to match big ones like Walker's. It was also one of several occasions when Motley flashed his old form, as the Cleveland fullback totaled 95 yards from scrimmage on just nine combined carries and receptions.

Perhaps two or three years earlier Motley would have scored. But his knees were bad and he was playing against men who were now as many as ten years younger than he was, and the Detroit pursuit caught up with him at the 5-yard line. Still, the Browns were in good shape, with four cracks to get the tying score.

But then the defense of the Lions came up big. On first and goal Motley was caught behind the line for a loss, then Graham was sacked at the 22 by the Lions' rampaging front line. After Graham was able to pick up only a yard on a scramble after again being pressured, setting up a fourth down, Brown took a calculated gamble. Figuring that his team would not get as good a chance the rest of the game, he eschewed a field goal and went for the touchdown.

The decision was a risky one. The odds of converting a fourth and goal from the 21 were not good in any circumstance, and Detroit was playing inspired defense when backed up against its own goal line. But even with a field goal, Brown reasoned, the Browns would still need a touchdown later. His defense was playing well so even if they came up short, there was a good chance Cleveland could get the ball back soon with the score still 14–7.

Besides, a field goal was no sure thing. Playing with cracked ribs, Groza was already zero for three on the day, although two of his misses were from the relatively long range of 44 and 47 yards (the other was from 28). So the Browns went for it. It was a doomed play from the start. With his downfield receivers all covered, Graham threw short over the middle to Motley well shy of the goal line, and the pass was batted down.

The defense did indeed dig in and force a punt, but Carpenter fumbled the kick and Harder converted from 36 yards a few plays later to put Detroit two scores ahead at 17–7. Still the Browns pressed on. Playing like true champions, they showed no signs of quitting and again drove all the way to the 8-yard line.

Graham passed to the end zone and for a brief moment the 50,934 fans let out a roar as Brewster caught the ball for an apparent touchdown. Only several minutes remained, but perhaps a miracle was still possible. But it was no touchdown. Brewster had caught the ball after it was tipped by Renfro. Under rules then in force, such a double touch by offensive teammates was an incompletion. Further Cleveland attempts failed, with Brown again passing on a field goal on fourth down, and for the sixth and final time the Browns were turned away deep in Detroit's end of the field. When the Lions ran out the clock, they were the new champions.

Renfro and Brewster played about as well as could be expected in place of Jones and Speedie. Renfro caught four passes for 26 yards and ran three times for 13 more. Brewster caught two passes for 53 yards. Jagade had a big day with 104 yards on fifteen carries, and Motley added 74 on just six carries and caught three passes for 21 more. Bumgardner and Lavelli each caught four passes.

Although Graham completed twenty of thirty-five passes, they were good for only 191 yards, or 5.46 yards per pass, a figure that is all the more striking in that Graham is football's all-time leader at 8.98 yards per attempt. The absence of Speedie and Jones forced the Browns to go with a more conservative, short-range passing game. Then again, the Lions had completely shut down the Browns with Speedie and Jones and a healthy Groza in the lineup in their regular season matchup.

"I've been saying all along that Detroit had the best club in the league," said a stoical Paul Brown afterward. "I guess this proves it."

The Lions win came nine days after Bobby Layne's twenty-sixth birthday, and the Lions quarterback later said that "nothing was ever as good as that. That was the happiest I ever was in football."

In addition to his field goal record, Groza finished third in scoring with 89 points, and Gillom's 45.7 punting average was again the best in the NFL. Graham was fourth in passing and Speedie first in receptions. Home attendance was up slightly to just over 40,000 per game. That was an increase of over 8,000 per game from the low water mark of 1949.

Groza parlayed his outstanding kicking and line play into selection to all of the major all-pro teams. Ford also was a unanimous choice while Graham, Speedie, Gatski, and Willis were named first-teamers on at least one all-pro team. Lahr and Thompson were second-teamers. Graham, Groza, Willis, Ford, Gillom, and Gibron were selected to the Pro Bowl.

The decline of the running game, the continued unavailability of players because of military obligations, and injuries to key players on both sides of the ball that kept some of them out of numerous games, most notably the Championship Game, hurt the Browns throughout 1952. Two straight seasons had ended in frustration, and more and more veteran players had retired or were approaching retirement. But the Browns were by no means dead; far from it. 1953 would prove to be a momentous year in the history of the franchise. After an offseason of upheaval, the team would play as well as it ever had, only to experience still more frustration.

CHAPTER **12**

Groza and Gillom

What has more recently come to be known as "the kicking game" has been an integral part of pro football since the first game was played. From the days of the dropkick and the quick kick to the modern era of specialists, kicking the ball with skill has always been of the utmost strategic value to winning. Teams that have been outplayed in other areas of the game have always been able to make up that difference if they had players who possessed superior punting and placekicking (or dropkicking) skills.

There were no specialists in the first four decades of the pro game. The players who did a team's kicking were just that: players who, in addition to their skills as tackle, end, guard, or back, also did the team's kicking. The only exception was Ben Agajanian, whose kicking skills enabled him to play in three different pro leagues in three different decades.

By the time tackle and placekicker Lou Groza and end and punter Horace Gillom joined the Browns, a number of outstanding kickers had made their mark in the game. Paddy Driscoll, Jack Manders, and Parker Hall were some of the best kickers of pro football's first quarter century. Still active in 1947 were Ward Cuff (three times the NFL's field goal leader and soon to be four), Sammy Baugh (who set punting records that stand to this day), and Bob Waterfield and Bill Dudley (players whose kicking skills helped them become among the first members of the Pro Football Hall of Fame).

Although coaching and strategy were less sophisticated and thorough in the 1940s than they later became, stripped to their essentials, the objectives of both punting and placekicking were the same then as they are today: distance and accuracy. The best punters kicked the ball far and, depending on field position, toward the sidelines. Quick kicks also required that a punter be able to kick without benefit of a full approach and, occasionally, on the run.

Placekickers had to be able to get consistent depth on kickoffs, be able to make a high percentage of extra points and short field goals, and be able to occasionally connect from long and medium-long range. Although it was by no means a hard and fast rule, the best teams tended to have above average, and sometimes exceptional, kicking games. Baugh's Redskins and Cuff's Giants were perennial championship contenders, the Bears teams Manders played on won four conference crowns in eight years, and the Rams were contenders throughout Waterfield's career.

Lou Groza did not change the technique of or approach to placekicking; he simply did it better than anybody had done it before. Teams had always known that the farther and more accurately a placekicker could kick, the more valuable he was to the overall goal of winning. Groza not only raised the bar on both accuracy and distance, he also raised it at a faster pace than anybody had before or has since. Teams with poor, average, and even above average kickers suddenly found themselves at a huge disadvantage when they played the Cleveland Browns.

Although he did not become a consistently great kicker until 1950, Groza set the tone for what was to come in 1946. Driscoll had set the all-time single-season pro record of twelve field goals in the sixteen-game season of 1926. Groza passed that mark in his rookie year with thirteen in a fourteen-game season.

Before Groza, Driscoll also held the record for field goals of 50 or more yards with two, a feat he accomplished in a ten-year, 118-game career. Groza equaled that mark in his first year and passed it in his third in his twenty-seventh career game. Groza was not knocked from his perch as the career leader in field goals of 50 yards or more until the era of the kicking specialist was well into its second generation in 1973.

Paul Brown was as incredulous as anyone in 1946 when he first saw Groza warming up his leg any time the Browns offense reached midfield. After Groza proved himself more than capable of hitting from long distances, however, the Cleveland coach was quick to take advantage of Groza's great range whenever possible.

"I reasoned that there are just so many . . . times when your offense has a chance to score," Brown said. "I wanted to take advantage of every opportunity. That's where a long-range field-goal kicker like Groza helped us put a lot of games out of reach of the opposition which didn't have a kicker like him."

The numbers bear Brown out. For example, as thoroughly as they dominated the AAFC, the Browns would not have been anywhere near as dominant without Groza. Points that he put on the scoreboard with his kicking were the difference between a win or a tie or loss in 15% of the team's games in four years. The percentage was even higher in the six NFL years of Cleveland's dynasty, and last-minute kicks by Groza won both the Eastern Conference playoff and NFL Championship Game on successive weeks in 1950.

"Everybody started to pay attention to field goals when the Browns started to win games with them," said Pat Summerall. Summerall was one of the better placekickers in football during his ten-year career, a career in which he played against Groza twice a year and thus saw up close what a potent weapon he was for the Browns. In a career that lasted almost as long as Groza's, Ben Agajanian was also familiar with the Cleveland kicker and the effective way he was utilized by Brown.

"He's the first coach in the history of pro football that used the field goal as an offensive weapon," Agajanian said of Brown. "He recognized that a field goal is half a touchdown and that if you get enough of them you can beat a team even if they score more touchdowns than you do." By contrast, Agajanian recalled that even after he set a new all-time record with fifteen field goals in 1947, a new coach the following year did not take full advantage of his kicking.

Few players at any position have put together the kind of dominant run Groza put together from 1950 through 1954. Groza led the NFL in highest field goal percentage three times and in field goals four times in that span. Three times he established a new NFL record for most field goals in a season. After establishing a new record in 1950 with thirteen,

Groza proceeded to shatter that mark with nineteen in 1952 and again in 1953 when he kicked twenty-three.

During those five seasons Groza also set the mark for most consecutive field goals made and became pro football's all-time career field goal leader. Perhaps most impressive was Groza's making twenty-three of twenty-six attempts in 1953. That 88.5% success rate shattered the previous record of 76.9% and stood as the single-season record for twenty-eight years.

In four different seasons Groza also accomplished something that has been done only thirteen times in history, something that is virtually impossible now, when he kicked 20% of his league's field goals. On five different occasions, Groza accomplished something else that will never be done again, something that no other kicker has ever done more than once, by kicking at least twice as many field goals as the average of the rest of the teams in his league. His 1952 and 1953 totals were 2.75 and 2.98 times higher than the average of the rest of the league, the two highest differentials since 1948. And in large part because of Groza, Cleveland's mark of kicking 1.75 more field goals per game than they allowed in 1953 is the second best mark ever, just a shade behind the 1.79 record established by Jim Turner and the 1968 Jets.

Groza was also one of the best offensive tackles in football during that portion of his career that he played that position, as he earned NFL all-pro honors six times. That he played for so long and at such a high level at a position like tackle makes Groza's accomplishments as a kicker all the more remarkable. He would spend play after play leading sweeps and pass protecting, blocking virtually every play against the likes of Gene Brito and Andy Robustelli, and then be called upon to kick field goals.

"I always admired Groza, grinding away at tackle" is how Ara Parseghian put it. "Then if the drive stalled, he'd move back into a kicking position. Remember, this was a long time before the soccer-style kicker. You'd have shoes that weren't as clean, from playing in the mud and snow. Before Groza would kick, he'd take a towel and wipe off his shoes. He wasn't all clean and rehearsed like the kickers of today."

"Lou never got all the credit he deserved for his tackle play, probably because his great kicking skills got him more notoriety," longtime opponent Robustelli said. "But while other offensive linemen rested, Lou kicked off and ran down to make tackles; kicked field goals and extra points; and then played left tackle on every offensive play, a truly remarkable achievement. He was a superb tackle whose strong point was pass blocking. Take it from someone who played against him, there is no denying his Hall-of-Fame spot."

Parseghian's and Robustelli's observations can also be applied to Groza's booming kickoffs. Groza was far above average throughout his career at being able to force touchbacks by sailing kickoffs into or out of the end zone. Groza deserves a lot of the credit for the remarkable fact that opposing teams did not return a single kickoff for a touchdown in a period of more than nine years beginning in 1946, a stretch of 137 regular and postseason games.

Finally, Groza was probably the best of his time in the often overlooked category of kicking extra points (a time when such kicks were not at all a given). He was either perfect or had the best extra-point percentage in twelve of his seventeen NFL seasons, and he also set a record by making 109 in a row from 1950 to 1953. As with virtually every other important placekicking category—points, field goals, field goal percentage—Groza held NFL career records for extra points and extra-point percentage for many years.

Horace Gillom was not only better than just about every punter that went before him, his skill also allowed the Browns to completely change the punting game. Although he kicked for tremendous distance, Gillom was like Groza in that he also positioned his kicks with great accuracy. This skill of Gillom's was particularly important on the numerous occasions when angling a kick toward the sidelines was as important or more important than the distance of the kick. Several Browns recalled that Gillom's ability to angle kicks without losing distance was especially effective in neutralizing the best punt returners of that era like Emlen Tunnell.

In addition, Gillom almost single-handedly introduced a whole new element to punting: hang time. The height Gillom got on his punts was as important for the prevention of good returns as either his positional or distance kicking skills. With Cleveland's coverage team better able to converge on punt returners, the Browns were able to force negligible returns or no returns at all with far greater frequency than other teams and thus gain yet another advantage over opponents.

"Horace Gillom was one of the best that ever came down the pike," Alex Agase said. "He not only kicked them far, he kicked them high. He was a great punter . . . just a super punter."

"Up to Yankee Stadium, people used to come out and just watch him kick the ball in the pregame warm-up," Dante Lavelli said.

"With most punters," Parseghian said, "the ball goes up and it comes down. But with Gillom, he'd just put the ball into orbit, it would level off and go for a while, and then it would come down. I'd match him with today's punters, all right."

"We didn't just go back 40 yards, we went back 50, 60 yards because he just kicked it so damn far and so high," said Otto Schnellbacher, who returned Gillom's punts as a member of both the Yankees and Giants.

"[H]e was the best punter that ever put a toe to the pigskin," Tommy James said, a sentiment that Paul Brown agreed with. "[T]here has never been a better punter than Horace," the Cleveland coach said.

In other subtle but important ways Gillom changed the face of punting. When he lined up to take the snap from center, for example, Gillom was able to stand 3 or more yards further back than was then the norm because of his powerful right leg. Rather than attempting to correct Gillom to conform to the standard procedure, Brown recognized the advantage to such positioning. Gillom's kicking power would make up for the difference in yards, Brown knew, and the deeper stance made it far more difficult for opponents to block Cleveland punts. And with the threat of an opponent getting to Gillom to block a kick greatly diminished, the coverage was better able to release and get down the field to stop a return.

"I never saw any equal in punting," Emerson Cole said. Cole also recalled another remarkable aspect of Gillom's punting ability. "He would tell us in the huddle, 'Go all out, because this one's going toward the other goal line,'" Cole said. "Other times he would say, 'Be under control, because this one's going to hit and come back.' He could control how the ball bounced."

Like Groza, Gillom was a force right from his rookie year. He averaged 44.6 yards per kick in 1947, a figure that was the fourth best of his ten-year career and just a fraction behind the AAFC leader that year. Also like Groza, however, Gillom really came into his own after the Browns joined the NFL. That may have been in part because Gillom saw far more action at end in 1948 and 1949 than he did at any other point in his career, catching forty-three passes, good for 15.2 yards per reception. In fact, when he was pressed into duty in 1948 because of an injury to Lavelli, Gillom relinquished his punting duties to Tom Colella.

Gillom's skills at end were such that his coach and teammates were convinced he could have been an outstanding player at that position had he not been playing on a team with Lavelli and Speedie. At the peak of his career, Brown was certain that every other NFL team would have benefited from having Gillom as an offensive end, a sentiment that James heartily agreed with.

"If he'd played for any other team but the Browns during his years, he'd have been playing offense because he was a great receiver," James said of a player he had to cover in practice for nine years. James was also sufficiently impressed by Gillom's performance as a fill-in on defense, most notably when Len Ford was hurt in 1950, to call him "a great two-way end."

Gillom's athletic prowess is reflected in the fact that, like so many of his teammates, he excelled at other sports besides football, most notably basketball. His skills were such that Brown called Gillom "the best all around athlete I coached at Massillon Washington High School. He was successful at everything he did."

When Gillom retired, his 43.8-yard NFL average was the second highest in league history behind Baugh's still-standing record of 45.1. Punters playing in the era of specialization have since passed him, but five decades after his retirement Gillom still ranks among the all-time leaders. Gillom is one of only a handful of players to lead the NFL in punting in two consecutive years, and he finished second by fractions of yards on several other occasions.

Gillom was a model of consistency as well, as his average never dropped below 41.2 in his seven NFL seasons. He ranked in the top three in his league in six of his eight years as a full-time punter, including five times in succession from 1950 through 1954, the very same seasons Groza was at his most dominating. And like Groza, Gillom rarely had a kick returned for a touchdown in a career in which he punted well over five hundred times in 127 regular and postseason games. In fact, he had a streak of over four hundred punts from the start of his career before one was returned for a touchdown.

* * *

While Graham, Motley, Lavelli, and Speedie certainly overshadowed Willis and the rest of the players on Cleveland's terrific defense, they cast even longer shadows over the team's two great kickers. Brown and the team's other players knew what they had, however, and knew that Gillom and Groza were of the utmost value to the team's seven championships. So, too, did opposing players like Summerall, Tunnell, and Schnellbacher.

No one game better illustrated that value than the Browns' 8–3 triumph over the Giants in the 1950 playoff for the American Conference title. With virtually all of Cleveland's offensive weapons rendered ineffective because of an outstanding New York defense, winter winds, a frozen field, and cold temperatures, Groza and Gillom tilted the balance of the game the Browns' way. Groza staked Cleveland to an early 3–0 lead and then won the game with a second field goal, while Gillom had a tremendous day, pinning New York down with poor field position that was a huge factor in keeping the Giants to just 3 points. Gillom may also have saved the day early in the game when he chased down a snap that sailed over his head and got off a punt on the dead run that traveled deep into New York territory.

Few teams have been fortunate enough to have either one of the very best punters or placekickers on their roster; far fewer still have had all-time elite players at both of those positions simultaneously for any length of time. Yet for *ten years*, including nine of their dynasty years, the Browns had precisely that in Gillom and Groza. The Kansas City Chiefs' great tandem of Jan Stenerud and Jerrell Wilson, teammates for eleven seasons, is the only one in football history that compares to Groza and Gillom.

13

Big Changes and a Third Straight Championship Game Loss

New in 1953: Doug Atkins (DE), Tom Catlin (LB), Don Colo (DT), Gene Donaldson (G), Ken Konz (DB), Chuck Noll (G/LB), Billy Reynolds (HB), Don Steinbrunner (T)

Gone From 1952: Rex Bumgardner, Emerson Cole, Hal Herring, John Kissell, Bert Rechichar, Ed Sharkey, Don Shula, Joe Skibinski, Mac Speedie

Remaining from 1946 (8): Gatski, Graham, Groza, Houston, Lavelli, Motley, Willis, Young

T HE 1953 OFFSEASON was one of the most eventful in Browns history. In a span of just a few months the franchise was sold, two starting players including one of their very best left for Canada, the team engineered one of the biggest trades in football history, their star quarterback held out, and players continued to go in and out of the military. In the player draft came a future

Hall of Fame defensive end and lots of other defensive help, although little of that help would manifest itself in 1953.

Shortly after being called to testify before the Senate's Kefauver Commission investigating organized crime, Mickey McBride decided to get out of football. He sold his majority interest in the Browns to a group headed by Davy Jones, Bob Gries, Ellis Ryan, Homer Marshman, and Sol Silberman for $600,000, twice as much as any sports franchise had ever sold for.

Ryan was a part owner of the Indians, Marshman had been one of the owners of the Rams in the 1930s before the team was sold to Dan Reeves, and Silberman was the owner of Randall Park Race Track. Jones was the majority owner and remained so for the next eight years. The team's success would continue, but Paul Brown's relationship with the new owners was occasionally rocky.

Not long after the sale, for example, Silberman began calling Brown for updates on the team and scouting reports on upcoming games. Suspecting that Silberman might be betting on games, Brown reported the calls to Commissioner Bert Bell. A short time later Silberman was forced to sell his interest in the team.

Looking in particular to strengthen his defense, Brown packaged ten players in a trade with the Colts. Shula, Sharkey, and Rechichar were among those who went to Baltimore in exchange for defensive tackle Don Colo, linebacker Tom Catlin, defensive back John Petitbon, middle guard Mike McCormack, and guard Herschel Forester. Although Petitbon, McCormack, and Forester were all in the military and only Colo and Catlin played for Cleveland in 1953, it was a great trade for the Browns and helped solidify them as a top team for the rest of the decade.

In McCormack and Colo, Cleveland got the two best of the fifteen players involved. McCormack would go on to the Hall of Fame, and Colo was a mainstay for seven years. Catlin and Forester played capably if not spectacularly for four seasons each, while Petitbon was a backup in the secondary for two seasons when he eventually joined the team in 1955. On the other side, four of those traded away never played pro football. Rechichar and Art Spinney, who was in the military and had never played for Cleveland, would play in the Pro Bowl, and Taseff, Rechichar, and Spinney would still be Colts during Baltimore's championship seasons in 1958 and 1959.

The acquisition of Colo was especially important because Gain was unavailable due to military obligations, and Kissell left to play in Canada. Gain would not return until the tail end of 1954, missing almost two full seasons. Free agent guard Harold Bradley was likewise unavailable until 1954 while he finished a tour of duty in the Marine Corps.

"I knew our guys did not like to play against him," Brown said of Colo. "That made him the kind of player I wanted for our team." Brown called Colo "a rough, almost brutal type of defensive tackle who punished offensive blockers." Longtime opponent Lou Creekmur of the Lions seconded that sentiment, saying, "Don Colo was a fierce competitor, a great defensive tackle with Cleveland."

Colo's presence on the Browns further muddies the popular notion that Cleveland was simply a finesse team markedly different from old-school brawling teams like the Bears and Lions who liked to intimidate with rough play. That finesse was supposedly a reflection of their cerebral, intellectual coach, who, after all, was a former quarterback, as well as the professorial assistant Collier. That notion is true as far as it goes, but as the team's rough play in the 1951 rout of the Bears illustrated, it is not the whole story.

In contrast to the Browns, Lions head coach Buddy Parker had been a linebacker, and his assistants included two former Monsters of the Midway, Aldo Forte and George Wilson, as well as Buster Ramsey and Russ Thomas. All were players out of the rough and tumble mold who brought that attitude to their coaching. Similarly, Halas and his assistants with the Bears like Hunk Anderson were throwbacks to a more primitive style of play.

But while it's true that Brown and his teams brought a great deal of finesse and intellectualism to football, they also had players who dished out more than their share of physical punishment. Colo, Gain, Kissell, Ford, Adamle, Willis, and Thompson were just some of the players from the NFL period of the team's dynasty years who made the defense one that could go toe to toe with any other, either in the trenches or in a brawl. Jim Brown noted that the Browns were a lesser team by decade's end when most of the players he endearingly referred to as "brawlers," "thugs," and "maniacs" were gone.

Newcomer Catlin epitomized Cleveland's deadly combination of aggressiveness and smarts as well as anyone. "Catlin, I think, was the most intelligent linebacker I have ever seen," McCormack said. "He just studied and analyzed everything . . . he just knew where to be—knew his defense, knew his coverage." And, McCormack added, Catlin "was tough."

Catlin would be a significant contributor to Cleveland's ascent back to the top of the football world. However, his stint with the team was interrupted by military service that cost him two full seasons and most of a third. Like so many of the Browns of that era, he had a long career as an assistant coach after his playing days.

The good news on the military front was that defensive backs Gorgal and rookie Konz were available, both after missing two years. They would team with Lahr and James and strengthen a secondary weakened in 1952 by their absences and the retirement of Cliff Lewis. Konz also impressed with his punt-returning skills and would eventually lead the league in that category.

Like his secondary mates, Konz had great speed. In fact, at that point, Konz, Lahr, and James were probably the fastest players on the team behind Renfro. Like Lahr and James, Konz had been an outstanding college player on offense as well as defense. Putting him at defensive back rather than on offense, where there were actually openings because of the departures of Bumgardner and Cole, was Brown's philosophy of utilizing great speed on defense at work again.

Of the rookies, first-round draft choice Doug Atkins, a defensive end from Tennessee, attracted the most attention. In an era when Len Ford, the end on the other side of the defense, was one of the NFL's biggest players at six foot five and 260 pounds, Atkins was something else altogether at six foot eight and 275. He was tremendously strong and not the least bit shy about taking an extra shot or mixing it up when necessary.

Perhaps most impressive, though, was how athletic Atkins was at that size. Players marveled at his quickness, speed, and agility. On several occasions during his brief tenure with the Browns, Atkins hurdled completely over an opponent attempting to block him on his way to the quarterback.

"Doug was probably the most talented defensive end I ever ran across," Derrell Palmer said, high praise from someone who played with and against such giants at the position as Ford, Andy Robustelli, Gino Marchetti, and Gene Brito. "That old boy had a lotta talent."

But Atkins also had an individualistic streak that Brown eventually found intolerable. Although he had proven time and again with the exceptions that he made that the rules were far from inflexible, Brown was not very flexible in Atkins's case. Brown traded Atkins after two years to the Bears for draft choices used on players who never played a down for the Browns and who yielded nothing in return when they were gotten rid of.

Of the other newcomers, Billy Reynolds would contribute as a running back and as a kick returner. Out of Dayton University, Chuck Noll played on offense at guard but became a linebacker after several years and made his biggest contribution on defense. Like Moselle three years before, he was an extreme longshot to even make the team as a twentieth-round draft choice from a school that was hardly a football power.

"He was a very bright and determined player who became a tremendous technician," Brown said of Noll. "No one ever worked harder in practice to perfect his skills." In the 1970s Noll was head coach of a Steelers team that was another of the game's great dynasties, consistently besting his old coach, who was then the head coach of the Cincinnati Bengals. His coaching accomplishments earned him a place in the Hall of Fame.

Two players who eventually became starters were unavailable in 1953. Defensive end Carlton Massey was drafted in the eighth round but was unavailable until 1954. Similarly, the Browns' thirteenth-round choice, linebacker Galen Fiss, did not join the team until 1956 because of military obligations and a brief excursion into professional baseball.

Unhappy that the contract offered to him was less than what he earned in 1952, Otto Graham decided not to report until Brown upped the team's offer. The holdout did not last long; Graham's options were few. Brown let anyone who asked know that even with the pay cut, his quarterback was the league's highest paid player. Graham knew that that did not negate the fact that he was one of the biggest bargains in all of sports. He eventually reported, all too aware that his only real leverage was to have a great season and hope for something closer to his actual value.

Lost somewhat amid all the coming and going was the biggest of all the offseason developments, the departure of Mac Speedie. Like a growing number of departures in the Paul Brown era, a number that would grow ever larger over the years, Speedie's departure for Canada was acrimonious. Speedie and Brown apparently never spoke or reconciled in the thirty-eight years from the time Speedie left until Brown's death.

In 1953, Canadian teams were in the midst of a concerted effort to sign players and draft choices by offering salaries that were far higher than the NFL was paying. NFL player salaries had dropped precipitously since the AAFC merger and remained far below the levels of 1946 to 1949. For players like Graham and Speedie, who were certain they were underpaid, playing in Canada presented a new but risky alternative.

In addition to Speedie and teammate Kissell (Carpenter would also leave the Browns for Canada in 1954), NFL standouts Arnie Weinmeister, Bud Grant, Gene Brito, Eddie LeBaron, Lowell Wagner, Ray Poole, and Tex Coulter all signed with Canadian teams during the brief period of competition for playing talent. Dante Lavelli was offered more than double what Cleveland would pay him in 1953 to jump, and when he asked Speedie what he had signed for, the figure Speedie told him was the same.

When they lost Speedie, the Browns lost one of the greatest receivers in the history of pro football. Paul Brown knew that better than anyone. But Brown was also a management reactionary, someone who believed more firmly than most in the personnel relations of the time that so overwhelmingly favored owners in every way.

His dealings with Graham during his best player's brief holdout underscore that fact as well as anything. It was both just and necessary that management could cut, trade, bench, blackball, and own in perpetuity anyone and everyone that it wanted, according to Brown. But any player who sought to better his means by negotiating in an open market was violating some sacred trust.

And never mind that Brown had used offers and overtures from employers other than the Cleveland Browns to improve his own contract. As players and observers have noted, Brown's attitude toward personnel relations is the main reason that Browns players were a key force in the origins of the NFL Players Association.

"I'll tell you what kind of negotiator he was," Dub Jones said of Brown. "You took a cut in salary and felt happy about it."

There was something else about Speedie in addition to his playing talent that made it not at all surprising that he went to Canada. He was independent to a degree that made Brown uncomfortable. He was a renegade in the words of one teammate, a rebel according to another.

"He was one of the ones that Paul Brown picked on quite a bit," Carpenter said of Speedie, touching on another subject that also undoubtedly wore on Speedie. "He'd get on Speedie's case for no particular reason, but he knew he could get on certain players and it's not gonna hurt their play any. And it was the same every week. Same players."

Brown's criticisms of Speedie in practice and in film sessions persisted, Carpenter recalled, despite Speedie's great play and the team's tremendous success. It was undoubtedly for this and other reasons (Brown's uncompromising negotiating habits, for example) that Speedie reportedly kept a pet skunk for a brief time that he called Paul.

So Speedie was Paul Brown's employee but not one of Paul Brown's guys. He had seen many talented teammates come and go by 1953. He had heard Brown's threats and barbs many times in seven seasons: "We'll keep you until we can replace you," "Maybe you should be in another profession," "What do you plan to do next year?" and "You are like an apple on a tree—when you get too ripe, you're going to fall off." Best receiver in football or not, those remarks had been directed at him on more than one occasion.

And when he slipped enough, Speedie knew, all of the all-pro recognition, pass-catching titles, championships, and other accomplishments wouldn't prevent Brown from getting rid of him. By then it might be too late to get the kind of salary he rightfully deserved. Perhaps that day was nearly at hand with Brewster on the roster. So Speedie jumped. He took his lawyer to meet with Brown, listened as Brown refused to budge from an offer that was half what some semblance of a market had determined he could earn, and he jumped. And Paul Brown never forgave him.

Kissell's departure north of the border was less dramatic and less acrimonious. He would, in fact, return to the Browns after one season. But Kissell's departure left a hole in the middle of the defense that seemed all the more problematic with Gain unavailable. The burden of filling that hole fell to veteran Palmer, second-year man Helluin, and newcomer Colo. The trio proved more than equal to the task, and the defense was its dominating self again in 1953.

The Dallas Texans had been an abysmal failure in 1952, and by season's end the franchise was under the control of the league office. Faced with lawsuits filed by Baltimore officials angered at the termination of the Colts after just one NFL season, the league resolved matters by awarding the city a new team, also to be named the Colts, that began play in 1953. The roster was made up of a number of players who played for the Texans. By 1957, the Colts would be one of the best teams in the league, and they remained so for most of their tenure in Baltimore.

After years of franchise upheaval, rival leagues, and general instability, the NFL had finally achieved a certain equilibrium. The twelve teams that took the field on opening day of 1953 remained in place through 1959, and no new teams were added. Remarkably, that stretch of seven seasons with exactly the same look—no franchise moves, no team or league mergers, no expansion—is the longest such stretch in NFL history.

The Browns went 4–1–1 in the preseason. Included in those games was a fourth straight exhibition win and fifth overall over the Bears, 20–14, and back-to-back games in San Francisco (a 20–7 win) and Los Angeles (a 27–9 loss). The extended preseason California stay was a Browns tradition that lasted for most of the next two decades.

The season began with the Browns clicking on all cylinders in a 27–0 win over the Packers in Milwaukee. Graham played three quarters and went eighteen of twenty-four for 292 yards and ran for two scores, while Renfro caught six passes for 97 yards. The defense held the Packers to eight completions, 66 passing yards, and 159 total yards and intercepted three passes in recording the fifteenth shutout in franchise history in ninety-one regular season games. Among the other teams in the renamed Eastern Conference, all but the Redskins lost, so immediately Cleveland was a game up on the Giants and Eagles, the two teams most likely to challenge them for first place.

Graham and the defense continued to sparkle as the Browns ran roughshod over their next two opponents. In a 27–7 win over the Cardinals, Graham was fifteen of twenty-two for 310 yards, with touchdown passes of 55 and 34 yards to Lavelli and 48 to Renfro. He then went twenty of thirty for 328 yards in a 37–13 rout of the Eagles in a Saturday-night home opener before a crowd of 48,502. Jagade scored twice, Groza kicked three field goals, and Helluin ran 42 yards with a Philadelphia fumble for the game's last score. Graham equaled Sid Luckman's record of throwing for 300 yards in consecutive games, a mark that stood until 1963 when John Unitas did it three times in succession.

The Browns widened their lead over second-place Washington to a game and a half with a 30–14 win at Griffith Stadium on October 18. Groza kicked three more field goals, and Cleveland amassed 407 yards of offense that included 197 on the ground. Renfro led the rushing attack with 101 yards on just seven carries, and Lavelli hauled in his fourth touchdown catch of the season. With the win, the Browns raised their all-time record against the Redskins to 6–0.

The 1–3 Giants tried to upend the high-flying Browns the following week by leaving the Polo Grounds field uncovered during a driving rainstorm that fell prior to and throughout the game. New York succeeded in slowing down the Browns but still lost, 7–0. Playing in a quagmire, players on both teams were soaked and covered with mud from the opening minutes. The game's only points came when Graham scored after the Giants were offside on a Groza miss. The Browns were 5–0 for the first time in the NFL and for the fourth time in their eight seasons.

47,845 were on hand at Municipal Stadium to see the Browns defeat the Redskins for a second time, 27–3. Graham scored on two short runs, and rookie Reynolds continued to impress with a 14-yard touchdown run. James led the defensive charge with three interceptions as 24 of Cleveland's points came off turnovers. At the halfway mark of the season, the defense had two shutouts, had allowed just over 6 points a game, and had not allowed any opponent to score more than 14.

The Steelers were Cleveland's next victim, 34–16, as the Browns overcame an early deficit with 24 second-quarter points. The Graham-Lavelli tandem clicked for their fifth touchdown, but it was Renfro who sparkled brightest. Renfro was playing the combination running back/wide receiver role that Elroy Hirsch and, to a lesser extent, Renfro's teammate Dub Jones had initiated.

In just a few years, Frank Gifford and Lenny Moore would become two of the most dangerous players in football in that role. Against Pittsburgh, Renfro rushed for 67 yards on nine carries and a touchdown and caught three passes for 35 yards. Most dramatically, he helped turn the game Cleveland's way for good when, with the score 24–16, he blocked a field goal and picked up the ball and ran 79 yards to score.

"Ray didn't get the recognition he deserved," Groza said of Renfro. "He made a lot of big catches for us." Although Hirsch, Gifford, and Moore all had more productive careers, Brown considered Renfro "the real artist of the flankers I know." Chet Hanulak recalled that even at 185 pounds, Renfro was a good blocker, while Konz said the experience of covering his teammate in practice made him a better player.

The November 15 game against the 49ers was one of the biggest in the NFL that year. The Municipal Stadium crowd of 80,698 was by far the largest in Cleveland's four NFL seasons, and it remained a team high until 1960. It was also the fifth time in the six regular season games the two teams had played in Cleveland that they had drawn over 70,000. Five of the seven largest crowds in Browns home games up to that time had been in games against San Francisco.

The 49ers were involved in another dogfight in the West and went into the game in a first-place tie with the Lions and Rams at 5–2. San Francisco remained a team driven primarily by its offense. Albert, Beals, Standlee, Strzykalski, Vetrano, and Eshmont were gone, but AAFC veterans Tittle, Banducci, and Perry were better than ever.

Perry was on his way to the first of two consecutive rushing titles, seasons in which he became only the second runner to twice reach the 1,000-yard mark. In addition, the offense included standouts Billy Wilson, Gordy Soltau, Bob St. Clair, and second-year sensation Hugh McElhenny. San Francisco would surpass Los Angeles in scoring in 1953, ending the Rams' three-year run as the NFL's best in that department.

Although still not as good as its offense, San Francisco's above average defense was led by future Hall of Famer Leo Nomellini and a rookie linebacker on his way to the Pro Bowl named Art Michalik. Against the Browns, however, Michalik made a mistake that would help fuel a Cleveland victory. Michalik's cheap shot against Otto Graham and Graham's recovery from it would add still further to the legend of the Cleveland quarterback.

A Reynolds touchdown run and a Groza field goal gave the Browns a 10–7 second-quarter lead. Then Michalik hit Graham in the face with a forearm after the Browns quarterback had run out of bounds after scrambling for a short gain. While several Browns went after Michalik,

Graham was tended to by the team medical staff and then helped to the locker room.

After a cut on his lip was sewn up with fifteen stitches, Graham was fitted with a face mask. He thus became one of the first players to ever wear a device that before long became mandatory. Graham returned to the game and threw a 34-yard fourth-quarter touchdown pass that increased Cleveland's lead to 20–7. On the day, Graham was seventeen of twenty-four for 286 yards.

Behind McElhenny and Tittle, San Francisco rallied. But Groza's third field goal of the day was just enough to hold off the 49ers as Cleveland won, 23–21. Lavelli finished with six receptions for 137 yards. Groza increased his field goal total to fifteen, just four shy of the record he set in 1952; extended his record of consecutive field goals to twelve; and scored in his forty-first straight game, another NFL record. Groza would break the all-time pro record of fifty-three set by Vetrano in the AAFC in November of 1954.

Michalik, meanwhile, was worked over for the rest of the game by Cleveland's offensive line. Afterward in the locker room, his eyes were blackened and he could barely lift his head. Graham accepted Michalik's apology, but some of his teammates were in a less forgiving mood.

"We got pretty steamed up when Otto got hurt," linebacker Tommy Thompson said after the game. "If it had been anybody else, it probably wouldn't have made us so mad. But they couldn't do that to Otto and get away with it. Not old Otto."

Graham's gutsy performance was one of the best of a great season. He was throwing the ball with tremendous accuracy as well as for distance in leading the team to an 8–0 start. His 64.7% completion percentage and 10.55 yards per pass for the season were tops in the league and among the very best marks ever.

And although it was not in use at the time, Graham scored 99.7 on the passer rating system in use today, the third highest mark in history up to that time, trailing only his own marks of 112.1 in 1946 and 109.2 in 1947. Brown called it the best season of his quarterback's career. Even more impressive was the fact that Graham's rating was almost twice as good as the cumulative mark of 50.7 compiled by the rest of the league's quarterbacks. That degree of superiority was the second best of Graham's career behind only his best season in 1946.

"He was so darn consistent and accurate with his passes," Carpenter said of Graham. "And sometimes I wouldn't quite make a good block and he'd take the blame for it. He was a super guy and a great quarterback."

Graham had not lost the fire that had made him and his team so good for seven years. He was the kind of leader who inspired the kind of support voiced by Thompson and Carpenter, and his return in the second half against the 49ers was typical of the determination he played with throughout his career.

Graham was fully recovered the following week as he threw for 220 yards and touchdowns to Renfro and Brewster, and the Browns beat the Steelers, 20–16. Groza kicked two more field goals of 50 and 41 yards, but the victory was a costly one as Thompson suffered a career-ending injury to his right knee. At the start of the season, Brown had called the Cleveland captain "the best middle linebacker in the game" on the basis of his play the previous year, and he was playing even better in 1953 until his injury.

Many observers obviously agreed with Brown's assessment. Despite missing the final quarter of the season, Thompson was named to the first team of the AP and UPI all-pro teams. He returned to training camp in 1954 in a game but ultimately doomed effort to come back. At the time of his injury, Thompson was just twenty-six years old.

The Browns clinched the Eastern Conference title on November 29 when they defeated the Cardinals, 27–16, and the Eagles lost at the Polo Grounds. The Browns took a 10–0 lead and then rallied after Chicago took a 14–10 lead into the fourth quarter. Graham was nineteen of twenty-eight for 276 yards, including three completions for 55 yards on a fourth-quarter drive that ended with a Renfro touchdown that put Cleveland ahead 20–14. James added an insurance touchdown with a fumble return for a score late in the game. The Browns' first-place finish was their eighth in a row and fourth in a row in the NFL, tying the league record set by the Bears from 1940 through 1943.

Kicking records continued to fall as Groza continued to amaze. Against the Cardinals, he equaled his nineteen field goals of the year before and broke Waterfield's NFL career record of sixty, a total it took Waterfield eight years to accumulate. Groza surpassed it in less than four. Counting his AAFC years, Groza's total stood at ninety-one. Equally impressive was the accuracy with which he was kicking in 1953. In a season in which all other NFL kickers made good on 41% of their field goal attempts, Groza made twenty-three of twenty-six for an 88.5% mark.

First place was clinched and a second perfect season was still a possibility, and the Browns moved a step closer with a 62–14 destruction of the Giants in Cleveland. It was an overwhelming all-around performance, most notably on offense. Ratterman played most of the game and finished fifteen of twenty-seven for 235 yards and three touchdowns, while Graham chipped in with 116 yards and a touchdown.

Brewster caught seven passes for 182 yards, including scoring grabs of 22, 23, and 36 yards, and both Carpenter and Renfro scored rushing and receiving touchdowns as the Browns racked up 495 yards of offense. Renfro got in on the passing game by throwing a scoring toss, and the defense again scored when Michaels returned an interception 34 yards in the third quarter.

The scoring binge and rout were a marked contrast to the many close defensive battles the two teams had engaged in over four seasons. Only once in eight previous games had the Browns been able to score more than 14 points against the Umbrella Defense and variations thereof deployed by New York.

"Against Cleveland, it was one hell of a leaky umbrella," said Frank Gifford, who was used primarily as a defensive back that season. It was a frustrating season for a Giants team that had been right on Cleveland's heels the three previous years. New York finished 3–9, and Steve Owen was fired after the season after twenty-four years as the team's head coach.

Through eleven games, the Browns had been as dominant as they ever had before, in either the AAFC or the NFL. They had allowed just 120 points, or 10.9 per game. The second best mark in the league was the Eagles' 188, which averaged out to more than 6 points more per game. In addition, the Browns had outscored the opposition by 18.3 points per game.

However, Cleveland's hopes for a perfect season came crashing down in the final twenty minutes of the finale in Philadelphia. The Browns built leads of 10–0 and 20–14, but the Eagles rallied both times. Philadelphia scored touchdowns on four consecutive possessions in the second half to overwhelm the Browns, 42–27. It was the most points Cleveland had allowed in the NFL and the second highest total after San Francisco's 56 in 1949.

Brown viewed the loss as somewhat of a blessing in disguise. After two consecutive Championship Game losses, his team was already under enough pressure. The pressure that had built up around the possibility of the NFL's first perfect season would have been all the greater if his team had gone into the title game at 12–0, the Cleveland coach reasoned. In addition, he rested some of his players against the Eagles, and the team was able to avoid injury. That was in striking contrast to 1952, when the Browns had to fight to the very last regular season play and played the Lions for the title with so many key players missing or hobbled due to injuries.

A dogfight for the eighth consecutive year, the West was settled on the final day by Detroit's 27–16 win at the Polo Grounds. Winners of their final six games, the Lions were able to hold off fast-charging San Francisco. The 49ers closed with four straight wins of their own but were unable to make up for two early season losses to the Lions and the loss to the Browns. San Francisco's three losses were by a combined total of 9 points. So for the sixth time in the twenty-year history of the NFL Championship Game, the same two teams would play for the title in consecutive years.

Cleveland's and Detroit's combined regular season record was one of the best in the history of pro football championship play. Previously only the 1942 matchup between the Bears and Redskins (21–1, .955) and the 1947 AAFC game between the Browns and Yankees (23–3–2, .885) were better than the Browns' and Lions' combined mark of 21–3 (.875).

In the five decades since, that .875 mark has been surpassed only four times: in the 1962 NFL title game and in the Super Bowl matchups after the 1972, 1976, and 1984 seasons. Bert Bell went so far as to say beforehand, "Here possibly are the two best teams ever to meet for the championship." For the Browns, where the 1952 loss to the Lions had been the most frustrating in team history, the 1953 title match would prove the most heartbreaking game the team has ever played.

Although the Lions won ten games in 1953, they were more an opportunistic team than an overpowering one. Layne had been bothered by a sore passing arm for much of the season, and the team's offensive production was down from 1952. Cloyce Box had led the NFL with fifteen touchdown catches on forty-two receptions in 1952 but had only sixteen catches and two touchdowns in 1953. The team's other top end, Leon Hart, had been bothered by injuries all year. Six of Detroit's wins were by 7 points or fewer.

But win they did, and they did it mainly on the backs of Layne, Walker, an excellent offensive line, and a defense that was second only to Cleveland's. Chris's Crew led the league in interceptions by a wide margin with thirty-eight (more than three per game), and Christiansen snared a league-leading twelve. And the team's best new face was rookie Joe Schmidt, on his way to a thirteen-year career in which he was one of the best linebackers to ever play the game.

It was thirty-four degrees as 54,577 people filled Briggs Stadium on December 27. Although a sizable number of Browns fans had traveled the short distance from the south side of Lake Erie to the north side, the vast majority of the crowd was there to root for a colorful Lions team that had captured the fancy of one of the country's best sports towns. Not only were the resurgent Lions going for a second consecutive championship, the Tigers were consistently competitive, and the Red Wings were in the midst of a remarkable run in which they finished first in the National Hockey League seven years in a row and won the Stanley Cup four times.

Schmidt made his presence felt early in the game when he forced a fumble on a sack that the Lions converted into a Doak Walker touchdown. A short time later Layne was swarmed under at his own 2-yard line, and it appeared Cleveland might get the ball in great field position. However, Colo was called for unnecessary roughness on the play, and the Lions subsequently reached Cleveland territory before punting. With both yards and points difficult to come by throughout, the penalty and resulting swing of 50 yards in field position was the kind of thing that hurt the Browns all day.

On their next possession, the Browns reached midfield, but the drive stalled after an incompletion on a play that was similar to one that had occurred in the previous year's title game—a double-touch pass. From the Cleveland 49, a Graham pass went off Brewster's hands, sailed just over Jack Christiansen's fingertips, and landed in the arms of Billy Reynolds. Reynolds ran to the Detroit 17, but the play was nullified and the Browns eventually punted.

Then, in what seemed like another flashback to the meeting a year earlier, the Browns failed to take full advantage of a tremendous break that set them up deep in Detroit territory. Late in the first quarter, Ford recovered a fumble at the 6 and the Browns appeared poised to tie the game. But they were unable to move and wound up settling for Groza's 13-yard field goal. The key play in the sequence was a Graham pass to Lavelli in the end zone. For a moment it looked like a touchdown, but Yale Lary arrived just as the ball did and broke up the play.

A short time later another Graham pass that went off a receiver's hands—this time Carpenter's—was picked off by Jim David and returned 37 yards to the Cleveland 20. The Browns held, but Walker kicked a field goal that boosted Detroit's lead to 10–3. Then Cleveland was again foiled by the great defense of the Lions in the waning moments of the half.

After Jagade returned the ensuing kickoff 29 yards to the Cleveland 49, another sack resulted in a loss of 11 yards. Jagade made 18 yards on a screen, but too much yardage had been lost on the sack and Cleveland came up short of a first down. Groza then missed a field goal attempt from 51 yards, and just as they had in 1952 the Lions went to the locker room with a 7-point advantage.

Jagade was running well, and he accounted for most of the yardage on a third-quarter drive, capping things off with a touchdown run from the 9 that tied the score at 10–10. On the ensuing kickoff, Sherman Howard stood Jug Girard up at the 17 and forced an apparent fumble. After a scramble Brewster recovered for Cleveland at the 4, but the play had been blown dead and Detroit took over at the spot of Howard's hit.

After the defense again stopped the Lions, the Browns got the ball back near the end of the third quarter and launched a drive that reached the Detroit 7. They were in great shape to take a 7-point lead that eventually, given subsequent events, would have become 10 had they gotten a touchdown. Instead they ended up with only another short field goal.

As they had on so many occasions the year before, the Lions stiffened when the Browns neared their end zone. From the 7, Graham threw outside to Renfro near the goal line. As with the earlier pass to Lavelli, it looked as if the Browns might have a touchdown. But this time it was Bob Smith who arrived in the nick of time to make a big play, knocking the ball out of Renfro's grasp. After the incompletion, Graham was stopped on a third-down run, and Groza came on and gave Cleveland a 13–10 lead.

Lavelli has said that one of the reasons the Browns lost three straight title games is because Brown's play-calling was too conservative. Having Graham run a keeper on third and goal from the 7 may have been an example of the conservatism Lavelli referred to, but with his defense playing well and his quarterback having a poor day, Brown went with the percentages. Rather than risk a possible interception and come away with no points, he called for a run and then sent in Groza for a field goal that gave his team the lead.

After trailing throughout to an outstanding team, getting the lead in that situation that late in the game was imperative. The real problem was not the call on third down so much as it was the team's overall inability to push over touchdowns, both earlier in that sequence and in several other situations. Still, when Groza added another field goal from 43 yards with about four minutes remaining, the Browns increased their lead to 16–10.

So even with all the near misses and mistakes, the fact is the Browns had a 6-point lead in the fourth quarter. For a while it looked as if the running of Jagade and the other backs might be enough to offset the passing deficiencies. In all, Cleveland gained 182 yards rushing and averaged 5.1 yards per attempt. Jagade exactly duplicated his totals from the 1952 title game with fifteen carries for 104 yards and scored Cleveland's only touchdown.

Still, all of Cleveland's fourth-quarter points were on field goals. A touchdown on either of their two drives would have probably put the game out of reach. The upside was that Groza's third field goal put the Lions in a position where a field goal would do them no good. In all likelihood, if the Browns had held Detroit one more time, the championship would have been theirs.

And although Layne had five solid years as a starting quarterback and a championship ring to his credit, he was still a great quarterback in the making. In big moments of big games past, Cleveland had gone up against Ace Parker, Frankie Albert, Spec Sanders, Y. A. Tittle, Bob Waterfied, Norm Van Brocklin, Charlie Conerly, and Tommy Thompson and won practically every time. Still, although a field goal would not help the Lions, a 6-point lead was fragile, capable of being erased by one drive down the field—one big play.

With their 16–10 lead, the Browns kicked off and the Lions took possession on their own 20. Eight plays and two minutes later, Bobby Layne was no longer just a great quarterback in the making. Hart had left the game early, unable to play because of his injuries. His replacement at end was Jim Doran, a third-year player who played seven games during the season and caught six passes for 75 yards and no touchdowns.

Layne and Doran connected for 17 yards on the first play, but two incompletions followed to set up a third and 10 from the 37. There were still over three minutes to play at that point, and Parker later said he decided before the play that he would have punted if the Lions had come up short. But Layne again found Doran for 18 yards, and the Lions were at the Cleveland 45.

Layne next hit Box for 9, but Hoernschmeyer was stopped for no gain, bringing up another third down. With the ball at the Cleveland 36, only a yard to go, and the two-minute warning approaching, there were no more thoughts about punting. Layne got the first down himself with a run to the right—the side of the field where Doran was lining up opposite Lahr—that gained 3 yards. After the play Doran told Layne he could beat Lahr on a go pattern after first faking like he was blocking on another run to his side.

The play worked just as Doran had suggested it would. Lahr went for the fake and came up for what he thought was a run. That allowed Doran to break clear by several steps, and he caught Layne's pass just past the goal line. The touchdown tied the game, and Walker's conversion put the Lions ahead 17–16 with 2:08 to play.

After Carpenter returned the kickoff to the 28, Graham and the offense came on the field one last time. It was a situation much like the one they had been in three years before against the Rams: starting in their own territory, about two minutes to play, down a point, and needing only a field goal to win the championship. It was just this kind of predicament that Graham had led them out of so many times.

Brown had briefly pulled Graham in the second quarter in favor of Ratterman, but he never seriously considered keeping Graham on the bench in spite of his poor play. With the game's greatest kicker on their side, a drive of 50 yards would have given the Browns an excellent chance at victory. They might not even have needed 50. Groza had already hit from 43 yards and a drive of about 35 yards would have been enough for another attempt of that distance. They could have gotten that on two or three completions.

But it was not to be. On the first play, Karl Karilivacz intercepted Graham and the Lions ran out the clock. For the second straight time against the Lions and the third overall, the Browns lost in the NFL Championship Game. In the same way the Browns had established their greatness by playing their best in big games, so had the Lions. And much as Graham had established himself as the greatest quarterback of his era with clutch play at the end of those big games, so had Layne with two years of clutch play of his own.

Dissections of the game, both at the time and in the years since, often focus on Doran's performance against Lahr on the winning drive. That is fair enough as far as it goes; a big play or even just a stop by Lahr in one of several key spots (or by any other member of the Browns defense, for that matter) could have produced a different outcome. But the fairest conclusion is to put the burden of responsibility squarely on the shoulders of the offense.

For one thing, the Cleveland defense was outstanding. Their performance was good enough to win most games, and it still might have been enough against the Lions had the opposing quarterback been just about anybody but Bobby Layne. Save for his 1-yard touchdown run, Walker was completely shackled throughout. He finished the day with one reception for 10 yards and three carries for 7 yards. All told, the Lions rushed thirty-nine times for 129 yards, an average of just 3.3 yards per attempt.

For fifty-six minutes, the defense also kept Layne in check. The Browns intercepted two of his passes (both by Gorgal) and allowed Detroit only 87 net yards through the air until the game's final moments. Cleveland also recovered two fumbles. That total of four takeaways was matched by Detroit's defense, which also intercepted two Graham passes and recovered two fumbles.

The Cleveland turnovers were part of a bigger problem on offense. Graham's performance was the worst of his career, and the Browns were unable to do anything through the air as the Cleveland quarterback completed just two of fifteen passes for 20 yards. The two second-year men who had played so well all year, Renfro and Brewster, were completely shut out in the passing game.

Although Graham injured his passing hand at some point during the game, he noted that it affected his throwing at times without making excuses for his poor play. "I just played a lousy game," he said. "I was the main factor in losing. If I had played my usual game, we would have won." Immediately after the game, he wanted to "jump off a building" for having let his teammates down.

Graham's bad day was attributable in large part to the Detroit defense. The Lions not only had the best secondary in football, they also consistently pressured Graham, both with the charge of their front line and with blitzes. Lavelli, however, felt that poor decisions by Graham were the biggest factor in Cleveland's poor passing performance.

"Their pass defense wasn't especially difficult," said Lavelli, who caught one pass for 13 yards. "I was loose a lot. We just didn't throw to the right man at the right time." Lavelli also felt that Brown should have passed occasionally in short yardage situations and on other plays when Detroit was keying on the run.

"[H]e'd go down to basic football and try to get a three- or six-point lead and hold onto that," Lavelli said of Brown. That conservatism didn't just turn potential touchdowns into field goals or no points at all, Lavelli felt. The lack of points also put extra pressure on the Cleveland defense. In fairness to Brown, however, the running game was working and the passing game was not. Jones, Carpenter, Reynolds, Graham, and especially Jagade were running well, but Cleveland never got its passing game going.

In fact, the offense as a whole was inconsistent throughout, even with the large total of rushing yards. In addition to stalled drives, turnovers, and missed opportunities after takeaways, the Browns made only eleven first downs to eighteen for Detroit and ran only fifty-two plays to sixty-five for the Lions. Cleveland undoubtedly had a similar disadvantage in time of possession given that 62% of Detroit's plays were runs.

The two tipped passes were indicative of the kind of day it was for the offense. On both plays the intended receiver was open, and on both plays Graham threw the ball too high. One resulted in an incompletion that killed a drive, while the other was intercepted and returned deep into Cleveland territory, leading to a Detroit field goal.

Not only did Cleveland's inability to score more than 16 points put pressure on the defense, their inability to control the ball did as well. On the series just before Groza's last field goal, the Browns had a second and 4 with about five minutes remaining and failed to pick up the necessary yards in their next two plays. Had they done so, and then gotten two more first downs, or even one, that, too, might have run the clock down sufficiently and produced a different result.

One prime result of the disparity in plays, first downs, and time of possession was that the Cleveland defense spent a lot of time on the field. Lahr was beaten cleanly by great Detroit execution, so perhaps how worn down he or any of his mates may have been is irrelevant. Still, prior to the game-winning drive, Layne was just eight of nineteen for 102 yards and the Lions had gained an average of only 4 yards per play. Then on that possession, Layne went four of six for 77 yards and Detroit averaged 10 yards per play. Even with the final drive, Cleveland's defense had again played superbly, something it did on a regular basis in postseason play (Detroit's other touchdown drive came after the fumble forced by Schmidt's hit on Graham and went for all of 12 yards).

For while the postseason feats of Graham and Motley and Groza are much better known, among the many credentials that support the supposition that Cleveland's was the greatest defense ever is the fact that they allowed only 160 points in twelve postseason games in their dynasty years. Layne and his mates were a great team that came through in the biggest of spots, but it is also at least partly true that the Cleveland defense had been asked to do more than can be asked of even the very best.

For the third straight year an outstanding Browns team had finished just short of a sixth championship. They were not in the same boat as their baseball contemporaries, the wait-'til-next-year Brooklyn Dodgers, but the team's frustration was definitely on the rise. That frustration could only be alleviated by another championship, and no one knew that better than Otto Graham. And as the world of professional football would soon find out, no one was more determined to get back to the winner's circle than Otto Graham.

Graham again won both the passing title and the MVP award in 1953. He led the league in passing yards for the second straight year with 2,722, completion percentage with a 64.7% mark, and yards per pass with 10.55. The last two were the second highest in NFL history in those categories behind records set by Sammy Baugh and Sid Luckman.

Despite all of his record-shattering, Groza finished second in the scoring race as Soltau had another outstanding season for the 49ers. Gillom was likewise a bridesmaid as he finished second in punting average, missing out on a third straight punting title despite an excellent 43.8 average when Pittsburgh's Pat Brady had an outstanding season.

Groza's 88.5% success rate not only smashed Bill Dudley's previous mark of 76.9%, it stood for an incredible twenty-eight years, well past the point when the game's placekickers had become specialists. Also noteworthy is the fact that Dudley's record was set on thirteen attempts and Groza's on twenty-six. Groza would build on his all-time career total for fourteen more years. Counting his AAFC field goals, kicks that are not recognized in the NFL's official totals, Groza was the game's field goal leader until 1971 when he was dethroned by George Blanda, whose kicks from his ten years in the AFL are counted. In several more years Groza would pass Don Hutson and become the all-time leader in points, a record he likewise held until the 1970s.

Graham, Groza, Gatski, and Ford were unanimous first-team all-pro choices, while Lavelli, Thompson, and Gorgal were consensus first-team picks. Willis and Gibron were each selected to one of the first teams, while Jagade, Lahr, and Colo were second-team selections. Ford, Gibron, Graham, Groza, Jagade, James, Lavelli, and Renfro were all picked for the Pro Bowl game as eight Browns were selected for the third time in four years. And for the second time since the team joined the NFL, Brown again won Coach of the Year honors, this time from both the UPI and the *Sporting News*.

Home attendance was up for the fourth year in a row as the Browns continued to be one of the NFL's leaders at the gate. Just under 46,000 fans per game paid to see Cleveland in their six dates at Municipal Stadium. And a month after their loss to the Lions, the Browns won the right to the first pick by winning the lottery for the bonus draft choice, a special selection made before the beginning of the rest of the draft. That and the expectation that Gain, McCormack, and Forester would all be available were additional reasons for the franchise to look forward to 1954 despite the third straight disappointing ending in 1953.

14

Willis and Motley Depart

THE YEAR 1953 marked the end of the road in Cleveland for both Bill Willis and Marion Motley. They had made history together in 1946, and both were among the team's most valuable players during the Browns dynasty. In the face of all of the hostility directed toward them because of their skin color, they didn't only persevere, although that alone would have been a singular accomplishment; they achieved greatness.

Both Willis and Motley were among the very best at their respective positions for most of their careers. Almost sixty years after their pro debuts, each is also still spoken of with the utmost respect for what they were as players and as human beings by men who played with and against them. And both were accorded the highest individual honor a pro football player can receive, induction into the Hall of Fame.

Willis was thirty-two and still near the top of his game when he played his last game. In each of the eight years he played he had made somebody's all-pro team. And for most of those eight seasons, Willis was the best player on the best defense in the history of the game.

There were other things Willis wanted to do, however, in addition to play football. He was very popular in Ohio, especially in Cleveland and Columbus, and he spent many years working with youth in both cities. As great a player as Bulldog Turner spoke of Willis in glowing terms.

"The first guy to convince me that I could not handle anybody I ever met," Turner said, "was Bill Willis."

Motley's departure from Cleveland was not as amicable as Willis's. He went to training camp in 1954 determined to play a ninth season, only to be informed by Brown near camp's end that he was not going to make the team. Brown had newcomers Maurice Bassett and Curly Morrison in camp competing for Motley's fullback position, and the coach told Motley he should retire rather than wait to be released. Motley begrudgingly agreed.

Motley was thirty-four by then and had suffered serious injuries to both knees. He had had only one really productive season since 1950, and he had not carried the ball a single time in his last game as a Brown, the previous year's Championship Game. He was certain he could play another year, but to Brown the cold evidence was that he was no longer the man for the job. As with about everything else having to do with the Cleveland Browns, Paul Brown made a decision based on that cold evidence and not sentiment, and that decision was law.

Still convinced he could play, Motley joined the Steelers in 1955 after sitting out a season. He played seven games, mostly at linebacker, and mostly ineffectually. He retired for good at the end of the season with hopes of remaining in football.

The end of Motley's career with Cleveland could have been just another unfortunate interlude, yet another case of a player wanting to play when it was clear to most observers that it was time to retire. Had the Browns offered Motley a job, perhaps that's what it would have been—a temporarily difficult interlude before a second long and productive career in the game that he loved for an organization to which he had given so much. But the bitterness Motley felt about the end of his career was compounded when his inquiries about a coaching job were spurned. Perhaps more cutting than the rejection was Brown's suggestion to Motley that he look for a job in a steel mill.

Fullback Emerson Cole, Cleveland's fifth black player, joined the Browns in 1950. While he is quick to pay tribute to Paul Brown for hiring black players, Cole expressed feelings about other elements of racism that may partly explain Brown's unwillingness to hire Motley as a coach or scout.

"The trouble I had with him was he didn't think blacks had much intellect," Cole said of Brown. "He certainly admired their physical ability, but he never gave them much credit for thinking and intelligence."

Motley did work briefly as a scout for Cleveland in the 1960s after Brown was fired, but he left feeling that he had been hired as a token. Motley felt the same sting of rejection a short time later when he approached Otto Graham, then head coach of the Redskins, about a coaching job and was again turned down. He worked for the postal service and then for the Ohio lottery and remained an imposing figure well into his seventies.

Except for his still-standing lifetime record of 5.7 yards per carry, his yardage totals seem almost paltry by today's standards, but teammates and opposing players invariably speak of Motley in the awed tones reserved for the very best. Many who got to know him also speak with great fondness of Motley as a human being. And from the distance of time, as the impact of what he, Willis, Kenny Washington, and Woody Strode did has become clearer, many also speak with tremendous respect for what Motley and the others went through as trailblazers.

"Motley was one of a kind," Cole said. "He didn't have a lot of education, but what he didn't have in education he made up in mother wit. He made wise decisions that helped to perpetuate the integration of football and baseball."

"Definitely one of the very best," said George Terlep.

"There used to be a sign in the stadium that said, 'The World's Greatest Fullback,' and I tell you, he was," Ken Konz said.

At Motley's funeral in 1999, Joe Perry, another of the game's greatest fullbacks and one of the first blacks to play pro football after the breakthrough of 1946, said, "I had to come. Marion's my man. He was the greatest all-around football player there ever was."

CHAPTER 15

A Defense for the Ages

HE RETIREMENTS of Bill Willis and George Young after the 1953 season left the Browns with no original 1946er who was primarily a defensive player. When Derrell Palmer also retired, James and Lahr were the only players left from the defense who had been with the team in the AAFC, although Adamle was coaxed out of retirement a week into the 1954 season. That degree of turnover makes the defense's great play over more than a decade all the more remarkable.

Unlike defensive units that came along after pro football's popularity surged to far greater heights, Cleveland's did not have a memorable nickname. Their numbers did not include any particularly colorful or outrageous personalities. Their accomplishments predate NFL Films and the game's marriage with television and thus were neither captured by high-tech cameras or broadcast for tens of millions of people nationwide to see. For the same reason, their exploits are also not part of the menu on the many channels that televise sports programming twenty-four hours a day, 365 days a year.

In addition, the Browns defense made its mark just before a Giants unit that was not as good or anywhere near as dominant made its mark in the media capital of the world and also made defense popular in a way it never had been. The Browns' excellence was apparent enough in the final scores of the team's games and in the standings, but at the time only aficionados, some of the team's legion of fans, and close readers of Cleveland's newspapers were likely to recognize that the Browns unit was something truly special. Almost as remarkable as their accomplishments is the fact that the Browns defense is rarely if ever mentioned with the 1950s Giants, the Purple People Eaters, the Doomsday Defense, and the Steel Curtain in discussions of the best ever.

In looking at a long stretch of years rather than a few spectacular seasons, however, a strong case can be made that the Browns defense was the best ever. Some of the evidence is so overwhelming that a case could, in fact, be made that the issue is not even close. What the Browns did in a twelve-season period that actually transcends their 1946–1955 dynasty, both as it is reflected in statistics as well as in victories and championships, is nothing short of mind-boggling.

And like the team's overall achievements, the defense's greatness includes their years in both the All-America Football Conference and the NFL. Although there was a slight drop-off in the degree of dominance after 1949, for almost every year from 1950 until 1958 Cleveland's was the best defense in the NFL. The team's .766 winning percentage, seven first-place finishes, and three championships in the eight-year period from 1950 through 1957 offer ample but still only partial evidence of that defensive dominance.

Year after year, the Browns were first in their league in multiple defensive categories. Most striking is the fact that the Browns led their league *ten times* in twelve years in fewest points allowed. Six of those years were in a seven-season stretch in the NFL. Some of those years they didn't just finish first, they were far ahead of every other team. In 1953, for example, the Browns allowed almost 4 fewer points per game than the second best team and almost 11 fewer points per game than the rest of the league. In 1949, they allowed 13.6 points per game while the other AAFC teams allowed 24.1.

In the two years they did not lead in scoring defense, 1950 and 1952, the Browns were second both times. They went into the final game of both of those seasons in first place in fewest points allowed, only to be passed at the wire. Cleveland thus missed a perfect *twelve defensive scor-*

ing titles in twelve years by a mere 2 points per game in those two years combined.

What is remarkable is that Cleveland's defense was allowing exceptionally low numbers of points in one of the highest scoring eras in football history. One way of understanding how superior Cleveland's defense was year after year is the degree to which their points allowed was better than the league average. Only fourteen teams since 1933, NFL, AAFC, and AFL, have allowed fewer than half as many points as the rest of their league's teams. The 1946 Browns team that allowed 9.8 per game compared with 21.2 by the rest of the AAFC is the eighth best on that list. Put another way, their defense was 2.16 times better than the average of the rest of the league that year (the 1944 Giants posted the all-time best mark at 2.56).

In their first NFL season of 1950, the Browns came within a whisker of repeating that feat, allowing 12 points per game while the rest of the league averaged 23.9. Cleveland's defense could thus be said to have been 1.99 times better than the average of the rest. That mark is the fifteenth best in history. Cleveland posted eight of the top sixty marks since 1933 during their dynasty years—three in the AAFC and five in the NFL, missing only in 1952 and 1955. In posting eight of the best defensive seasons ever in nine seasons, the Browns put together a stretch of dominance that is by far the best all-time.

Cleveland was also tops on numerous occasions in yards allowed per rush, yards allowed per pass, completion percentage allowed, total yards allowed, yards allowed per play, and takeaways. In 1948 the Browns were first in seven of the major defensive categories; in 1946, 1954, and 1955 they were first in six. Seven times in twelve years they were first in at least four major categories, and they were first in at least two in all twelve years.

Some of the numbers are unbelievable: 4.4 yards allowed per pass in 1946, 3.5 yards per play that same year, 4.2 yards per play in 1950, 2.8 yards allowed per rush and 236 total yards allowed per game in 1954, 39% pass completion percentage allowed in 1955 and 39.5% in 1949. All of those numbers are far ahead of the rest of the league in those years. In 1954, for example, Cleveland's 236 yards per game average was 117 better than the rest of the NFL (50% better), and the 2.8 yards per rush was 46% better than the rest of the league's 4.1.

Cleveland also had an incredible number of shutouts in the twelve years of their defensive dominance. They recorded twenty in 150 regular season games from 1946 through 1957, a shutout in 13.3% of games played. Included in that total are four in both 1946 and 1951. Only the Steelers' five in 1976 has topped that total in the last fifty-four years, and Pittsburgh's mark came in a longer season than in 1951. Narrowing the scope down to the 93 regular season games the team played from 1946 through the first month of the 1953 season, the Browns registered sixteen shutouts. That means Cleveland shut out the opposition in 17.2% of those games. That averages out to about two shutouts per season over more than seven seasons. All of that was accomplished in an era that was one of the highest scoring in history.

Statistics that measure a football defense, like any statistics, can tell only part of the story. And sometimes they can be deceptive. A team may lead the league in fewest rushing yards allowed because their pass defense is so porous that teams rarely run the ball against them.

Yards per play and comparing how a team ranked, say, in yards per pass with how it ranked in yards per rush can sharpen the analysis. If a team leads in fewest passing and rushing yards *in the same season*, as the Browns once did, then you know it has a superlative defense. What is ultimately most telling in Cleveland's case, then, in addition to how long they were the best, is how often the team finished first in so many varied categories.

For example, the Browns were league leaders seven times in fewest yards per pass allowed *and* three times in fewest yards per rush allowed. When they led the AAFC in seven of the main categories in 1948, they led in both fewest yards allowed per rush and per pass. And they scored a rare trifecta in 1954 when they became the first team in history to lead the league in fewest rushing yards, fewest passing yards, and fewest yards. Only the 1959 Giants, 1963 Bears, and 1969 Chiefs, three of the best defenses in history, have done that since.

In both 1954 and 1955, the Browns defense led the league in fewest points and fewest yards allowed, a feat only a handful of teams have accomplished. No team before the Browns had done it in two consecutive years. In the fifty years since, only the 1969 and 1970 Vikings and the

1985 and 1986 Bears, two more of the most storied defenses in history, have replicated Cleveland's accomplishment of finishing first in those categories twice in a row.

Only a handful of teams have had single seasons on defense that were more dominant than Cleveland's in the best of its twelve-year run. The 1963 Chicago Bears, for example, led the NFL in all of the major categories and a few minor ones as well. But the Bears were very much a one-year wonder. They were first in exactly one of those same categories, for example, in the four combined years immediately before and after 1963.

The Minnesota Vikings defense of Purple People Eaters fame led the league in a number of categories over a prolonged period of time. In the seven seasons from 1969 through 1975, they were league leaders in about twenty categories. By comparison, Cleveland led in fifty categories in twelve years. Not only did the Browns lead in more categories per season, their period of dominance lasted almost twice as long.

The difference between the Browns defense and others heralded as among the best is even more extreme. The Giants of the late 1950s and early 1960s, the Packers of the 1960s, and the 1970s Steelers came nowhere near even approaching Cleveland's defense, either in all-around dominance or in length of time as a dominant unit.

In fewest points allowed, the Packers were first three times during their dynasty. The Steelers led in that category exactly twice in the entire decade of the 1970s. The long-term run that comes closest to Cleveland's was posted by the Giants, who led the NFL five times from 1935 through 1944. Defenses of more recent vintage with impressive multiyear streaks atop the NFL are the Vikings with three years in a row from 1969 through 1971 and the Bears with three in the four seasons from 1985 through 1988.

Despite posting five shutouts in 1976, the Steelers were not able to put together a string of years in which they excelled in that department, despite the fact that the mid-1970s was the lowest scoring era since World War II. The Pittsburgh defense was terrific, and the team was able to post nine shutouts in one stretch of eighty-eight games. But compare that with the Browns, who posted nine shutouts in a stretch of fifty-five games from 1950 to 1954 in a much higher scoring era. Beginning in their very first NFL season, in other words, the Browns posted shutouts in 16.4% of their games across almost five complete seasons.

* * *

And because the Browns' accomplishments in the AAFC are still largely considered questionable, it is important to point out again that Cleveland's defense was almost as dominant in the NFL. Again looking at the years through 1957, they led in lowest completion percentage allowed five times in the NFL and four times in the AAFC and in fewest yards allowed per pass four times in the NFL and three times in the AAFC. Cleveland was first in at least six different categories in 1954 and 1955 as well as in 1946 and 1948. And as has been mentioned, they had four shutouts in a twelve-game NFL schedule in 1951 as well as in a fourteen-game AAFC schedule in 1946.

The defense unquestionably benefited from the potent offense. Game in and game out for years, opponents found themselves behind on the scoreboard and having to change game plans to catch up. The disruption this caused opposing offenses was unquestionably beneficial to the Cleveland defense.

But the relationship was a symbiotic one. The great play of the defense aided the offense, too. Early stops, takeaways, and tilting the field-position balance were just some of the key ways the defense helped the offense to build, maintain, and expand leads. It is no more accurate to claim that the Cleveland offense made the defense look better than it actually was than to claim the reverse. The Browns offense, like offenses throughout football history, simply got more attention than the defense.

The gaudy numbers, while extremely impressive and helpful in quantifying the achievements, are just one part of the story. The other part is the players, the men who did the work that those numbers reflect. The unit was never exactly the same from year to year; only Willis, Young, Lahr, James, and Ford played in more than five of the dynasty seasons, and no defensive player played in more than eight. But it was a tremendous group of players who played together at an exceptionally high level.

That the defense could be great for so long despite the constant turnover of players is also further proof of the greatness of Brown as a coach, an organizer, and a selector of talent. The system that he developed, the coaches he hired to implement that system, and his ability to find and develop new players as needed were the impressive foundation for the defense's achievements. Every time a player retired or slipped, another about as good or better took over his spot. That was true even in the case of Willis, Cleveland's best ever defensive player, who was more than capably replaced first by McCormack and then by Gain in the last years of the middle guard position.

In addition to Brown's approach and leadership, the other factor that enabled the defense to be so great for so long was a combination of lots of talented football players and their ability to work together. The unit was not stocked with players who were the greatest of all time. Other than McCormack, who played only one year of defense, and Atkins, who played only two years before being traded, only Willis and Ford are in the Pro Football Hall of Fame.

And it is not as though there are lots of others who have been unjustly slighted. Of the remaining dozens of other Cleveland defenders, only Gain can really be considered close to Hall of Fame caliber. There were a number of players besides Willis and Ford, however, who were outstanding.

Young and James (eight dynasty years) and Lahr (seven) played with distinction for long periods, while Kissell, Adamle, Lewis, Palmer, Thompson, Gain, Saban, Agase, Paul, Colo, Michaels, and Yonakor were also noteworthy contributors for part of the ten years. None, with the possible exception of Saban, was the very best at his position for more than a year or two, but all were among the better players at their positions at some point from 1946 through 1955.

And where outstanding defensive football often invokes images of violence and savagery, the Browns' reputation was that of a finesse team. None of them is remembered in the way contemporaries like Ed Sprinkle, Hardy Brown, Jim David, and Bucko Kilroy are remembered. Tom Landry, as accomplished a defensive strategist as ever lived, once remarked that opponents never felt beat up after a game with Cleveland the way they did after games with some other teams.

That may have been as much a result of the team's discipline as anything. Brown was one of the first to preach the importance of minimizing penalties, and in part that meant avoiding late hits and unnecessarily rough play. Still, the finesse label and Landry's characterization are not entirely accurate. The Browns had a number of players whom

Gain called "headhunters." Perhaps they were not headhunters in the manner of Sprinkle, but they were aggressive players who frequently punished opponents.

Kissell, Colo, and Gain himself, for example, made the middle of the Cleveland defense a particularly unpleasant and even dangerous place for ball carriers, quarterbacks, and blockers. And few players of that era went as hard or hit as devastatingly as Saban, Willis, Thompson, Ford, and Adamle.

Still, the Browns defenders *were* a finesse group in that they were highly skilled technocrats who were more organized, better coordinated, and more disciplined than the other defenses of their era. They were not wild men looking to intimidate with late hits or brawl at the drop of a hat. They were a group of strong, intelligent, and aggressive players molded by a cerebral coach and a professorial assistant. "Chess with muscles," Brown once said of football. And where hitting was the focus of defenses before, during, and after Cleveland's dynasty, the Browns' approach emphasized thinking as well.

So while there was no getting around the fact that size and strength were essential requirements for a player, for the most part Brown was interested only in players who were also intelligent and fast and, if possible, quick. Brown's genius in recognizing the importance of these qualities, and in developing and best utilizing them in a player, is exemplified in the person of Bill Willis. It is difficult to imagine that a player could play his entire career as an interior down lineman at 210 pounds even in the 1940s and 1950s.

But because Willis was smart, incredibly fast, and quick and had the strength of a much bigger man, he not only played for eight years but also was one of the greatest defensive players ever. Perhaps the most lasting defensive image of that era of Browns football is Willis, who lined up as a down lineman on the play, making up almost 5 yards on Choo Choo Roberts in a span of about 20 yards to prevent a touchdown in Cleveland's 8–3 playoff win over the Giants in 1950.

It was especially on defense that Brown looked for players who had both above average intelligence and football intelligence. That was one of the purposes of the tests Brown administered, tests that were another of his innovations that the old guard initially scoffed at. The tests measured both smarts and a player's ability to learn.

The defenses used by the Browns were not complicated by today's standards, but they did entail following assignments, diagnosing plays, and coordination. Mistakes on offense are frequently harmful, Brown often said, but mistakes on defense are frequently fatal. "Somewhere along the line the dumb guy will get your football team in trouble," the Cleveland coach once said, and he did everything he could to make sure that his players on defense had the necessary football smarts.

Like intelligence, speed was an essential ingredient in Brown's defensive philosophy. James and Lahr were outstanding offensive players in college who Brown switched to defense, and for a period of years, they were probably the fastest players on the team. When Konz joined the secondary in 1953, the team's fastest players, excepting Renfro, were all on defense. Like James and Lahr, Konz could cover. And like James and Lahr, Konz's speed was invaluable in preventing the long touchdown. Rarely in Cleveland's dynasty years did teams break big plays against them.

Others like Willis, Gorgal, and Michaels were faster than most of the players in football who played their position. And Cleveland defenders like those on the line who were not especially fast afoot were quick. Colo, Ford, and especially Gain had the ability to get off the mark ahead of the linemen trying to block them, and that gave them and the defense that much more of an advantage.

Ford was another player who, like James and Lahr, had excelled on offense before coming to Cleveland. Based on both his physical skills and his accomplishments in two years on offense with the Los Angeles Dons, it is easy to imagine Ford blossoming into one of the game's best receivers of the 1950s. Like Cleveland receivers Speedie, Lavelli, Gillom, and Brewster, Ford was an outstanding basketball player.

Ford played a season with the New York Rens, an outstanding all-black team in the years before pro basketball was integrated. In his two years as an outstanding receiver with the Dons, he was able to outposition defenders, shield them away with his size and strength, and go up for passes as a rebounder does. Plus, Ford was bigger and stronger than Speedie and Lavelli.

Brown saw those attributes in Ford and selected him in the 1950 AAFC dispersal draft after every other team passed on him. But Brown envisioned Ford as something other than a great receiver in the making. That was in part because he already had Speedie and Lavelli, but it was also because of Ford's combination of attributes. There were few players in the NFL in 1950 who were six foot five and 260 pounds, Ford's weight after he bulked up, and fewer still who were that size and were also as fast, smart, quick, and agile as Ford.

In addition to the fact that Ford was a rare and exceptional athlete, that was also because fewer players still played both ways by 1950. The requirements of the end position were evolving such that the qualities needed to play offense and defense were increasingly divergent. More and more, defensive-end play emphasized size and strength, while because of the rapid upsurge in the importance of the passing game, the most important qualities for an offensive end were increasingly speed, good hands, and shiftiness.

Despite the changes at the position, none of the NFL's best defensive ends circa 1950, with the exception of Larry Brink at six foot five and 235, was anywhere near as big as Ford. Sprinkle was six foot one and 205; Ray Poole was six foot two and 215; Tom Wham was six foot two and 215; and Pete Pihos, one of the few who was outstanding both ways, was six foot one and 210. Ford's impact would further accelerate the move toward bigger defensive ends that had begun, in part, because of the advent of two-platoon football. And again it was Brown's foresight that enabled him to understand this better and earlier than most of the football men of his time.

Whatever Ford may have been had he remained an offensive player, by his second year with the Browns he was the best defensive end in football. Thus Cleveland's defense went on as strong as ever as Ford replaced his very good predecessor, Yonakor. Like the adjustments made when standouts like Willis, Young, Saban, Thompson, Lewis, and Adamle retired, the move of Ford to defense allowed the Browns to roll on to still greater heights.

Bob Gain was another of Cleveland's best defensive players. Brown recognized this when Gain came out of college in 1951, and he engineered a trade with Green Bay for his NFL rights even though Gain was then playing in Canada. The Packers were experiencing financial difficulties, and a difference of just $1,000 cost the Packers Gain's services. Brown, on the other hand, satisfied Gain's salary needs and was thus again able to whisk a player away from a team that lacked the foresight to fully grasp that player's potential.

In addition to his stint in Canada, Gain's NFL career was further stunted by military obligations and an injury. Almost five years after winning the Outland Trophy as college football's best lineman in his senior year, he had played only eight regular season NFL games. But beginning in 1955, Gain was an outstanding player for ten years.

At six foot three and 255, Gain was ideally suited to play tackle. And before 1955 and for most of his career, that is where he played. As in the case of Ford, though, Brown saw that Gain could play other positions besides the one at which he had previously excelled.

Gain's versatility was such that, in addition to tackle, he was very good at end, middle guard, and linebacker, and Brown did not hesitate to deploy him at those positions as needed. When future Hall of Famer McCormack moved from middle guard to offensive tackle in 1955, for example, Gain moved to that position from tackle and played it at about the same level as McCormack. Gain's versatility not only allowed Brown to move McCormack to a position where he became one of the best of that era, it meant Colo and Kissell could continue to play tackle, Gain's best position, while adding Gain to the mix.

When the middle guard position became obsolete a short time later and Cleveland went to the 4-3 formation, with long-term linebackers Galen Fiss and Vince Costello added to the lineup, Gain moved not to tackle but to end. That not only filled a hole at end, it again meant two very good tackles who did not have Gain's versatility could remain in the starting lineup. Then when Kissell left and the team added ends Paul Wiggin and Bill Quinlan, Gain moved to tackle.

Although he played mostly tackle thereafter, Gain was also sometimes used at end as Brown maneuvered and juggled in search of the best combination. Through it all, Gain continued to earn spots on all-pro teams and in the Pro Bowl, and the Browns continued as one of the league's best teams. Gain and Lou Groza are the only Browns from the dynasty years who were still with the team in the championship season of 1964. Brown made some personnel mistakes with his line talent in the late 1950s and early 1960s, but it is also a testament to Gain's ability that the outstanding players that Brown traded away could not earn a starting spot with

Cleveland. Among those players were Quinlan, Floyd Peters, Jim Marshall, and Hall of Famers Henry Jordan and Willie Davis.

In his book *Dominance: The Best Seasons of Pro Football's Greatest Teams*, Eddie Epstein compares Gain to Art Donovan. He points to clear similarities between their accomplishments as well as those of their teams and questions a Hall of Fame process where Donovan but not Gain has gained induction. A similar comparison could be made to other Hall of Fame contemporaries like Jordan, who was second string behind Gain for two years in Cleveland.

Rather than helping him, Gain's ability to play four positions and play them well may be one of the things that's kept him from enshrinement in Canton. Moving about made it more difficult to appreciate his talents, for although he played all four positions well, Gain was not dominant at any, and dominant players are the ones who make it to the Hall of Fame. Had he played his whole career at tackle, he may have been able to establish that kind of dominance and earn the kind of recognizability and all-pro honors that make a surefire Hall of Famer.

As it is, Gain's Canton credentials are quite good. Achieving Pro Bowl honors and mentions on all-pro teams at three different positions is something not even many Hall of Famers have done. And while both Donovan and Jordan were the best tackles in football at some point during their careers, something that was not true of Gain, it's difficult to imagine either playing end as well as he did. It is more difficult still to imagine either playing middle guard or linebacker as effectively as Gain.

Hall of Fame considerations aside, Gain's versatility unquestionably helped the Browns win many games as well as three championships, including the last two of their dynasty. His talents and aggressiveness were certainly recognized by his coach, teammates, and those who played against him. Jim Brown for one bemoaned the fact that Cleveland did not have more rugged players like Gain in the late 1950s and early 1960s. And longtime opponent John Henry Johnson, as tough a football player as ever lived, paid tribute to old foe Gain in his Hall of Fame induction speech when he said, "I haven't been this scared since I was chased by Bob Gain and Don Colo."

* * *

Seven championships in ten years is perhaps the best indicator of the greatness of the Cleveland defense. Defense wins championships, after all, and while recognition has been somewhat lacking, the players on offense as well as defense knew of the tremendous contribution the defensive unit made to the team's dynasty. Still, as phenomenal as those seven championships are, they actually do not entirely capture how good that group of defensive players was.

That greatness only really becomes apparent when what the Browns did is compared with the defenses that are considered to be the best of all time. Changing circumstances—more teams, free agency, salary caps, parity—can be cited to explain why no team going back even as far as the Purple People Eaters and Steel Curtain has come close to matching the achievements of the Browns defense. But those explanations only limit the discussion, they do not illuminate.

For the fact is that in the same way that none of those more recent defenses comes at all close to Cleveland's, other great defenses from earlier eras don't, either. That is true of a great Lions defense that played in exactly the same 1950s NFL, it is true of a great Packers defense and a Giants defense that came shortly after the Browns dynasty ended—teams that played in an NFL that in lots of ways was very similar—and it is true of the great Bears defense of the 1940s that played in circumstances (fewer teams, lots of poorly run franchises) that were, in a lot of ways, *more* favorable to dynasties and long stretches of domination.

So while the legacy of the Browns defense is intertwined with the overall great success of the team, for the historical record that is only part of the story. Some of Cleveland's individual defensive seasons are among the very best of all time. More important, however, is the fact that over the long term, there is absolutely no question that they were the best in the history of pro football. Football has never seen its like and is not likely to any time soon.

CHAPTER

16

Back on Top

New in 1954: Maurice Bassett (FB), Harold Bradley (G), Herschel Forester (G), Chet Hanulak (HB), Don King (T), Carlton Massey (DE), Mike McCormack (MG), Curly Morrison (FB), Don Paul (DB)

Gone from 1953: Ken Carpenter, Gene Donaldson, Jerry Helluin, Lin Houston, Sherman Howard, Chick Jagade, Marion Motley, Derrell Palmer, Don Steinbrunner, Tommy Thompson, Bill Willis, George Young

Remaining from 1946 (4): Gatski, Graham, Groza, Lavelli

lthough not the largest in sheer numbers, the turnover of players in 1954 was the most dramatic in Cleveland's dynasty run. Four men who had been with the team since 1946—Motley, Willis, Young, and Houston—were not on the 1954 opening-day roster. Palmer and Thompson were two others who played with the team in the AAFC who did not return. All except Motley had retired for good.

Most but not all of the military news was good. Forester, McCormack, and Bradley were on hand to play a full season. Gain, however, did not fulfill his assignment until December. The postponement of a game until the end of the season allowed Gain to play in two games. That turned out to be a break for the Browns because two games was the minimum number required for a player to be eligible for the Championship Game.

Carpenter left for Canada and Kissell returned. With Willis, Palmer, and Young retired and Gain unavailable, Kissell's return was particularly important to the continued excellence of the defense. Carpenter's departure, the retirements of Motley and Howard, and the trading away of Jagade left holes in the running game that newly acquired Curly Morrison and rookies Maurice Bassett and Chet Hanulak were expected to fill.

McCormack's arrival was big news. Brown had said all along that McCormack was the key figure in the fifteen-player trade with the Colts. Born in Chicago and raised in Kansas City, McCormack was an outstanding player at Kansas. In 1951, he played well enough as a rookie with a poor New York Yanks team to be selected to the Pro Bowl.

When he arrived in Cleveland after missing two years, McCormack was a better player than ever. The best testament to that is the fact that he took over for Willis and the defense never missed a beat. It was McCormack's skills as an offensive tackle, however, that had really caught Brown's attention. Brown moved McCormack to offense in 1955, and he was one of the team's best players for the remaining eight years that he played.

McCormack had power, speed, great technique, and intelligence. He also played his entire career with a great deal of enthusiasm. Ten years after he retired, McCormack said that "they almost had to tear the uniform off me, I love the game so much."

Both his enthusiasm and his playing ability made an impression on teammate Bobby Mitchell. "He was a tremendous leader," Mitchell said. "He never made a mistake."

George Ratterman remembered McCormack for his speed and his work habits and said, "He was maybe the greatest lineman I've ever seen."

Bucko Kilroy played the line for thirteen years in the NFL and then worked for many more years as a player personnel evaluator. "I've seen him have games where if you were grading him he'd score 100," Kilroy said of McCormack. "Not one mistake, and his guy would never make a tackle."

Despite playing only one year of defense with Cleveland, McCormack made quite an impression. "No one took liberties with Mike when we turned him loose on the pass rush," coach Howard Brinker said. "He just crushed the middle."

"He could have very likely been a Hall of Famer as a defensive lineman," Galen Fiss said of McCormack. Chuck Noll was one of many others who seconded that statement. As it was, the man Paul Brown called "the finest offensive tackle who ever played professional football" made it to the Hall of Fame on the strength of his great play on offense. McCormack later was a head coach and longtime general manager for several NFL teams.

In the draft came Chet "the Jet" Hanulak from the University of Maryland in the second round and Maurice Bassett from Langston University in the third. Like so many others, Hanulak's career would be interrupted by military service, but not until after the 1954 season. He was a valuable contributor during that season and after his return in 1957.

Bassett's career was similarly brief, but he stepped into the breach at fullback created by the departures of Motley and Jagade. Almost as big as Motley at six foot one and 230 pounds, he made his mark both as a runner and a pass receiver.

The third newcomer in the backfield, Curly Morrison, came by trade from the Bears in exchange for Jagade. He was an Ohio native and an Ohio State graduate who had been a multipurpose player in four seasons with Chicago. In addition to being an above average back, Morrison returned kicks for the Bears and led the league in punting one year. He fit in nicely as the Browns continued with the backfield-by-committee approach in 1954 and then really blossomed in a full-time role in 1955.

Bradley's father Harold Sr. was one of thirteen African Americans to play in the NFL before the imposition of the color line in 1934. Harold Jr. and Forester teamed with Noll to fill the vacancy left by Houston's retirement at the guard spot on the other side of center from Gibron. They would do such a good job in 1954 that Brown was able to move Noll to defense in 1955 to fill a hole at linebacker. It was yet another example of the team's ability to take advantage of the talent on hand to tinker and adjust as necessary. Newcomer Massey played behind Atkins in 1954 and then took over the starting job for two years after Atkins was traded.

Fifth-year defensive back Don Paul arrived via a trade with the Redskins. Traded to Washington after four solid seasons with the Cardinals, seasons he spent mostly on offense, Paul's arrival was indication again that Brown's rules regarding personal behavior were not always as strict as he wanted people to believe. Shortly after being traded to the Redskins, Paul fell into disfavor with George Preston Marshall, who immediately unloaded him to Cleveland.

"Don Paul was a fine football player," Ken Gorgal said. "I think he'd gotten in a jam drinking or doing something, was drunk or something with Washington. Some kind of incident. And then Brown picked him up." Fiss said of Paul that he was both "really a character" and "a great defensive back."

Brown said of his decision to get Paul that Paul's reputation was undeserved and that his real problem was a lousy Cardinal team that won only thirteen of forty-eight games in his tenure with them.

"He simply did not like his losing team or its future," Brown said. "With the Browns, he became a driving force in both our daily practices and our games and turned into a team leader." In his five seasons with the Browns, Paul intercepted twenty-two passes, was named to three Pro Bowls, and got at least second-team all-pro recognition three times.

Brown again had an heir to Graham in mind when he used the bonus pick to select quarterback Bobby Garrett out of Stanford University. In a span of years when a number of Cleveland's high choices didn't pan out, 1954 was a banner year for busts. After selecting Garrett, Cleveland used its first-round choice to select John Bauer, a player who never played for the team and played only two NFL games. Obviously Brown knew talent. He had unearthed many pearls that other teams had overlooked. And Garrett was much heralded as a collegian, as he was selected to just about every All-American team.

But in an era when the player evaluation process was far less sophisticated than it later became, what Brown didn't know was that Garrett had a speech impediment that caused him to stutter. Brown wasn't alone; every other NFL team was ready to take Garrett if he was available. Apparently Garrett had managed to keep the stutter under control in college, and no one in pro football was aware of the problem until he got to Cleveland's training camp.

Amid the pressure of a pro training camp, pressure that was magnified by the talk of his perhaps being Otto Graham's successor, Garrett's stuttering problem surfaced. It got so bad that he was unable to call plays in the huddle or signals at the line of scrimmage. Brown's patience did not last long. Mystified that so little had come of the treasured bonus pick, Brown traded Garrett to the Packers for Babe Parilli, who was in the military at the time and did not join the team until 1956.

Like Garrett, Parilli had been an outstanding college quarterback who entered the NFL touted for greatness. Like Garrett, his stay in Cleveland was brief and undistinguished. Cleveland would reacquire Garrett a few years later in the hopes that he had overcome his stuttering. He had not, however, and the only time in the first fifty years of the Browns franchise that the team selected first in the draft turned out to be a complete loss.

The striking thing about the 1954 draft is how little it yielded for any of the NFL's twelve teams. A number of first-round picks were outright busts, and none had a distinguished career. The biggest sensation was caused by end Harlon Hill, the famously obscure choice from Florence State Teachers College in Alabama picked in the fifteenth round by the Bears. The entire draft of 360 players yielded only one player, twentieth-round pick Raymond Berry, who could be said to have had a great pro career. The best player selected by the Browns was guard Jim Ray Smith, a future choice at Baylor University, although because of the military draft he would not make an impact with the team until 1957.

After quitting in a huff after Brown's criticisms of the defense after the 1951 title-game loss, Tony Adamle devoted himself full-time to medical school. He was just about finished by the fall of 1954 and was working part time as a scout for the Cardinals. Brown had not allowed Adamle's mutinous remarks to go unpunished. After Adamle's outburst and retirement, Brown traded the linebacker to Green Bay, then the NFL's Siberia, a transaction Adamle ignored.

By 1954, the coolness had thawed and Brown engineered a transaction with the Cardinals to regain Adamle after the first game of the season. Adamle agreed to return, but only with the understanding that because of his studies he would practice only one day a week. He joined with Michaels and Catlin to give the Browns a linebacking corps about as good as the group Adamle had played with in the first five years of his career when his mates were Saban, Agase, Thompson, and Humble.

Although no long-term heir apparent was in sight, Graham informed Brown that 1954 would be his last season. The pressures of the game and the drudgery of training camp and practice had gotten to be too much for the great quarterback. Approaching thirty-three, Graham, like most observers, was certain he could play another four or five years. But aside from the quest for one more redemptive championship, there was little left to accomplish.

Graham was also driven by a desire to retire while still on top. In the decades after his retirement, Graham alluded on a number of occasions to the experience of Joe Louis that unfolded in the middle of Graham's playing career. After carving out a niche for himself as perhaps the greatest heavyweight boxer ever, Louis had his achievements tarnished by some very un-Louis-like performances in several fights after an ill-fated return to the ring.

Last but by no means least, both Blanton Collier and Weeb Ewbank left the Cleveland coaching staff for head-coaching jobs, Collier at Kentucky and Ewbank with the Colts. Collier, and not Ewbank, was actually Baltimore's first choice, but his preference for the Kentucky job opened the door for his colleague. Brown and Collier remained close for nine more years. The Cleveland coach apparently called his longtime right-hand man throughout Collier's eight-year stint at Kentucky for advice, player evaluations, and the like.

Brown and Ewbank's relationship soured somewhat before Ewbank even departed Cleveland, however. Dub Jones said that Brown "was terrible to his assistant coaches. . . . They were just as intimidated as the ballplayers were, more so." Whether or not that was the nature of Brown and Ewbank's relationship, Ewbank was unhappy when Brown tried to talk him out of accepting the Baltimore job. When Ewbank persisted with his interest, Brown told him he would never make it. For his part, Brown accused Ewbank of passing Cleveland's scouting information on to the Colts on draft day.

Ewbank certainly did make it. He built one of the best teams of all time in Baltimore, teams that won NFL championships in 1958 and 1959. He also won a championship with the AFL New York Jets and thus became the only coach besides Paul Brown to win titles in two major leagues.

Collier's term at Kentucky was largely uneventful, but he returned to the Browns as an assistant in 1962 and was very successful in eight years as Cleveland's head coach after he succeeded Brown. When he took the head job in Cleveland after Brown was fired, however, Brown curtailed their twenty-year friendship. Collier thus joined an increasingly large group of people that had once been close to Brown and then became alienated or even entirely cut out of the Cleveland coach's life. Joining the Browns' staff in place of Collier and Ewbank were Howard Brinker, an old Massillon player, and Ed Ulinski, a standout guard for the Browns in their four AAFC years.

After a 2–3 preseason that included yet another loss to the Lions and yet another win over a Chicago team (the Bears), the 1954 regular season began the way the 1953 regular season ended: with a decisive loss to the Eagles in Philadelphia. The Eagles dominated and won 28–10 behind four touchdowns through the air. Graham connected with Lavelli for Cleveland's only touchdown but otherwise had a subpar game reminiscent of the title game against the Lions nine months before.

As in 1948, a Municipal Stadium scheduling conflict arose because of an Indians World Series game. Game 5 of the Series between the Indians and Giants was scheduled for Sunday, October 3, the same day the Browns were scheduled to host the Lions. Brown resisted entreaties from Buddy Parker and the Lions owners to move the game to Briggs Stadium, scoffing at Detroit's guarantee that the Browns would be given a home team's share of the ticket money. The game was instead rescheduled for the open week between the end of the regular season and the Championship Game.

Football fans, especially those on either side of Lake Erie, were thus left to speculate as to whether the December 19 game between the two teams might be a prelude to a third consecutive title-game matchup. As it turned out, no game of any kind was played at Municipal Stadium on October 3. On Saturday the 2nd, the Giants completed a shocking four-game sweep of an Indians team that had won an all-time record 111 regular season games.

The prospect of another Browns-Lions title game did not appear very likely a few weeks later, at least not where the Browns were concerned. After the usual 31–7 rout of the Cardinals in which Graham returned to form with a masterful game, the Browns were routed for the second time in three games, this time by Pittsburgh at Forbes Field. Steelers halfback Ray Mathews piled up 235 yards from scrimmage and scored four times as Pittsburgh romped, 55–27.

Graham was twenty-two of twenty-eight for 298 yards and three touchdowns in the game, but he was also intercepted five times. Two of the interceptions were returned all the way. The Browns actually had a 14–7 second-quarter lead but were soon buried under an avalanche of Pittsburgh touchdowns. Perhaps because of the large roster turnover, or perhaps because of the loss of so many key veteran players all at once, Cleveland was 1–2 for the first time ever.

Or perhaps it was a case of several pissed-off teams finally striking back at their tormentors. Philadelphia's win was just its third in nine games against the Browns, and Pittsburgh's win was its very first ever against Cleveland after eight losses. Whatever it was, the Browns had allowed 90 points in three games and were in fourth place in the East, ahead of only the hapless Cardinals and Redskins. Even the most steadfast of fans must have had their doubts, especially with the Eagles off to a 4–0 start and both the Giants and Steelers sitting at 3–1.

"I was disheartened," said newcomer McCormack, "but I'll never forget Don Colo and Sandusky and a safety man named Ken Gorgal saying, 'No problem, we'll win it.'" The confidence even after two ragged performances struck McCormack. "[T]here was no doubt in their minds" that they would finish the season in first place.

Looking back, Brown felt that the postponement of the Lions game had been a break. With the team struggling, a game at that point against the best team in the league could very well have meant a 1–3 start. That not only would have meant a three-game deficit in the standings, it also would have dented the attitude of even the most confident of the Browns.

It helped that the Cardinals were up next, and Cleveland romped 35–3. The defense righted itself with a smothering performance, allowing only eight first downs, 160 yards, and no points after Pat Summerall's first-quarter field goal. Lavelli led the way with eight catches for 98 yards and a touchdown, while Graham and Bassett each scored twice on the ground. The Browns squared their mark at 2–2 and gained a game on the Eagles, who lost on Saturday night at Forbes Field.

Things tightened even more the following week when the Browns beat the Giants, 24–14, and the Eagles and Steelers lost. Graham again ran for two scores, and Lavelli caught his fourth touchdown pass of the year. Groza was again kicking with outstanding accuracy, and his fourth-quarter field goal after a Konz interception put the game out of reach.

Ratterman was outstanding in relief the following week in a 62–3 destruction of the Redskins. Those around the league who had thought hopefully three weeks earlier that Cleveland's dynasty had run its course were certainly dismayed by the team's performance against the Redskins. The defense held Washington to 64 total yards and four first downs and forced five turnovers. Gorgal scored the game's last touchdown with a 53-yard interception return.

The offense rolled despite Graham's absence for about half the game as Ratterman completed ten of eleven for 208 yards and three touchdowns. Brewster caught seven passes for 114 yards and two touchdowns, and Jones gained 84 yards on just ten carries and added 93 yards on three catches and a score. In all, Cleveland piled up thirty-three first downs and 515 yards.

The Browns continued their amazing mastery of the city of Chicago with another one-sided win, this time by 39–10 over the Bears at Wrigley Field. Groza kicked three field goals, Graham scored his sixth rushing touchdown, Lavelli caught his seventh touchdown pass, and Hanulak rushed for 90 yards and scored his first career touchdown on a 7-yard run. It was the twentieth straight victory over Chicago teams (twenty-six including preseason games), and the Browns had outscored the big, bad Bears 81–31 in their two regular season meetings.

The defense was again devastating, holding the Bears to 3 points until the final minutes. Ford nailed quarterback Zeke Bratkowski for a safety, and Lahr duplicated Gorgal's feat of the week before with a touchdown on an interception return. It was the fifth such return of Lahr's career and established a new NFL record, one that Lahr held until Herb Adderley broke it in 1967.

A year after being beaten for the touchdown that decided the previous Championship Game, Lahr was playing the best cornerback of his career. "He just got tougher," McCormack said of Lahr in 1954. Lahr was a big reason the Browns finished first year after year in pass defense. By season's end he would have five interceptions, the fifth of six straight seasons he had at least that many.

Few defenses of that era turned games around with touchdowns as frequently as Cleveland's, and Lahr was as good as any of his defensive mates at getting into the end zone. He did it in the game against the Bears, and he did it in consecutive crucial games at the end of 1950. And Lahr's speed, coverage skills, and touchdown returns should not obscure the fact that he was a solid all-around defensive player who was strong against the run and a sure tackler, an important reason Cleveland rarely gave up long plays.

"He was a good, solid defensive back," Derrell Palmer said. Groza remembered that Lahr was a "very smart football player" who "possessed great athletic skills" and packed a lot of muscle into his five-foot-eleven, 185-pound frame. Paul Brown echoed that sentiment. "He didn't look like much in street clothes," Brown said, "but his tremendous body just rippled."

Then in his sixth season, Lahr was probably Cleveland's top defensive back, and he continued as such for most of the rest of his career. In addition, Lahr was a leader and well liked by his teammates. In his eleven-year career, a lot of defensive backs played for the Browns, and Lahr was a steadying force in the secondary. That influence and his outstanding play enabled the Browns to be the NFL's best defense for most of the 1950s and a contending team even after the end of their dynasty.

Seemingly with nowhere to go but down, the defense went up to still greater heights with a 6–0 shutout of the Eagles on November 21. The Browns made two Groza field goals stand up by holding the same Philadelphia team that had put up 70 points against them in their two previous meetings to 110 yards and ten first downs. That made it 30 points allowed in the five games since the 1–2 start. Bassett led the offense with 95 yards rushing and three catches for 60 yards. Five straight wins had thrust Cleveland into first place with a 6–2 record, just ahead of the 6–3 Giants.

A big reason the Browns had been able to make up so much ground in so little time was the excellent play of Dante Lavelli, who was having one of the best years of an outstanding career. Two thirds of the way through the season, he was among the league leaders in all of the major receiving categories. Especially noteworthy were his seven touchdowns and 17.1 yards per catch.

Lavelli's value could not be adequately captured by numbers alone, however. He had a knack for coming up with his best days and making big plays when they were most needed. That was true in his rookie year of 1946 when Lavelli caught the championship-winning touchdown, and it was still true in 1954. His eight-reception day against the Cardinals came in a game the Browns needed to avoid a 1–3 start, while his touchdown catch a week later put the Browns in front for good in their win over the first-place Giants.

"Lavelli wanted to win in the worst way," said Lin Houston, a teammate at Ohio State and for eight seasons in Cleveland. "And the tougher it got, the tougher he got." Brown called Lavelli "Clutch" because "so many of his catches were big ones."

Lavelli is proof that success is 10% inspiration and 90% perspiration. He ran patterns for hours after practice with Graham so that the two of them could get their timing down just right. Their synchronization became so acute it got "to where Otto could tell by my shoulder pads which way I was going to go." The result was pass completions in games that often looked easy.

Lavelli had excellent speed and hands that were both incredibly strong and true. They were "the best hands the game has ever seen," according to Graham. He knew how to position himself, how to time his jump, and how to angle defenders away from the flight of a pass, and he went up determined that he and only he was going to come down with the ball.

Brown said, "Dante was the greatest guy at catching a ball in a crowd that I have ever seen," while Groza said that Lavelli "was absolutely fearless when going over the middle."

"Nobody can ever take the ball away from him once he gets his hands on it," Brown said when Lavelli was at the peak of his abilities. Looking back years later, Brown went so far as to say, "I can't remember him dropping a single pass."

Although while he was playing Lavelli said that it was his job "to go in a certain direction and be at a certain spot at the proper count," that is a somewhat overly mechanical description of his pass patterns. Years later he said that it was fairly common for him to break off from the intended route if there was an opening elsewhere. Lavelli and Graham worked on that in practice, too, and it made the Cleveland passing game all the more dangerous. In 1954, Lavelli would lead the Browns in receptions for the second consecutive year and the fourth time in his career.

First place was in hand, but Cleveland's lead was only a half game. With a season-ending game looming against a Lions team that was again leading the pack in the West, Brown and his players knew there was a long way to go. And the first game of the home stretch was a showdown with the second-place Giants.

Under first-year head coach Jim Lee Howell, New York was much improved over their fifth-place finish in 1953. After starting 4–1, the Giants had slipped, however, and were 6–3 as they prepared to host the 6–2 Browns. New York was coming off a tough 1-point loss to a good Rams team that was again very much in the hunt in the West.

On a cold, raw day at the Polo Grounds, the Browns took a big step toward a ninth straight conference championship with a 16–7 victory. The Cleveland defense continued its marvelous play with another dominating performance. They held the Giants to four first downs, 4 yards rushing, and 68 yards passing and blocked a Ben Agajanian field goal attempt. New York's only points came on a punt return by Herb Johnson.

After a somewhat slow start, Groza had again found his groove. He kicked three field goals against New York to give him ten in four games, and Graham and Brewster provided much of the team's offense. Graham completed sixteen of twenty-seven passes for 238 yards and ran for a touchdown, while Brewster caught eight for 126 yards. Despite the scoring return by Johnson, Gillom had an excellent day. He helped keep the Giants hemmed in with a 54-yard average, including one kick of 80 yards that was the longest of his career. The Browns thus entered December with a lead of one and a half games.

Cleveland clinched a tie for first place with a 34–14 victory against the Redskins at Griffith Stadium. Graham was thirteen of eighteen for 252 yards and rushed for 41 yards, while Lavelli caught five passes for 126 yards and Brewster hauled in six for 98 yards. The defense was again outstanding. They held the Redskins to 7 points until the final moments and again put points on the board as Konz returned an interception 25 yards for a touchdown.

The Lions clinched the Western Conference when they rallied for a 13–13 tie against the Eagles. It was the first time since 1946 that the race in the West was settled before the season's final day. So the Lions would have a shot at becoming the only team besides the Browns to win three consecutive championships. Still to be determined was whether that shot would come against the Browns themselves for a third straight time or whether it would come against the Giants, the fading Eagles having been eliminated.

Smelling blood, there was no stopping the Browns on December 12 against Pittsburgh as Hanulak had the biggest game of his rookie season. Playing against a number of former teammates from his Air Force team, Lieutenant Hanulak ran for 94 yards and three touchdowns as Cleveland avenged its 28-point loss with a 42–7 rout.

Cleveland rushed for 298 yards in all and finished with 469 yards from scrimmage. The defense held the Steelers to 171 yards, forced six turnovers, and did not allow Pittsburgh's only points until the score was 28–0. For the second game in a row, Konz scored on an interception return. During its eight-game winning streak, Cleveland allowed just 7.3 points per game and a total of seven touchdowns. And in one stretch of four games, the Browns defense scored more points than it allowed.

Like McCormack, Hanulak was in his first year with Cleveland. He had been aware of the team's prowess ever since seeing them manhandle a good Yankees team as a high school senior in 1949. And like McCormack, Hanulak was bewildered after the Browns started 1954 with two bad losses in the first three games. They had always been a terrific team, but what's more, all the winning that began in 1946 had created an aura about them.

"How could this be happening to us, the Cleveland Browns?" Hanulak said of his thoughts in October. He felt privileged to have been drafted by pro football's best franchise but was discouraged when the season started so poorly. Once the team righted itself, their play and Hanulak's mood improved dramatically.

"As the season went on, you got that old feeling back like nobody's gonna beat us," Hanulak said of the winning streak. The Browns ran roughshod over opponent after opponent in that span, winning the eight games by an average of 25 points. Still remaining were two games with the Lions, one meaningless one and one for all the marbles. All of the great play during the regular season would be for naught if the Browns couldn't figure out a way to beat Detroit.

Both Brown and Buddy Parker approached the season finale with a degree of trepidation. There was always a risk of injury, and each would limit the playing time of certain key players. And although the two teams already knew each other quite well by that point, both coaches figured to play it close to the vest with a much more important rerun scheduled a week later.

On the other hand, the Browns certainly could have used a victory against Detroit. Nowhere in Paul Brown's scientific football world of thorough scouting reports, game films, preparation, and execution did hexes or jinxes factor in, but even the great coach could no longer wave aside his team's poor record against the Lions. Actually, the notion of a jinx or a hex must have had at least some appeal to Brown, for the obvious alternative conclusion was that Parker's team was simply better than his, something that Brown was loath to admit.

For the Lions, on the other hand, there was little in the way of pressure as they approached the two games against Cleveland. Detroit not only was a great team, they clearly had an advantage over a team that had beaten them only once in eight games. More important, by winning the two very biggest of their matchups with Cleveland, they had gained football supremacy two years running. Their preseason and regular season wins over the Browns were great, but those two Championship Game victories provided the Lions all the psychological advantage they needed.

Snow blanketed Cleveland on December 19, ensuring that the two teams would play all the more conservatively. Despite being largely unable to move the ball, the Browns took a 10–7 lead into the final minutes. Graham scored his eighth touchdown of the season in the first quarter, and Groza kicked a 44-yard field goal through swirling snow to give Cleveland the lead in the third.

But in an ending that was eerily similar to the end of the previous year's Championship Game, the Lions drove down the field in the closing minutes. Layne connected with Jug Girard on an 11-yard touchdown pass with 0:50 seconds remaining and Detroit won, 14–10. Counting exhibition, regular season, and Championship Games, the win boosted Detroit's edge over the Browns to 7–1–1 and allowed the Lions to edge the Browns for the best record in the NFL for 1954, 9–2–1 to 9–3.

Graham was second in the league in passing behind Van Brocklin, Bassett was fifth in rushing, Lavelli fifth in receptions, Groza third in scoring and first in most kicking categories, Reynolds first in kickoff returns, and Gillom second in punting. The defense again led the league in numerous categories; perhaps the most impressive was allowing only four rushing touchdowns. Ford set a new league mark when he recovered an opposition fumble for the twelfth time in his five NFL seasons, a total he would increase to twenty by the end of his career. He remained the all-time leader in fumble recoveries until 1962 when Andy Robustelli broke his record.

After leading the NFL in field goals for a third straight year and fourth overall, feats no other kicker has ever accomplished, Groza was named the *Sporting News* Player of the Year. He also joined Graham and Ford as unanimous first-team all-pros. Gibron, Gatski, and five members of the defense—Colo, Catlin, McCormack, James, and Lahr—were second-team picks on at least one of the all-pro teams.

For the sixth time in eight years, Brown was somebody's Coach of the Year, winning the award from UPI. Groza, Gatski, Ford, Graham, Gibron, Lavelli, and Colo were selected to play in the Pro Bowl. But as far as the Browns were concerned, the Pro Bowl was a month away and could wait; there was far more important business at hand.

The Lions went home for a week of practice, and the Browns went back to work at League Park. Among those at the workouts was Bob Gain. Gain returned December 12 against the Steelers, the game that was the regularly scheduled season finale. Had he played in just that game, he would not have been eligible for the Championship Game; league rules required that a player play two regular season games to be eligible. When he played in the rescheduled game against the Lions, however, Gain became eligible for the title game, a break for the Browns.

The fact that it was the Eastern Conference champion's turn to host the title game was also a break for the Browns. For the fourth year in a row, the team with the league's best record would have to play on the road in the Championship Game. The preference for any team to play at home was even more pronounced in this case; Cleveland had never won so much as a preseason game at Briggs Stadium (later renamed Tiger Stadium) and never would in the twenty remaining years the Lions called it home.

Three straight Championship Game losses had punctured both Cleveland's and Paul Brown's air of invincibility. Among the players, Lavelli felt that part of the explanation for those three losses was offensive game plans that were too conservative. "[T]he three games we lost . . . is because Brown wouldn't throw the ball on 3rd and 2 or something."

In the three Championship Game losses, the Browns had scored only four touchdowns and 40 points. Even with so little production, they had lost the games by an average of only 6 points. And they had been alive until the last minutes in all of them.

No one was more aware of the offense's deficiencies in the three losses than Otto Graham. His poor play in the 1953 game especially gnawed at him. In fact, the ghost of that performance hovered over Graham all year, driving him to still greater levels of excellence in his determination to redeem himself for that performance. And although Graham was not the kind of person who would have said so at the time, he later acknowledged that he was glad that his chance for redemption had come against the Lions.

The night before the game, Graham called a meeting of the offense in a room of the Carter Hotel where the team was staying. Like Lavelli and some of the other players, Graham was concerned about Brown's conservative play-calling. Having announced that the game would be his last, Graham had less reason to fear the consequences for defying the coach. He proposed, and his gathered teammates agreed, that they would call their own plays when necessary if the team fell behind.

In addition to being justifiably confident, the Lions may have been feeling a bit dismissive of the Browns. In an era when publicly belittling an opponent was a very rare occurrence, the Lions made a mistake by belittling the Browns as "cheese champions." Looking for any advantage they could, the Browns may have inflated the comments beyond what was intended. But once the remarks appeared, several Lions amplified on them, and the comments became fodder for discussion in the days leading up to the championship match.

According to the Lions, the Browns were "cheese champions" because the West was the stronger of the two conferences. The Browns may have won five straight Eastern Conference championships since joining the NFL, the argument went, but they had done so against competition that was weaker than that in the West. The 11–1 regular season records that Cleveland had put together in 1951 and 1953, for example, had not stood up in the title game either year.

Carrying the argument a bit further, even if the Browns were an elite team, the thinking among some Lions was that they were the only such team in the East. Their comparatively comfortable margin in the standings in three of five years could be cited as evidence of that. By contrast, the Lions, Bears, Rams, and 49ers of the West were all annually considered to be championship timber.

On the surface, the "cheese champions" argument had some merit. The team finishing first in the West had won the championship three straight years, and the West's best teams had staged a series of compelling multiteam conference races since World War II. That was true before the AAFC-NFL merger and even more true once the 49ers emerged as a force in 1951. Plus the West had gone 8–3–1 in games between the two conferences in 1954, and the decisive 11–3 advantage the East had posted in 1950 was by then four years in the past.

The assertion of Western Conference superiority is contradicted by two sets of facts. First is the interconference advantage the East held over the West in the five seasons from 1950 through 1954. Although the 35–32–2 advantage is slight, it is real enough, and it is difficult to see how that record can be indicative of anything other than equality or a slight degree of Eastern superiority. The West's 8–3–1 advantage in 1954, while also real enough, was actually an exception considering that in every other season of that era the slate was either about even or heavily favored the East. Although four years in the past by 1954, the East's 11–3 advantage in 1950 was even more decisive than that 8–3–1 mark.

Even if the West was deemed to be the better conference, one other fact irrefutably destroys any notion that the Browns were "cheese champions" feasting only on inferior Eastern competition: Cleveland's record against the West. In fact, the Browns' 1950–1954 record against the West is dominant. In regular season games, they were 8–3 against the West: 2–0 against the Bears, 2–0 against the Rams, 2–1 against the 49ers, 1–0 against the Packers, 1–0 against the Colts, and 0–2 against the Lions.

Seven of Cleveland's wins were by decisive margins (15 or more points), and the average margin of victory in their wins was 21.9 points. The Browns' advantage in points in all eleven games was 297 to 151. Cleveland was 6–1 with a 223 to 116 advantage in points against the Rams, Bears, and 49ers, three of the West teams that were consistently contenders; that's a 2 to 1 advantage in points, and only one of the Browns' six wins against those upper-tier Western teams was close.

Extending Cleveland's performance to 1955, the last year of their ten-year dynasty, the Browns went 2–0 and had a 79 to 13 scoring advantage in their games against Western teams. That raised their record to 10–3, with a 16.3 per-game point advantage in six years. And since one of the 1955 wins was another blowout of one of the West's big four (38–3 over San Francisco), Cleveland's mark against the Rams, Bears, and 49ers over six years was 7–1, and they outscored those teams by an average of 18 points per game.

The only light in which the Browns' record against the West pales somewhat is when it is compared with their record against the East. Cleveland's record against the East through 1954 was 41–8, a winning percentage of .837. So at the same time the Browns dominated their Eastern foes, they also dominated the West, just not to the same degree. That and the East's overall record against the West clearly refute the notion that the West was better than the East or that the Browns' annual first-place finishes were those of "cheese champions." A team with a .769 winning percentage and a 376 to 164 scoring advantage, Cleveland's 1950–1955 record against the West, would have won a lot of championships in any era, but especially in that pre-expansion era, and none of them would have been made of cheese.

The Browns' problem was not a Western Conference problem, it was a Lions problem. A third straight Championship Game loss to Detroit (and fourth overall) would not only have more emphatically made that point but would also have been an embarrassment for a team as proud as the Browns. But while the Lions had every reason in the world to be confident, the ill-advised words of several of their players made the Browns that much more determined to vanquish their toughest foe.

No two teams other than the Browns and Lions have played for pro football supremacy three years in a row. The two previous meetings had been close, hard-fought games decided by a total of 11 points. Bert Bell had said the 1953 teams were the two best ever to play for football supremacy.

Bell may have been correct, but it's very possible that both teams were even better in 1954. Although they won one fewer game, Detroit's points scored and points allowed were substantially better than in 1953, and they won the West more decisively. Bobby Layne for one thought the 1954 Lions the best of their great teams from that era.

And it would be difficult to argue that any team had ever played as well as the Browns did over the last two months of the 1954 regular season. No team scored more than 14 points against them in their last nine games, and they allowed only 8 points per game in that stretch. Over that span, they outscored their opponents by an average of 22 points. Whether the teams were better, as good, or not as good, they figured to battle fiercely in the Championship Game for the third straight year.

The game did not begin well for the Browns, and many in the home crowd of 43,827 must have felt that it was again to be Detroit's day. On the very first play from scrimmage, Bill Bowman ran 49 yards to the Cleveland 34. An early deficit was temporarily averted when Kissell fell on a Lew Carpenter fumble, but after Schmidt intercepted a Graham pass on Cleveland's first offensive play, Detroit converted the turnover into a Walker field goal for an early 3–0 lead.

Cleveland did not do much offensively on their second possession, either. They wasted great field position after a long Reynolds kickoff return and were forced to punt. But Gillom was roughed after punting by Harley Sewell, and the Browns maintained possession. They immediately capitalized when Graham threw a 35-yard touchdown pass to Renfro.

The touchdown was the result of Brown's close examination of film of previous games between the two teams. Brown noticed that Detroit's cornerbacks came up in anticipation of a sweep any time Cleveland lined up in a tight T-formation. On the touchdown, Cleveland lined up in the tight T and the Lions overplayed the run just as Brown anticipated. Renfro circled out of the backfield to the left around the defense and caught Graham's pass well behind the secondary.

From that point on, it was a landslide of Cleveland scoring, scoring fueled by eight more takeaways as the Browns won 56–10. As he had throughout his career, Graham passed with great accuracy and for lots of yards per pass to lead the charge. He was nine of twelve for 163 yards and touchdowns of 35 and 31 yards to Renfro and 8 yards to Brewster. Those numbers translate into a 75% completion rate, 13.6 yards per attempt, and a passer rating of 116.7.

Graham also scored three rushing touchdowns. Three passing touchdowns and three rushing touchdowns—it was one of the best individual performances ever in a Championship Game or Super Bowl. Renfro was the other top offensive performer, with 94 receiving yards on five catches and two touchdowns. Brewster made his two catches count for 53 yards, and Morrison and Hanulak added scoring runs.

As magnificent as the defense had been all year, they were able to top their regular season excellence against the Lions. Ford became the only lineman ever to intercept two passes in a postseason game, returning one of them a Championship Game record 45 yards. Konz also had two interceptions as the Browns picked off six Layne passes in all, and Michaels added an interception and a fumble recovery that snuffed out a Lions drive. In all, takeaways led directly to five of Cleveland's eight touchdowns. And in addition to his long kickoff return, Reynolds ran a punt back 42 yards to the Detroit 12 to set up Cleveland's third score.

Perhaps the most bizarre and telling play of the game came in the second quarter. Having just scored to pull to 21–10, Detroit had the ball and was poised to chip away further at Cleveland's early lead. But McCormack rushed Layne and, upon grabbing the Detroit quarterback to tackle him, adeptly stole the ball out of his hands at the Detroit 31. Graham scored a short time later to boost the lead to 28–10. That one play amply captured Detroit's sloppy play and Cleveland's alertness and opportunism.

"The defense wanted to prove something to Paul Brown because of the way they had beaten us," said Konz. "We wanted to prove we had the best defense in the league."

Further testimony to the huge role played by the turnovers and the resulting Cleveland advantage in field position is the fact that other than in passing efficiency, the Browns had no discernible statistical advantages. They held a 17–16 edge in first downs, but the Lions actually had more yards, 331 to 303. Hanulak's 44 yards on five carries was the Browns' top rushing performance of the day, and Cleveland rushed for just 3.1 yards per attempt as a team. But time and again the Browns had a short field to work with, and the 303 total yards yielded 56 points.

After frustrating finishes to outstanding seasons the three previous years, the Browns were back on top. Graham's sojourn back from the despair of 1953 may have been more publicized, but every member of the team had worked hard to make the championship possible. Few teams before or since have put together as dominating a stretch as Cleveland did beginning with the fourth game of the season.

The game against the Lions was a breakout one for Renfro. The same man who had zero catches and zero yards rushing against the Lions the year before helped the Browns build their big halftime lead with his two scoring catches. "We killed them there," Graham said of the speedy Renfro's performance. "Ray was very fast and a very good receiver."

Near the end of the game, Brown sent Ratterman in to replace Graham. The Cleveland crowd rose and roared, voicing its appreciation both for the quarterback's great performance that day and for his fantastic career. In nine years he had led the Browns to nine Championship Game appearances and six championships.

"That almost made me change my mind," Graham said afterward of the impact his and the team's performance had on his plans to retire. Amid the locker room celebration, Brown asked a reporter rhetorically, "Why should a guy who can do what he did want to retire?" Later the coach added, "I don't want him to quit."

And with good reason. What the Browns accomplished against the Lions was about as great a moment as the franchise had ever had, ranking with the first championship in 1946, the perfect season in 1948, and the wins over the Eagles and Rams in 1950. When Brown addressed his team, he said, "On this given day, you were the finest team I have ever coached."

In fact, Graham had not yet played his last game. He would return for one more season. At the end of that season, both he and his team had solidified their claims as the best of their or any other time.

Seven Championships in Ten Years

New in 1955: Henry Ford (HB), Ed Modzelewski (FB), Sam Palumbo (LB/C), Pete Perini (FB), John Petitbon (DB), Bob Smith (HB), Chuck Weber (G/LB), Bob White (HB)

Gone from 1954: Tony Adamle, Doug Atkins, Ken Gorgal, Don King

Remaining from 1946 (4): Gatski, Graham, Groza, Lavelli

Remaining from 1950 (12): Ford, Gatski, Gibron, Gillom, Graham, Groza, James, Jones, Kissell, Lahr, Lavelli, Sandusky

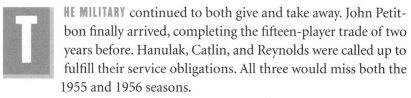

THE MILITARY continued to both give and take away. John Petitbon finally arrived, completing the fifteen-player trade of two years before. Hanulak, Catlin, and Reynolds were called up to fulfill their service obligations. All three would miss both the 1955 and 1956 seasons.

Those losses created holes in both the linebacking corps and the running game. Brown addressed Catlin's absence by moving Noll from offense to defense and by drafting Notre Dame linebacker Sam Palumbo in the fourth round. Palumbo played two seasons with Cleveland and made his most valuable contribution in the 1955 Championship Game.

Rookie halfbacks Bob Smith and Henry Ford made the team, although Ford was released after two games. He was the ninth African American to play for Cleveland. Former 49er Bob White played part of the season for the Browns and then was dispatched to the Colts. Fullback Pete Perini played half the season with the Browns after starting with the Bears as Brown maneuvered all season to make up for the loss of Hanulak and Reynolds.

Like Petitbon, Gain had finally fulfilled his military obligations, and 1955 was the first year that he played a full season with the team. He proved to be an extremely valuable player. McCormack was moved to offense and Gain stepped right into the middle of the Cleveland defense, a defense that once again would be the NFL's best.

Of particular value was the fact that Gain excelled at three different positions. As the league continued to evolve from the 5-3 to the 5-2 and eventually to the 4-3, many teams including the Browns used all three formations at different times. Depending on the situation, Gain played as a tackle, a middle guard, and a middle linebacker in 1955, something very few players were able to do. The defense was not as dominating as in previous years, but it again finished first in most of the important categories including fewest points, fewest yards, fewest yards per pass, and lowest completion percentage.

The versatility of third-year man Chuck Noll also proved a valuable asset to the defense. After two years at offensive guard, Noll's move to outside linebacker helped make up for the loss of Catlin and Adamle. He even became the defensive signal-caller.

The yield from the draft was very thin. None of the top five picks ever played for the team. Of the handful of draft choices who did make the Browns, none played more than two years and none ever became a starter. First-round pick Kurt Burris, an All-American center from the University of Oklahoma, went to Canada and never played in the NFL.

Brown used a third-round pick on Auburn University quarterback Bobby Freeman, who, on the surface, seemed to be another of those he hoped might succeed Graham. Freeman also opted to play in Canada, and Brown later claimed that he "never had any illusions that Bobby could be a quarterback with us," which made the use of the thirty-seventh overall pick of the draft on him a bit curious.

The real addition to the team and the newcomer who made the biggest impact was fullback Ed Modzelewski. "Big Mo" was a former teammate of Hanulak's in college on an excellent Maryland team and a former first-round choice of the Steelers. When Marion Motley came out of retirement and the Browns traded his rights to the Steelers, Modzelewski went to the Browns as compensation.

Although he arrived at the end of training camp, Modzelewski made an immediate impression and took away Bassett's starting job. He and Morrison teamed to give the Browns their best running tandem since Motley and Dub Jones in 1950, and they led the team to its best rushing season in five years. Modzelewski remained with the Browns for five seasons.

Adamle retired for good, and Gorgal was traded to the Bears. Gorgal had been a solid player in the three seasons he played bracketed around two years in the Army. He intercepted eleven passes in those three seasons and had two more in the 1953 Championship Game.

Gorgal also added some of the many intangibles that contribute to a prolonged dynasty like Cleveland's. He had the confidence that so impressed newcomer McCormack in 1954, and Brown called him one of the nicest men he'd ever known. "The players called him Gurgles Gorgal," Brown said, "because he added so much fellowship and good feeling to our team."

Business was business, however, and Brown traded Gorgal nonetheless. And while Gorgal did not hesitate to praise Brown's tremendous skills and cite them as one of the biggest factors in the team's success, he also harbored some resentment toward his former coach. For one thing, he was traded right after sustaining an injury. There was a connection, Gorgal felt, and the implication was that it was a player's responsibility to avoid injury.

Also, Gorgal felt the Cleveland coach "was kind of hypocritical" when it came to players who supposedly didn't fit the Brown mold. "He always said, 'They're not our kind of people,' we were all supposed to be straight shooters," Gorgal said. But that was not true in the case of players on the team who were known to be carousers and heavy drinkers, and, according to Gorgal, it was not true in the case of Brown's acquisition of Don Paul, the player who took Gorgal's place.

And while there was room for players whose drinking was so problematic that it affected their play, there was no room for Doug Atkins, one of Gorgal's best friends on the team. Like Gorgal, Atkins was dispatched to the Bears. "He could be disruptive to the coaching staff, but you knew he was going to be a great football player," Gorgal said of Atkins. "Better than they had."

Although most Cleveland players knew Brown well enough not to be surprised when he got rid of Atkins, the fact that he got rid of such a talented player for just a few draft choices baffled some of them. Like Gorgal, many of them looked back at the trade as a mistake.

"Doug was a hellraiser, but he wasn't worse than the rest of us at the time," Colo said. Colo disagreed with Gorgal in one sense, though, when he said, "With Doug, he had someone to replace him, obviously." That someone was Massey. However, given that Massey played just two more seasons with Cleveland and five overall, while Atkins had a seventeen-year Hall of Fame career, Gorgal was far more accurate in his assessment of the impact of the trade than Colo. Massey may have replaced Atkins, but he was nowhere near as good.

Brown's explanation for the trade was simply that Atkins's "lifestyle became incompatible with our philosophy." Brown apparently never admitted that there was a double standard at work, nor does he seem to have realized that a number of his players accepted his philosophy to a great degree simply because he was their boss and not because they believed it represented some high moral standard worthy of their respect.

For example, Len Ford was a great player and, like Atkins, a future Hall of Famer. But a number of teammates also spoke of Ford's heavy drinking (one remembered Ford coming to practices reeking of alcohol), his taste for the night life, and his questionable practice habits. The fact that Cleveland kept Ford for eight years and got rid of him only after he was a shadow of his perennial all-pro self is further evidence of a double standard. If prohibitions against such "lifestyles" were really the issue, Ford would have been gone long before his playing skills were in decline.

It is not surprising that there would be inconsistencies. What is surprising is that Brown would continue to claim to uphold some unbreakable set of rules long after it was glaringly obvious that that set of rules was full of holes. Ford, after all, while perhaps the most obvious flaunter of those rules, was not the only one. Former Browns recalled that more than a few of their teammates were heavy drinkers, carousers, and/or troublemakers.

For example, Dante Lavelli spoke of another player whose drinking was as out of control as Ford's. He, too, was a quality player who remained in the starting lineup until he could be replaced. Several players spoke of another teammate who, like Ford, came to practices reeking of alcohol. Teammates nicknamed him Smitty, according to one, because of his largely unsuccessful efforts to camouflage the smell of alcohol on his breath with a steady supply of Smith Brothers cough drops.

Perhaps Ford's habits didn't take hold or surface until after he had established himself as a great player, and Brown, as most coaches would have, made a choice to keep him. Perhaps Brown was willing to tolerate some players who did not abide by his rules and drew the line at a point where Atkins was one too many. Either way, Brown tolerated a lot of players whose lifestyles were incompatible with the philosophy he claimed to cherish so dearly, and his players knew it. Through 1955, the Browns just kept on winning championships, despite both the obvious inconsistencies in the philosophy and the playing talent that was lost in part because of it. But in a few short years both would catch up with Brown and his team in a big way.

At least somewhat in defense of Brown, despite Atkins's occasionally awesome play and the raves of some players of that era, he was not the consistently dominating player he might have been given his size and physical skills. And the main reason for that would appear to be his work habits. Marchetti, Ford, Robustelli, Brito, Deacon Jones, Willie Davis, and Carl Eller were defensive ends who were contemporaries of Atkins, and all arguably had better careers.

Still, Atkins was a force for seventeen years, and when he was at his best he wreaked havoc on offenses. Considering how many times the Browns came up just short of winning it all in the years from the end of their dynasty until Atkins retired, it is certainly plausible that they would have won more titles had he been a Brown during that time. That is especially true given that their defense was never a particularly strong one after 1957.

Part of what may also have bothered Brown is that Atkins had a penchant for playing outside the rules on the field as well as off. It was a style—intimidating, nasty, dirty at times—that allowed Atkins to fit in perfectly with the roughhouse Bears. One difference between the dynasty-era Browns and later Cleveland teams that Jim Brown said hurt the team was a shortage of exactly those qualities. Whatever the unevenness of his play over the years, there is no question that Gorgal was right when he said that Atkins was "better than they had."

Ray Renfro was one of the few players from the Browns dynasty years who played through the less successful years that followed and whose time with the team extended beyond Paul Brown's. By the time Brown was fired in January of 1963, the Browns were coming off a particularly disappointing season and were seven years removed from their last championship. By then, the unloading of talent, for lifestyle incompatibility and other reasons, had taken an undeniable toll on the team.

"I always thought Paul lost his biggest asset when he found he couldn't handle certain types of players, fellows who liked to stay up late and have a good time," Renfro said shortly after Brown was let go. "Just look around the league. There's an awful lot of horses that used to belong to us. So they weren't Paul's kind of people? But they could play football."

It was one thing to trade an unproven rookie like Art Donovan because solid established players like Kissell and Palmer played the same position, or even to trade someone considered to be a bad apple like Atkins. But by the early 1960s, in addition to Donovan and Atkins, Willie Davis, Henry Jordan, Dick LeBeau, Jim Marshall, Bobby Mitchell, and Floyd Peters had all slipped through Cleveland's hands with no player of note who ever played for the Browns coming in return. A lot of horses indeed.

Otto Graham did not stand firm in his decision to retire. He told Brown that he would return if the team stumbled and if no quarterback emerged to do the job in training camp. Graham later joked that Brown didn't try very hard to find a replacement, and after a 1–5 preseason in which no quarterback made an impression, Graham rejoined the team. He was reportedly the highest paid player in the NFL with a salary of $25,000.

One of the preseason defeats was a 30–27 loss in the College All-Star Game. Arch Ward was not on hand to witness the stunning upset, however. He had died just a month before the game and thus did not get to experience the satisfaction of seeing the collegians defeat the team and the coach whose one-sided win four years earlier had so upset him. For his part, although disappointed at the loss, Brown had bigger worries that summer. He could only hope that Graham was what his floundering team needed.

Graham's presence did not help against the Redskins at Municipal Stadium as the Browns lost on opening day for the second year in a row, 27–17. Graham was rusty and connected on just three of nine passes for 30 yards and was intercepted twice. Brown eventually pulled him in favor of Ratterman, who threw two touchdowns as Cleveland rebounded from a 13–0 deficit to close to within 20–17. But despite Cleveland's 221 rushing yards that included 117 and a 7.8 average by Morrison, the Redskins prevailed. It was Washington's first ever win over the Browns after nine straight defeats.

The Cleveland ship righted itself in a big way the following week as the Browns blasted the 49ers at Kezar Stadium, 38–3. It was a stellar performance on both sides of the ball as Morrison rushed for 80 more yards and Graham went seven for eleven for 140 yards. The defense, meanwhile, held the Million Dollar Backfield and the rest of the San Francisco offense to eight first downs and 134 yards. A blocked punt by Noll set up a touchdown that put the game out of reach at 24–3.

Cleveland had a tougher time in their third game but rallied for a home win against the Eagles, 21–17. The winning score was a 5-yard Graham to Lavelli pass with just over a minute to play. As he had so many times in the past, Graham displayed skills on the winning drive that set him apart from so many other quarterbacks.

With the Browns facing a do-or-die possession from their own 13 with just over three minutes to play, Graham led them to the winning score. His running and passing accounted for almost all of the team's yards. Among Graham's big plays on the drive were a 14-yard completion on fourth and 6, an 18-yard run on third and 3, and a 44-yard run to the 8-yard line.

The Browns moved to 3–1 by avenging their loss to Washington with a 24–14 win at Griffith Stadium. Modzelewski scored his fourth and fifth touchdowns, and the defense continued its history of putting points on the board as Michaels ran an interception back 25 yards for a touchdown that put the game out of reach. The defense forced five turnovers in all and held Washington to 51 yards passing.

It was another all-around effort the following week as the Browns buried the 3–1 Packers, 41–10, and knocked Green Bay out of first place in the West. The Browns had a twenty-one to nine edge in first downs and a 454 to 161 edge in total yards, and the defense held the opposition to less than 200 yards of offense for the fourth consecutive game. Graham continued to pile up lots of yards on a small number of passes as he went seven of twelve for 187 yards, while Ratterman chipped in with two fourth-quarter touchdown passes.

"It's those tackles and Gibron," Green Bay head coach Lisle Blackbourn said after the game. "That's the difference between our teams." Indeed, Cleveland's offensive line was as strong as ever, in part because of the shift of McCormack to right tackle. But although tackles McCormack and Groza were future Hall of Famers, the best players on the line in 1955 were Gibron and center Frank Gatski, a future Hall of Famer himself.

Although a number of outstanding linemen had come and gone in the franchise's first decade, including Lou Rymkus, Weldon Humble, and Lin Houston, the unit never slipped very much along the way. In fact, it was probably stronger than ever in 1955. Cleveland's offense was far and away the best in the league that year in large part because of the line's play.

After six years of excellent play, Gibron had his best year in 1955. As much as anything, his great play was responsible for the Browns having their best season rushing since Motley was in his prime. Both Morrison and Modzelewski finished the season among the league's rushing leaders.

"The best guard in football," Brown said of Gibron. "Every time we need yardage, we ride his shirttails." No one looking at the stocky, comparatively short Gibron would have guessed that great quickness and tremendous bursts of speed were among the attributes that made him so good. But they were, and together with extremely wide shoulders, great strength, and outstanding technique, they made Gibron one of the best blockers of his era.

"Gibron was a mean, low-slung fire-blocker who caught them underneath and crumpled them" is how Paul Zimmerman put it. "Huge upper body, thin legs, blazing speed. At 4.75 perhaps the fastest of any of them."

"Out of a dead three-point stance, he outran everybody for 20 yards on the ballclub including Ray Renfro, who was a sprinter . . . myself, everybody," Ken Konz said of Gibron. "For 20 yards he would lead the pack. That's how quick he was getting out of his stance."

"Sometimes he'd get called offsides because the rest of the line couldn't charge as fast as him," Gain said. "And it wasn't because he was offsides, he was just so damn quick out of the start."

"His reactions on offense were like Willis's on defense," Brown said of Gibron, comparing him to the player who may have been the quickest of that era.

"He was the ultimate offensive guard," said Herschel Forester, the guard who played on the other side of center in 1955 and who eventually stepped into Gibron's shoes. "At his best, he was the best offensive guard I ever saw."

In his tenth season, Gatski, like Gibron, was playing the best football of his career. He had played every game in franchise history, the only player besides Graham who could make that claim. Although at center he was somewhat anonymous, Gatski's value was something that his teammates recognized.

"He was as durable and tough as any player I've ever known," Brown said of Gatski. Like many Cleveland players, McCormack looked on in admiration as Gatski, for most of his career the only center on the team's roster, went about his business in the obscurity that is part of an offensive lineman's fate.

"He was an iron man," McCormack said. "He came to work and did his job. That was it."

"He was so precise," Ken Carpenter said of Gatski. "He held his own against anybody."

Gatski was in the middle of Cleveland's great pass protection, the famous "cup" the first generation of Browns linemen had introduced to football. That protection was one of the main reasons Cleveland's passing game was vastly superior to the rest of the league's. In two of the most important passing categories, Cleveland had wide advantages over the rest of the league in 1955: 55.6% to 47.4% in completion percentage and 9.5 to 6.4 in yards per pass. In the passer rating system used today, Cleveland's advantage was 98.3 to 57.1.

Going up against the likes of all-pro linebackers and tackles Chuck Bednarik, Ernie Stautner, Roger Zatkoff, Dale Dodrill, Lavern Torgeson, and Wayne Robinson game in and game out, Gatski himself was selected to every all-pro team in 1955, as was Gibron. With Groza and McCormack also garnering similar honors, the Browns became the first team to ever have four offensive linemen named as first-team all-pros in the same season since selection of separate offensive and defensive units became the norm in 1951. Only the 1962 Packers have matched that feat in the years since.

Before 29,471 fans at Comiskey Park in the sixth week of the season, the Browns continued to score in a variety of ways as they defeated the Cardinals, 26–20. Don Paul ran a punt back 60 yards for a touchdown against his old team, and Noll tallied a safety on another blocked punt as the Browns built a lead of 21–3 before the Cardinals tallied twice to make the final score more respectable. The Browns' running tandem continued to click as Modzelewski rushed for 121 yards and Morrison added 70 as Cleveland stuck mainly to the ground game on a rainy day. With the win, Cleveland moved into sole possession of first place at 5–1, a game ahead of the Steelers.

Although the 2–4 Giants arrived in Municipal Stadium in last place on November 6, they gave the Browns all they could handle before Cleveland prevailed, 24–14, in front of 56,524, the largest Cleveland crowd of the season. It was an especially brutal game between two teams that had forged one of pro football's best rivalries. New York fullback Alex Webster was carried off the field on a stretcher, and Graham left the game after being tackled after a scramble.

Ratterman again played well in relief of Graham, throwing for two second-half touchdowns and running for a third to rally the Browns from a 14–3 halftime deficit. After allowing 217 yards on defense and doing very little on offense in the first half, the Browns turned the tables on New York after halftime. Renfro caught a scoring toss of 30 yards, Brewster caught one of 14, and Ratterman's bootleg on fourth and goal from the 4 iced the game. New York managed just 5 yards of offense in the second half. The game ended with Colo swinging at Charlie Conerly and just missing.

The Eagles brought the Browns back to earth the following week with a scoring spree reminiscent of the 1953 finale, 33–17. The Browns shot out to a 17–0 first-quarter lead, but Philadelphia rallied with 10 points in the second quarter, 6 in the third, and 17 in the fourth. Cleveland turned the ball over seven times and saw their record fall to 6–2, one game better than the Redskins'.

Cleveland bounced back with a 41–14 rout of Pittsburgh before 53,509 home fans. The Browns again did most of their damage on the ground with 199 yards and rushing touchdowns by Modzelewski, Graham, and Bassett. Morrison led the way with 140 yards and an 8.2 average, while Lavelli and Konz also had big days. Lavelli caught touchdown passes of 6 and 42 yards, while Konz ran an interception back 15 yards for a touchdown and set up Graham's score with a 42-yard punt return. After starting the season 4–1, the loss dropped Pittsburgh to 4–5 and virtually ended the Steelers' hopes for a first ever conference championship.

On the Sunday after Thanksgiving, the Browns and Giants closed the NFL chapter of the storied history of the Polo Grounds with one of the most exciting games ever at the old ballpark, a 35–35 tie. After a 1–4 start, the Giants had improved to 4–5 with three wins in their previous four games. The tie eliminated New York from the conference race, however. Hard feelings left over from the team's previous game and the rivalry that would soon explode as the game's best helped attract a crowd of 45,699, New York's biggest of the season.

Graham had a big day with seventeen completions on thirty-one attempts for 319 yards and touchdowns of 16 and 41 yards to Brewster and 42 to Renfro. Noll again made his presence felt with a 14-yard interception return for a fourth-quarter score that gave Cleveland a 35–28 lead. After the Giants tied the game, Graham again performed his magic as he led the Browns on a 59-yard drive in the final moments, a drive that included a 28-yard bootleg.

The drive was for naught, however, as Groza's attempt at a game-winning field goal from the 21 with 0:30 seconds left was blocked. That capped a tough day for the Browns' kicking game as the Giants blocked two field goal attempts and a Gillom punt. The tie dropped the Browns' record to 7–2–1 and left them just a half game ahead of the surprising Redskins.

Matters were settled the following week when Cleveland took apart the Steelers for a second time, 30–7, while Washington lost to the Giants. Again it was the running game and the defense that did the job for the Browns. They rushed for 273 yards, with Morrison leading the charge with 104 and an 8.0 average. The defense held Pittsburgh to eight first downs and 123 yards, intercepted four passes, and did not allow any points as the Steelers only score came when another Gillom punt was blocked and recovered in the end zone.

Graham passed only twelve times but connected on scoring tosses to Renfro and Brewster, while Groza kicked a season-high three field goals. So for the tenth consecutive season, the Browns clinched a berth in their league Championship Game. It is a mark unsurpassed in the annals of pro sports.

The Browns' 35–24 win over the Cardinals the last week of the season improved their record to 9–2–1 and marked the eighth time in those ten years that they finished with the best regular season record in their league. For the ten years, the Browns' record was 105–17–4, a winning percentage of .861.

The race in the West again went to the final day of the season. The Lions had suffered through an injury-plagued season and fell off sharply after three straight conference championships. They finished last at 3–9, a game behind the equally disappointing 49ers. The upstart Colts and Packers were alive as late as the penultimate weekend, but ultimately matters came down to the Rams and Bears.

The Rams clinched their fourth conference title in seven years with a win over Green Bay in front of over 90,000 at the Los Angeles Coliseum. The Bears finished half a game behind, undone yet again by a late-season loss to the crosstown rival Cardinals. So for the third time in six seasons, the Browns and Rams would square off for NFL supremacy. In their six NFL title-game appearances, in fact, the Browns had been matched with only the Rams and Lions.

1955 also marked the fifth consecutive season that the team with the league's best record would have to play the Championship Game on the road. That streak would extend two more years. In ten of the twelve title games played from 1948 through 1959, in fact, the team with the best regular season record had to play the NFL's biggest game on the road. The only exception in that period was in 1950 (in 1958, the Colts and Giants both finished 9–3).

Although none of them would say so publicly, some of the Browns players were glad their foe was the Rams and not the Bears. The Browns knew no matter what that they would have to play the title game on the road, and the Coliseum was the largest stadium in use in the NFL. Its seating capacity was more than double that of Wrigley Field.

Los Angeles was also far from the wintry northeastern quadrant where most of the league's teams played, and relatively mild weather made a big turnout in the huge stadium a distinct possibility. The bigger the gate, the players knew, the bigger their payday. Such considerations were important in an era when players could earn as much as two thirds of their season salary in one game. Many players of the twenty-first century, by contrast, actually earn less in the Super Bowl than they do per regular season game.

Although not as powerful as their great teams of 1949 through 1951, the Rams were still a formidable opponent. Waterfield had retired, but the passing game still featured Van Brocklin, Hirsch, Fears, and Bob Boyd. Sid Gillman was in the first year of his great career as a head coach. He would carry the postwar passing innovations of the Browns and Rams into the 1960s.

For the second year in a row, some ill-advised remarks by the opposition may have added an edge to Cleveland's preparation. As Bob Gain recalled, "I remember Les Richter making a remark, 'Oh, we'll beat the Browns' butts. They're fat and happy now because they won last year. They think they've got it made.'"

More instrumental to Cleveland's success were two offensive innovations put in just for the game. One was the use of a hurry-up offense. Several players had suggested it as a way to keep the Rams off guard, and Brown, showing again that he was not as inflexible as is often claimed, put it in the game plan. Using it frequently throughout, the Browns kept the Rams defense off balance and thus accomplished exactly what was hoped.

Perhaps more important, the Browns successfully utilized a double wing formation. The alignment created additional confusion among the Rams regarding their coverages and also allowed Cleveland to get its four outstanding receivers—Lavelli, Brewster, Renfro, and Jones—into their pass routes more quickly.

"I think it sort of surprised them," Gain said of the double wing. "Paul was very innovative."

The weather cooperated and 87,695 fans were on hand for the game, which was played on a Monday afternoon the day after Christmas. It was the biggest crowd ever in the twenty-three-year history of pro football postseason play and was also the first Championship Game ever played on a day other than a Sunday.

Like the year before, things did not begin well for Cleveland. Chuck Noll, so valuable at linebacker all season, went down with an injury in the first minute and was done for the day. He was replaced by rookie Palumbo. Then Van Brocklin led the Rams deep into Browns territory. But as in 1954 against Detroit, the Browns quickly turned things their way and then stepped on the gas. In a portent of things to come, a Konz interception stopped the Los Angeles drive and led to a Groza field goal.

Cleveland's Don Paul broke Len Ford's Championship Game interception return record of the year before with a 65-yard score after pilfering a Van Brocklin pass early in the second quarter. That increased the Browns' lead to 10–0. Then after a Los Angeles touchdown, Konz intercepted another pass and Graham and Lavelli connected on what was probably the game's biggest play.

With under a minute to play before the half, Cleveland was at midfield trying to at least get close enough for a field goal attempt. They got more than that, however, when Lavelli broke free behind the Rams defense and took in Graham's pass for a 50-yard touchdown. As he did so often in his brilliant eleven-year career, Lavelli got open by improvising.

"When I went down and out, half the Rams were there waiting for me so I went the other way," Lavelli said. "I'm 30 yards wide open by myself, caught the touchdown, got in at the half, and Brown says, 'Lavelli, you broke the pattern.' I says, 'Yeah, but we're up by 10 points.'"

Coming just before the half, the touchdown gave the Browns a big lift and deflated Los Angeles. The second half was all Cleveland. Every time the Rams tried to get something going, somebody from Cleveland's back line was there to make an interception. They intercepted seven in all, six off Van Brocklin and one off Bill Wade, who came on in relief late in the game.

It was a remarkable exhibition of ball-hawking by the Browns. The seven interceptions bested by one their performance against Detroit the year before. It was one off the all time mark for a Championship Game/Super Bowl, and the Browns also hold two of the next highest spots with their six in 1954 and the five they intercepted in 1950.

The play of the defensive line had a lot to do with the secondary's success. Ford, Kissell, Colo, Massey, and Gain kept after Van Brocklin and Wade all game and disrupted the timing that was so important to the success of Los Angeles's aerial game. Ford and Kissell sacked Wade on successive plays at one point, while Hirsch and Fears were held to one catch each for a total of 25 yards. Boyd, one of the fastest players in football and a dangerous deep threat, did not catch any.

But again the biggest story of the game was Otto Graham. Playing in what, in fact, turned out to be his last game, Graham had another big day. In many ways, it exemplified his entire brilliant career. Spectacular at times but mostly coolly efficient, Graham led the Browns as they rolled over a very strong opponent. In addition to his pass to old buddy Lavelli, he added a second touchdown toss of 35 yards to Renfro and also ran for scores from the 15 and the 1.

Graham finished the day fourteen of twenty-five for 209 yards with 21 yards rushing. Not awesome, perhaps, but the important thing, as it always was with Graham and the Browns, was that Cleveland cashed in on their opportunities and won the game. On several occasions Graham converted fourth downs into first downs. And he expertly kept the Rams off balance by mixing plays on two decisive third-quarter drives that put the game completely out of reach. Those touchdown drives made the score 31–7, Cleveland scored again in the fourth quarter to increase their lead to 38–7, and then Los Angeles scored the last points of the game to make the final 38–14.

Graham cited Brown's willingness to deploy the new looks on offense as part of the reason for the team's performance. "[W]e told him a spread offense would really murder them," Graham said, "and he agreed to put it in. We always took a great deal of pride in feeling that we were architects of that great victory."

As he had the year before, Brown sent Ratterman in near game's end to replace Graham. And although the partisan crowd was undoubtedly disappointed at the way Graham had just helped take apart the home team, they stood and cheered as the great Cleveland quarterback walked off the field for the last time. There was no Championship Game MVP award then, but had there been, there's a good chance Graham would have won it, as he likely would have in 1950, 1954, and on at least several occasions in the AAFC.

"Nothing would induce me to come back," Graham said afterward, and this time he made his retirement stick. Few athletes in sports have ever exited on such a high note. Graham had led his team to two consecutive championships to close his career and seven in all, ten straight Championship Game appearances, a 9–3 postseason record, and a 114–20–4 record overall, and he accounted for five touchdowns passing and five touchdowns rushing in the last two title-game wins.

If a player as great as Graham had really needed to redeem himself, the three straight Championship Game losses and his poor play in the 1953 game in particular were atoned for. No quarterback—not Sammy Baugh, not Sid Luckman, not Bobby Layne, not John Unitas, not Bart Starr, not Joe Montana, not John Elway, not Tom Brady, none—has ever played two such dominant games in consecutive Championship Games or Super Bowls.

The same could almost be said about the Browns as a whole. They had won the 1954 and 1955 titles by a combined score of 94–24, an average margin of victory of 35 points. No team since has approached that mark, and only the 1940 and 1941 Bears have topped it. Cleveland's victory against an overwhelmed Rams team was a fitting exclamation point to ten years of unmatched greatness.

Appropriately enough, Graham again was the NFL passing leader and MVP. It was the third time he had been named MVP in six NFL seasons. Curiously, no MVP award was given in 1950 or 1952, years in which he certainly would have been in the running. Graham was also again a consensus first-team all-pro in 1955.

Groza was displaced as league field goal leader by Green Bay's Fred Cone but finished second in that category and fifth in points. Morrison was third in rushing yards with 824, while Modzelewski placed ninth with 619 and second with eight touchdowns. Renfro also scored eight touchdowns that came on just twenty-nine receptions, and he led the league with a 20.8 yards per catch average. Gillom continued his strong punting with a 41.2 average.

Groza and Gatski were unanimous first-team all-pros, while Ford and Gibron joined Graham as consensus first-teamers. McCormack, Colo, Morrison, and Paul were all named to at least one first team, while Gain, Renfro, Konz, and Lahr were picked to at least one second team. Gatski, Groza, Colo, Morrison, Gibron, Konz, Brewster, Massey, and Michaels were selected for the Pro Bowl.

18

The Browns and Other Dynasties Compared

T here are four dynasties in the history of pro football that are Cleveland's competitors for the title of the best ever: the 1940–1946 Chicago Bears, the 1961–1967 Green Bay Packers, the 1974–1979 Pittsburgh Steelers, and the 1981–1989 San Francisco 49ers. The Browns and these four teams all won at least four championships in a period of ten seasons or fewer. That is an accomplishment that sets them apart from others that were very good, but not quite as good, as these five.

Thus, as great a team as the 1952–1957 Detroit Lions was with three championships in six seasons, they come up a bit short and miss the cut. Then there are the Packers of the period 1929–1936, who actually won four championships in eight seasons; if we stretch their run to 1939, Green Bay won five titles in eleven seasons. Perhaps unfairly, they will not be included in this discussion.

The reason is the gap of five years between championships from 1931 to 1936. In football terms, that is a very large amount of time, too large for those Packers to be considered one continuous dynasty. For one thing, the Packers did not so much as win the Western Conference in the interlude. For two of those seasons, in fact, they slipped appreciably, posting a combined record of only 12–13–1 in 1933–1934 and finishing a combined eleven games off the conference pace those two years.

In addition, 85% of the Packers on the 1931 team were gone by 1936. That turnover is huge for a five-year period and is far too large for the Packers to be considered a dynasty in the same sense as the other five teams. And none of the other teams experienced a down interlude anywhere comparable to Green Bay's in 1933 and 1934.

The 49ers dynasty is an interesting case because they won another championship in 1994, five years after the fourth and last of the 1981–1989 period. However, that five-year gap is just too long given that the 49ers failed to make it to the Super Bowl in the four seasons from 1990 to 1993. There is no comparable gap without a Championship Game/Super Bowl appearance in the trajectories of any of the other dynasties.

Also coming up short are teams that put together a long stretch of years of excellent play but who did not bunch together four or more championships. The Baltimore Colts, for example, had a tremendous run from the late 1950s to the early 1970s. Not only did they win three championships in that span, there were two other years in which they lost the Championship Game or Super Bowl and a number of others where they had an outstanding regular season record.

Similarly, the Dallas Cowboys put together a stretch of excellence that extended from 1966 into the 1980s. In addition to winning two championships, the Cowboys had a number of fine seasons in that span. Like the Colts, however, they did not string together a series of championships. As a result, what they did also does not constitute a dynasty.

Given that the five dynasties under discussion range from the era of one postseason game to the modern era's labyrinthine system, it raises an obvious question: Was it more difficult to win a championship in the Browns' day when a team either finished with the best record in its conference or went home, or in the post-1966 period when a team had to win at least three playoff games? Winning three or even four playoff games certainly sounds more difficult, but remember that numerous teams from the more recent period have won championships in seasons in which they either did not finish with the best record in their conference or, once teams began to be seeded, as the number one seed. Included in that group are Packers, Steelers, and 49ers teams from their dynasty years, as will be discussed further below. In fact, the Steelers did so twice. Things have changed to such a point that in today's NFL a team could finish with the thirteenth best regular season record in its conference and still win the Super Bowl.

A sixth-place conference finish in Cleveland's day, on the other hand, earned a team not a playoff berth but the top pick in the draft. Another point in favor of the proposition that the Browns faced a more difficult road, also discussed further below, is the fact that until thirty years ago home field advantage in the postseason had nothing to do with a team's regular season record.

Chicago Bears, 1940–1946

The Bears won four championships and appeared in a fifth title game in a span of seven seasons. They were an awesome team that put together some of the most dominating seasons in history in the early 1940s. Coached by George Halas and peopled with the likes of Bulldog Turner, Sid Luckman, George McAfee, Joe Stydahar, and Bronko Nagurski, the Chicago roster reads like an NFL who's who of the 1940s. The Bears also had a number of other outstanding players who were somewhat overshadowed by their better known teammates, men like Ray Bray, Lee Artoe, Bill Osmanski, Ken Kavanaugh, George Wilson, and George Musso.

The 1942 and 1941 squads posted per-game point differentials of 26.6 and 22.6, respectively, that are the two largest in history. The first three of the Bears' championships were likewise won in dominating fashion by scores of 73–0, 37–9, and 41–21. They also won a conference play-off game by a score of 33–14 and capped their great run with a 24–14 title-game victory in 1946.

The Bears also posted a series of multiyear regular season winning percentages that are among the best of all time. From 1940 through 1943, for example, the Bears went 37–5–1 for a winning percentage of .881. In the three years beginning in 1941, they lost only two regular season games (30–2–1) for a .936 mark. Both marks are second only to ones posted by the Browns.

The Bears were also the first team in history to play in four straight Championship Games/Super Bowls. More than sixty years later, the Browns are the only team to surpass that mark, with the 1990–1993 Buffalo Bills having matched it. The Bears were also an elite team for an extended period before 1940, although their championship that year was their first in seven years.

Like the Browns a few years later, the Bears also had to contend with having to play Championship Games on the road in years that they had the best regular season record. It happened in 1946 when they prevailed over the Giants anyway, and it happened in 1942, when they weren't so fortunate. That year was the year they posted the highest point differential in history and a perfect record. Based just on the regular season, the 1942 Bears were the best team of all time. But as happened in their perfect 1934 season, the 1942 Bears had to play the Championship Game on the road, and they lost to the 10–1 Redskins, 14–6.

More than any of the other dynasties, the question of what might have been surrounds Chicago's. After Pearl Harbor, Bears players began entering the military until, by 1944, a number of the team's best players were no longer with the team. Even founder, owner, and coach Halas left for several years. The Bears fell to 6–3–1 and second place in 1944, then to 3–7 and fourth place in 1945.

When Halas and most of the draftees returned in 1946, the Bears again won the NFL championship. Even though they were no longer as strong as their teams of the early 1940s, the Bears continued to be one of the best in the NFL. The years immediately after 1946, however, were marked by a series of agonizingly close finishes (second by one game in 1947 and 1948, second by percentage points in 1949, defeated in a playoff in 1950, one game out in 1951), and the Bears did not make it back to the title game until 1956.

Probably no team in history was as dominant as Chicago was in the early 1940s. Some of the standards they set in both regular season and Championship Game play may never be surpassed. And the Bears may very well have been able to win one or more additional championships had many of their key players not gone into the military.

For the purposes of this discussion, however, the Bears have to be judged in the same way as the rest of the teams: by what they did and not by what they might have done. So while one and probably several of Chicago's seasons are arguably the best ever, their dynasty is not.

Green Bay Packers, 1961–1967

Green Bay's five championships in seven seasons tops all of the other challengers and is second only to the Browns. They also won the Western Conference in 1960, and their run of six conference titles in eight years is also second only to Cleveland. Not surprisingly, Green Bay's multiyear regular season winning percentages are among the best ever. Their .787 mark from 1961 through 1967, for example, is the third highest seven-year mark in history, behind only the Browns and the 1964–1970 Colts.

Besides the five championships, perhaps the Packers' most impressive feat is their record nine-game winning streak in the postseason. That mark tops even Cleveland's seven straight wins from 1946 through 1950, and while Green Bay won two fewer championships than Cleveland, their Championship Game winning percentage during their dynasty is better.

Unlike the Browns, the Packers were not negatively impacted by the rotating home field system for postseason games. Twice they were able to overcome having to play on the road in seasons that they had the league's best record: against the Giants in 1962 and the Cowboys in 1966. They also benefited from that system on two occasions when they hosted postseason games against teams that had better regular season records: the Browns in 1965 and the Rams in 1967. The Packers won both games.

The Packers also had an outstanding season in 1963, a year in which they finished second in the Western Conference, a half game behind the Bears. Green Bay was 11–2–1 that year, with both losses coming to Chicago. They tied for second in the somewhat less successful 1964 season in which they were 8–5–1 and finished three and a half games behind Baltimore.

Those two second-place finishes, but especially 1963, again highlight the differences between the postseason before the mid-1960s and what it has evolved into in the years since. Because while the fact that a team must win more playoff games is often cited as an argument as to why recent dynasties are more impressive, the expanded playoffs of recent decades have aided the latter-day dynasty teams when they finished down in the regular season conference rankings.

Until the mid-1960s, a team either finished with the best record in its conference or it went home. The "postseason" consisted of the Championship Game and nothing more unless there was a tie atop a conference. Beginning in 1967, by contrast, a team with the *fifth* best record in its conference could still make the postseason and thus have a chance at winning a championship. Today, a team that finishes 5–11 and has the thirteenth best record in its conference could win its division, qualify for the postseason, and win the Super Bowl.

So while the Packers went home at the conclusion of the regular season in 1963 with an 11–2–1 record, there is little question that they were better that year than the vast majority of playoff teams of the last thirty-five years. Like the rotating home field in the Championship Game, that is an often overlooked circumstance that makes the accomplishments of teams from earlier eras more impressive.

Had the rules in 1963 and 1964 included second-place teams, for example, the Packers would have earned a playoff berth and a chance at a championship both years. Although they would not have been the favorites either year (although who would have been willing to bet against them in 1963, even in a third matchup with the Bears), there have been numerous occasions in recent years when the team that won the championship was one that did not have the best regular season record in its conference. And with the further NBA-ization of the NFL postseason beyond even the current twelve of thirty-two teams an inevitability, championship teams are increasingly likely to be ones that finish down in the conference seedings.

Of course the converse of the previous hypothetical scenario is also true: The Packers (or the Browns, for that matter) might have won fewer championships had they had to navigate a more labyrinthine playoff system. Still, the system of earlier years rewarded regular season excellence and made it very difficult for a team to get to the Championship Game if it faltered at any point during the season, either because of injuries or any other reason. And while over the last three-plus decades the higher seeded team wins a playoff game well over half the time, the three dynasty teams from that era—the Packers (1967), Steelers (1974 and 1979), and 49ers (1988)—have all won championships in years when they were not the best regular season team in their conference. In fact, three of those teams were only the third best regular-season team in their conference.

Unlike the 1940s Bears, the 1960s Packers did not remain among the game's best teams after their dynasty ended. Head coach Vince Lombardi's departure was a big reason, but it's also clear that the best players who were still around were in decline by 1968. A remarkable eleven players who played for Green Bay from 1961 through 1967 are members of the Hall of Fame, more than any of the other dynasties. All eleven of those players—Herb Adderley, Willie Davis, Forrest Gregg, Paul Hornung, Henry Jordan, Ray Nitschke, Jim Ringo, Bart Starr, Jim Taylor, Emlen Tunnell, and Willie Wood—played on Green Bay's 1961 team, the highest number of Hall of Famers to play for the same team in the same season.

That the Packers are widely *perceived* to be a greater dynasty than the Browns has less to do with what the two teams actually accomplished and more to do with Green Bay being the first dynasty of the television era. The number of people who saw the Packers in any one of their Championship Game or Super Bowl appearances is many times the number who saw the Browns in their ten Championship Games *combined*.

Baby boomers who were young at the time of the Packers dynasty and became football fans at that time numbered in the millions. A nationwide development of that many fans had never occurred before. Compared with that of the 1960s, the post–World War II surge in football's popularity was tiny. And for most of the four decades since the Packers dynasty, baby boomers who came of age during Green Bay's reign have been the majority of pro football's opinion makers.

For many of the same reasons, Lombardi has been elevated to iconic status. He was *the* coach during the very years that pro football became *the* sport. By contrast, far fewer modern-day fans know of the accomplishments, the impact, and the greatness of Paul Brown. If a poll were held today among a random sample of football fans asking who among the two was the greater coach, Lombardi would undoubtedly win in a landslide. That's despite the fact that Brown won two more championships and posted a winning percentage about as good (.766 to .753) in a tenure that was almost twice as long (seventeen years to nine).

While a debate about Lombardi and Brown is a close and compelling one, the one about their respective teams is not. The evidence and the record are clear, and there is still no known way to make five championships better than seven. The Packers dynasty is greater than the Bears', but it is definitely somewhat less than Cleveland's.

Pittsburgh Steelers, 1974–1979

In addition to winning four championships in six years, the Steelers made it to the playoffs in all six of those years and in 1972 and 1973 for a total of eight years in a row. A defense that was one of the greatest in history was the foundation for their first two championships in 1974 and 1975, while the excellent passing triumvirate of Terry Bradshaw, Lynn Swann, and John Stallworth could be said to have driven Pittsburgh to two more titles in 1978 and 1979. One constant throughout was Franco Harris, consistently one of football's best rushers during the team's dynasty years.

Pittsburgh head coach Chuck Noll played guard and linebacker for Cleveland in the final three years of the Browns dynasty, including the 1954 and 1955 championship seasons. Noll made it to the Hall of Fame as a coach, and he is joined there by nine of his players: Bradshaw, Harris, Swann, Stallworth, Joe Greene, Jack Lambert, Jack Ham, Mike Webster, and Mel Blount.

In a curious twist, the Steelers actually benefited from both the old and the new home field advantage rules. On one hand, unlike the Browns, they never had to contend with going on the road in seasons when they had the best regular season record. The 1975 rule change made that an impossibility, while before that they got to play home games in 1972 and 1974 that they didn't deserve. In 1974, in fact, the last year of the old system, they caught a huge break in the first-round playoff schedule that might very well have paved the way to their first championship.

Those points are important because, as might be expected, Pittsburgh's home record in the postseason was drastically better than its record on the road. If the arbitrary, rotating basis for determining home field had been in place through 1979, the Steelers might not have won four Super Bowls. That is not to say that they *couldn't* win on the road; they did so twice in the postseason during their dynasty, including in

1974 against a strong Oakland team. However, it is eminently clear that they won with far greater frequency at home.

Looking more closely at the 1974 postseason in the AFC, the Steelers not only played a home game they wouldn't have been awarded had the division winners been seeded by regular season record, they also got to play the weakest of the four AFC playoff teams in the first round. The 10–3–1 Steelers opened in Pittsburgh against the 9–5 wildcard Bills, a game Pittsburgh won handily. Meanwhile, the two best regular season AFC teams, Miami (11–3) and Oakland (12–2), played each other in one of the great games of all time. The Steelers then beat the Raiders to advance to the Super Bowl.

Had the much fairer seeding procedure that began the following year been in place in 1974, the opening-round AFC playoff games would have pitted Buffalo and the Raiders in Oakland and Pittsburgh at Miami against the two-time Super Bowl champion Dolphins. The winner of the latter game presumably would have then played the Raiders in Oakland. Clearly a game in Miami against the Dolphins that year was a much tougher assignment than a home game against the Bills. And had they beaten the Dolphins, a road game in Oakland a week after a road game in Miami would certainly have been a more difficult road than the actual one the Steelers traversed. In such a scenario, it is certainly possible that the Steelers wouldn't have been NFL champions that year.

In no way does that diminish Pittsburgh's 1974 championship. They beat the team with the league's best regular season record on the road to win the AFC and then won the Super Bowl. Pittsburgh's 1974 experience is raised only because it contrasts so starkly with that of the Browns. That becomes clear with a closer examination of the extremely negative impact that the rotating home field advantage system had on Cleveland's chances for even greater success in their dynasty years.

The wisdom of awarding home field advantage in the postseason on the basis of regular season performance is such an integral part of modern-day football, not to mention most every other sport, that younger fans may be astonished to discover that this system is a fairly new one. But up until thirty years ago, with two exceptions, home field advantage in postseason football had nothing to do with which of the teams involved did better in the regular season.

Perhaps patterning itself after the baseball World Series, the NFL instituted a rotation system when it began postseason play in 1933. When the AAFC and the AFL were formed, both followed suit. For over three decades, the site of league Championship Games alternated between the home field of the two conferences in all three leagues.

When the postseason was first expanded in the 1960s, the same rotation system was used for playoff games for conference supremacy. The only times home field advantage was determined by regular season performance was in the AAFC in 1949 and in the first round of the AFL playoffs in 1969.

When the postseason was expanded further in 1970 after the NFL-AFL merger, home field advantage was still done on a rotation basis until 1975. Thus situations like the one in 1974 discussed already were fairly common. In the AFC in 1972, for example, in a scenario similar to the one the perfect Bears teams of 1934 and 1942 faced, the 14–0 Dolphins had to play the conference championship game on the road against the 11–3 Steelers. Unlike those Bears teams, Miami was able to prevail anyway.

In baseball, a rotation system made sense in the era before interleague play. Teams from the two baseball leagues did not play each other during the regular season so it wouldn't necessarily have made sense to base home field advantage in the World Series on the regular season records of the two pennant winners. In addition, the World Series is precisely that, a series of games, and each team is assured of at least two home games.

Postseason football, on the other hand, is not a series of games between two teams but a one-shot deal. The importance of home field advantage is thus magnified greatly. Considering the vast difference in December and January weather between California or Florida on the one hand and Wisconsin, Ohio, or Michigan on the other, where games are played is of even greater importance.

In addition, unlike baseball, teams from different conferences in football *always* played each other during the regular season right from the 1933 realignment. In the 1933–1965 period, the number of intraconference games was regularly as high as 33% or 40% in the NFL, and it was even as high as 50% in one season.

AAFC teams actually played the *majority* of their games against teams from the other conference, as did AFL teams for eight of that league's ten seasons. With that kind of mixture of games on the schedule, it never made sense for pro football to rotate home field in its league Championship Game. With so much intraconference activity, a much fairer system would have automatically awarded home field advantage to the team with the best regular season record.

Part of the thinking behind the rotation plan was also undoubtedly to avoid having the same team host the Championship Game three, four, or more years in a row. The rotation plan ensured that the title game would be spread around in the event a team put together a series of seasons with the best regular season record in a short span of time. As it turned out, only one NFL team of the 1933–1965 period—the 1941–1943 Bears—posted as many as three straight seasons with the best regular season record.

Whatever the intentions, whether good or misguided, the rotating system was fundamentally unfair. In essence, it penalized excellence. If a team posted the best record during the regular season, it should have played at home, as is the case today. The way to make it more difficult for any team to dominate was not to force it to go on the road with the best record but rather for other teams to get better. If there was a sense that one conference was substantially better than the other—easily measured by combined intraconference records—then an alternative system could have been implemented.

The result was a peculiar one in which the team with the best regular season record had to play the league Championship Game on the road about as often as it got to play it at home. From 1933 through 1965, the last season before the advent of the Super Bowl, there were forty-three league Championship Games played in the NFL, AAFC, and AFL. Twice the two combatants had the same record. In the other forty-one games, the team with the best regular season record in its league had to play the Championship Game on the road nineteen times, or just under half the time. With a rotating system, that's about what would be expected.

On six of those nineteen occasions, that team was the Browns. That's 32% of all instances *for one team*. Six is by far the most instances for any team. Two franchises in existence for far longer than the Browns, the Bears and Giants, share the second highest total with three. No other team had to do so more than once.

On eight of those nineteen occasions, the team with the best record won anyway despite having to play on the road. The Browns did so twice, in 1947 and 1955. So in all, eleven teams had to play on the road in the Championship Game despite having the best record in their league, and they lost. That doesn't mean they lost *because* they had to play on the road, only that they did.

On four of those eleven occasions, or 36% of the time, the losing team was the Browns. Again that is the most of any team. Cleveland lost Championship Games in that scenario in 1951, 1953, 1957, and 1965. 1965 falls outside of Cleveland's dynasty, but 1957 is included in this discussion because had the Browns won that year, their dynasty would have extended to include that season. A fourth NFL championship in eight years and an eighth overall in twelve years is a greater accomplishment than what even the Browns actually did achieve. Another NFL title would also have been further counterweight to those who insist on disregarding or downgrading Cleveland's AAFC championships.

The 1954 Browns are among the teams that could be said to have benefited from the system. They hosted Detroit and won that year although the Lions had the best regular season record. The Lions also had to play in Cleveland in 1952 despite a superior record, but they won anyway.

So the crux of the discussion as far as the Browns are concerned comes down to four seasons: 1951, 1953, and 1957 on the one hand and 1954 on the other. The most mechanical analysis—a simple reversal of the outcomes of the four games—would up Cleveland's dynasty to nine championships in twelve years. Again, that is clearly better than what even the Browns actually accomplished.

And since that hypothetical increase in championships involves seasons from the NFL and not the AAFC, transforming Cleveland's NFL run to five titles in eight years, it also goes a long way toward boosting the Browns dynasty among those who downplay their AAFC accomplishments. Even if we disregard a reversal of the 1957 game on the grounds that it was so one-sided it wouldn't have mattered where it was played (Detroit won 59–14), we would have to do the same with Cleveland's 56–10 victory in the 1954 game for the same reason.

In the 1951 and 1953 games, however, it is very clear that home field advantage might have turned defeat into victory for Cleveland. Both games were decided in the final minutes, and the Browns lost them by a combined eight points. At 17–16 the 1953 game was as close as a game can be, and 1 point is less than the advantage generally factored in for home field advantage.

The Rams won the 1951 Championship Game in Los Angeles, 24–17. They broke a 17–17 tie with a late touchdown and then snuffed out a Cleveland drive in the final minutes, so by any measure the game was very close. And as far as the home field advantage question is concerned, there are several important things to keep in mind, besides the obvious one that teams win far more often at home than on the road.

First, the difference in the regular season records of the two teams that year was not some minimal amount like a half game or even one game. Cleveland was 11–1 and Los Angeles 8–4, a difference of three full games. That is the second highest gap between Championship Game combatants in the era of the twelve-game season. It is therefore extremely difficult to imagine any argument in favor of the Rams being the best regular season team that year, whether it be intraconference record or any other.

Second and perhaps more important are the implications of playing in Los Angeles instead of Cleveland at the end of December. There is no way to know if the result would have been different had the game been played in Cleveland. What is known is that warm-weather teams like the 1951 Rams are even far more likely to lose on the road in the postseason in a cold-weather venue than the norm. Warm-weather teams were a combined 0–9 in postseason games in cold-weather cities until San Francisco won in Minnesota in 1970. With their pass-oriented offense, the Rams of the early 1950s were in many ways the embodiment of a warm-weather team, and they did, in fact, lose both of the postseason games they played in cold weather in those years.

And although it may be stating the obvious, it should be noted that the Browns in their dynasty years, like the vast majority of teams, were better at home than on the road. During their dynasty years, they posted a winning percentage of .887 (55–7–1) in Cleveland and .833 (50–10–3) on the road. In postseason games, the difference is far larger: .875 (7–1) at home and .500 (2–2) on the road. And in just the NFL, the discrepancy in the postseason is even more dramatic: .750 (3–1) in Cleveland and .333 (1–2) away from home.

In contrast to the Browns, the Steelers and 49ers never had to play any kind of a playoff game on the road against a team that finished with an inferior record in the regular season. And considering the disparity in Pittsburgh's and San Francisco's home and away postseason records, it's a good thing for them that they didn't, for if they had there's a very good chance each would have won fewer championships.

How, for example, would a Steelers team that was 7–0 at home but just 2–2 on the road in the postseason from 1974 through 1979 have done had they had to play on the road on a rotation basis like Cleveland? Similarly, how would the 49ers have done playing more frequently on the road considering that from 1981 through 1989 they were 8–1 at home and just 1–2 on the road? (Note that in each case, those home and away records are almost exactly the same as Cleveland's).

Although there is no way to say so with certainty, it is very possible that Pittsburgh and San Francisco would have won fewer than four championships under the old rules. However, since the point is not to question their validity as great dynasties, let's look at it from a Cleveland perspective. Contrary to what appears to be the popular opinion, the Cleveland dynasty likely would have been *greater* had they played under the post-1974 system, and the gap between the Browns and the other dynasties would likewise be greater.

But all of the discussion about how games might have gone had they been played in other places is just speculation. Football supremacy is decided in only one venue, on the field, and that is absolutely as it should be. As unfair as rules seem from the distance of time, each team had a chance to win and the results are what they are.

Still, the rules enacted in 1975 and in force ever since *are* fairer, so much fairer, in fact, that there would be an uproar if anything remotely resembling the old rotation system were even suggested today. More important, closer examination allows us yet another perspective on how great Cleveland's accomplishments during their dynasty years were. Of the other dynasty teams, only the Bears were negatively impacted by the home field advantage rules at all, and even then to nowhere near the degree as the Browns.

The years the Packers benefited (1965 and 1967) are balanced somewhat by the years they could have been unfairly impacted (1962 and 1966). With their entire dynasty coming under the better rules, the 49ers were not negatively impacted at all. In the case of the Steelers, however, they not only were not negatively impacted by the old rules, they clearly benefited from them, as the breakdown of their previously outlined 1974 championship path makes clear.

And, as mentioned, 1974 was not the only one of their four championship years that the Steelers did not finish as the top seed in their conference. They were the number two seed behind San Diego in 1979 but didn't have to play on the road because the Chargers were knocked off in the first round. That is another way that they benefited from the expanded playoffs; during their dynasty, by contrast, the Browns never made the playoffs by finishing second in their conference.

One last piece of the puzzle that will forever be left to speculation is how Pittsburgh (and, for that matter, the 49ers) might have done had the rotation system remained in force after 1974. In such a scenario, there would have been seasons in which the Steelers would have played playoff games at home against teams with better regular season records, games they could conceivably have won. And there might have been more seasons like 1974, ones in which teams with better records than Pittsburgh's knocked each other off while the Steelers were scheduled against a weak team.

The point, however, is to look at the different eras in their entirety. The upshot for the Browns is that they played a very high number of Championship Games on the road that they would have played at home under the post-1974 rules—five, if we count 1957, or 45% of their total of eleven. It is perfectly reasonable to think that the 1951 and/or 1953 Championship Games in particular would have gone the other way had that been the case.

Put another way, suppose the Browns had home field advantage in the Championship Game in all seasons in which they finished with the best record in their league during their dynasty years, plus 1957. That translates into home field advantage in every game from 1946 through 1951, plus 1953, 1955, and 1957. Only the title games of 1952 and 1954 would have been on the road.

Projecting their postseason home and road winning percentages in their dynasty years (.875 at home, .500 on the road) onto that number of games, it works out to an 8–1 record in the nine games at home and a 1–1 record in the two on the road. As mentioned, that hypothetical total of nine championships is significantly better than the seven that they actually won.

For the Steelers, on the other hand, it is difficult to imagine them doing any better than four championships had they been playing under the old rules; the greater likelihood is that they would have won fewer than four. Every year where they might have beaten teams with better records in the friendly confines of Three Rivers Stadium is balanced by ones in which they might not have made it out of the AFC. Might Pittsburgh, for example, have won it all in 1976 with home field advantage throughout the AFC playoffs? It's possible, but it seems just as likely—probably more so—that they would not have gone all the way in 1975 had they had to play the AFC Championship Game on the road in Oakland.

The real point again is that *never* in their dynasty years did the Steelers have to play a team with an inferior record on the road in the postseason. The Browns, on the other hand, had to do so numerous times. As mentioned, Cleveland's total of five just from 1947 through 1957 is more than any other team ever, and it is also far more than the number of times they hosted teams with better records.

A comparison of the rules giveth, but it also taketh. Those who assume that more recent dynasty teams have won under more difficult circumstances because they have played in eras of bigger leagues and more playoff teams are off the mark. An analysis of the old home field advantage system and who did and did not achieve regular season conference supremacy over the years leads back to the same conclusion as so many of the other analyses: The 1946–1955 Cleveland Browns and nobody but the 1946–1955 Cleveland Browns is the greatest dynasty in pro football history.

Pittsburgh's teams in the years just after the end of their dynasty were not quite as good as Chicago's post-1946 teams but better than Green

Bay's post-1967 teams. They made the playoffs several times but did not play for a championship again until sixteen years later. Pittsburgh's dynasty rates about even with Chicago's and somewhat behind Green Bay's and Cleveland's.

San Francisco 49ers, 1981–1989

Although the 49ers had a number of excellent teams in their first thirty-five years, their teams of the 1980s that were led by Bill Walsh, Joe Montana, Ronnie Lott, and Jerry Rice won the first championships in franchise history, four in all from 1981 through 1989. The team won another championship and made it to the playoffs eight times in the nine seasons after 1989. The 49ers' winning percentage from 1990 through 1998 was actually higher than their mark from 1981 through 1989. In all, San Francisco made it to the playoffs sixteen times from 1981 through 1998, compiled a winning percentage of .742 in that span, and averaged 11.5 wins per year for eighteen years.

That is a remarkable record. The 49ers remained a top team for a period of time after their dynasty equal to the length of the dynasty itself. Playing in the last years before the advent of the salary cap, more fluid free-agency rules, and ever more expansion, the 49ers dynasty may be the last of its magnitude for a while. Even if a team is able to bunch together as many as four championships in the modern era, it's highly unlikely any team will be able to put together an eighteen-year run like the 49ers under the present circumstances.

However, as remarkable as San Francisco's run was, the Browns actually put together a *longer* run with a *higher* winning percentage. In the twenty-four seasons from 1946 through 1969, Cleveland compiled a winning percentage of .752 (227–75–10). San Francisco's 11.5 wins per season is a great mark, but it serves as a basis for comparison only with teams playing in the era of the sixteen-game schedule, which began in 1978. More relevant is the fact that the Browns won a higher percentage of their games over six more years. San Francisco's winning percentage during its dynasty was .750, and its best ten-year record during its eighteen-year run is .757, marks that are far lower than Cleveland's for the same lengths of time.

The 49ers record was compiled at a time when anywhere from 36% to 43% of teams made it to the playoffs. In thirteen of those eighteen seasons, teams from San Francisco's conference made it to the playoffs with a winning percentage of .563 or worse, including one that won only half of its games (one made it to the expanded playoffs of 1982 with a winning percentage of .444).

In other words, making it to the postseason generally meant being a little better than average. By comparison, making it to the postseason during the Browns' ten dynasty years required a team to be far more than a little better than average. *Fourteen teams* that finished .545 or higher finished behind the Browns and went home at the end of the regular season during Cleveland's ten dynasty years. Included in that group are the 1948 49ers (12–2, .857) and the 1951 Giants (9–2–1, .818).

Amid the twenty-four-year stretch mentioned previously, there were five occasions that the Browns finished with a winning percentage of .583 or higher and did not make it to the postseason. Included among those were seasons when they posted marks of 8–3–1 (.727), 10–4 (.714), and 9–5 (.643). Although those seasons came after Cleveland's dynasty, the point simply is that San Francisco's great playoff streak came at a time when "making it to the postseason" was far easier than it was in earlier eras. If all a team had had to do to make it to the postseason from 1946 through 1969 was be in the top 43% of teams or compile a .563 winning percentage, Cleveland would have made it in twenty-three of those twenty-four seasons instead of seventeen.

In fairness to the 49ers, none of their sixteen playoff appearances came with anything less than a .625 winning percentage. And their regular season records in three of their four championship seasons from 1981 through 1989 were exemplary (the best in football, in fact). In 1988, though, they finished 10–6 (.625) and tied with four other teams for the third best conference record. They earned the second seed on tiebreakers and because one of the teams with a better record (Minnesota) did not win its division and thus could not be seeded ahead of the 49ers.

So in 1988 the 49ers had the kind of season—.625 winning percentage and third best record in their conference—that would have sent a team in the 1950s packing at the end of the regular season. Yet because of the expanded playoffs, San Francisco was able to garner a division crown, earn a first-round bye, play at home in the second round, and parlay three straight solid games at the most important time of the season into a Super Bowl title. Like the Steelers in 1974, San Francisco's 1988 season goes a long way in illustrating how the Browns played under more difficult rules than the latter-day dynasty teams.

Again, by no means is this analysis meant to diminish the 49ers' many great accomplishments; the point is to put them in perspective. Compared with the vast majority of teams, the 49ers hold up very well. Compared with the 1946–1955 Browns, they definitely have to take a backseat.

The analysis also underscores the fact that a playoff appearance in an era when a team could qualify for the playoffs with a .500 winning percentage doesn't tell us much. So that San Francisco made it sixteen of eighteen times while Cleveland made it only twelve of eighteen times, or seventeen of twenty-four times, while literally true, obscures more than it illuminates. When comparing a team from an era when .500 playoff appearances are possible to a team from an era when a winning percentage of .857 could and did earn nothing but a trip home at the end of the regular season, the number of playoff appearances is shown to be a particularly unenlightened way of getting at the essence of two team's comparative greatness.

The upshot of the comparisons is that the Browns best all the challengers. They won regular season games and championships with greater frequency, and they did it under circumstances that were at least as difficult, and probably more difficult, than the others. As to how Cleveland's AAFC titles rate, the fact is that they rate very well, as has already been discussed at length.

Since they won more times than the rest, the Packers would rate a slight edge over the others, while there's not much to differentiate between the Bears, Steelers, and 49ers. That may be unfair to the Bears because of the World War II interruption, but they can take some consolation from the fact that in 1941 they were the most dominant championship team ever.

CHAPTER 19

The End of an Era

THE **1955** SEASON marked the end of the Cleveland dynasty. The Browns would remain among football's best teams until the end of the 1960s, but their reign as the game's dominant power ended with the Championship Game win over the Rams. Otto Graham, Lou Groza, Dante Lavelli, and Frank Gatski had been there for the entire ten years, and those four plus Horace Gillom, Dub Jones, Tommy James, Warren Lahr, Len Ford, Abe Gibron, and John Sandusky had been there for the whole NFL portion of the team's dynasty.

The Browns' ten straight Championship Game appearances is unsurpassed in the annals of pro sports. In 1955, the second best mark was the five straight World Series appearances by the 1949–1953 Yankees. In the fifty years since, the Boston Celtics have matched Cleveland's ten. In pro football, the second best mark is the four accomplished by the 1940–1943 Bears and the 1990–1993 Bills.

Similarly, no team in football history can match Cleveland's seven championships in a span of ten seasons. The next highest mark is the five won by the Packers in a seven-season span in the 1960s. Of the major pro sports, only the Celtics won more than seven titles in a span of ten years.

Cleveland's cumulative winning percentages during those years are likewise football's best ever. The Browns hold the record for best winning percentage for every increment ranging from one season to ten. Their .861 record over ten seasons far outdistances the second best .787 record posted by the 1934–1943 Bears. Boiled down to a season, those two marks are the equivalent of records of 13–2 and 11–3, a full one-and-a-half-game difference.

Even taking just the six NFL years of their dynasty, the Browns' winning percentage was .817. That's higher than any team has posted over six seasons in the last sixty years. Even if a modern-day team went 13–3 every year for six straight years, they still would not match Cleveland's record from 1950 to 1955. In NFL history, only the 1939–1944 Bears' mark of .823 is better over six years than Cleveland's .817, and the teams actually have exactly the same .8125 winning percentage if the more accurate modern means of calculation is used. Had the AAFC Browns simply played at the same level as the team did from 1950 through 1955 (.817 rather than .922), Cleveland's winning percentages for seven, eight, nine, and ten years would still be the highest ever.

Although not as well known as winning percentage, average point differential is a very good measure of a team's strength, and a look at the marks posted by the 1946–1955 Browns further cements their place as the game's greatest dynasty. Eight of the forty best per-game point differentials in pro football history (NFL, AAFC, and AFL) are held by Browns teams from their dynasty years—that's 20% of the best by one team in a span of just ten years. The only other team to have as many as five of the best forty *in its entire history* is the Bears.

Three of those five by the Bears came during the Chicago dynasty of 1940–1946. Dynasties like the 1961–1967 Packers, the 1974–1979 Steelers, and the 1981–1989 49ers each hold exactly one of the top forty spots. Seven times in their ten dynasty years, Cleveland was first in its league in per-game point differential. As with their number of championships won, no other team in history was first anywhere near as many times in that number of years. And since the quality of the AAFC will undoubtedly remain an issue, it is important to note that five of those years as the best were in Cleveland's six NFL seasons, while only two were in the AAFC.

The Browns slipped badly in 1956 and finished 5–7 and in fourth place in the East. In the wake of Graham's retirement, the biggest problem was at quarterback. But there were other holes as well, holes created by veterans of the dynasty years who were at the end of their careers.

Dub Jones and Tommy James were also gone in 1956, and Dante Lavelli, Frank Gatski, Horace Gillom, John Kissell, and Abe Gibron played their final seasons that year. And for each season thereafter more players retired or were traded away until by 1964 only Lou Groza and Bob Gain remained from the 1955 team. Groza, one of the players who had been there in the very beginning, was the last from the dynasty teams to hang it up. He played his last game in 1967.

The player losses were not insurmountable, however. For ten years the team had experienced the departures of a number of outstanding players and continued winning. Behind rookie Jim Brown, in fact, the Browns bounced back in 1957 and made it to the Championship Game, where they lost to the Lions. But consistently drafting at the end of the line, wasted draft picks, and a series of bad trades eventually caught up with Cleveland. In addition, powerhouse teams soon emerged in Baltimore and Green Bay to write their own tales of football glory.

Still, the Browns remained one of football's best teams after the one down season in 1956. They eventually reclaimed the NFL championship in 1964 and played for the NFL title three more times in the 1960s. Paul Brown was not there to experience any of that success, however, because in 1963 the unthinkable happened: He was fired from his job as coach and general manager.

Fittingly, Graham and Brown were the first two men from the Browns organization to be elected to the Pro Football Hall of Fame. To date, Brown and nine players who played for Cleveland in the 1946 to 1955 period have been so honored: Graham, Marion Motley, Lou Groza, Len Ford, Dante Lavelli, Bill Willis, Doug Atkins, Mike McCormack, and Frank Gatski. Weeb Ewbank, Don Shula, and Chuck Noll have also been enshrined for their accomplishments as head coaches.

Cleveland Browns Composite Roster, 1946–1955

Adamle, Tony (1947–1951)
Adams, Chet (1946–1948)
Agase, Alex (1948–1951)
Akins, Al (1946)
Allen, Ermal (1947)
Armstrong, Quincy (1954)
Atkins, Doug (1953–1954)
Bassett, Maurice (1954–1955)
Blandin, Ernie (1946–1947)
Boedeker, Bill (1947–1949)
Bradley, Harold (1954–1955)
Brewster, Pete (1952–1955)
Bumgardner, Rex (1950–1952)
Carpenter, Ken (1950–1953)
Catlin, Tom (1953–1954)
Cheroke, George (1946)
Cline, Ollie (1948)
Cole, Emerson (1950–1952)
Colella, Tom (1946–1948)
Colo, Don (1953–1955)
Coppage, Alton (1946)
Cowan, Bob (1947–1948)
Daniell, Jim (1946)
Dellerba, Spiro (1947)
Dewar, Jim (1947)
Donaldson, Gene (1953)
Evans, Fred (1946)
Fekete, Gene (1946)
Ford, Len (1950)
Forester, Herschel (1954–1955)
Gain, Bob (1952, 1954–1955)
Gatski, Frank (1946–1955)

Gaudio, Bob (1947–1949, 1951)
Gibron, Abe (1950–1955)
Gillom, Horace (1947–1955)
Gorgal, Ken (1950, 1953–1954)
Graham, Otto (1946–1955)
Greenwood, Don (1946–1947)
Grigg, Chubby (1948–1951)
Groves, George (1946)
Groza, Lou (1946–1955)
Hanulak, Chet (1954)
Harrington, John (1946)
Helluin, Jerry (1952–1953)
Herring, Hal (1950–1952)
Horvath, Les (1949)
Houston, Lin (1946–1953)
Howard, Sherman (1952–1953)
Humble, Weldon (1947–1950)
Jagade, Chick (1951–1953)
James, Tommy (1948–1955)
Jones, Dub (1948–1955)
Jones, Edgar (1946–1949)
Jones, Tom (1955)
Kapter, Alex (1946–1947)
King, Don (1954)
Kissell, John (1950–1952,
    1954–1955)
Kolesar, Bob (1946)
Kosikowski, Frank (1948)
Konz, Ken (1953–1955)
Lahr, Warren (1949–1955)
Lavelli, Dante (1946–1955)
Lewis, Cliff (1946–1951)

Lund, Bill (1946–1947)
Maceau, Mel (1946–1948)
Martin, Jim (1950)
Massey, Carlton (1954–1955)
Mayne, Lew (1947)
McCormack, Mike (1954–1955)
Michaels, Walt (1952–1955)
Modzelewski, Ed (1955)
Morrison, Curly (1954–1955)
Moselle, Dom (1950)
Motley, Marion (1946–1953)
Noll, Chuck (1953–1955)
O'Connor, Bill (1949)
Oristaglio, Bob (1951)
Palmer, Derrell (1946–1953)
Palumbo, Sam (1955)
Parseghian, Ara (1948–1949)
Paul, Don (1954–1955)
Perini, Pete (1955)
Petitbon, John (1955)
Phelps, Don (1950–1951)
Piskor, Ray (1947)
Pucci, Ben (1948)
Ratterman, George
    (1952–1955)
Rechichar, Bert (1952)
Renfro, Ray (1952–1955)
Reynolds, Billy (1953–1954)
Rokisky, John (1946)
Rymkus, Lou (1946–1951)
Saban, Lou (1946–1949)
Sandusky, John (1950–1955)

Scarry, Mo (1946–1947)

Schwenk, Bud (1946)

Sensanbaugher, Dean (1948)

Sharkey, Ed (1952)

Shula, Don (1951–1952)

Shurnas, Marshall (1947)

Simonetti, Len (1946–1948)

Skibinski, Joe (1952)

Smith, Bob (1955)

Smith, Gaylon (1946)

Speedie, Mac (1946–1952)

Spencer, Joe (1949)

Steinbrunner, Don (1953)

Steuber, Bob (1946)

Sustersic, Ed (1949)

Taseff, Carl (1951)

Terlep, George (1948)

Terrell, Ray (1946–1947)

Thompson, Tommy (1949–1953)

Ulinski, Ed (1946–1949)

Weber, Chuck (1955)

Willis, Bill (1946–1953)

Yonakor, John (1946–1949)

Young, George (1946–1953)

A Key to the Nicknames

These are the players who are referred to by nickname in the introduction:

Rivet: Cliff Lewis
Rabbit: Ray Renfro
Rock: Billy Reynolds
Lou the Toe: Lou Groza
Lou the Heel: Lou Rymkus
Captain Lou: Lou Saban
Lil' Abner: Frank Gatski
Chet the Jet: Chet Hanulak
The Kid: George Ratterman
Special Delivery: Edgar Jones
Dub: William Jones
Mo: Mike Scarry
Mo: Maurice Bassett
Big Mo: Ed Modzelewski
Dippy: Fred Evans
Dopey: Don Phelps
Iggie: Marshall Shurnas
Chubby: Forrest Grigg
Curly: Fred Morrison
Chick: Harry Jagade
Pinky: John Harrington
Flip: Ermal Allen
Spud: Ray Terrell

Sources

Interviews and Letters

Ben Agajanian (Eagles, Steelers, Dons, Giants, Rams, Chargers, Texans, Packers, Raiders; 1945, 1947–1949, 1953–1957, 1960–1962, 1964): July 3, 2004

Alex Agase (Dons, Rockets, Browns, Colts; 1947–1951, 1953): February 10, 2003

Charlie Ane (Lions; 1953–1959): December 19, 2003

Vince Banonis (Cardinals, Lions; 1942, 1944, 1946–1953): January 3, 2004

Hub Bechtol (Colts; 1947–1949): May 28, 2004

Bill Boedeker (Rockets, Browns, Packers, Eagles; 1946–1950): March 2, 2004

John Brown (Dons; 1947–1949): September 28, 2005

Ken Carpenter (Browns, Broncos; 1950–1953, 1960): June 11, 2004

Emerson Cole (Browns, Bears; 1950–1952): February 9, 2006

Ken Coleman (Browns broadcaster; 1952–1965): March 13, 2003

Lou Creekmur (Lions; 1950–1959): December 9, 2003

Ray Ebli (Cardinals, Bills, Rockets; 1942, 1946–1947): December 21, 2004

Dick Erdlitz (Eagles, Seahawks; 1942, 1945–1946): May 11, 2004

Gene Fekete (Browns; 1946): March 25, 2004

Henry Ford (Browns, Steelers; 1955–1956): February 14, 2005

Herschel Forester (Browns; 1954–1957): January 3, 2004

Bob Gain (Browns; 1952, 1954–1964): December 10, 2003

Frank Gatski (Browns, Lions; 1946–1957): February 8, 2003

Ken Gorgal (Browns, Bears, Packers; 1950, 1953–1956): December 10, 2003

Billy Grimes (Dons, Packers; 1949–1952): August 6, 2004

Ed Gustafson (Dodgers; 1947–1948): July 3, 2004

Chet Hanulak (Browns; 1954, 1957): December 19, 2003

George Hekkers (Seahawks, Colts, Lions; 1946–1949): May 10, 2004

Jerry Helluin (Browns, Packers, Oilers; 1952–1957, 1960): March 3, 2004

Sherman Howard (Yankees, Yanks, Browns; 1949–1953): August 31, 2005

Duke Iverson (Giants, Yankees, Yanks; 1947–1951): June 8, 2005

Tommy James (Lions, Browns, Colts; 1947–1956): March 1, 2004

Edgar Jones (Bears, Browns; 1945–1949): December 19, 2003

Ken Konz (Browns; 1953–1959): December 5, 2003

Dante Lavelli (Browns; 1946–1956): November 29, 2003

Verl Lillywhite (49ers; 1948–1951): June 30, 2004

Chick Maggioli (Bills, Lions, Colts; 1948–1950): December 21, 2004

Mike McCormack (Yanks, Browns; 1951, 1954–1962): May 23, 2005

Ed Modzelewski (Steelers, Browns; 1952, 1955–1959): November 11, 2005

Dom Moselle (Browns, Packers, Eagles; 1950–1952, 1954): December 6, 2003

Fred Negus (Rockets/Hornets, Bears; 1947–1950): December 21, 2004

Derrell Palmer (Yankees, Browns; 1946–1953): December 19, 2003

Don Panciera (Yankees, Lions, Cardinals; 1949–1950, 1952): August 9, 2004

Ara Parseghian (Browns; 1948–1949): December 16, 2003

Ollie Poole (Yankees, Colts, Lions; 1947–1949): May 27, 2005

Ray Poole (Giants; 1947–1952): May 26, 2005

Dom Principe (Giants, Dodgers; 1940–1942, 1946): letter, November 24, 2004

George Ratterman (Bills, Yanks, Browns; 1947–1956): February 10, 2005

Lester Rodney (*Daily Worker* sports editor; 1936–1957): August 9, 2004

Lou Saban (Browns; 1946–1949): letter, January 10, 2003

John Sandusky (Browns, Packers; 1950–1956): July 17, 2004

Mo Scarry (Rams, Browns; 1944–1947): March 13, 2004

Bob Schnelker (Eagles, Giants, Vikings, Steelers; 1953–1961): February 15, 2005

Otto Schnellbacher (Yankees, Giants; 1948–1951): May 13, 2004

Dean Sensanbaugher (Browns, Bulldogs; 1948–1949): April 13, 2004

Joe Signaigo (Yankees, Yanks; 1948–1950): June 30, 2004

Gordy Soltau (49ers; 1950–1958): April 7, 2004

Lou Sossamon (Yankees; 1946–1948): June 11, 2004

Dick Stanfel (Lions, Redskins; 1952–1958): February 10, 2005

George Taliaferro (Dons, Yanks, Texans, Colts, Eagles; 1949–1955): September 21, 2005

George Terlep (Bills, Browns; 1946–1948): May 11, 2004

Al Wistert (Eagles; 1943–1951): February 5, 2005

Paul Zimmerman (sportswriter, *New York World-Telegram & Sun, New York Post, Sports Illustrated*): letter, August 5, 2002

Newspapers

Brooklyn Daily Eagle

Chicago Tribune

Cleveland News

Cleveland Plain Dealer

Cleveland Press

Daily Worker

Detroit News

Los Angeles Times

New York Daily Mirror

New York Daily News

New York Herald Tribune

New York Sun

New York Times

New York World-Telegram

New York World-Telegram & Sun

PM

San Francisco Chronicle

San Francisco Examiner

Articles

Braunwart, Bob, and Bob Carroll. 1982. "Big Mac of the Browns' Attack." *The Coffin Corner* 4 (1).

Grosshandler, Stan. 1980. "All-America Football Conference." *The Coffin Corner* 2 (7).

Grosshandler, Stan. 1996. "The Day Dub Jones Ran Wild." *The Coffin Corner* 18 (4).

Piascik, Andy. 2002. "Marion Motley." *The Coffin Corner* 24 (4).

Piascik, Andy. 2005. "Why the AAFC Cleveland Browns Were the Best Team in Football from 1946 through 1949." *The Coffin Corner* 27 (3).

Piascik, Andy. 2005. "World War 2 and the Hall of Fame." *The Coffin Corner* 27 (4).

Smith, Thomas G. 1989. "Outside the Pale: The Exclusion of Blacks from the National Football League, 1934–1946." *The Coffin Corner* 11 (4).

Ziegler, Jack. 1988. "Eight Tries at the End Zone: The Giants-Browns 1950 Playoff Game." *The Coffin Corner* 10 (3).

Ziegler, Jack. 1994. "Podunk versus Gotham: The 1946 Browns-Yankees Rivalry." *The Coffin Corner* 16 (2).

Books

Ashe, Arthur, Jr. 1988. *A Hard Road to Glory. Football: The African-American Athlete in Football.* Amistad.

Brown, Jim, with Steve Delsohn. 1989. *Out of Bounds.* Zebra Books.

Brown, Paul, with Jack Clary. 1979. *PB: The Paul Brown Story.* Atheneum.

Carroll, Bob, Pete Palmer, David Pietrusza, and John Thorn. 1998. *The Hidden Game of Football: The Next Edition.* Total Sports.

Carroll, Bob, Michael Gershman, David Neft, and John Thorn, eds. 1997. *Total Football II: The Official Encyclopedia of the National Football League.* HarperCollins.

———. 1999. *Total Browns: The Official Encyclopedia of the Cleveland Browns.* Total Sports.

Clary, Jack. 1973. *Cleveland Browns.* MacMillan.

Cohen, David. 2001. *Rugged and Enduring: The Eagles, the Browns, and 5 Years of Football.* Xlibris.

Coleman, Ken, and Dan Valenti. 2000. *Talking on Air: A Broadcaster's Life in Sports.* Sports Publishing.

Epstein, Eddie. 2002. *Dominance: The Best Seasons of Pro Football's Greatest Teams.* Brassey's.

Eskenazi, Gerald. 1976. *There Were Giants in Those Days.* Grosset & Dunlap.

Gildea, William. 1994. *When the Colts Belonged to Baltimore: A Father and a Son, a Team and a Time.* Johns Hopkins University Press.

Godin, Roger. 2002. *The Brooklyn Football Dodgers: The Other "Bums."* St. Johann's Press.

Gordon, Roger. 2002. *Cleveland Browns A to Z.* Sports Publishing.

Gottehrer, Barry. 1963. *The Giants of New York: The History of Professional Football's Most Fabulous Dynasty.* Putnam.

Green, Jerry. 1973. *Detroit Lions.* MacMillan.

Grossi, Tony. 2004. *Tales from the Browns Sideline.* Sports Publishing.

Groza, Lou, with Mark Hodermarsky. 1996. *The Toe: The Lou Groza Story*. Kendall/Hunt.

Herskowitz, Mickey. 1974. *The Golden Age of Professional Football: A Remembrance of Pro Football in the 1950s*. MacMillan.

Hoppel, Joe, Mike Nahrstedt, and Steve Zesch, eds. 1989. *Greatest Sports Dynasties*. Sporting News.

Huler, Scott. 1999. *On Being Brown: What It Means to Be a Cleveland Browns Fan*. Gray.

Keim, John. 1999. *Legends by the Lake: The Cleveland Browns at Municipal Stadium*. University of Akron Press.

Korch, Rick. 1993. *The Truly Great: The 200 Best Football Players of All Time*. Taylor.

Landry, Tom, with Gregg Lewis. 1996. *Tom Landry: An Autobiography*. Zondervan.

Leuthner, Stuart. 1988. *Iron Men: Bucko, Crazylegs, and the Boys Recall the Golden Days of Professional Football*. Doubleday.

Levy, Alan. 2003. *Tackling Jim Crow: Racial Segregation in Professional Football*. McFarland.

Levy, Bill. 1965. *Return to Glory: The Story of the Cleveland Browns*. World.

Littlewood, Thomas. 1990. *Arch: A Promoter, Not a Poet. The Story of Arch Ward*. Iowa State University Press.

Moon, Bob, ed. 1995. *The Cleveland Browns: A 50-Year Tradition*. SporTradition.

Morgan, Jon. 1997. *Glory for Sale: Fans, Dollars, and the New NFL*. Bancroft.

Murray, Mike, ed. 1993. *Lions Pride: 60 Years of Detroit Lions Football*. Taylor.

Natali, Alan. 2001. *Brown's Town: 20 Famous Browns Talk amongst Themselves*. Orange Frazer Press.

Neft, David, Roland Johnson, and Richard Cohen. 1974. *The Sports Encyclopedia: Pro Football*. Grosset & Dunlap.

Newhouse, David. 2000. *The Million Dollar Backfield: The San Francisco 49ers in the 1950s*. Frog.

O'Connell, Kevin. 1997. *City of Champions: The Story of the 1948 Cleveland Barons, Browns and Indians*. Green Road Press.

Parker, Buddy. 1955. *We Play to Win! The Inside Story of the Fabulous Detroit Lions.* Prentice-Hall.

Pluto, Terry. 1997. *When All the World Was Browns Town.* Simon & Schuster.

Robustelli, Andy, with Jack Clary. 1987. *Once a Giant, Always . . . My Two Lives with the New York Giants.* Quinlan Press.

Rosen, Charley. 2001. *The Wizard of Odds: How Jack Molinas Almost Destroyed the Game of Basketball.* Seven Stories Press.

Ross, Charles K. 1999. *Outside the Lines: African Americans and the Integration of the National Football League.* New York University Press.

Schmidt, Raymond. 2001. *Football's Stars of Summer: A History of the College Football All-Star Game Series of 1934–1976.* Scarecrow Press.

Schneider, Russell. 1999. *The Best of the Cleveland Browns Memories: Players, Coaches, and Games.* Moonlight.

Shelby, Strother. 1988. *NFL Top 40: The Greatest Pro Football Games Ever Played.* Penguin.

Silber, Irwin. 2003. *Press Box Red: The Story of Lester Rodney, the Communist Who Helped Break the Color Line in American Sports.* Temple University Press.

Slone, Kay Collier. 1985. *Football's Gentle Giant: The Blanton Collier Story.* Life Force.

St. John, Bob. 1991. *Heart of a Lion: The Wild and Wooly Life of Bobby Layne.* Taylor.

Steadman, John. 1997. *From Colts to Ravens: A Behind-the-Scenes Look at Baltimore Professional Football.* Tidewater.

Thorn, John. 1981. *Pro Football's Ten Greatest Games.* Four Winds Press.

———, ed. 1982. *The Armchair Quarterback.* Scribner's.

Treat, Roger. 1977. *The Encyclopedia of Football.* Doubleday.

Whittingham, Richard. 1984. *What a Game They Played.* Harper & Row.

Zimmerman, Paul. 1984. *The New Thinking Man's Guide to Pro Football.* Simon & Schuster.

Other

All-America Football Conference information booklet, 1946

All-America Football Conference record manuals, 1947, 1948, and 1949, and supplement to the 1949 record manual

"All-Pros: The First 40 Years," by John Hogrogian and the editors of the
    Professional Football Researchers Association (PFRA)
Cleveland Browns media guides, 1946–1956
"Game by Game Summaries and Linescores: All-America Football Con-
    ference 1946–1949 and National Football League 1950–1955" (PFRA)
"Progression of NFL Records," compiled by Ken Pullis (PFRA)

Index

About the Author

Andy Piascik is a long-time activist for peace and social justice. He has written articles about labor history, African Americans in sports, and other subjects for a variety of publications. *The Best Show in Football: The 1946–1955 Cleveland Browns, Pro Football's Greatest Dynasty* is his first book.